Sofia Coppola

THE ICONIC FILMMAKER AND HER WORK

IAN NATHAN

Unofficial and unauthorised

Quarto

First published in 2026 by White Lion Publishing,
an imprint of The Quarto Group.
One Triptych Place, London, SE1 9SH,
United Kingdom
T (0)20 7700 9000
www.Quarto.com

EEA Representation, WTS Tax d.o.o., Žanova ulica 3, 4000 Kranj, Slovenia
www.wts-tax.si

A catalogue record for this book is available from the British Library.

ISBN 978-1-80570-279-5
Ebook ISBN 978-1-80570-280-1

10 9 8 7 6 5 4 3 2 1

Design: Sue Pressley and Paul Turner, Stonecastle Graphics
Copy Editor: Nick Freeth
Publisher: Jessica Axe
Editor: Izzy Toner
Editorial Manager: Jennifer Barr
Senior Designer: Renata Latipova
Senior Production Controller: Rohana Yusof

Printed in Guangdong, China TT062026

MIX
Paper | Supporting responsible forestry
FSC® C016973

Sofia Coppola

THE ICONIC FILMMAKER AND HER WORK

IAN NATHAN

Unofficial and unauthorised

WHITE LION PUBLISHING

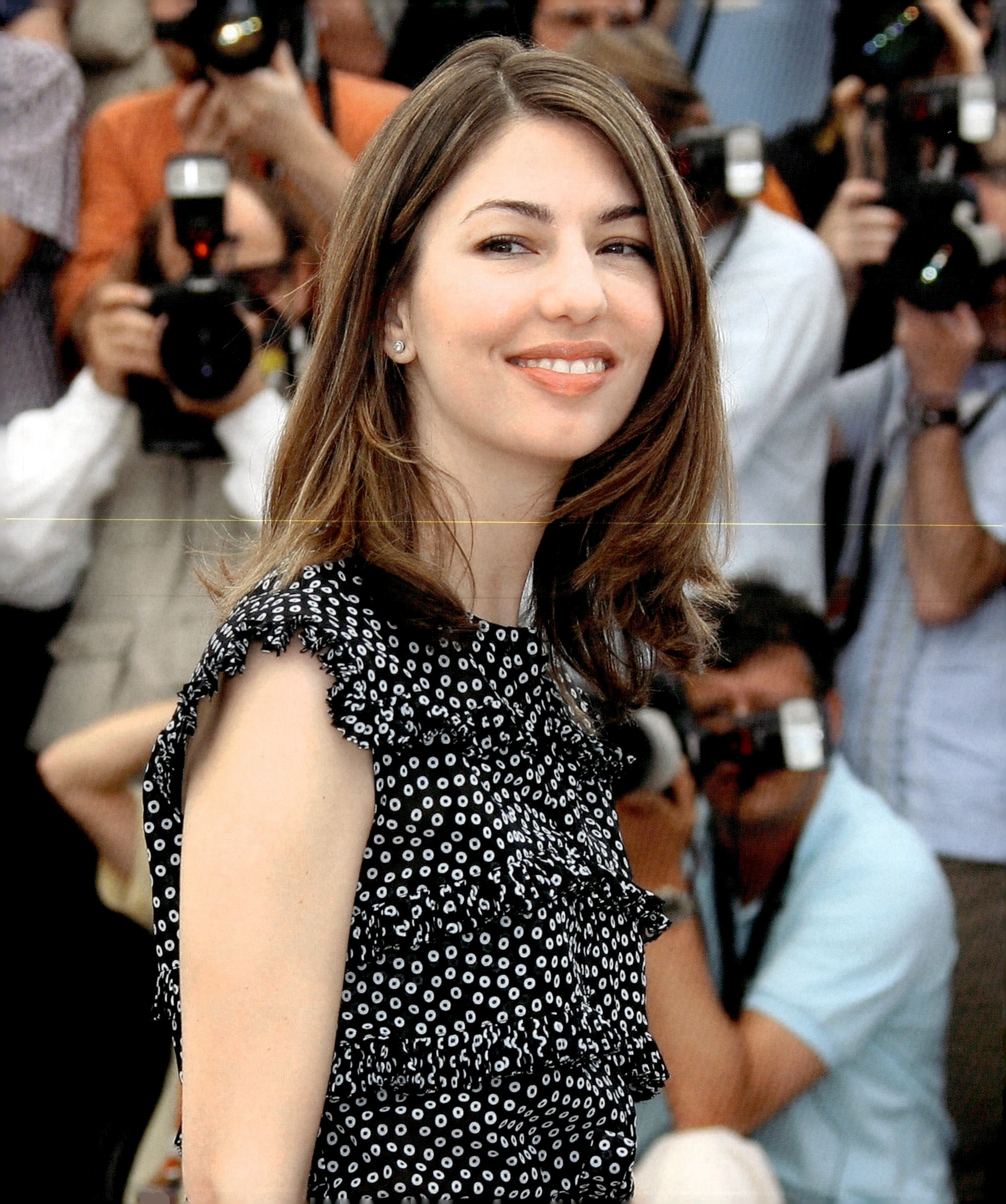

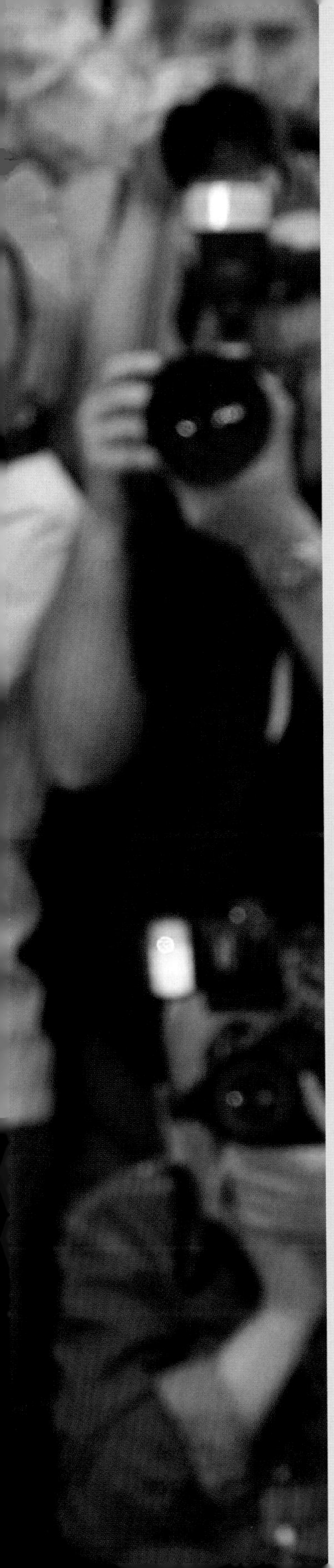

CONTENTS

INTRODUCTION

When you try and describe any one of Sofia Coppola's films it is always easier to say how they make you feel, rather than pin down a plot. We tend to talk about how they look and sound, how they have the quality of music to soothe or haunt, or both. Maybe we would even describe how they taste.

During the brief time Coppola dated Quentin Tarantino in the 2000s, following a brief marriage to Spike Jonze, she showed him her mood book for the ambitious biopic of *Marie Antoinette* (still her most expensive production). He marvelled at how neat it was, this handmade but exquisite creation, clearly the work of 'the loving hands of a fine artist.'[1] His own scripts came written in a frenzy of felt-tip pen. He paused over a page filled with photos of glazed pink donuts.

'What's with the donuts?'[2]

It was simply the shade of pink, she replied, she was imagining a sofa in just that colour.

'And when I saw the film,' he recalled, 'sure enough, I wanted to eat the goddamn furniture.'[3]

Such is Coppola's aesthetic, so beguilingly tactile, almost aromatic, that her films have become a fetish. Even her period pieces – *Marie Antoinette*, *The Beguiled*, and *Priscilla* – come glazed in Sofia. We eagerly await the next, mostly for the chance to taste her aesthetic again.

Each of her eight films to date began with such imagery, which forms an atmosphere – once she has her atmosphere she has her film. It is only then she writes a script. Scripts that are written while listening to music and gazing out of hotel windows and conjuring up yet more images. Scripts that only serve as blueprints for a feeling.

When you try to write about how she makes films you are writing about how she makes us feel.

Coppola became a great director both because of and despite her heritage. True enough, being a scion of such a distinguished family offered a rarefied gateway into the movie business (though she has never been a Hollywood director): her DNA is entwined in a cinematic legacy that stretches across aunts and cousins and back in time to her struggling grandparents. A great American story of Italian immigrants who forged a dream out of poverty and those irrepressible genes. Yet her style was shaped by her resistance to the world she was born into. From the start, her films were an act of defiance against the accusations of nepotism they inevitably engendered. They were an attempt to express her own identity. To find her own voice.

It wasn't something she had ever planned, she implored in interview. Nevertheless it feels like gravity. She instinctually moved in creative circles:

Previous pages: *The inescapable lenses - Sofia Coppola stands before the photographers at the Cannes Film Festival in 2006, where* Marie Antoinette *was making its debut.*

Opposite: *Going her own way (on the set of* Somewhere *in 2010) – Sofia Coppola has forged a career, and more potently a style, that is entirely her own. Despite her famous family name, she is a singular filmmaker.*

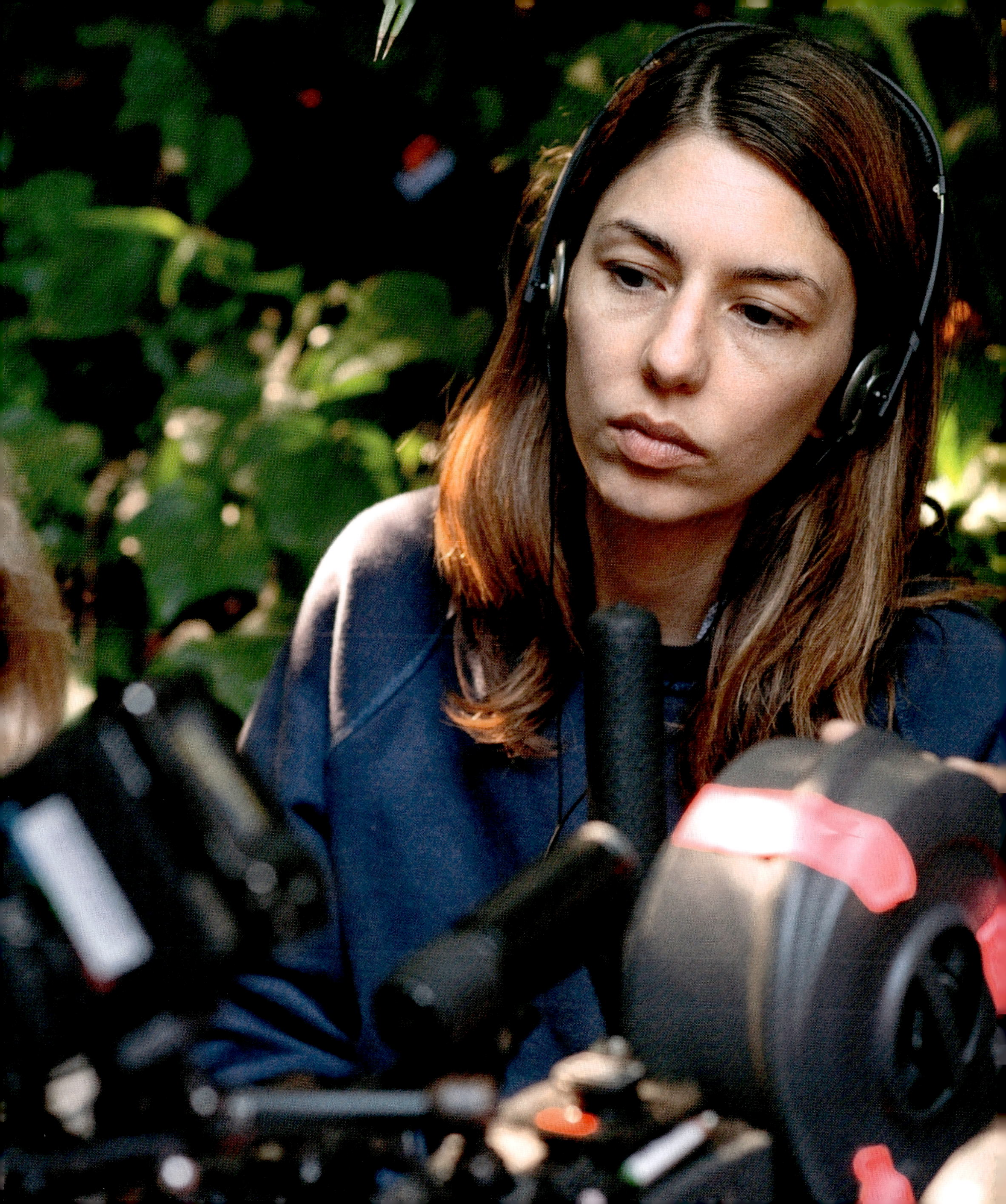

artists, actors, musicians, photographers, fashion designers, wannabe directors, relatives. It was Sofia who encouraged her cousin Jason Schwartzman to audition for Wes Anderson's *Rushmore*.

As we will see, the idea of filmmaking took shape with the urge to adapt Jeffrey Eugenides' *The Virgin Suicides* – they were one and the same thing. As soon as she read the book, she knew how it would look. In ways she couldn't fully articulate (except on screen), this story of the inexplicable suicides of the teenaged Lisbon sisters was about the death of her brother Gio in a boating accident, only twenty-three, never allowed to grow old. Something her father would have told her is that there comes a time when the art chooses you, even possesses you. She was twenty-seven.

A one-off became a vaunted career.

Like all those we label auteurs, and all those I have written about, her work is indivisible from her personality. As Sofia herself has an elusive, shimmering quality, a still surface with a hint of deep waters beneath, so does her filmmaking. If her life were a fiction, she would be the perfect director to bring it to the screen.

Her creativity is defined by her background (a life, lonely and fabulous, written into the fabric of her films), but she is an unlikely director by the old formula of outraged men pouting like infants. Her illustrious father was known to fake fits to get his way. She seeks serenity on set, a fish-tank tranquillity in which to express herself. But by her own description is 'superopinionated.'[4] By directing films, she realized, she could have the world exactly as she wanted it.

What is undeniable is that today no one thinks of Coppola as anything but an extraordinary talent in her own right. In fact, these days the most revered Coppola is Sofia, with her suite of absorbing, funny, melancholic films.

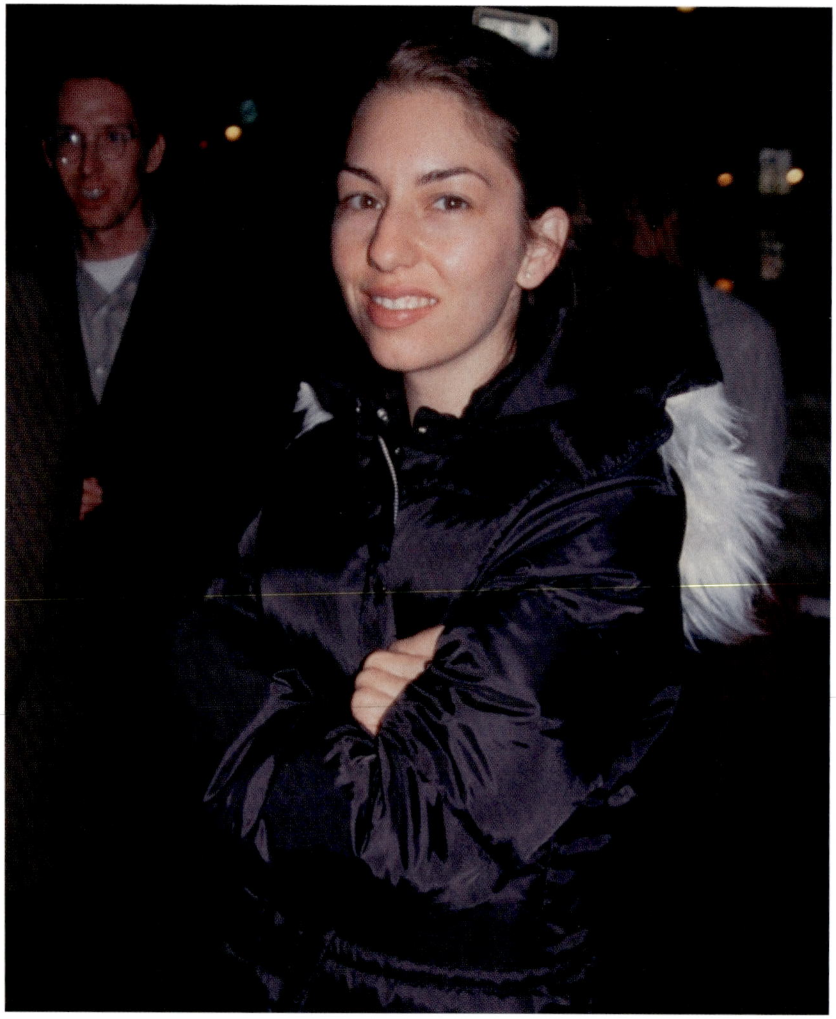

Above: *The neophyte artist – Sofia Coppola photographed in Los Angeles at the New York Film Festival premiere of her friend Wes Anderson's* Rushmore *in 1998. This was the time she was beginning to realize that directing was her calling.*

Each of which is a feast of pop-cultural citations. 'I grew up without TV reception…' she recalled, remembering a childhood, at least in part, sequestered in the cradle of Napa Valley. 'All I had to watch was my dad's laser disc collection.'[5] She saw *Breathless* when she was twelve, and still turns to Godard's rule-swerving caper when she begins anew on a film. To recall how to be both romantic and natural. To keep the camera as close as possible to the emotions. And it isn't simply callbacks to film alone: photographs, art, music, fashion, and advertising contribute to the softly postmodern veneer of her storytelling, never to announce her cleverness, but as a means to express something.

Coppola has become a figurehead in a generation of visually distinctive filmmakers, the new New Hollywood of Wes Anderson, Noah Baumbach, Paul Thomas Anderson, Spike Jonze, and even Tarantino. They are now in their fifties, or even older, but still exude a vigour for the medium, inspired by her father's generation. She works within this independent spirit that is still imbued with a love of Hollywood. Though of course, Sofia smarts at categorization: 'It makes it easier to write about you, I guess.'[6]

Themes move slowly and subtly through her work like the currents of a stream – a stream of thought. Coming of age and the mysteries of youth (not necessarily the sole province of the young). Desire, connection, alienation, and the search for intimacy. Wealth and its languorous traps. Celebrity and its burdens. Fathers and daughters, a hint of mothers, and the flow of something across generations. Bill Murray by night, Kirsten Dunst in sunlight, hotels, palaces, mansions and bedrooms – Coppola nearly always shoots on location. She has to be there.

She has been criticized for a fascination with affluence, all those five-star milieus, but that is arguably the allure of her films, where comfort is infused with loss. She uses superficiality as a weapon.

She has always been more fashionable than famous.

After a chapter on an extraordinary coming of age, this book will take each film in turn, exploring its genesis and creation, while reflecting upon its influence and meaning, and the interconnectedness that lies between all her work. Fundamental to any study of Sofia is an appreciation of what it is like to lose oneself to her sumptuous, ethereal, charming, and finally haunting films. Is that not vital to the weaving of her spell? The idea that we may never know exactly what her films truly mean. Only how they make us feel.

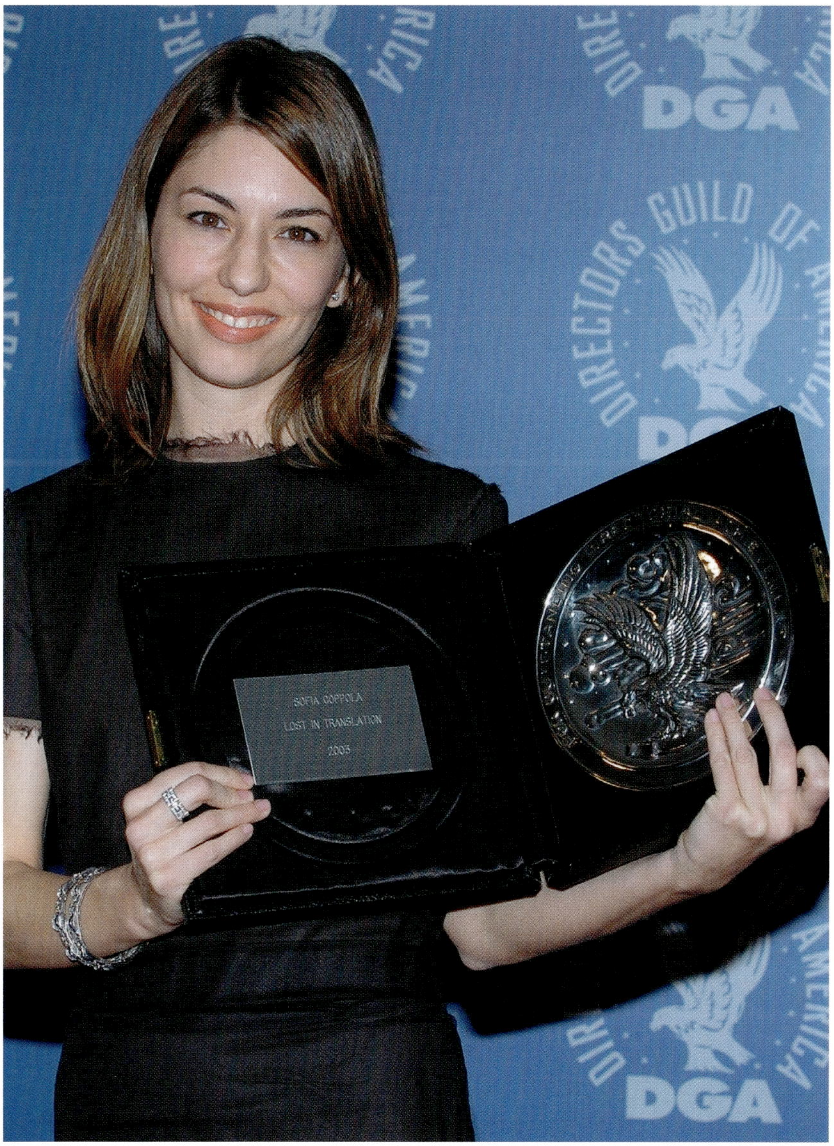

Left: *The established auteur – Coppola's nomination from the Directors Guild of America for* Lost in Translation *left no doubt that this was who she was.*

FAMILY TIES

The formative years, *Life Without Zoë* (1989), *Lick the Star* (1998)

Her father was one of the most famous directors in the world. That brought wealth, privilege, and some great hotels. But how do you escape such a shadow to become your own kind of Coppola?

Sofia Coppola gave her first interview when she was five years old. It was her father, Francis Ford Coppola, asking the questions, and it was mostly for fun, but also for posterity. He wanted Sofia (for clarity's sake, we will refer to her by her first name for the time being) to address her answers to her future self.

What are you going to be like, he asks, when you're a big girl?

'Well, I can make-believe what I want to be like,'[1] she answers. She pictured being a teacher or a nurse. 'I like being Sofia because there are a lot of fun things I know how to do,'[2] she adds. Perhaps it was a little difficult at this stage to imagine she could or would want to join the family business.

Some context. They were conducting the interview in the family's small, humid house in Manila. It was 1977, and they had upped sticks and moved to the Philippines for the endless struggle known to the world as *Apocalypse Now* – one of Sofia's first memories is riding in a helicopter. She attended school there with the local kids, learned to count in Cantonese, chased frogs in the garden, and sometimes came to set – observing something that wasn't so much a job as a way of life. Her grown-up self would come to know that feeling.

She was born into filmmaking – quite literally. Before she had taken a breath she was on camera. With the news that the baby was on the way, her father grabbed his Camcorder and filmed the delivery at a Manhattan hospital on 14 May 1971, during the tumultuous production of *The Godfather*. 'When they say, "It's a girl," my dad gasps and nearly drops the camera,'[3] she laughed. Only months later, she would make her inaugural performance in that fictional saga, as Michael's baby nephew during the climactic baptism.

It was the first credit in a sporadic acting career mostly in her father's films (she played 'Child on Ship' in *The Godfather Part II*) that brought its torments. For the record, she also appeared wearing a blonde wig in Tim Burton's early short *Frankenweenie*, in Jefery Levy's comedy *Inside Monkey Zetterland*,

Opposite: *Like father, like daughter – director Francis Ford Coppola poses with his young daughter on the* Life Without Zoë *segment of* New York Stories *in 1989. It marks Sofia Coppola's first screen credit as writer.*

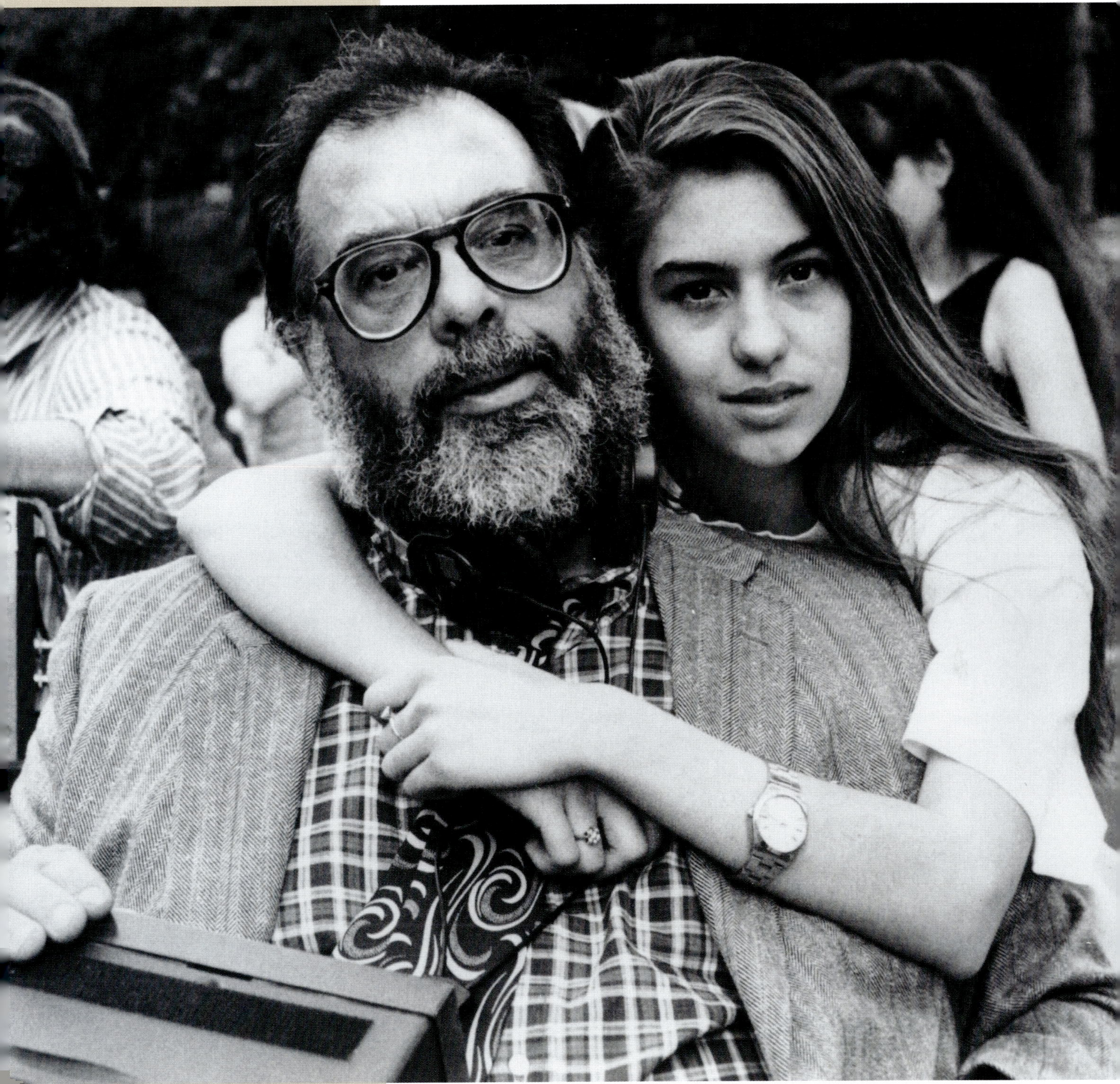

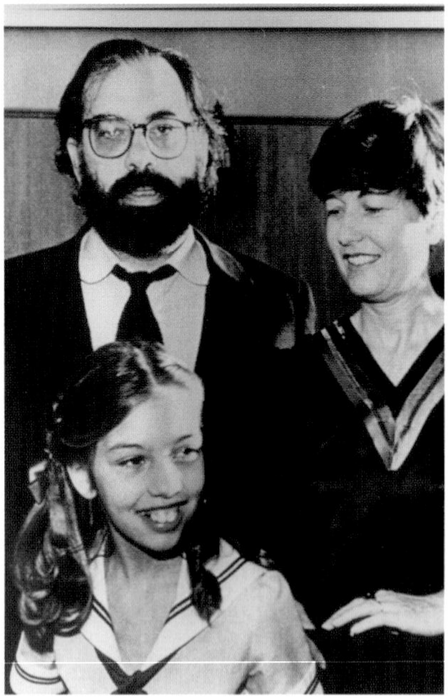

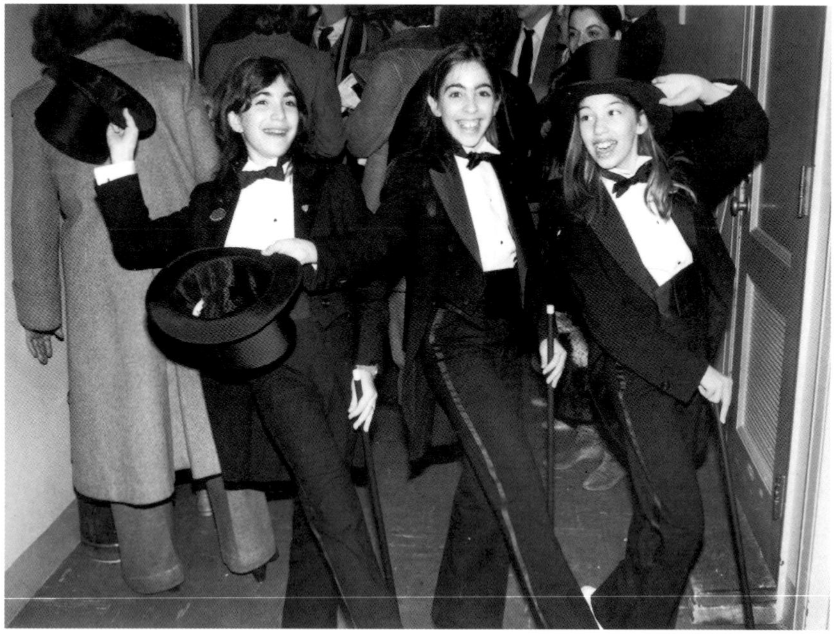

Above left: *Life through a lens – Sofia Coppola quickly had to get used to being pictured with her famous father and mother.*

Above right: *Not immune to the spotlight, a top-and-tailed Sofia (right) performs for the camera, with sisters Jenny and Jilian Gersten (daughters of the producer Bernard Gersten) at the premiere of her father's ill-fated romance* One from the Heart *in 1982.*

and as a Naboo handmaiden in *Star Wars: Episode I – the Phantom Menace*, but never truly felt at ease before the camera.

Her mother, the artist Eleanor Coppola, earthier than her husband, so much calmer, and so disdainful of Hollywood values, used the birth footage as part of a feminist installation in which Sofia would sit in a room watching her own birth over and over again. Such cool ideas, thought Sofia, were 'the opposite of my dad's world.'[4] It might be that the mother had a bigger influence than the influential father.

What chance did Sofia have of a normal upbringing? That dilemma echoes through her work – the way celebrity and wealth and expectation eat away at her characters. The search for identity can be so much harder if it is handed to you as a birthright. She has been more than aware of what people say. How it was all nepotism, privilege, doors held wide open. That she got her breaks without breaking a sweat. Which isn't wholly true: there has been struggle, but she recognized that there have been gifts.

Her childhood was in so many ways a blessed time, and thrilling. She would sit at the dinner table in their Napa Valley home with the likes of Wim Wenders, Steven Spielberg, Uncle George Lucas, and Akira Kurosawa talking film with her father. How could that not rub off on you? A sense of the possibility this medium held for expressing the personal. She once accompanied her father to Studio 54 in New York and ended up sitting on Andy Warhol's lap.

She still holds her father as the 'best film teacher,'[5] filling his children's eyes and minds with the best of world cinema and having them on set with him. Much of her childhood and teenage years were spent travelling like part of a circus between those sets: *The Conversation, The Outsiders, Rumble Fish, The Cotton Club, Peggy Sue Got Married* (in which she had a more significant role as Kathleen Turner's younger sister). In this, he may have influenced her in unspoken ways. Did her need for calm sets, where the primary demand is that voices never be raised, come as a response to the furies that often inflamed her father's creative process? What Eleanor described as his 'Italian approach.'[6] The fact he took the family to the brink of bankruptcy on more than one occasion for the sake of his art.

Her world may be relatively harmonious by comparison, but like her father, Sofia has resisted the pull of the studios and all their pernickety, wrongheaded, money-obsessed demands. 'I learned it's better to do your own thing,'[7] she insisted. Creative control is all-important. There is a cynicism to her beatific films, a knowledge of how the world can confine you. And she is subtly stubborn in getting what she wants. She never instructs actors, but is clear about what doesn't work.

Sofia was always quick to recall how encouraging her father had been of his daughter's career from the very first: helping her get films made, but knowing when to stand back. Aside from the cameos, her first serious collaboration with him had been on *Life Without Zoë*, the elder Coppola's segment of the much ballyhooed (and then much derided) 1989 triptych *New York Stories*. The other two segments were directed by fellow luminaries Woody Allen and Martin Scorsese, though no one came out of the experimental jaunt with their reputations exactly enhanced.

Looking back through a Sofia-curved lens, what is startling is how this film-within-a-film foreshadows the daughter's work more than the father's. She was only seventeen years old, and credited as co-writer on the screenplay for filling her father in on the psychology of precocious tween Zoë (Heather McComb), who lives at the prestigious Sherry-Netherland hotel while her wealthy parents remain largely absent.

Below: *Loved ones and future collaborators – the Coppola clan pictured at the Cannes Film Festival in 1979. From the left: Carmine and Italia (Sofia's grandparents), Francis, Gian-Carlo (known as Gio), Eleanor, Roman, and the young Sofia in front.*

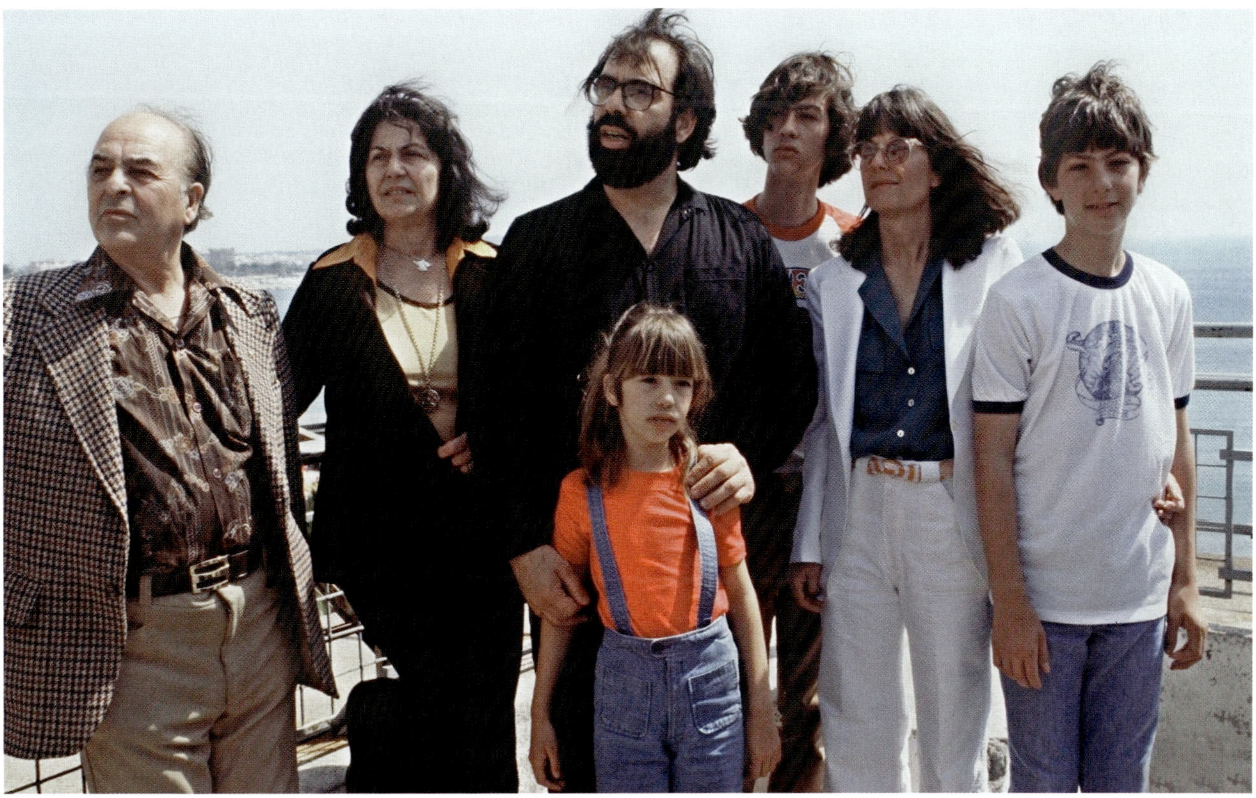

With heavy-handed symbolism, Zoë's father (Giancarlo Giannini) is a famous flautist (just as Sofia's grandfather Carmine had been – he even cameos as a street musician), and her mother, a player in the fashion industry, is filled by Sofia's real-life aunt (and onscreen mother in *The Godfather*) Talia Shire. Moreover, the Coppolas had an apartment at the Sherry-Netherland, one of a portfolio of five homes at the time. To wit: the Sherry, the Napa Valley Victorian, apartments in Los Angeles and San Francisco, and a beachside retreat in Belize.

During the writing, Francis had whisked his daughter to Las Vegas (just as Johnny does with Cleo in *Somewhere*), ordering room service as they collaborated on the screenplay. 'It was his scriptwriting workshop with me,'[8] she recalled.

Make it personal, he urged.

Though *Life Without Zoë* would stir grumbles from critics – 'The entire sketch seems without purpose,'[9] complained Roger Ebert in the *Chicago Sun-Times* – we can see something greater stirring. The out-of-joint aura of hotels, lost girls, the lonely adornments of wealth. Which also provided grist for those future commentators who would find Sofia's focus on privilege to be suspicious. Writing in *Jacobin* magazine on the release of *On the Rocks* (with its sleek New York scene and abandoned daughters), Eileen Jones ran with the headline: 'Sofia Coppola Wants You to Feel Bad for the Very Rich and the Very Sad.'[10] It is notable that the director claimed her most difficult shoot to be *The Bling Ring*, because it literally took her out of her comfort zone.

Below: Life Without Zoë *was Francis Ford Coppola's contribution to the triptych* New York Stories *(1989). The story centred around the twelve-year-old (Heather McComb, far right), and Francis Ford Coppola sought the collaboration of Sofia on the mindset of a girl.*

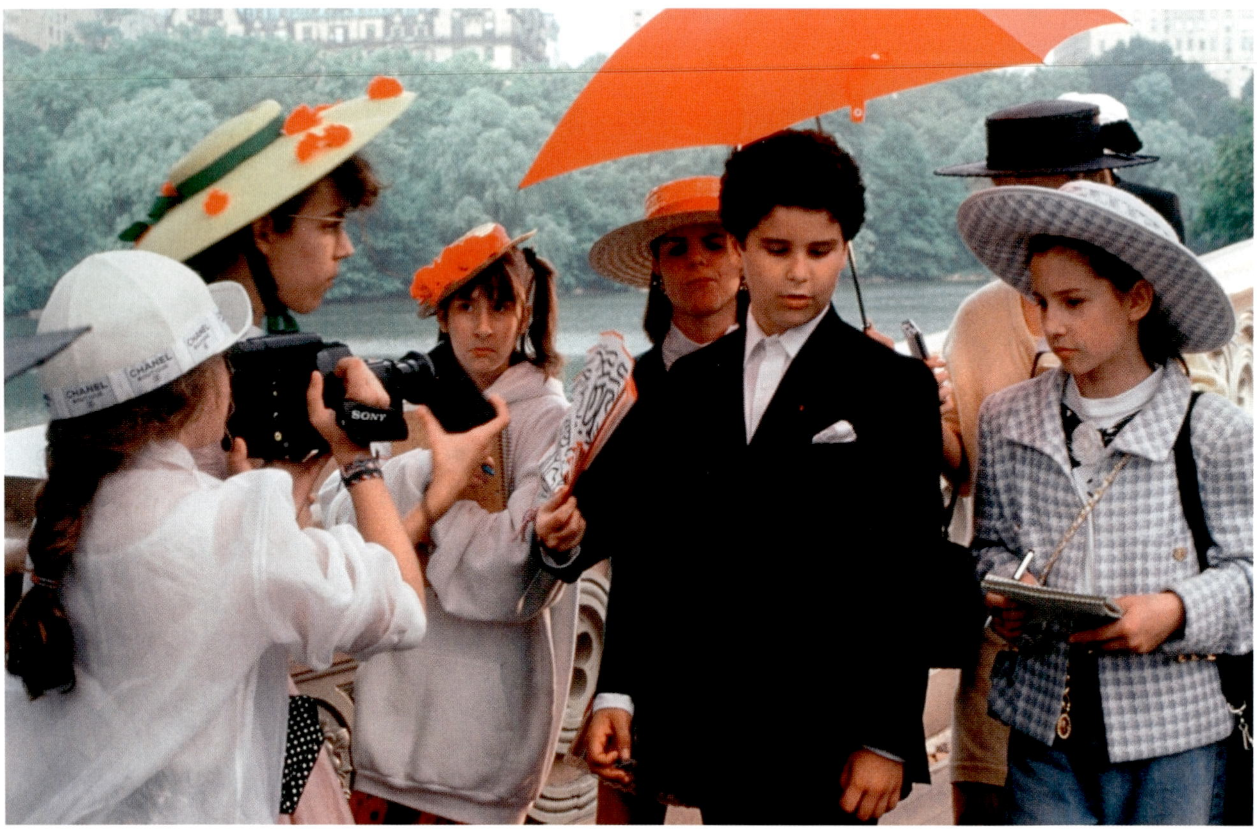

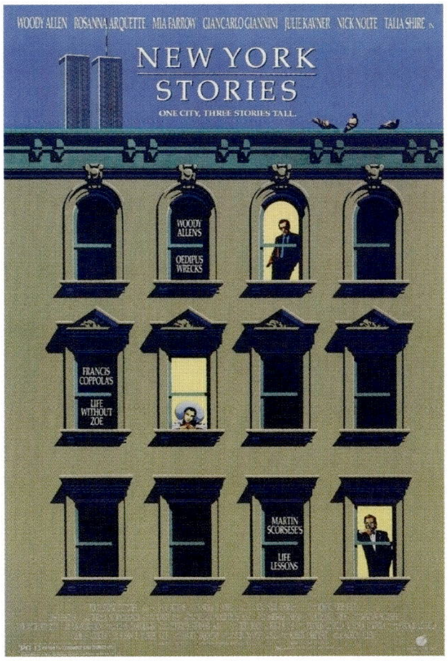

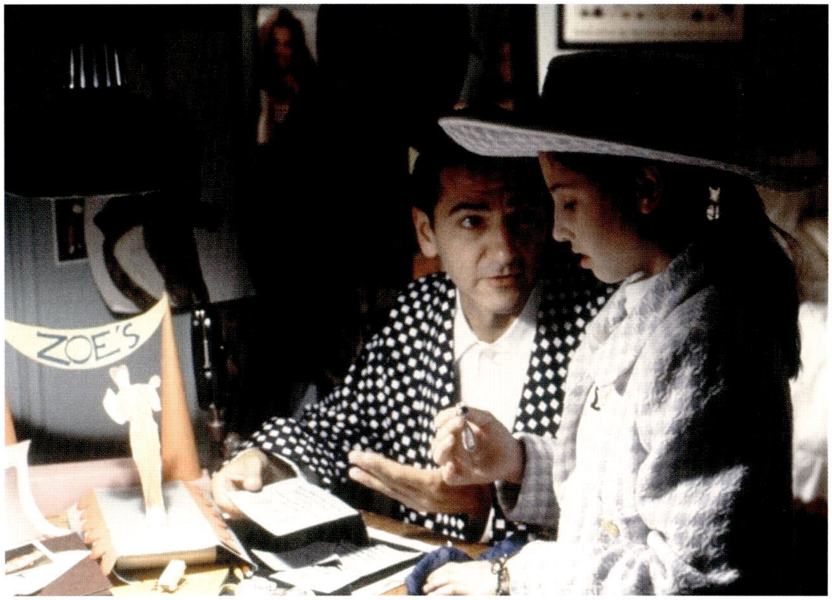

There is no doubt that family proved a great positive. Her father's deep knowledge and contacts, her mother's steady guidance, her brother Roman's invaluable assistance (he is still her closest collaborator, the first person she turns to with any script), her cousin Jason Schwartzman's performance in *Marie Antoinette*, her niece Gia's comradeship – Gia Coppola has now directed three films of her own.

But you have to be yourself. Whoever that might be. Like any teenager (and notably those she portrays), she went her own way, desperate to swerve her destiny. At first, this naturally tended toward fashion. Even as a child she had cut photographs from magazines like French *Vogue* to decorate her room, fostering big opinions on the latest trends.

Aged fifteen, with the help of her father's connections (Yves Saint Laurent was also a family friend), she was offered an internship at Chanel in Paris. However, just before she was due to leave, her older brother Gian-Carlo, known to all as Gio, was killed in a boating accident during another of her father's shoots, *Gardens of Stone* in Washington D.C. Such a loss would, of course, find its way into the melancholic aura of her films, and it feels significant that she was still allowed to go to Paris amid tragedy. Accompanied by family friend Susie Landau Finch (daughter of actor Martin Landau), Sofia found herself adrift in an alien city. When Gio's fiancée Jacqui de La Fontaine (pregnant with Gia) joined them, they spent long hours sprawled in their apartment, dazed in grief, a prelude to the Lisbon girls in *The Virgin Suicides*.

While being honoured by New York's Museum of Modern Art (the fabled MoMA) years later in 2025, and thus falling into the august company of Martin Scorsese, Quentin Tarantino, Cate Blanchett, Tilda Swinton, and Guillermo del Toro, Sofia gave a humorous, naturally self-deprecating speech.

'When I started, I was in my 20s and it was the nineties in LA where I was known as the daughter of. This was before Nepo babies were charming and most of them ended up in rehab, and I was the amateur actress who single-handedly ruined *The Godfather*.'[11]

Above left: *Uniting the reputations of Woody Allen, Martin Scorsese, and Francis Ford Coppola,* New York Stories *(1989) was ultimately viewed as indulgence.*

Above right: *Art reflecting life? Onscreen father and daughter Claudio (Giancarlo Giannini) and Zoë (McComb).*

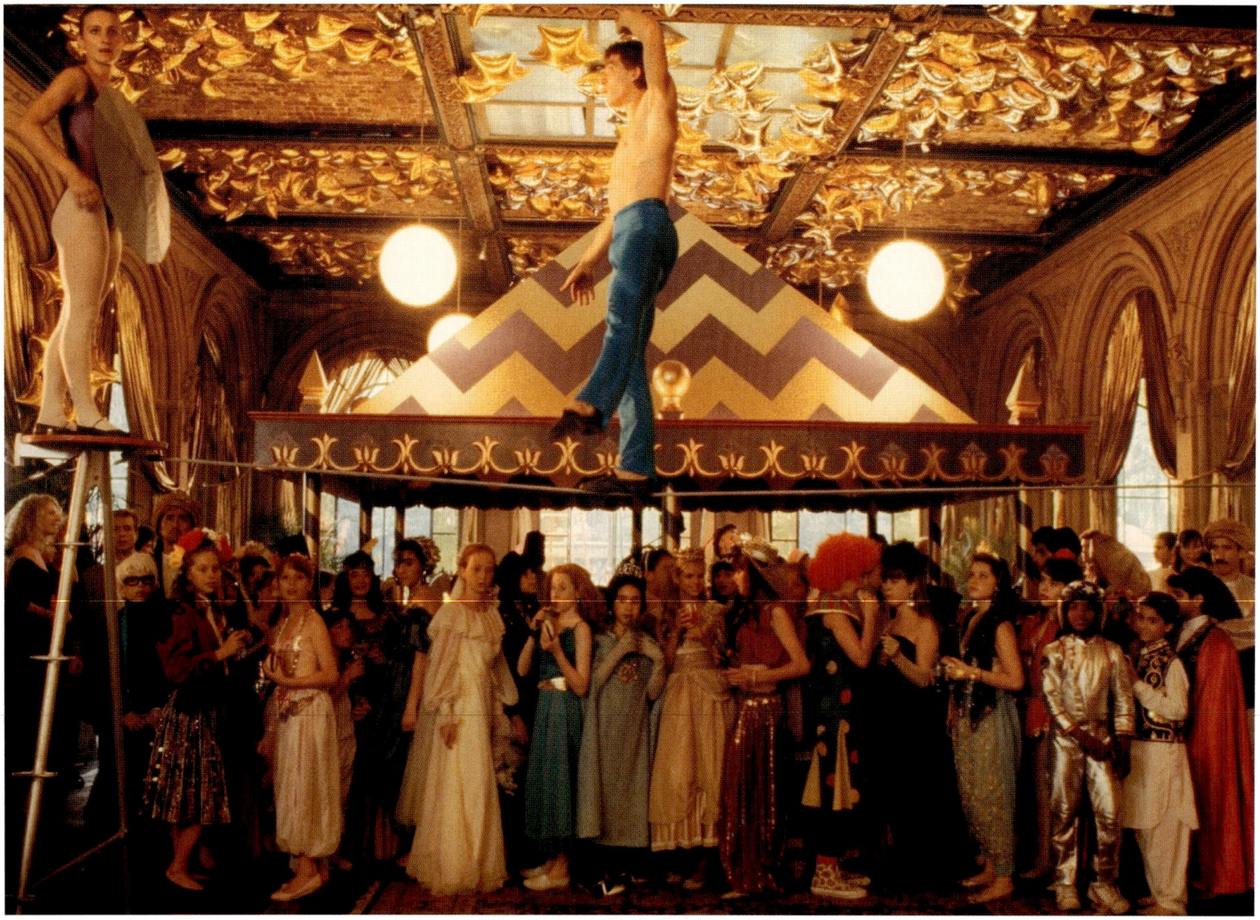

Above: *The* Life Without Zoë *part of* New York Stories *(1989). Prefiguring Sofia Coppola's later preoccupations, here was a film set within the strangeness of a luxury hotel.*

If we are looking for the inciting incident in her career, then we could look no further than Sofia's infamous return to the *Godfather* franchise as Michael's doomed daughter Mary in *The Godfather Part III*, a film already stymied by a hurried production and an inferior script. To cut a long, much-told story short: Winona Ryder had been cast in the part, but dropped out at the eleventh hour, citing exhaustion. Her previous production, *Mermaids*, had run into delays – and, arriving in Rome without a break, she had collapsed in her hotel room.

The third *Godfather* was already underway and they had to move quickly. Julia Roberts' dance card was already full and Madonna was deemed too old for the part, so Coppola turned to his daughter, with him in Italy for a winter break from Mills College in Oakland, where she was studying art history and beginning to feel her way toward an artistic temperament.

There was method in her father's madness. Sofia had served as an inspiration for the character and played the part during the early read-throughs. For Francis it was expediency, and perhaps an unforeseen blessing. How much more symbolic can you get than casting the director's daughter as the Godfather's cherished progeny, extending the trilogy's *King Lear* phase beyond the fringes of the screen? Furthermore, like

Mary she was equally the offspring of an Italian father and a WASP mother. But there were still those on the production who tried to warn him – they knew how the press was going to react. The studio was reluctant, but the director adamant. The call came through on 28 December 1989 – could Sofia come to set immediately.

She had wanted to do her best by her father and found herself swept up in a whirlwind of acting and voice coaches, costume fittings, and the pressure of sharing filial scenes with Al Pacino and romantic moments with Andy Garcia, as well as working with a father under intense pressure himself. The critics were savage. *Time* decried a performance of 'gosling gracelessness.'[12] She faced the ignominy of winning the Golden Raspberry Awards for both Worst Supporting Actress and Worst New Star.

Like many of Sofia's artistic endeavours, that fateful performance has come to be re-evaluated. Even at the time, *The New Yorker's* Pauline Kael, never one to go easy on foolhardy actors, offered some solace. 'It's obvious that this teen-age girl is not a trained actress; she seems uncomfortable at times… But she has a lovely and unusual presence; she gives the film a breath of life, and I grew to like her.'[13] Perhaps wrong for the film with all its dramatic weight and the cinematic legacy it was living up to, but there is a strange realism about her Mary – a ghostly charisma we can't quite take our eyes off. She is like one of her own characters wafting through her father's *Grand Guignol* epic.

Below: *The calm before the storm – director Francis Ford Coppola and Sofia Coppola as Mary Corleone on the set of the controversial* The Godfather Part III.

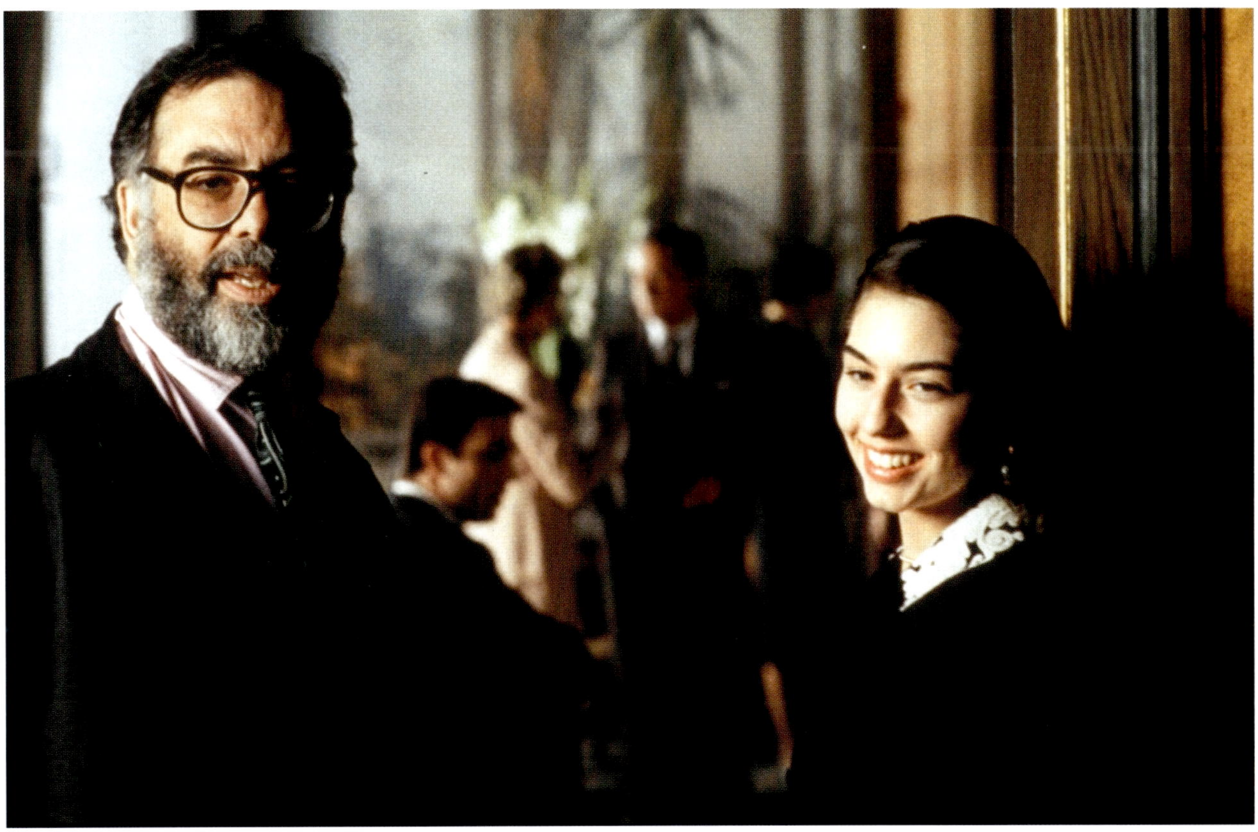

Right: *Love among the Mafia – one of the challenges Sofia Coppola faced in taking over the role of Mary in The* Godfather Part III *was creating a believable romance with her character's cousin Vincent, played by a charismatic Andy Garcia.*

Below: *The operatic climax of the film at the opera, where Mary will ultimately meet her doom.*

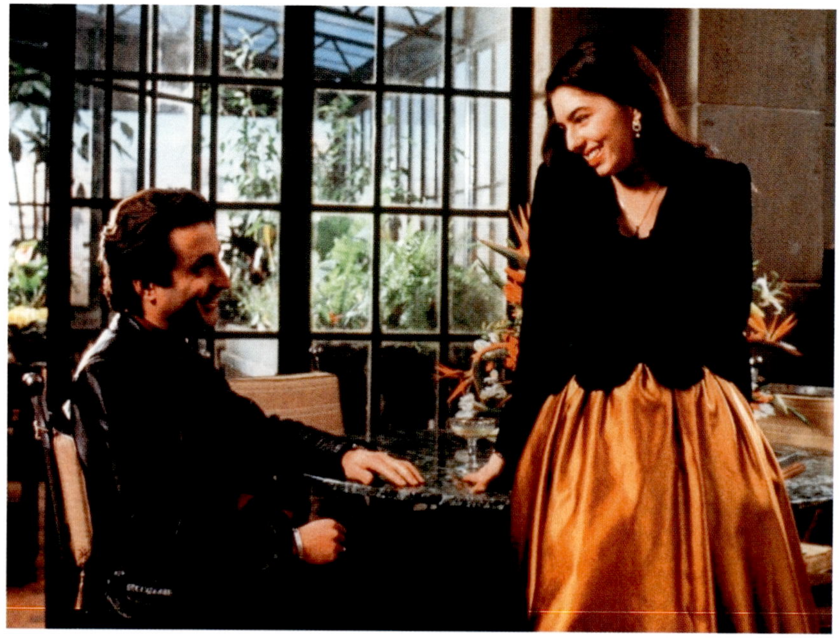

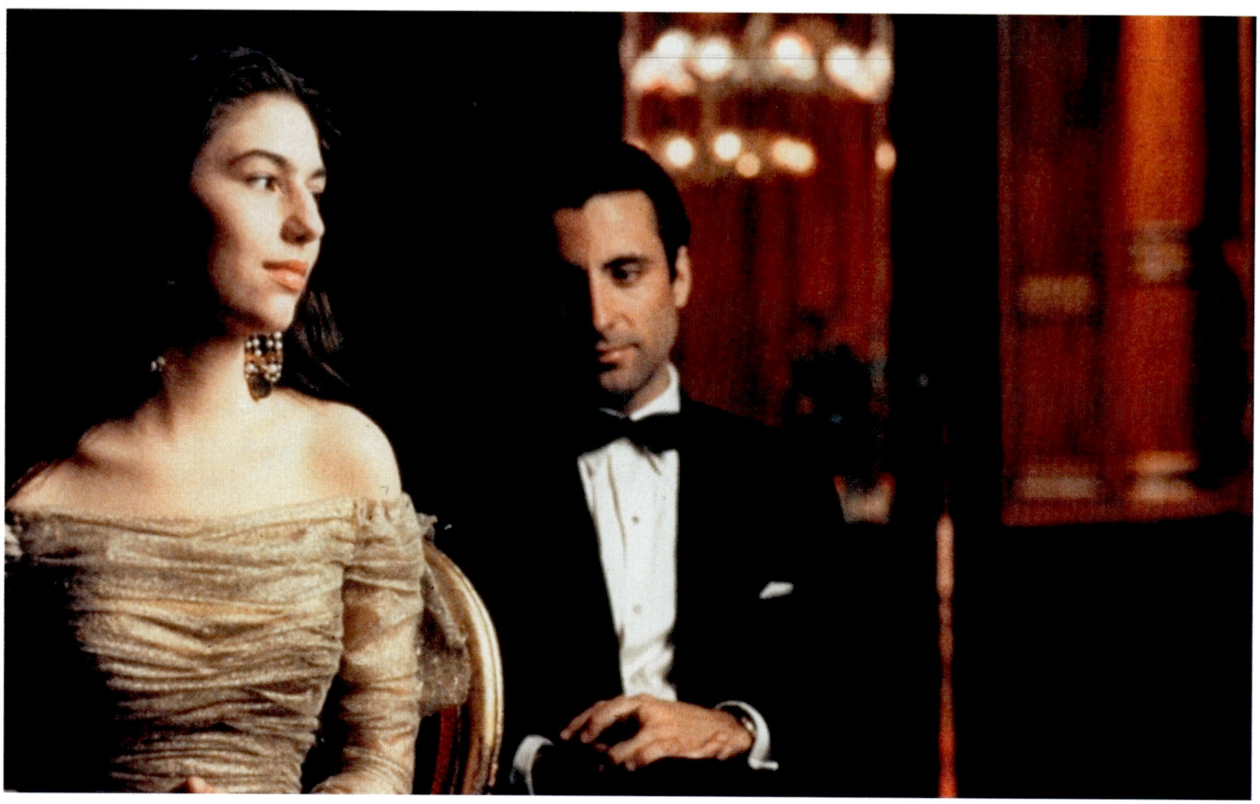

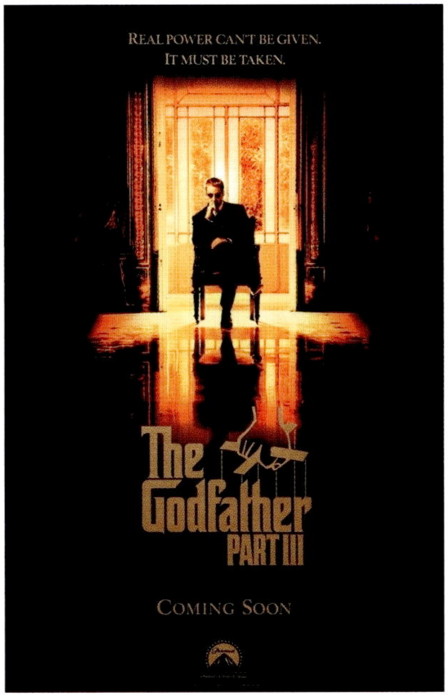

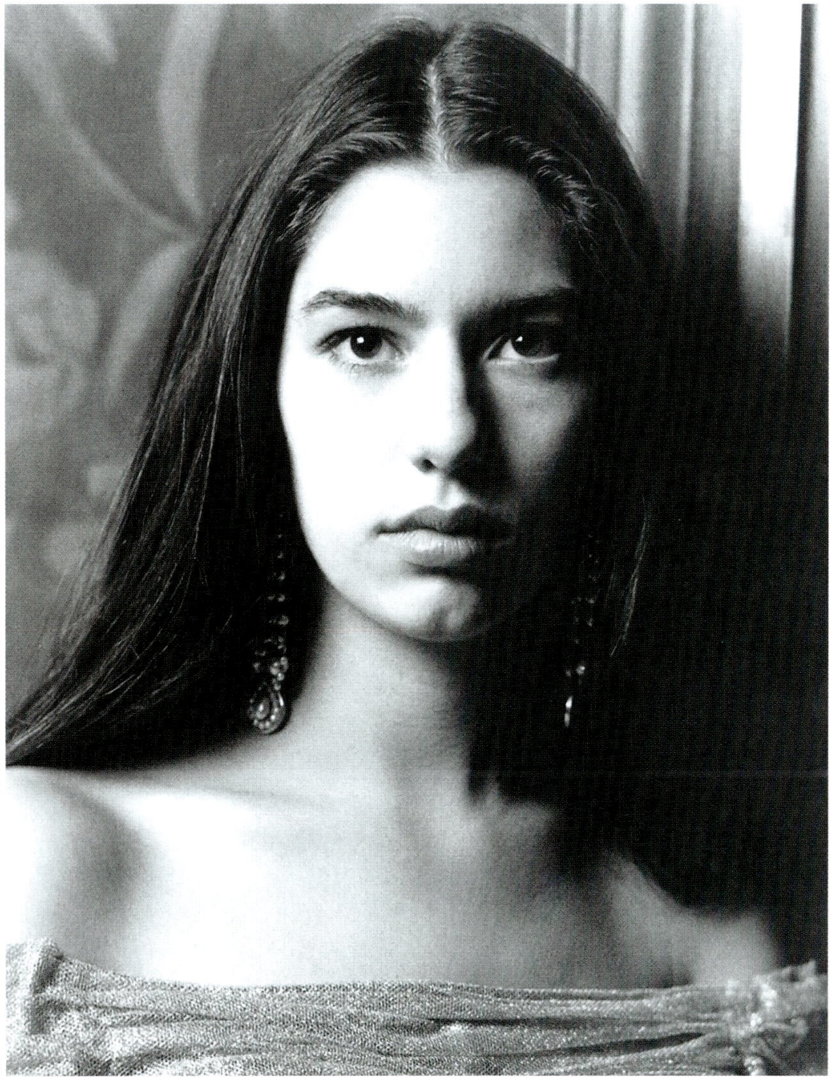

What emerged most firmly from this baptism-by-Hollywood was a decision. Acting was officially not for her. She claimed not to have been devastated, it was more the embarrassment of having supposedly ruined her father's film that left her wounded. 'It probably toughened me up,'[14] she said, reflecting on the 'freak show thing.'[15] You suspect it cut deeper than she lets on, she is still so sensitive to criticism, saving a weary sigh for the umpteenth time Mary Corleone is brought up in interview. On some level, she wouldn't be the director she is without that experience. She knows what it means to be exposed in front of the camera. And that fame could be a poisoned cup, being dragged from hotel to hotel around the world, including the Park Hyatt in Tokyo, to promote her great failure.

There followed a period of no fixed bearing as she tried to find herself outside of the family trade, only to be slowly pulled back in (the metaphors formed their own *Godfather* cliché). 'I was in my 20s, and it felt like there was a freedom to do whatever you wanted,'[16] she said. She dropped out of a CalArts course on oil painting, when they firmly told her she was no painter. Transferring to the ArtCenter College of Design in Pasadena, she studied photography with Paul Jasmin, who had pioneered a commercial aesthetic – a kind of glossy truth. He offered overdue encouragement. 'He told me my point of view was worth exploring,'[17] she said, now set on being a visual artist of some sort.

Above left and right: *There were many more flaws than just Coppola's performance in* The Godfather Part III. *Indeed, the presence of the delicate Mary has come to be reassessed over the years. But the criticism she received for it was a wound she would carry for many years.*

So much of what she learned about photography was simply transferred into filmmaking. Indeed, her work has been repeatedly slammed as superficial, but that is part of the deception. So much stirs beneath the limpid surface. 'I don't understand why looking at superficiality makes you superficial!'[18] she later said. It's the looking that is important.

She became part of a subset of musicians, actors, and artists, left-field Hollywood drinking beside the pool at the Chateau Marmont, living and partying on the hip fringes of the scene. Why not, she was in her twenties. She thought of herself as a 'dilettante,'[19] and for a while Sofia Coppola was best known as a style icon, driving about town in a jet-black Cadillac Seville (just as *Somewhere's* Johnny aimlessly prowls LA in a jet-black Ferrari). She was drawn to kindred spirits, fellow children of famous parents like Zoe Cassavetes, daughter of director John Cassavetes and actress Gena Rowlands, with whom she hosted the short-run comedy series *Hi Octane* on Comedy Central.

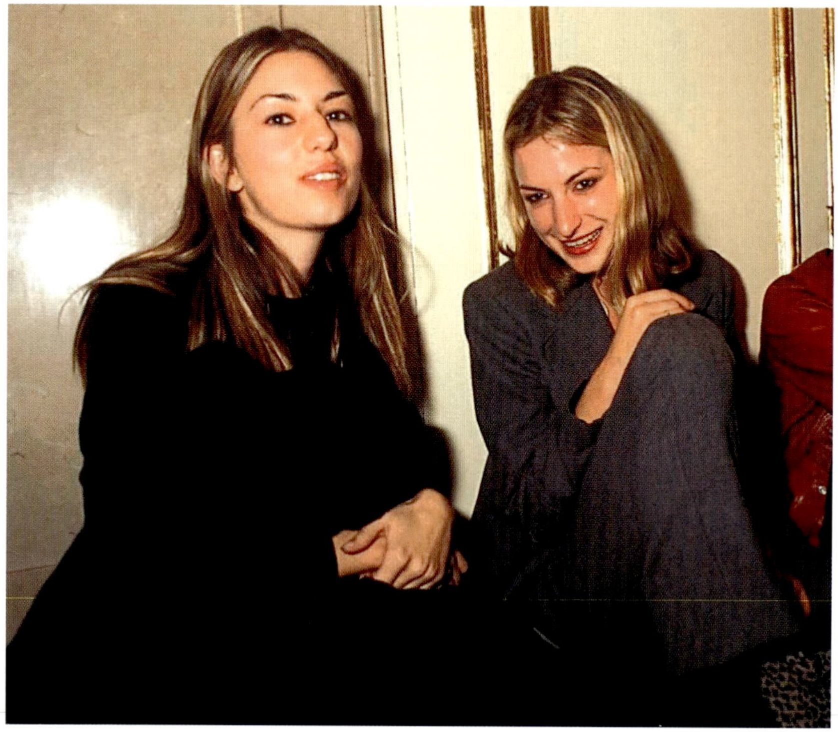

Above: *The cool kids – Sofia Coppola with friend and collaborator Zoe Cassavetes (daughter of director John Cassavetes) backstage at a 1986 fashion show.*

Opposite left: *She's in fashion – Coppola could add working as a model to an extensive résumé. Here, she's working the runway of a Donna Karan fashion show in 1994.*

Opposite right: *Cover girl – confirming her status as one of the It girls of the noughties, Coppola made the cover of the December 2004 edition of* French Vogue.

Shot on handheld Hi8 video, it was an unlikely (certainly in terms of Sofia's forthcoming raptures), ahead-if-its-time blast of unfixed motorhead-music-fashion reality TV in which the friends talk cars and bikes with Nicolas Cage and Keanu Reeves, and the future of cinema with Gus Van Sant and Sofia's ever-willing father, who happened to be floating in a swimming pool. 'I wanted to do a magazine that I'd want to see, that I'd be interested in,'[20] she explained in 1995. She didn't want celebrities talking about their latest character, she wanted to know what they were listening to, what they were reading.

Inevitably almost, it ran for only four episodes, but there are faint signals of what is to come. The intense first-person camerawork, cars streaming through cities, that rush of emotional spontaneity – everything on a whim. Sofia makes for an unconvincing host, the wacky, bad-girl groove something of a put-on, but there is a hint of good old-fashioned rebellion about it all. This was hardly what we had come to expect from a Coppola.

If not a teacher or nurse, or a director, the 'big girl'[21] Sofia could see herself as a magazine editor, working with the best photographers, curating a vibe. During the making of *One from the Heart*, aged ten or so, she launched her own gossip magazine with her friends called *Dingbat News*, which she distributed to the cast and crew.

In the same year as *Hi Octane*, 1994, she launched a far more successful clothing line MilkFed with friend Stephanie Hayman. Something that grew naturally out of her love of fashion. 'We started as amateurs, and I really like the amateurish-ness,'[22] she claimed with breezy humility in 2002. The designs were playful, cool casual wear in warm colours aimed at the young, an aesthetic that extended to cosmetics and

> **Designing the MilkFed line is something I enjoy doing, but it's not my main goal, creatively.**
> ***SOFIA COPPOLA***

stationery. Boutiques were opened in Los Angeles, Osaka, and most successfully (and tellingly) the Heaven 27 store in Tokyo, where the clientele could hang out reading magazines and listening to catchy pop music.

'Designing the MilkFed line is something I enjoy doing,' she remarked, 'but it's not my main goal, creatively.'[23] Film was waiting to sweep her up, but she has remained a part of fashion, both as icon and designer, creating lines for high-end brands, and lending her vibey name and sleek photography to their campaigns. It is an extension of her aesthetic needs, but also an acknowledgment of her father's warning – don't count on the movies to make you money. His career-ballast came with wine, hers with fashion. Film was the risk.

What all this resembles – music, television, fashion, art, and acting – is a mood board for the career to come. Out of her gilded, peripatetic youth came an aesthetic assurance. If she didn't yet know what she wanted to make, she knew how it should look.

'And then, when I made my short film, I realized it was a way to work with all of it.'[24] *Lick the Star* is the point where everything begins to come into focus. Made with MilkFed collaborator Hayman, this fourteen-minute black-and-white short, while not yet a declaration of intent in career terms, showed her a way forward – by accepting the past. She was born to this.

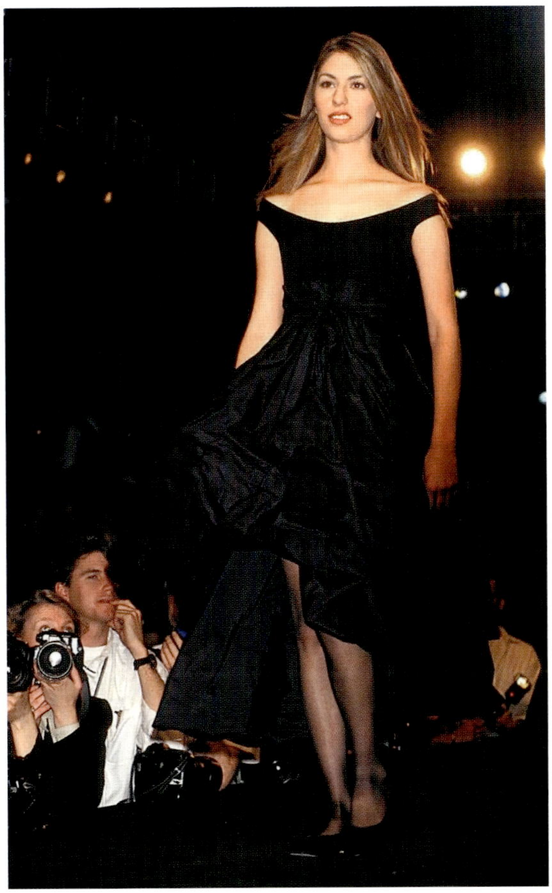

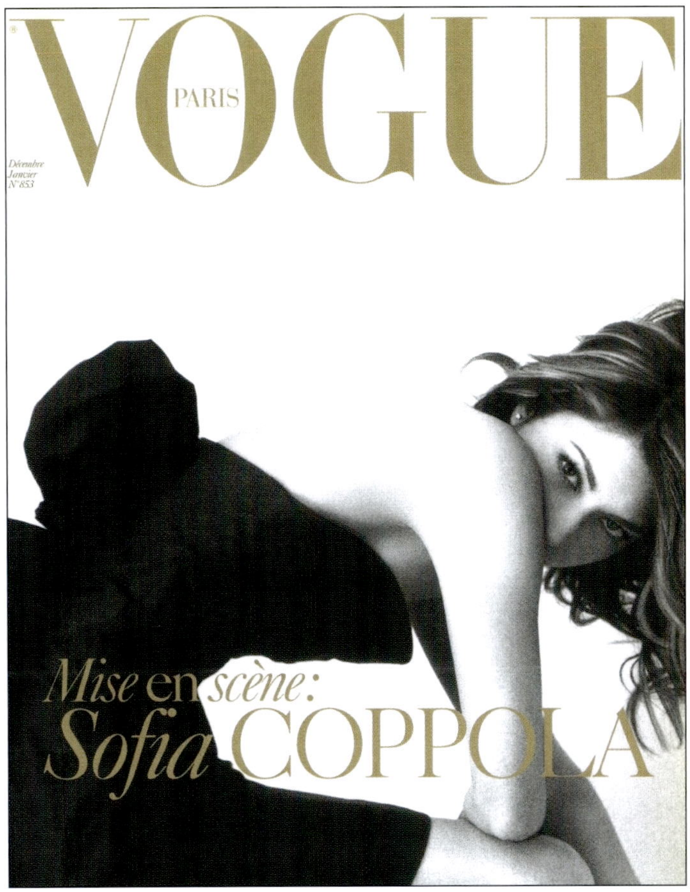

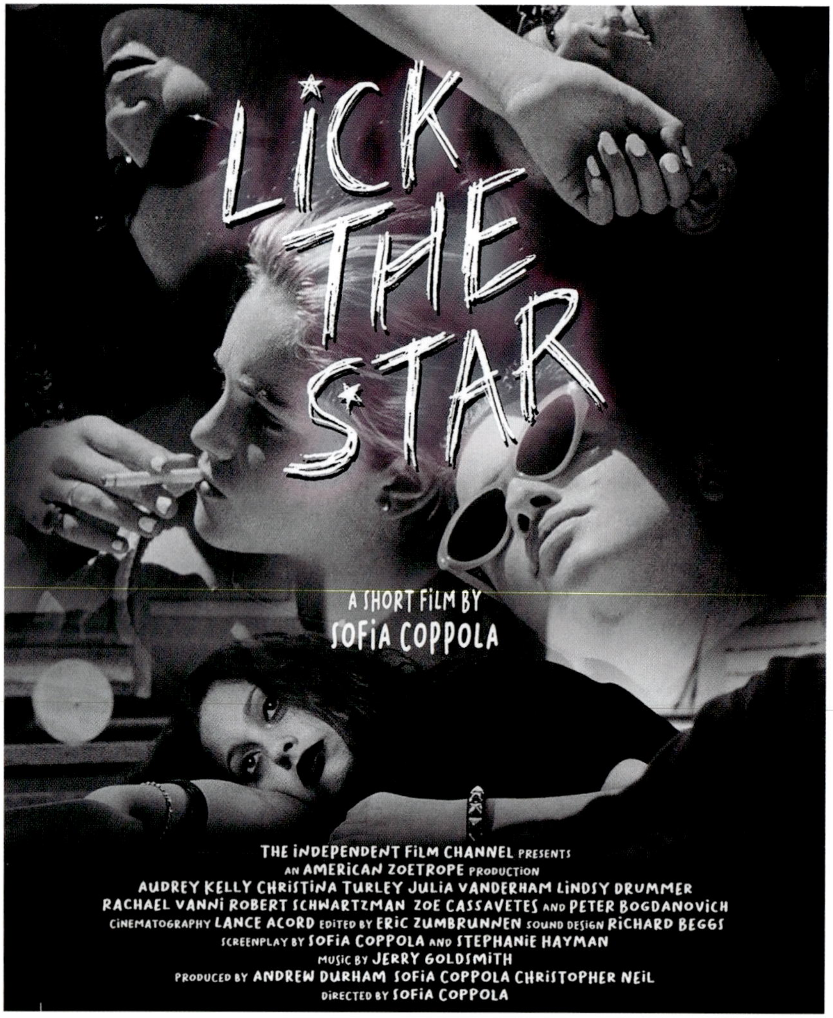

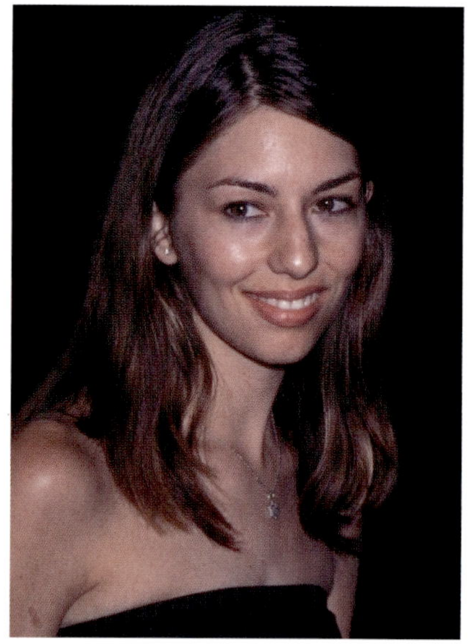

Above: *Coppola in 1998, on the verge of accepting her fate – she was destined to take up the family trade and make extraordinary films.*

Left: *The short teen drama* Lick the Star *(1998) marks Sofia Coppola's official debut as film director, though at the time she was simply exploring the possibilities of personal expression.*

There are hints of *The Virgin Suicides*, *The Bling Ring*, and even *The Beguiled* in its take on the shifting hierarchies of a clique of waspish teenage girls who turn on their coven leader. The story is told from the intense perspective of seventh-grader Kate (Christina Turley), fretting about her social station after returning to school after breaking her foot – she provides the voiceover that acts as our guide. Chloe (Audrey Heaven) is the ringleader who is brought to heel by the power of gossip and misunderstanding.

Along with the themes and already coherent style is an idea of the familiar, comfortable teams she would assemble around her projects: Lance Acord served as cinematographer (as he would on *Lost in Translation*), her brother Roman worked as second-unit director (as he would on just about everything), while Zoe Cassavetes and her cousin Robert Schwartzman (brother of Jason) were among the cast.

When the short debuted at the Venice Film Festival, there was no doubt that her surname was both a burden and boon. Nevertheless, *Lick the Star* is a compact experiment in the possibilities of Sofia-film and fixing her own sensibility as a filmmaker: the dynamic, realistic performances from teenagers; the visual flourishes; that feeling not of observing but stepping inside adolescence. The lush, haunting sense of loneliness and estrangement comes straight from the big girl's heart.

MOOD BOARD

The tell-tale motifs of the Sofia style

1. Hotels
A familiar haunt for Coppola's muse, they are worlds within worlds, luxurious alien settings where everyone is a kind of exile. See: *Lost in Translation, Somewhere,* or *On the Rocks*.

2. Cities by Night
There is a real contrast between the vibrant life of her neon-lit cityscapes and the loneliness of an observer, adrift on electric currents. See: *Lost in Translation, The Bling Ring, A Very Murray Christmas*, or *On the Rocks*.

3. Those Windows
The signature Sofia shot – figures lost in their thoughts as they gaze out of a window of a hotel or a cab or anywhere. But is it the scene beyond or their reflection that has stirred a reverie? See: *Lost in Translation, Somewhere*, or *A Very Murray Christmas*.

4. Spirit Animal Cars
Cars become vessels of transformation for Coppola's characters, carried along in cabs or driving somewhere – anywhere. See: Trip's Chevrolet in *The Virgin Suicides*, Felix's Alfa in *On the Rocks*, or Priscilla's Mercedes driving her to freedom in *Priscilla*.

5. Subdued Colours
Long essays have to be written on Coppola's palette, a muted spectrum of visual codes for the inner life of her characters. See: the soft pinks and despairing blues of *The Virgin Suicides*, the distant, unfocused neons of *Lost in Translation*, or the cornucopia of pastels in *Marie Antoinette*.

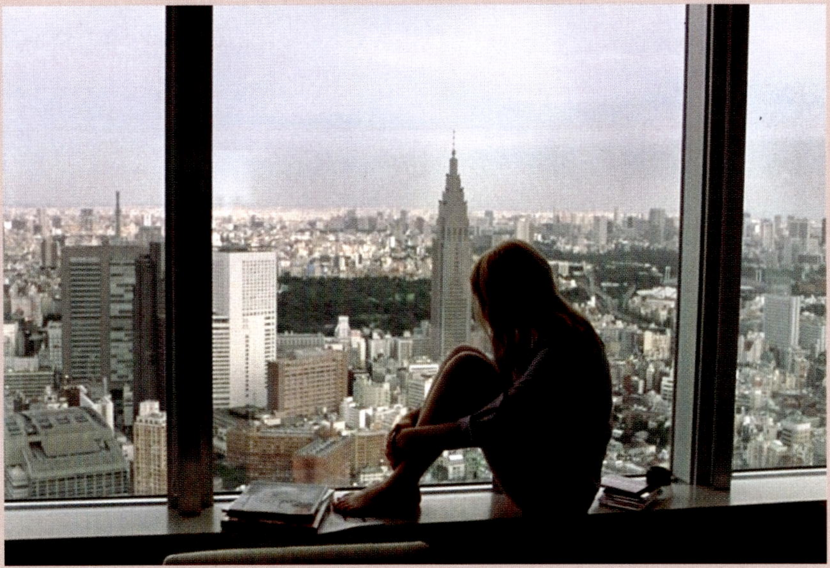

Above: *The signature shot – Scarlett Johansson's Charlotte takes in Tokyo from her hotel room in* Lost in Translation.

6. Haunting Songs
The director-curated playlists are as vital as dialogue within Coppola's aesthetic, acting as another gateway into character. Such that the soundtracks have taken on a life of their own, extending the films' ambience into the lives of the viewer. Listen: *The Virgin Suicides, Lost in Translation,* or Somewhere.

7. Table Scenes
Perhaps reflecting her family's dinnertime rituals, Coppola often locates dramatic and comic moments at a dinner table (or the equivalent). They are tricky to mount (those interminable eyelines), so often it can be only two for dinner. See: dining with the Lisbons in *The Virgin Suicides*, the ice-cream scene in *Somewhere*, or the fatal night in *The Beguiled*.

8. The Fabrics
It isn't simply a matter of costumes that make the characters, but the very fabrics they wear (remember Coppola is a fashion designer herself). She brings something tactile to her storytelling, as her camera closes in on the all-important clothing. See: the floral patterns and muslin smocks of *The Virgin Suicides*, the chintz gowns of *Marie Antoinette*, or the faded cotton dresses in *The Beguiled*.

9. The Pools
Arguably a mark of Coppola's predisposition for privilege, but there is a depth (no pun intended) to her use of swimming pools. We sense something cleansing about them, an attempt to shake off the ennui, or give in to it. See: *Lost in Translation, Somewhere*, or *Priscilla*.

10. Those Open Endings
Coppola never likes to close a book fully, and leaves us to ponder the afterlives of her movie characters forever. See: the boys haunted by the lost Lisbon girls in *The Virgin Suicides*, Bob's whisper in *Lost in Translation*, or where Johnny might be headed in *Somewhere*.

THE LOST GIRLS

The Virgin Suicides (1999)

With its haunting mood and sensitive portrayal of teen life, adapted from a literary darling, her debut film defined a style

Sofia Coppola had adapted *The Virgin Suicides* in secret, as if telling anyone would break the spell. She wasn't ready to admit, even to herself, that she wanted to transform this strange book into a film, which meant being a director. Making *Lick The Star* had brought together so many of the things she loved: photography, fashion, and music. Something was stirring, but admitting she wanted to be a filmmaker? That was too close to home.

Jeffrey Eugenides' 1993 novel had been passed on by Thurston Moore from Sonic Youth, one of Coppola's coterie of edgy-hip Californian friends. It was simply a great read, Moore had told her. She was immediately struck by the cover, a cascade of blonde locks without a face. She had no backing from a production company, or any kind of permission from the author to attempt a script. In fact, Muse (led by producers Chris and Roberta Hanley), the company which held the rights, had already commissioned a script from Nick Gomez, who had directed *Laws of Gravity* in 1992 with a snarling East Coast verisimilitude.

Coppola wrote a screenplay out of a pressing but indefinable need, highlighting passages with a marker, convinced she would only experiment with a few chapters, but like a junkie finding herself unable to stop. She was so connected with the material that she 'had no choice.'[1] She could see the film in her mind, which meant she could feel it, all her senses alerted to its incipient style: the gilded, elusive mood; its blend of enchantment and commonplace. 'The way it was written just felt cinematic,'[2] she said.

It was as if the novel expressed something she already knew, even though the suburbs of Grosse Pointe, Michigan in the mid-seventies were far removed from her own experience. The ennui of the Lisbon sisters resonated like a tuning fork, and she knew by instinct that this was when a film chose you.

Of Greek and Irish descent, indeed tracing a family tree back to Asia Minor via Kentucky, Brown alum Eugenides was inspired to write his first novel by the strangeness of life. He was visiting his brother in Grosse Pointe and got talking to the family's teenage babysitter, who idly mentioned that she and all her sisters had attempted suicide, but she couldn't exactly say why, only that 'they were under a lot of pressure.'[3] The novel was born from the exoticism of this sibling suicide pact and the airy nonchalance of its root cause.

Opposite: *Kirsten Dunst faces the camera as troubled Lux Lisbon, one of the five sisters at the dark heart of* The Virgin Suicides. *Sofia Coppola captures them as both high school girls and angels.*

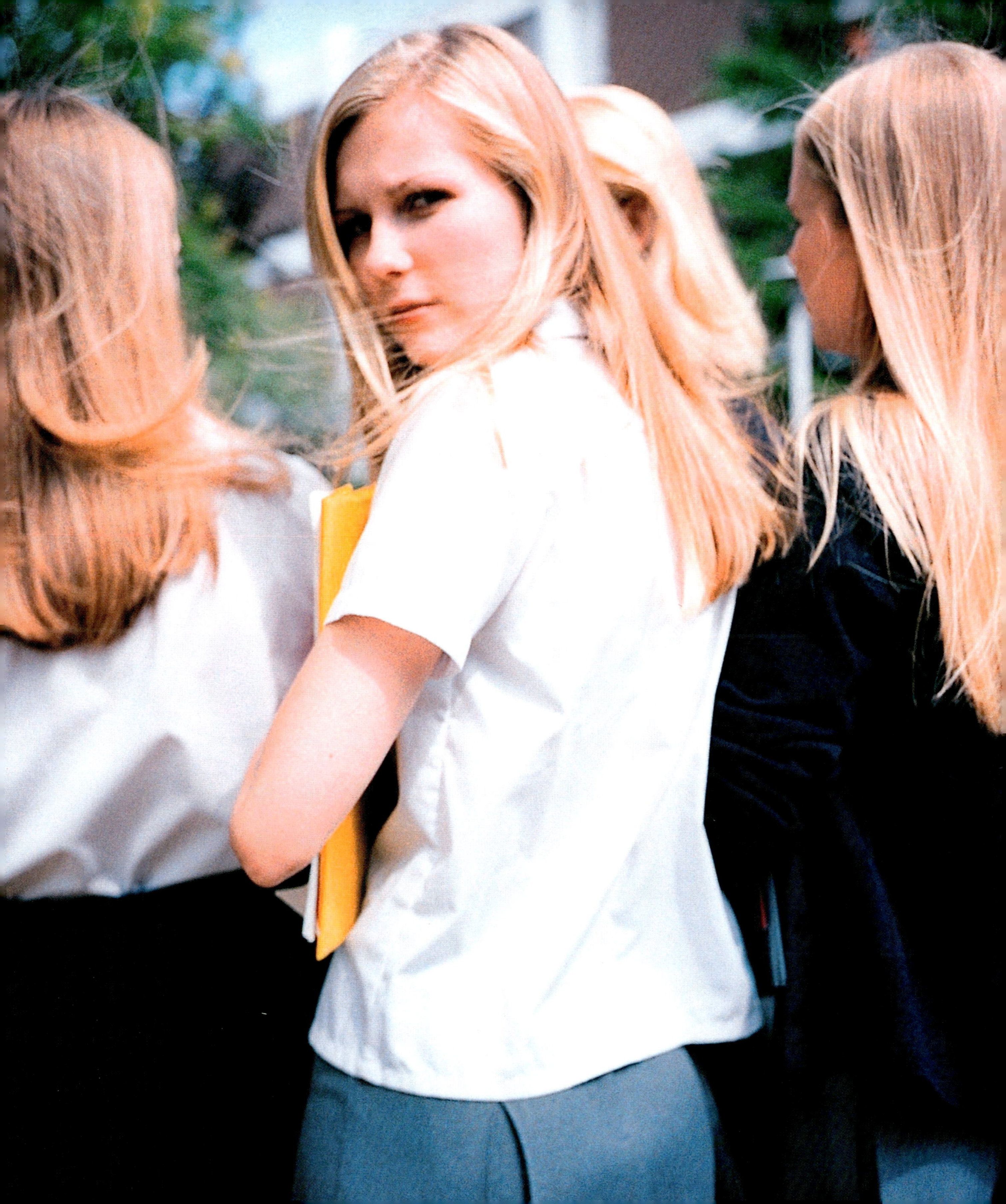

As soon as he wrote the first sentence, he knew the story needed to be told by 'another consciousness'[4] – the collective memories of the young men, now slumped in middle age, who adored the sisters as all teenage boys adore teenage girls. The title came with the first paragraph.

'I think psychologically, emotionally, the real influence was growing up in Detroit,' noted Eugenides, recalling a city in decay like a fallen empire. 'Things, giving into entropy.'[5] Life was impermanent, he reflected, and it is our fate to be haunted by some ideal vision of the past.

As recalled by four neighbourhood boys (collected into the stoic voice of Giovanni Ribisi's narrator), the Lisbon sisters, Lux, Therese, Mary, Bonnie, and Cecilia, grow up in a loving but fiercely protective Catholic household in Grosse Point as the seventies drift by, each in her own way yearning for release, for love, for experience. At various stations of teenage life, each blonde sister will commit suicide. The narrator coolly informs us of the how and the when, but the why remains the eternal, unanswerable question. With the brief romance between Lux (Kirsten Dunst), most rebellious of the Lisbons, and school heartthrob Trip Fontaine (Josh Hartnett) forming the catalyst of the tale, that mystery has haunted the boys for the rest of their lives.

Eugenides wrote with a great sense of innocence, not yet an author weighed down by definitions, uncertain the book would ever be published. You are writing, he said, because you want to. Coppola would direct her adaptation with a similar rush of heroic naïveté. It was not because she thought of herself as a director, but because she owed it to the Lisbon girls.

The problem was that she had written a script for a film she had no possibility of making. This was when serendipity (or fate, or talent, or family) intervened. Muse were unsatisfied by Gomez's script. It was too dark, too cold, he had missed the essential musicality of the novel, its elegiac groove.

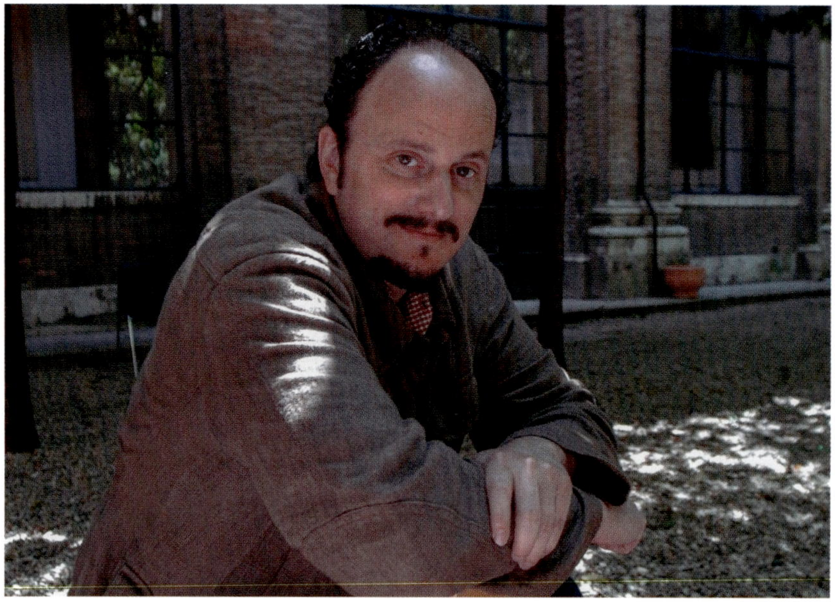

Above: *Author Jeffrey Eugenides in 2003. His first novel,* The Virgin Suicides, *captured his youth on the margins of a declining Detroit, and his sense of the impermanence of life.*

Opposite: *Madonna's break-out film performance in* Desperately Seeking Susan *(1985) was a significant influence on the film. That need for escape...*

'Well, the story is not really an exploration of suicide,' Coppola would later posit, never comfortable with locking her films down to definitions, least of all this one. 'It's not really about that. It's using it as a metaphor for these boys, you know? Confusion and the loss of innocence, and growing up. It's not in the realistic style.'[6]

She was also planning to shift the story away from the novel in a subtle but significant direction. Her camera would take us beyond the romantic speculations of the boys, where the girls remain angelic apparitions, framed in a corona of golden hair; a fantasy built of fragments, and ultimately a reflection of their own long-lost adolescence. The film will actually enter the private realm of the sisters' bedrooms that the boys will never see, but the director does, revealing the tragic chasm between mystery and reality. As critic Megan Abbott mused, Coppola infuses her film with 'impressionistic, unnarrated peeks into the sisters' world on its own terms.'[7]

'I was really motivated to make something sensitive and accurate to a teenage girl,'[8] insisted Coppola.

'We felt the imprisonment of being a girl,' mourns the narrator in Coppola's script, 'the way it made your mind active and dreamy.'[9]

Words to this effect would eventually sway Muse to let Coppola direct her first film. Having heard that they had dropped Gomez, she felt the electric surge of the now-or-never moment, and pushed hard for a meeting. They obviously knew who she was, and there was no missing the fact her father would serve as producer, an ardent supporter of the film sensibly visiting the set for only a few days before departing with his long shadow.

All the same, her pitch was centred on the aesthetic. The film needed to carry an air of detachment, the not-quite-thereness of being a teenager; and this aura of distant, almost embalmed nostalgia, as if the entire story was a flashback. Memories, she instinctually understood, were intensely cinematic (and a theme to bind a career). 'I didn't want it set in the seventies, but to be more about these boys looking back at this time of their life in the seventies,'[10] she explained.

After months of deliberation, doing wonders for Coppola's nerves, Muse granted her a budget of $6.1 million and she began making plans. How she would shoot on location, treading lightly with the milieu. She tightly aligned herself with cinematographer Edward Lachman (who had cultivated the yearning in *Desperately Seeking Susan* and *Far from Heaven*), as she would with all her cinematographers. This was to be a world viewed in mythical tableaux, where the dappled light of Terrence Malick's *Badlands* and gauzy otherworldliness of Peter Weir's *Picnic at Hanging Rock*, those requiems to doomed youth, were mixed with the 'backlit style of '70s *Playboy*'[11] and the languid flatness of Bill Owens' photographic studies of suburbia.

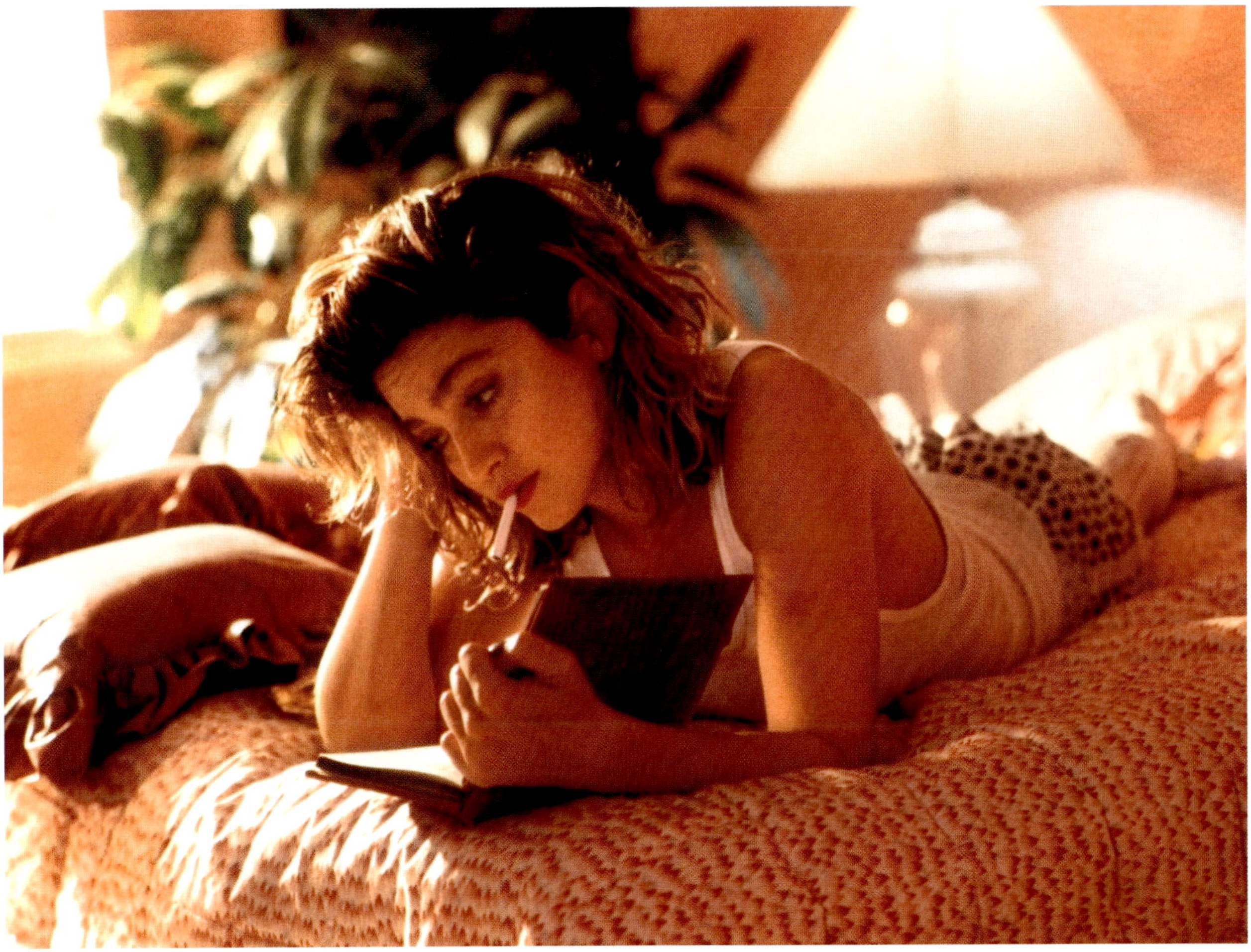

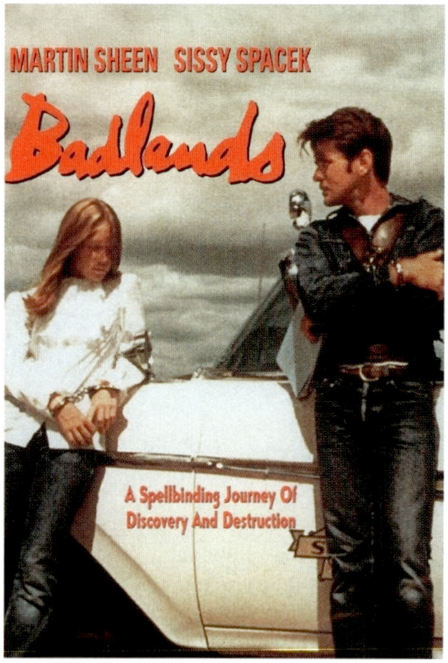

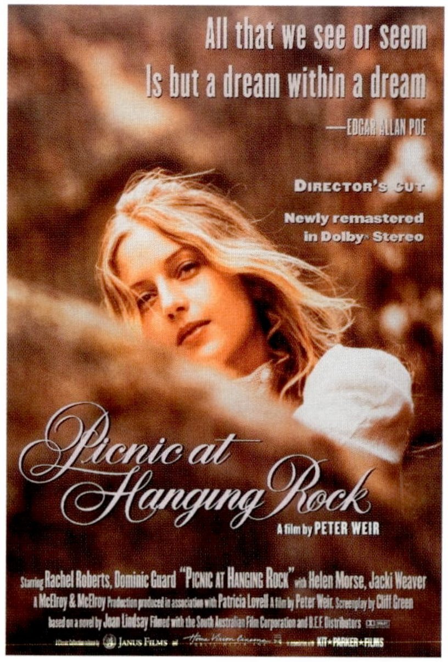

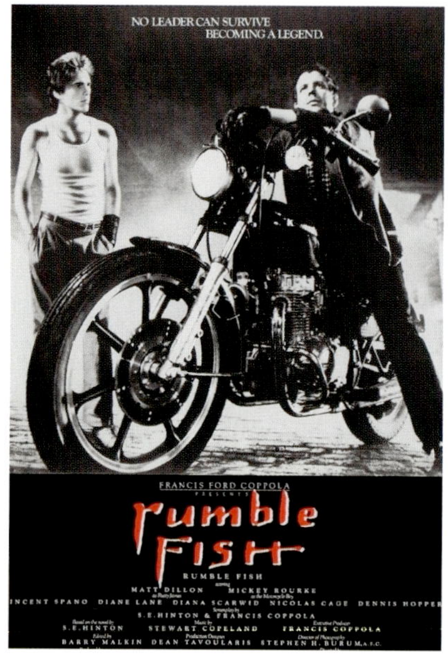

Above: *Throughout her career, Sofia Coppola has readily turned to older films for inspirations. In this case, the haunting, youth-focused auras of Terrence Malick's* Badlands *(1973), Peter Weir's* Picnic at Hanging Rock *(1975), and her own father's* Rumble Fish *(1983).*

From the beginning, she established a process of assembling mood boards, in this case collages of girlish memorabilia with which to build the inner world of the Lisbons, as well as looks for the homes, high school, and manicured neighbourhood streets lined with elms. It was a form of divination, a way of seeing the movie in her head. Collage was an artistic outlet long before directing, cutting out images from old magazines, assembling them, unaware she was telling stories, indeed editing together films. She had an innate specificity born of her training in photography and her love of art.

As production began in the hot summer of 1998, Coppola was faced with a new dilemma – getting what she wanted. 'I spent most of my twenties worrying, "Oh no. I don't know what I want to do",'[12] she admitted. Whether had she accepted it yet or not, directing would finally define her. With that came the burden of the family name. Expectation reared its ugly head. She was a Coppola. But what exactly did that mean for her?

There was a positive influence. After all, this was the family trade, even a genetic trait. She loved that her father had made an art film about teenage life in *Rumble Fish* – a stylish, haunting film in which she had appeared and which was now an inspiration – in the era of *Porky's*. There was the simple osmosis of sitting at the kitchen table with Spielberg, Kurosawa, Scorsese or whichever great was paying a visit. And there were times she just listened to the man who had given her life.

'He was always talking about filmmaking to my brothers and I as if we were all going to be filmmakers. He's always talking about writing structure and actors, and included us in his projects, so I got an incredible education.'[13]

When Francis Ford Coppola came to set he was surprisingly nervous. He sweetly tried to offer advice, father to daughter, director to director. Shout 'action' louder, he warned, to make sure they understood who was in charge. She smiled back, 'But dad, this is how I do it.'[14]

Nevertheless, she would sit beside the camera, as her father had advised, where the actors can see you. And she knew to be careful of high or low angles, and used the 40mm camera he suggested, the same type he had used on *The Godfather*.

Being a Coppola had side effects. She could see that growing up in a household filled with strong male presences had pushed her toward a more feminine style. Such a macho environment, she laughed, made her 'cling to that part of my identity.'[15] But it was something you didn't see too much of in film. It had an originality. Her brother Roman would still serve as second-unit director and creative confidant.

The influence of her mother, Eleanor, was no less significant. They were closer in personality: more reserved, contemplative, but no less strong-willed. She had that same Zen but unshakeable spirit. Eleanor's bohemian glow is also to be found in the lonely Lisbon sisters.

Of course, Coppola still feared the accusation of nepotism and reigniting the backlash she had endured in the wake of *The Godfather Part III*, when she was barely older than the characters in her film. But she was doing this on her terms, certain of how she wanted to tell this story. The film was as much an act of rebellion against that legendary name she couldn't shake, a chance to define herself as an artist. To be more Sofia and less Coppola.

Shooting in the suburbs of Toronto, she made a point of wearing a dress to set. She had noticed that what few women directors there were tended to be pictured 'dressed like guys,'[16] and she was determined to emphasize her femininity. 'I was trying to rebel against the norm of set fashion,'[17] she admitted, but was soon aware there were times you need to be practical: open-toed sandals and heavy equipment don't mix.

It was tough, she had a month to meet the needs of the film in her imagination, but as the camera turned at last she felt the exhilaration of being able to shape the world exactly as she wanted it. And

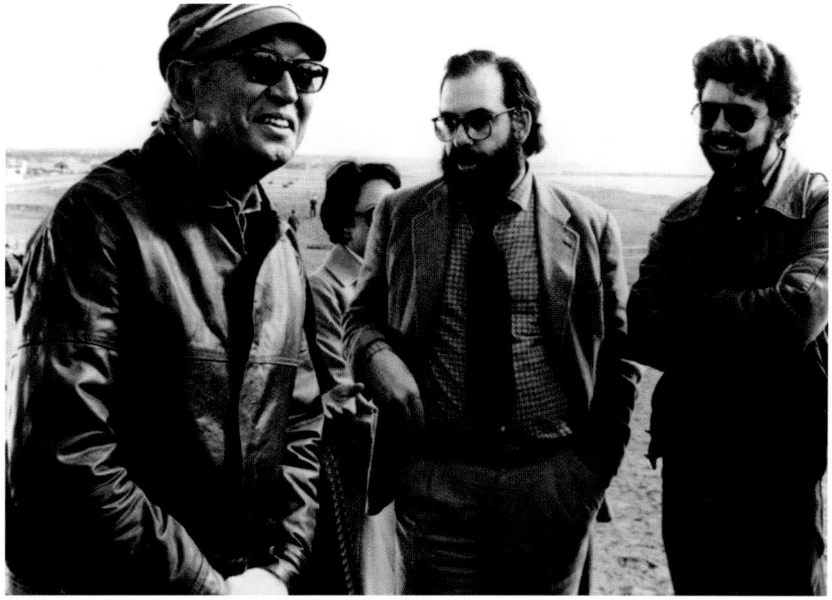

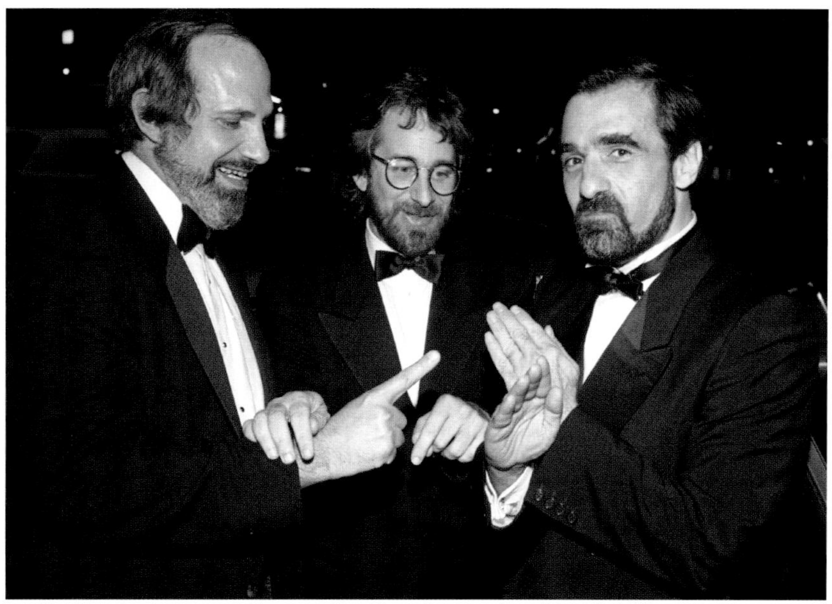

Top and above: *The male gaze – her father, Francis Ford Coppola, had been at the very epicentre of the industry. Here pictured with fellow directors Akira Kurosawa and George Lucas on the set of* Kagemusha. *And a shot of fellow Movie Brats Brian De Palma, Steven Spielberg, and Martin Scorsese.*

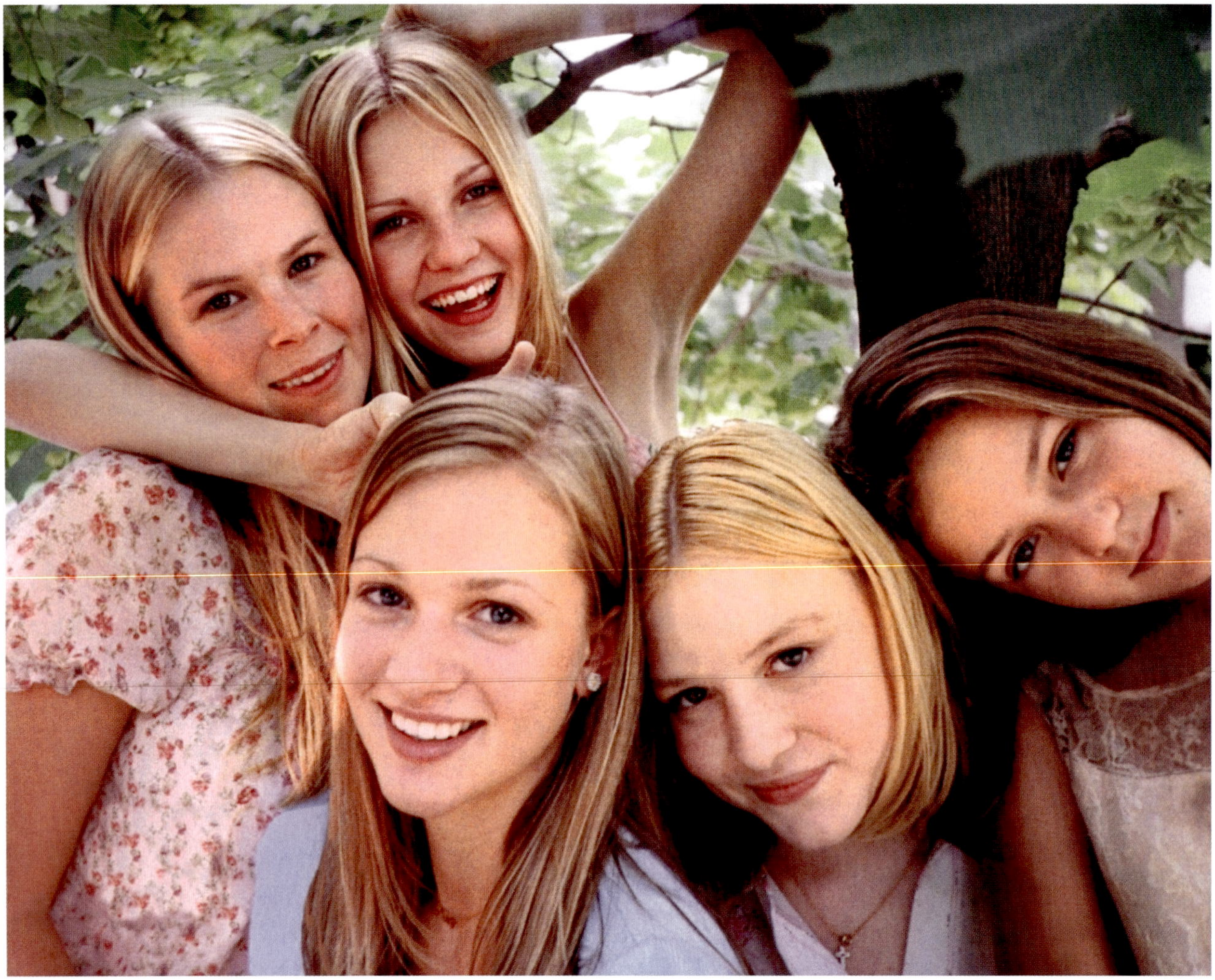

Above: *The Lisbon cast, with their uncanny resemblance. Back row: Therese (Leslie Hayman) and Lux (Kirsten Dunst). Front row: Mary (A.J. Cook), Bonnie (Chelse Swain), and Cecilia (Hanna R. Hall).*

what she didn't want was movie teens, who were usually touching thirty.

Born in Point Pleasant, New Jersey, of German and Swedish descent, Kirsten Dunst had been acting since she was six. Firmly established as a child star (*Interview with the Vampire, Little Women, Jumanji*), at sixteen she had never made a film about growing up. It was vital to Coppola that all her Lisbons would be as close to the ages of their sisters as possible and 'going through the same thing.'[18] She wanted that resonance. Dunst happened to be shooting a comedy in Toronto while they were doing preproduction, and Coppola arranged her first meeting with her first star.

'What I love about her is that she looks like this all-American blonde cheerleader but has this depth behind her eyes that contrasts her look,'[19] she said. So much of the film takes place in those eyes.

Coppola had auditioned others, but it was the rapport that made her so certain. Coppola sensing the reflection of her own life – it wasn't so long ago she was sixteen – and a willingness to be vulnerable. They were in this together. Dunst, on her part, felt the truth lying beneath the cool surface of the script. 'It was a lot of things that I was feeling that I hadn't expressed.'[20]

Her vivid performance as Lux marks the first of what would become a distinctly Coppola mode of expression, a merger of self, character, and a refraction of the director. Though the director didn't know it yet, *The Virgin Suicides* was the start of a thematic trilogy, vastly different in era and location, interpreting a female rite of passage. Significantly, Dunst would lead two of those films.

The Lisbons were all blonde and clearly identifiable as sisters, but each had to have her own identity. Besides the rebellious Lux, who gasses herself in the garage, there was Leslie Hayman's Therese, the oldest at seventeen, bookish and thoughtful, who mixes sleeping pills with gin; A.J. Cook's Mary, prim and pretty and keen on the vantage point of a tree branch, who takes sleeping pills; Chelse Swain's Bonnie, docile middle child, who hangs herself; and Hanna R. Hall's Cecilia, the youngest at thirteen, an oddball, who leaps from a second-floor window onto a spiked fence. Cecilia is the first to take her life, calling to her sisters to follow.

Against her producers' wishes, Coppola would do long takes, using up expensive film stock for scenes of the girls just lolling in their messy bedrooms like Pre-Raphaelite divines, caught in the daze of youth. Gradually, the actresses would grow bored and let their guard down, and the camera would catch the naturalism. What Coppola termed 'moments when you're not on.'[21] The Lisbons will attend prom, against their parents' better judgment, a brief, precious gasp of what life has to offer. But after Lux strays beyond curfew, they will be wrenched from school and shuttered away, left to play ELO and Carole King records down the phone to the forlorn boys, then one by one choosing death as the way out.

Below left: *Sisterhood – Coppola and star Kirsten Dunst take a moment on set. No one was missing the fact that the actress and character were a version of the director.*

Below right: *Coppola made a point of dressing in a feminine way during the shoot, determined to break free of the male stereotype of a director.*

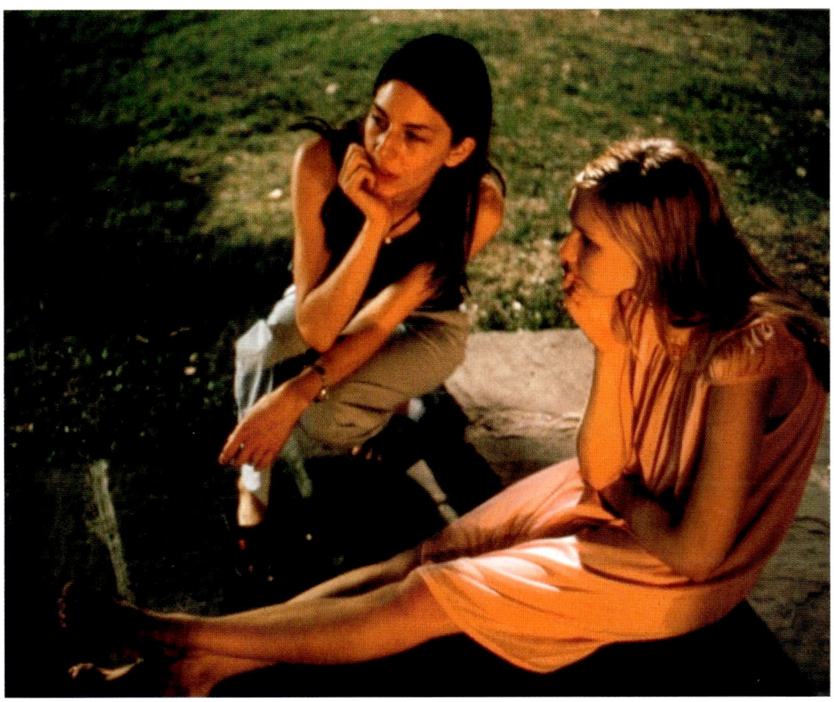

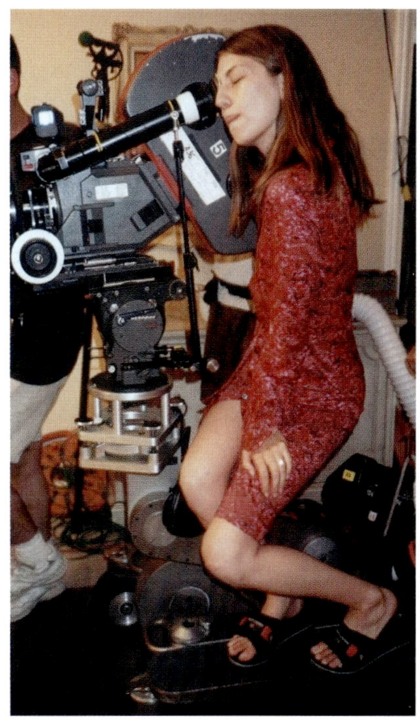

It was only in hindsight that Coppola realized her connection with *The Virgin Suicides* had a lot to do with the loss of her older brother Gio. He had died in a boating accident when she was only fifteen.

The Lisbons' fate is connected with the nascent romance between Lux and Trip. Hartnett would stride onto set, self-conscious in his seventies wig (real life providing the key to unlocking the insecurity within the class hunk), and bringing the production to a standstill. Eugenides had sent Coppola a Xerox of his school yearbook. The guy that Trip was based on had a sunset decorating his page.

Whenever she screened her film, it was the moment of Trip striding down the school hall to Heart's *Magic Man* when she knew she had her audience. She still has that ludicrous wig, stored away like a historical artefact. The stolen tryst in Trip's car was the first onscreen kiss for either Dunst or Hartnett; they had never felt so nervous on set. Coppola wanted to capture the tumultuous feeling of first love.

Her instructions to Dunst were simple. She had to jump onto Hartnett's lap at the wheel of his parked Chevrolet Camaro, kiss passionately, and trade the piece of gum she was chewing. It was perfectly excruciating. 'I remember his wig fell off one time. I was so embarrassed,'[22] recalled Dunst, presenting the film at a 25th anniversary screening, insisting she was a young sixteen. 'It all was very real,' she continued. 'The timing of it was real, which gave you that kind of anxiety watching it.'[23]

Here was Coppola's gift at work, capturing life, spontaneous and awkward and magical. She was born to this.

Not yet a star, nineteen-year-old Hartnett (playing seventeen) was another for whom the film felt like a step into adulthood. Born in Saint Paul, Minnesota, a mix of Irish, German and Swedish blood, he had featured in giddy horrors *Halloween H2O* and *The Faculty*. He admitted to taking himself rather seriously at the time, this 'hyper-vigilant' young actor arriving on set fully prepared, having read the novel alongside the script. He was met by harmony.

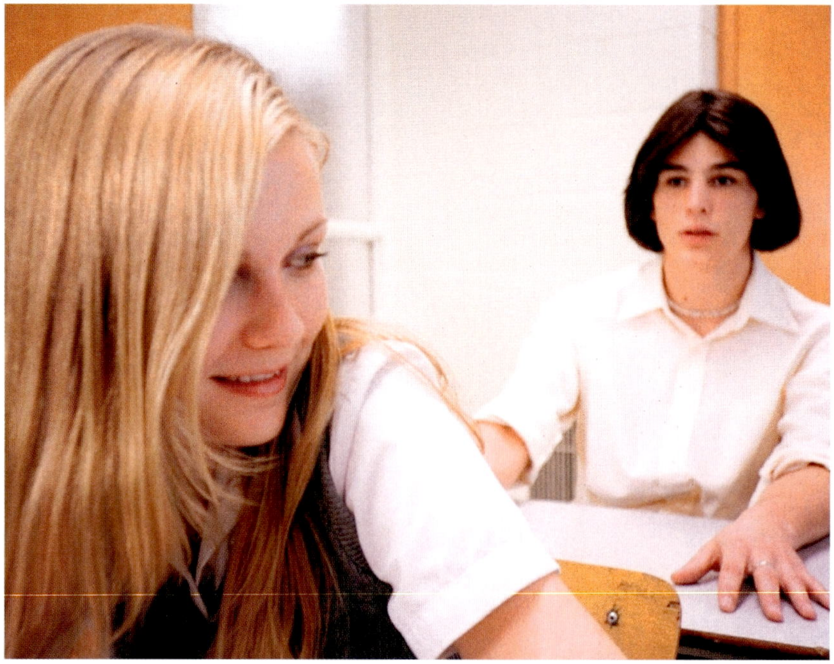

'It was the most pleasant arena to do anything,'[24] he marvelled. Coppola called it summer camp. This was to be another of her defining qualities as director: never to raise her voice – not even to say 'action' – while cultivating a relaxed air on set that would seep into the fabric of the story. An atmosphere so opposite to the 'the mad breath of conflict,'[25] as critic David Thomas put it, that so often consumed her father's sets. Dressed in their vintage clothes, the young cast would hang out on the balmy lawns between set-ups, as deep in the world off-camera as under its gaze. They were all lost in the film.

James Woods and Kathleen Turner are unusually sympathetic as the girls' bewildered parents. Both the ineffectual father and caring but controlling mother

> **It was a lot of things that I was feeling that I hadn't expressed … The timing of it was real, which gave you that kind of anxiety…**
>
> ***KIRSTEN DUNST***

Opposite: *Teenage dreams – Kirsten Dunst's Lux experiences the highs and lows of first love with class heartthrob Trip Fontaine (Josh Hartnett). Hartnett's era-specific wig would be the source of great amusement on set.*

Right: *Hartnett's Trip contemplates the universe at his leisure. Pools would grow into a regular motif for Sofia Coppola, as vessels of contemplation and transformation.*

Below: *The illusions of youth – almost all of* The Virgin Suicides *is seen from the perspective of the local boys, haunted forever by their encounters with these elusive girls.*

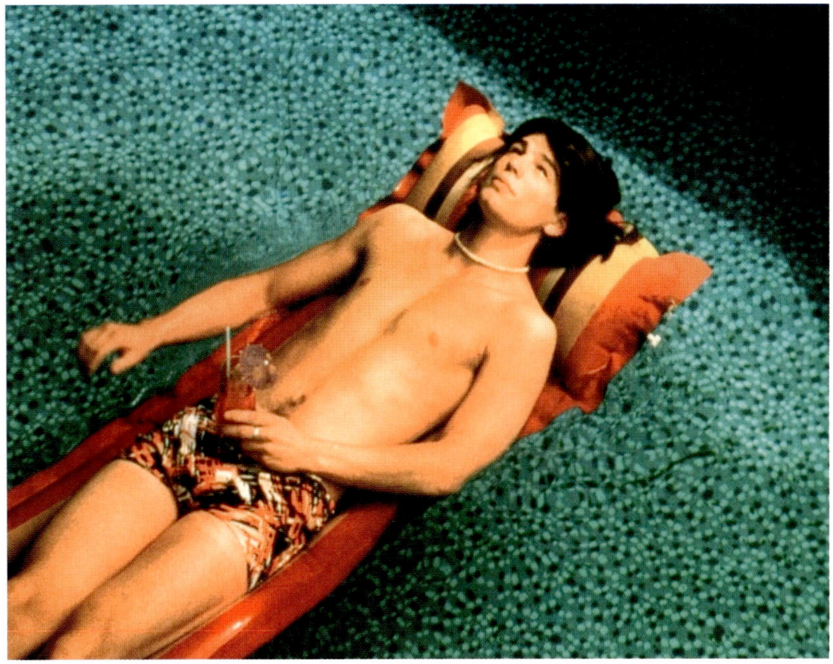

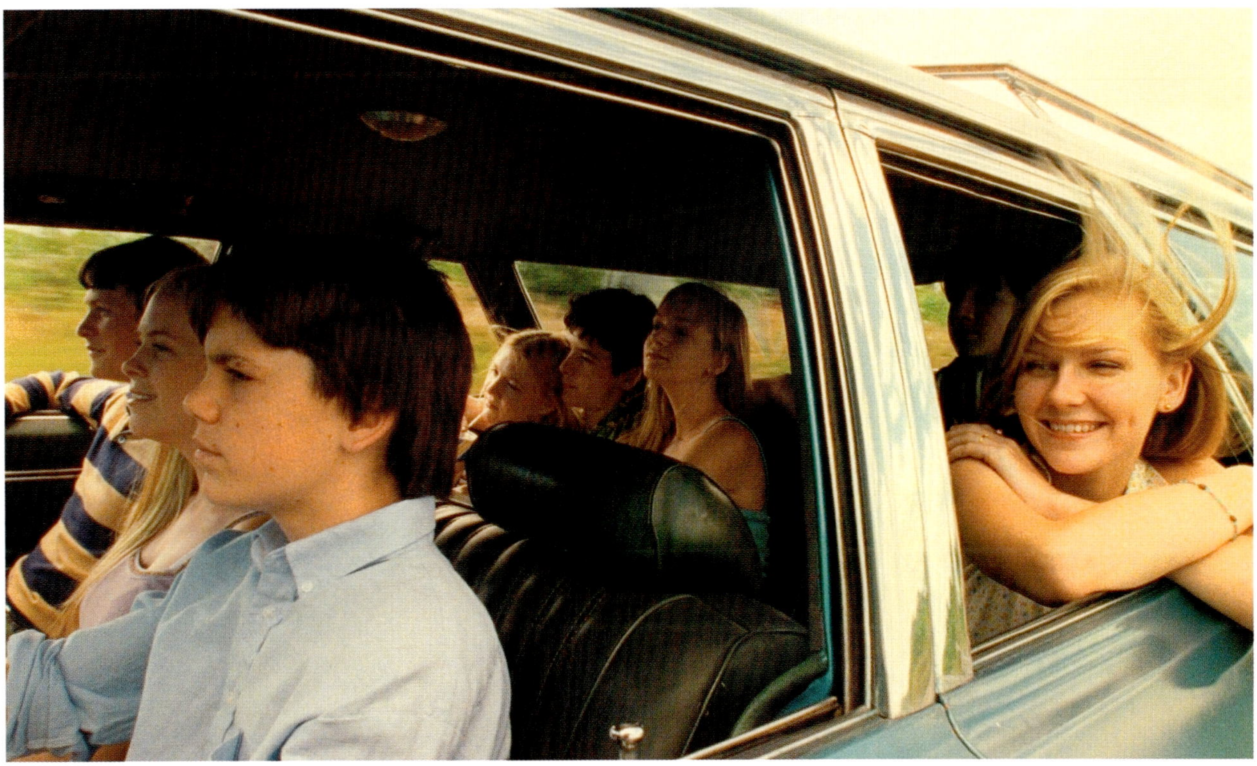

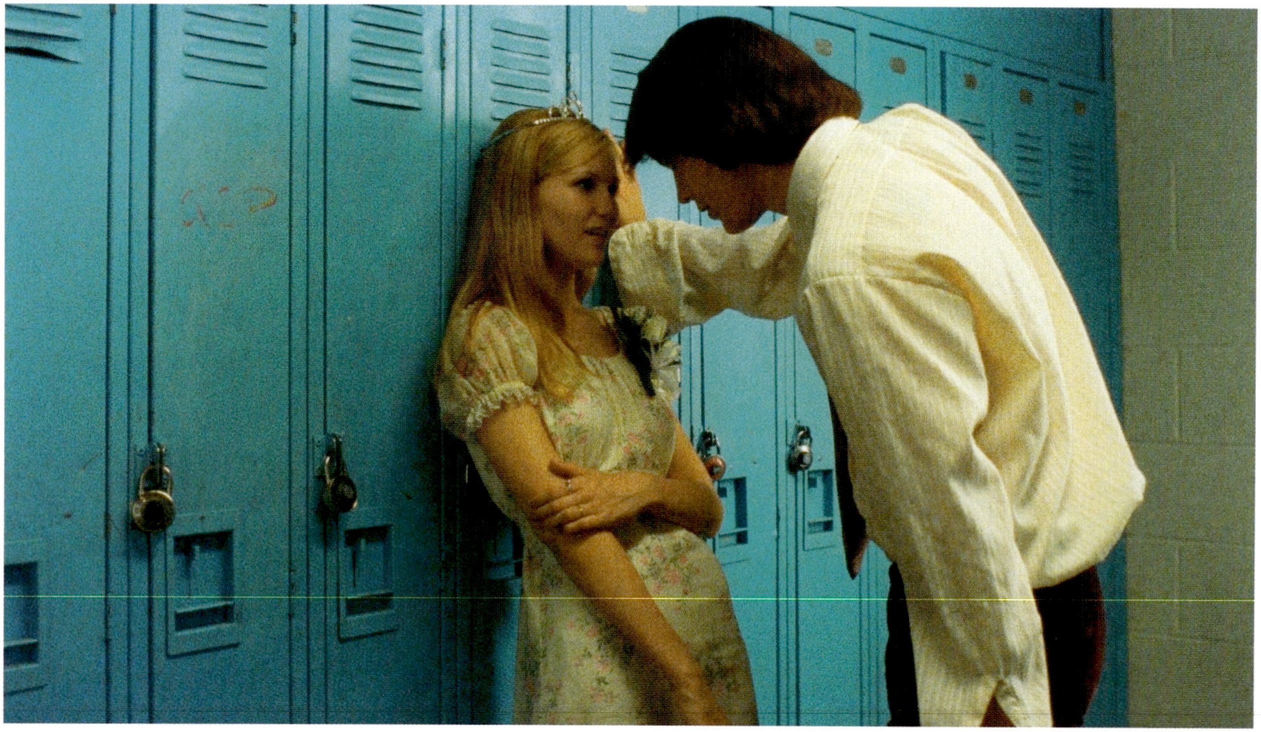

Above: *Lux (Kirsten Dunst) and Trip (Josh Hartnett) on their prom – one of Sofia Coppola's motivations with* The Virgin Suicides *was to capture teen girls as they truly are, not how they have been portrayed in endless teen movies.*

are never demonized. They are, in a sense, themselves victims lost to unaccountable tragedy. Coppola sought the experience and name recognition; landing an old pro like Woods had secured the financing. Her father had reached out to the actor, who responded to the dark humour in the script and a chance to play someone far removed from his metier of tough guys in suits.

Coppola coaxed the performance out of him like a snake charmer, his big personality, all that famous intensity, subdued into this meek, quietly touching maths teacher.

Turner was family of a kind. She and Coppola had played sisters in *Peggy Sue Got Married*. The uptight, religious Mrs Lisbon is more complex than her unprepossessing husband, in equal parts strict, unyielding, a little paranoid, and haunted by the possibility that she might be a cause of the terrible effect. 'None of my daughters lacked for any love, there was plenty of love in our household,' she remonstrates. 'I never understood why.'[26]

Returning to Los Angeles for postproduction, Coppola went in search of an aural texture to match her ethereal mood, another distinctive layer in a materializing style.

Brian Reitzell, an LA musician and composer who happened to be dating her best friend Stephanie Heyman, would serve as musical supervisor. Coppola's instructions were clear: she didn't want a score per se, and there were already cuts from specific seventies artists for a quasi-diegetic effect. What she was looking for was a dreamlike sound that would float over the era non-specifically, an extension of the boys' longing. To which Reitzell suggested Air, the French synth duo whose lush, space-age debut, *Moon Safari*, had caused such a stir on the electronic scene. Nicolas Godin and Jean-

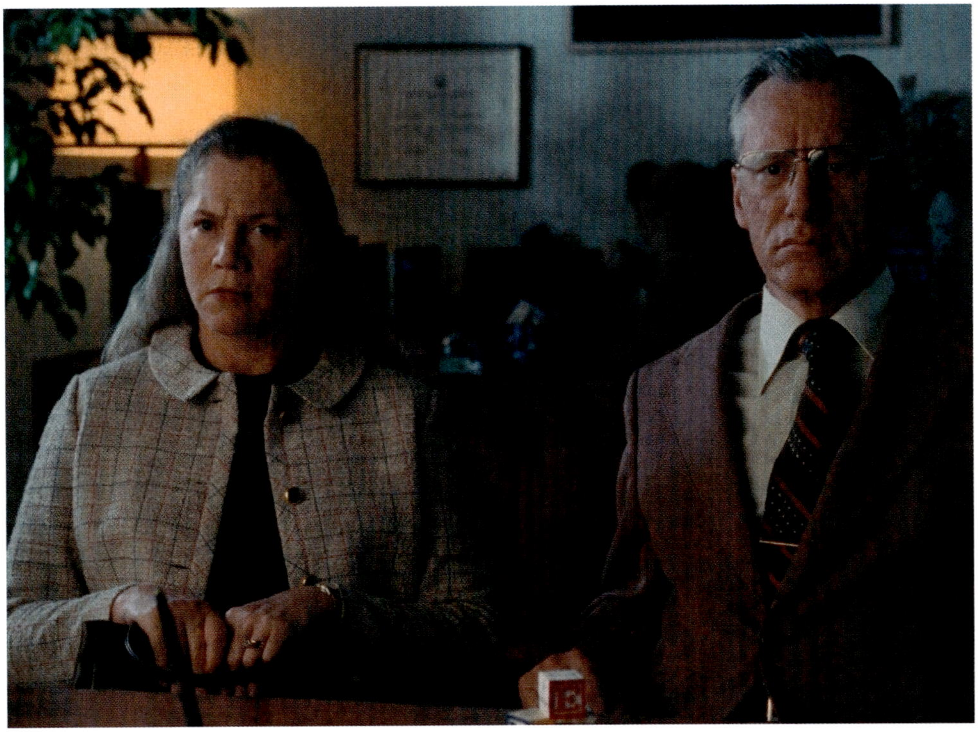

Left: *The torments of parenthood – the good fortune of landing Kathleen Turner and James Woods as Mr and Mrs Lisbon allowed them to emerge as stern but sympathetic characters.*

Below: *In casting Turner, Coppola was consciously referencing her father's time-travelling comedy* Peggy Sue Got Married *(1986), which starred Turner, Don Murray, Barbara Harris, and herself (bottom right) as the happy-ish family.*

Benoît Dunckel would prove to be very Coppola. Moreover, their video director Mike Mills happened to be sharing an office with her brother Roman.

It was all so quick. They had nothing but dailies and the novel to go on, but they caught on. 'There's something about boredom in Sofia Coppola's films,' explained Dunckel. 'She doesn't make boring movies, but they capture the feeling of being bored.'[27] They had a similar experience growing up in the suburbs of Paris, the sensation of not knowing what to do with your life, or where you might be going.

Unhurried, mildly jazzy, wounded, spiritual, epic, and existential, Air's music liberates the film from its era, but is inseparable from Coppola's images.

Exhilaratingly and terrifyingly, *The Virgin Suicides* was accepted into the Directors' Fortnight strand of the Cannes Film Festival. Whether or not the family name had helped

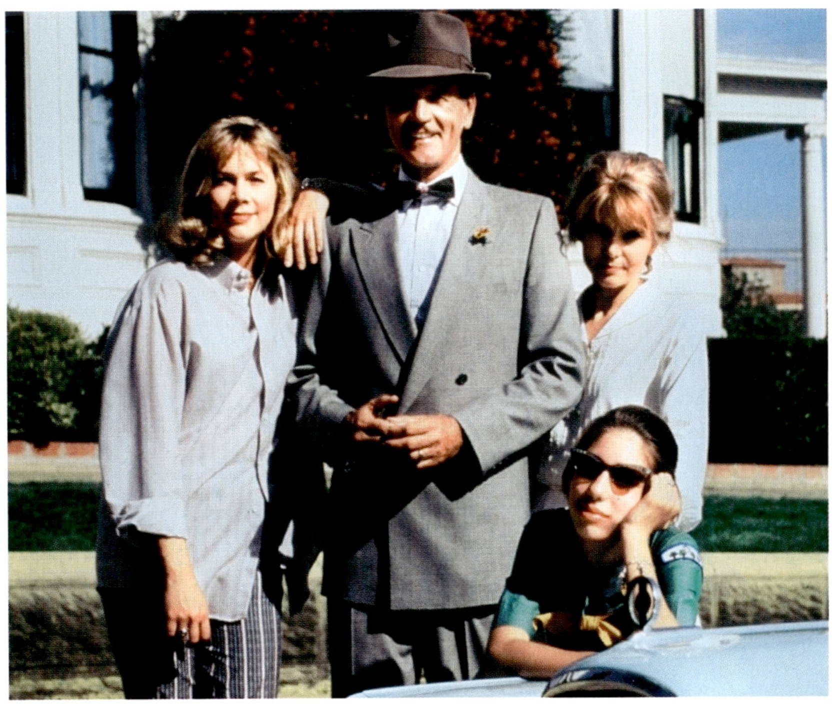

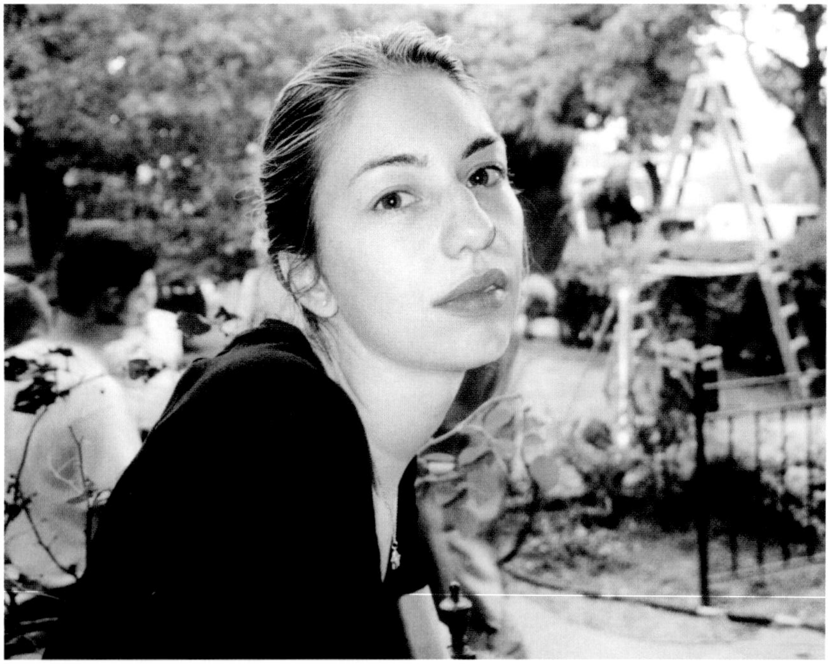

Left: *A twenty-eight-year-old (when she began) Sofia Coppola poses on the set of her first film. She hadn't chosen to become a director, she simply had to tell this story.*

Below: *Director Sofia Coppola finds her shot. From the start she was an artist driven primarily by images, making the film match the one she could already see in her head.*

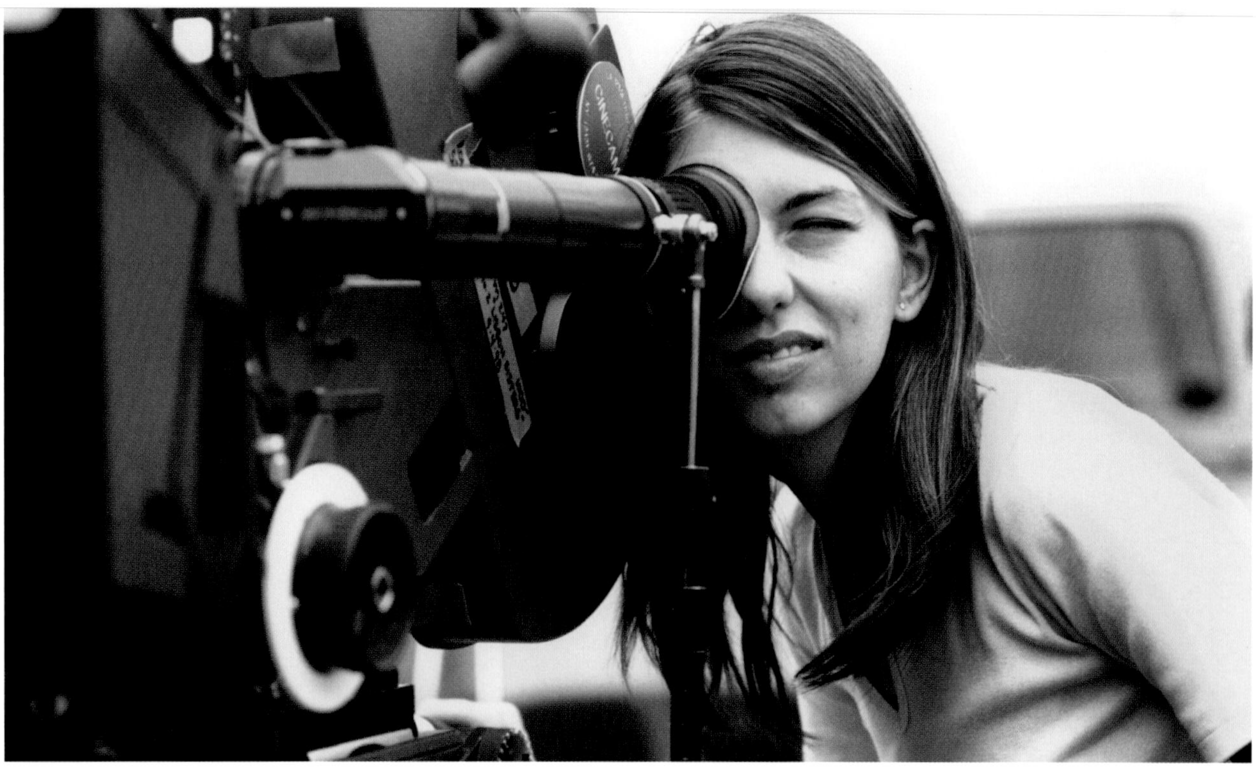

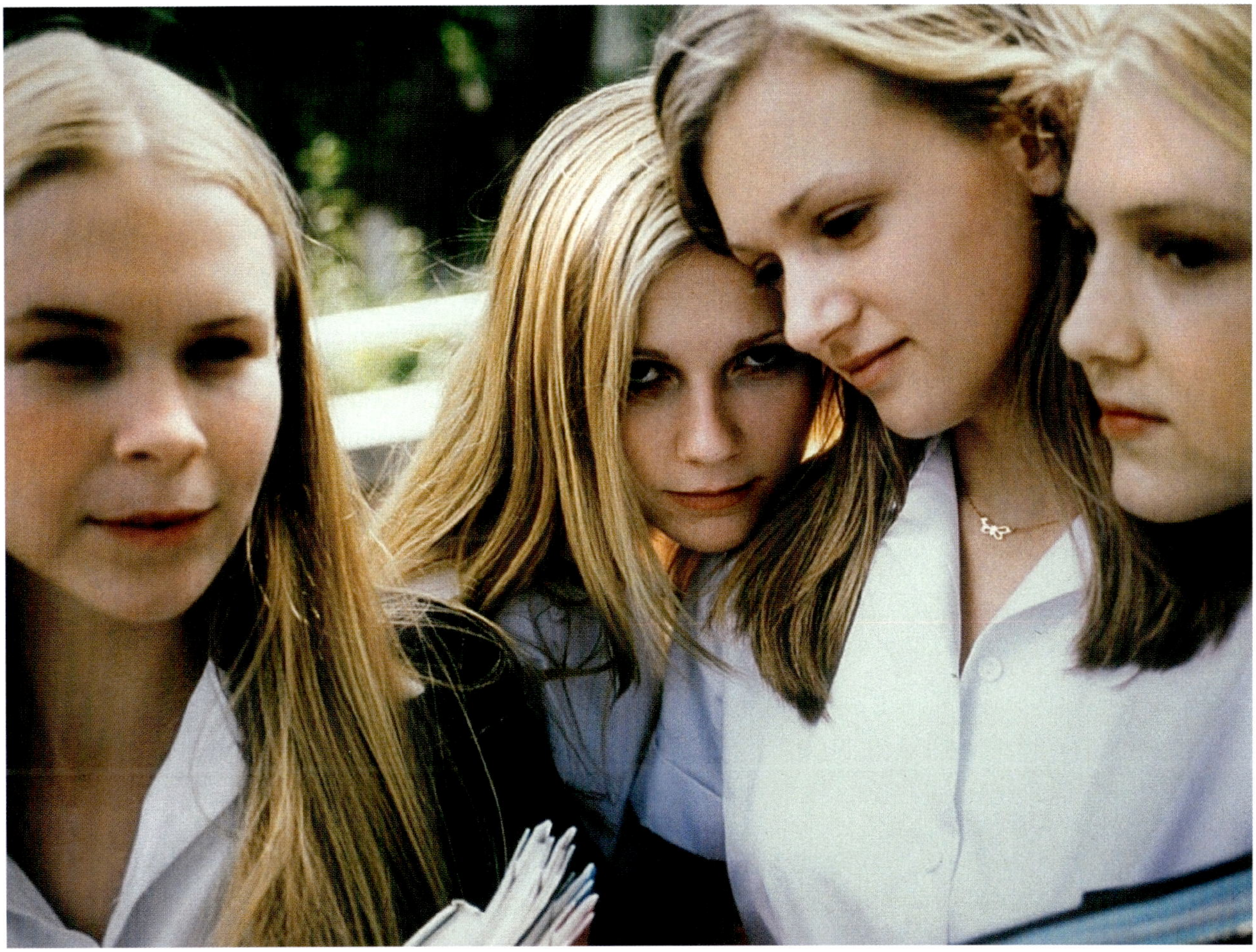

Above: *Sisterhood of sorrow – stars Leslie Hayman (Therese), Kirsten Dunst (Lux), A.J. Cook (Mary), and Chelse Swain (Bonnie) pose for the publicity camera, but still very much in character.*

procure the invitation, it was a double-edged sword. The introverted Coppola was suddenly on display, the daughter heading to the festival where her father had made such a noise. She only wished for her film to be judged for what it was.

But what kind of film was it exactly? Critics and marketing experts took to terming it a psychological romantic drama, but it never feels especially dramatic, at least not on the drowsy, luminous, hypnotic surface. The effect is both ephemeral and unforgettable. The classification they were reaching for is a Sofia Coppola film. And critics were cottoning on.

There was some sniffing about style over content – *Premiere* wrote it off as 'disarmingly wispy.'[28] But there was no denying the groundswell of appreciation. Duality was singled out. In the *New York Times*, A.O. Scott praised how it caught 'both the triviality and the grandeur of youth.'[29] A gift for milieu was lauded. In *Sight & Sound*, Mark Olsen talked up its 'magic-realist American suburbia.'[30] And it drew a touch of the poetic from the pens of reviewers. Ever wise, Roger Ebert of the *Chicago Sun-Times* saw it as a hymn to the loss of innocence, appreciating 'the mystery and loss that hangs in the air like bitter poignancy.'[31]

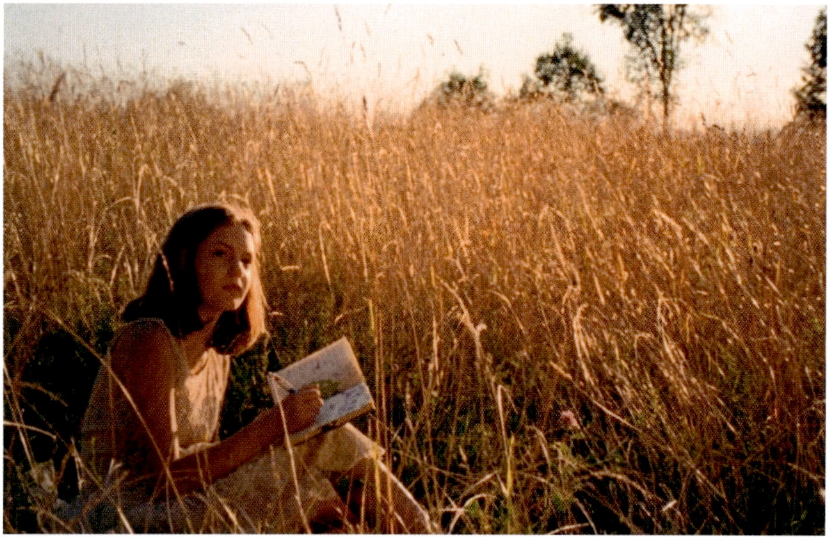

Left: *Hanna R. Hall as Cecilia finds a moment of solace. As well as telling the story, Sofia Coppola was forming an aesthetic, influenced by the world of fashion photography.*

Below: *Dream girl – Kirsten Dunst as Lux capturing the trademark Coppola faraway look.*

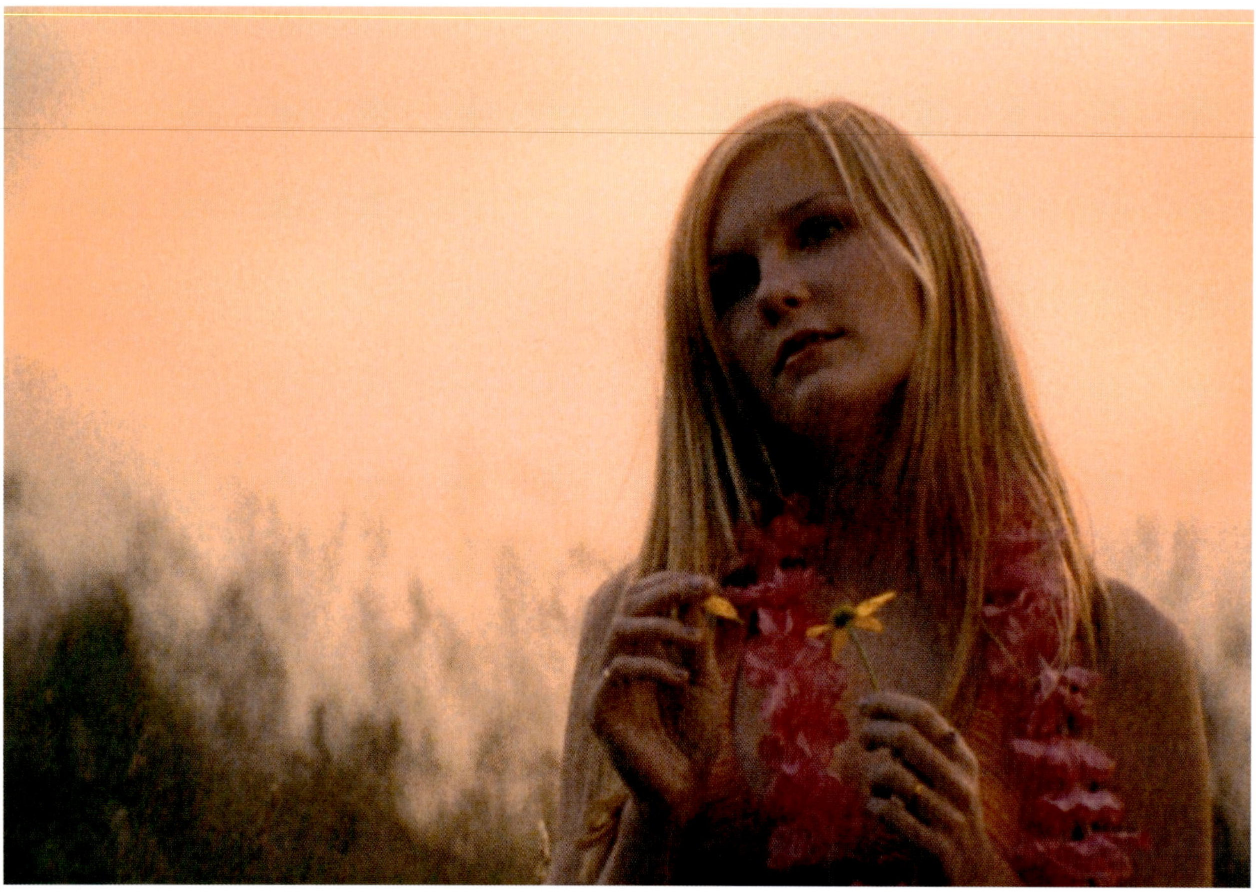

The heartbreak came with how it was handled on its release on 19 May 2000, a deflating year after its debut in Cannes. The studio, Paramount (through its then Classics arm), didn't know what to do with it. There was a genuine fear that the film would give rise to an epidemic of teen suicides. 'I think that kids know it's metaphorical,'[32] sighed Coppola. A tentative roll-out resulted in barely $10 million at the box office, but the film refused to fade away.

During filming on *The Bling Ring* in spring 2012, the actress Leslie Mann casually mentioned how much her daughter, Maude Apatow, loved *The Virgin Suicides*. It was as if Coppola had suddenly tuned into a radio station. Teenagers would come up to her, eager to explain how much the film meant to them, and she would marvel that they weren't even born when she made it. It was as if the film knew something about them. Online, fans spent hours trying to capture the gorgeous melancholia of Coppola's montages of the Lisbons in selfies, holding flowers, hair covering their eyes, then posting them up on Instagram. The film had taken on a life of its own, and is arguably her most pondered creation.

She wonders if it is the sincerity with which she approached the story that captivates new generations. Her innate understanding that teenagers are complex beings. What she called 'the mystery of that age.'[33]

With life and art entwined like a braid of golden hair, that idyllic shoot in 1998 would leave Coppola with a concomitant sense of loss and yearning. She would chase that same blessed experience through all the shoots that have followed. Of course it was stressful, filmmaking is stressful – she knew that well enough from her childhood. But that balmy, collaborative summer was like a coming of age, this second teenage that set her on a path for her life. '*The Virgin Suicides* made me a filmmaker,'[34] she acknowledged, and there was no turning back.

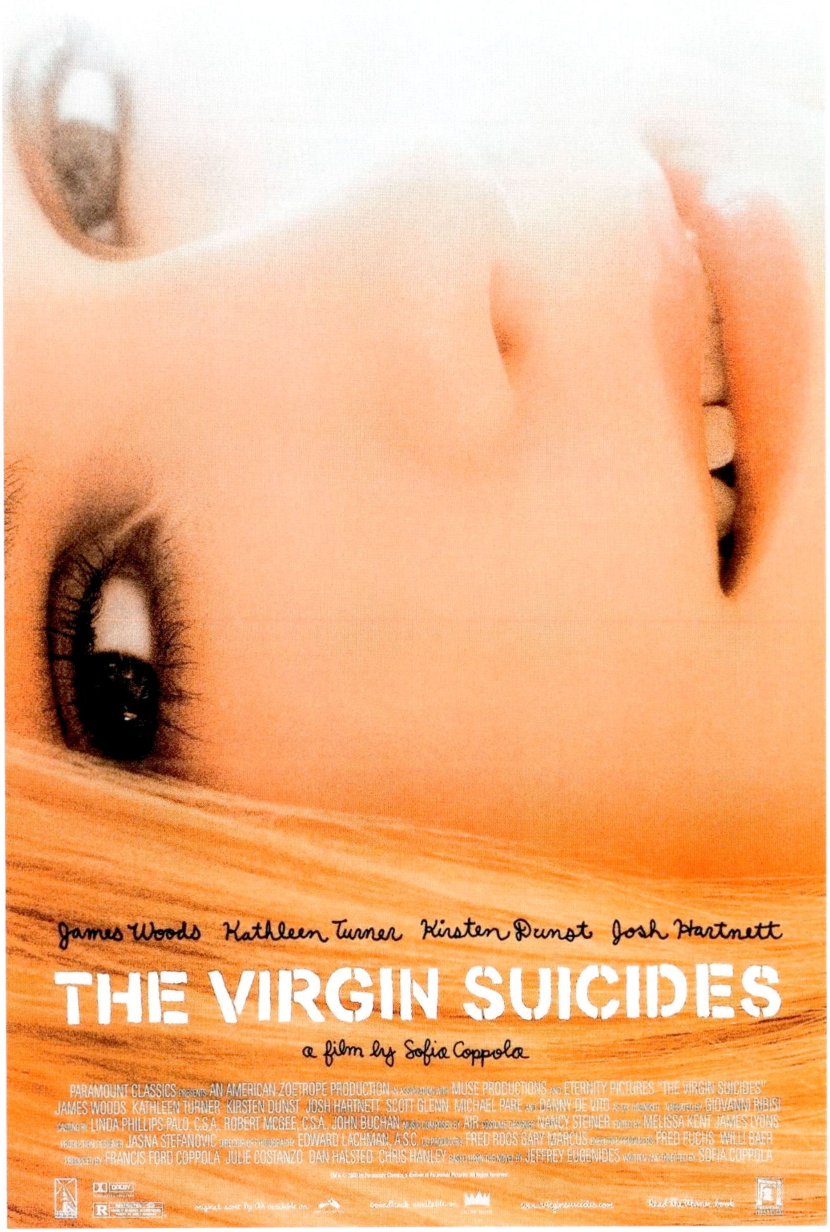

Above: *While not very successful on release, Coppola's debut subsequently evolved into a cult film that has helped define her career.*

THEY MEET, THEY BREAK UP

Lost in Translation (2003)

Her second film imagined a not-quite love affair between two lost souls adrift in a faraway hotel. She had worried it was indulgent, but her Tokyo story has defined her career

You never forget the ending. That famous embrace. A moment so ambiguous yet complete, this resolution without resolving anything tangible. Where the characters in what might or might not be a love story make both the bitterest and sweetest of partings on the corner of Chuo-dori and Sanbangai Street with the oblivious masses flowing past as if they were rocks in a stream. By now they are familiar. Disillusioned actor Bob Harris, who has the unmistakable mien of Bill Murray. Unhappy newlywed Charlotte Wells, so much younger, though not in spirit, with the beautiful, becalmed face of Scarlett Johansson. Even so, tears fill her eyes. Bob clutches Charlotte tighter still and whispers something to her so private, so secret, we will never be allowed to hear.

'It's a moment of acknowledgment, but viewers can make up their own minds about it,'[1] commented Sofia Coppola, pushed to explain the film's final, hushed mystery; another cherished Coppola Image.

She recalled her sixteen-year-old niece's response with a smile: 'I hope he gave her his email address.'[2]

Not knowing is the point.

There had been many hotels in her life, but the Park Hyatt was different. Or maybe it was that Tokyo's shimmering five-star tower on the west side of the Shinjuku district defined all the hotels she had ever stayed in: the luxury, the anonymity, the sense of being sealed off from the flow of life. How you kept running into the same people over and over again, and the strange camaraderie that develops between strangers.

'I wanted to shoot a movie in that hotel,'[3] she said. It was one of those passing thoughts that paused in her imagination. A ghost of a story took shape about these two people whose paths cross on the plush carpets of the Hyatt, with the neon-glazed streets of Tokyo outside. Two very different people who will answer a deep need in one another. A chance encounter that becomes a profound event.

At the age of 32, Coppola was now a director, which conferred on her a sense of self she had never previously experienced. While promoting *The Virgin Suicides*, she was pressed about what she might want to make next. She didn't exactly have an answer. She was toying with an ambitious biopic of the notorious French queen Marie Antoinette, but there

Opposite: *Opposites attract – the iconic couple of* Lost in Translation, *Bob (Bill Murray) and Charlotte (Scarlett Johansson) enjoy the moment.*

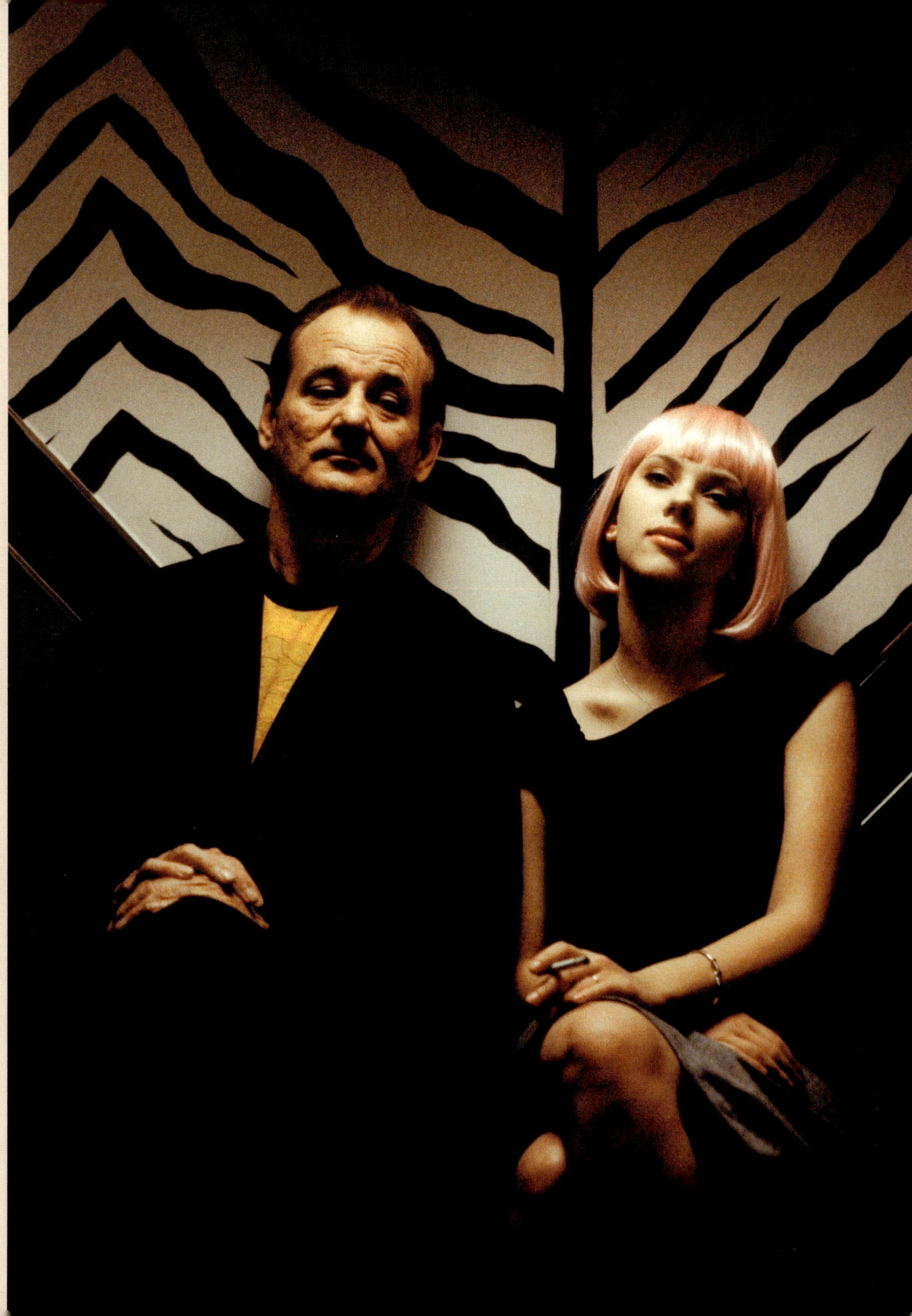

Below left: *With* Lost in Translation, *Sofia Coppola sought to capture the otherworldly feel of first coming to the electric streets of Tokyo.*

Below right: *The iconic future of the Los Angeles of* Blade Runner *(1982) was heavily influenced by Tokyo. Indeed, Coppola was struck by how much Tokyo resembled Ridley Scott's film.*

was this other idea that had whispered a title to her – *Lost in Translation*.

Arguably, the true inspiration for *Lost in Translation* was not the Hyatt or Bill Murray's solemn face, but a man named Charlie Brown singing *God Save the Queen* at God knows what hour. Charlie Brown was not really called Charlie Brown, but local fashion editor Fumihiro Hayashi loved the character almost as much as he loved finishing a night out with karaoke, and without fail picking The Sex Pistols' raucous aria as his number. Joining him on one such outing, Coppola had witnessed his commitment to the punk anthem and knew she wanted to preserve that moment on film. She was now thinking in images, pieces of a moving collage, things to include in a future movie. Hayashi singing his heart out is another of the stream of unforgettable moments that make up *Lost in Translation*.

She and Hayashi had become friends during a promotional visit for *The Virgin Suicides* when he served as a guide through the alternative Tokyo scene. The truth was, Coppola had been to Tokyo so often over the years it had grown familiar: first with the family, a pitstop on her father's adventures; then to promote *The Godfather Part III*, then in the early 2000s developing her clothing brand Milkfed, even opening shops.

She called it the *Blade Runner* city, it was like another world. 'I felt so free there and full of discovery.'[4]

She was struck by how Western culture had insinuated itself into the city to the point of absurdity. All those air-brushed A-list faces like Kevin Costner, Brad Pitt or Harrison Ford promoting coffee or beer from a vending machine or billboard. All those Western songs strangulated in midnight bars. It was almost surreal. The juxtaposition of cultures would become a central theme of the movie.

There were always personal connections. Coppola's father had even featured in a

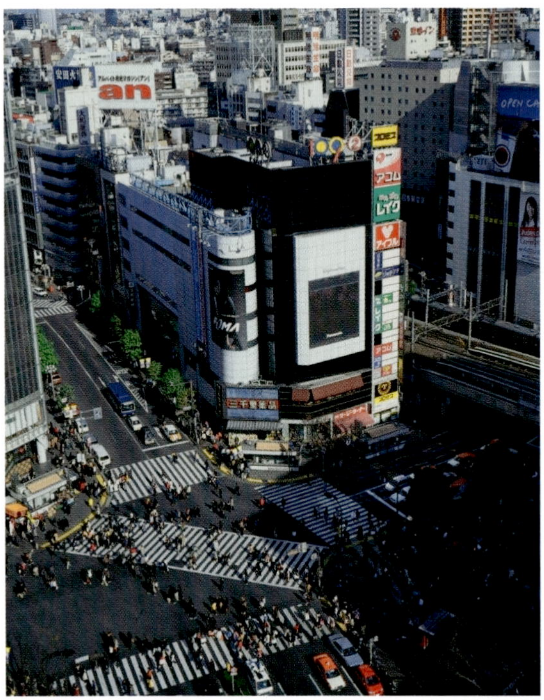

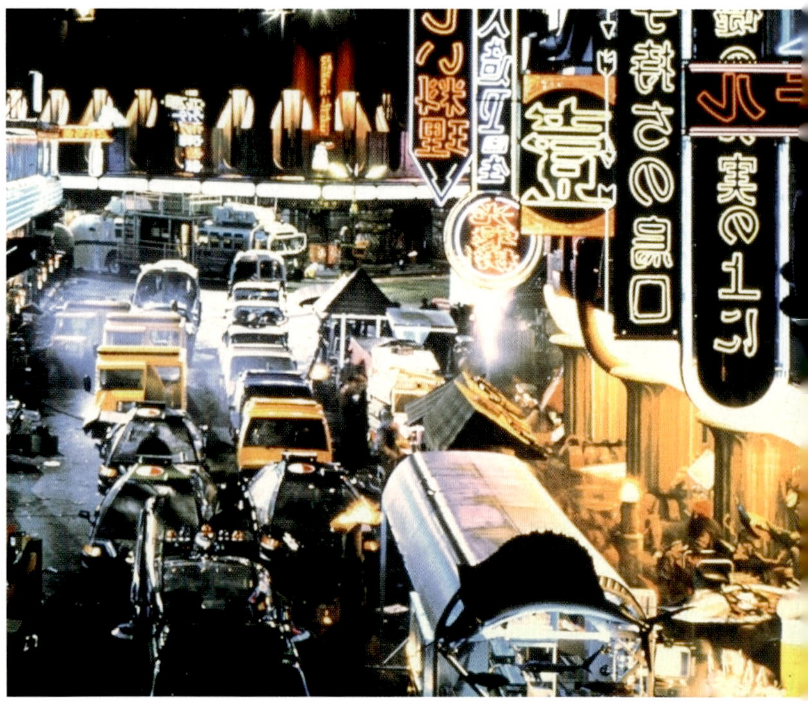

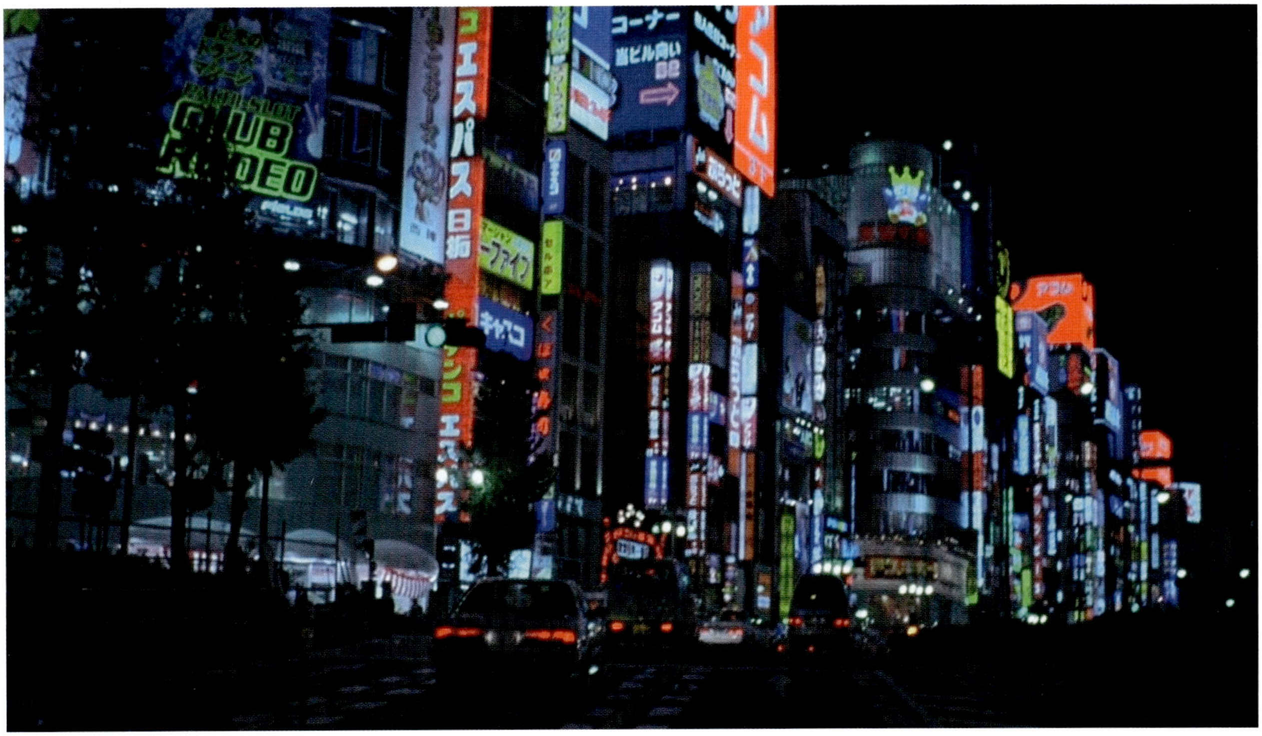

Above: *Neon dreams – Bob's taxi takes the journey to the Park Hyatt, opening his eyes to the splendour of the city. It is a vision both familiar and completely new.*

1979 Japanese commercial for Suntory whisky. Which translated into Bob being an ageing actor who has come to Tokyo to shoot a $2 million commercial for Suntory, bemused by his Japanese director's hectic demands followed by the translator's somewhat brief summary. Coppola recalled giving interviews for *The Virgin Suicides* in Tokyo, when the translator would give lengthy speeches for her short answers, or reduce her more elaborate explanations to almost nothing. She laughed, 'Even though she explained that the language was very different, I couldn't help feeling paranoid.'[5]

The comic situation (and the film's title) summed up Bob's malaise: his stagnating career has left him alienated and alone in this vast city.

She began the script at her home in Los Feliz, discussing its possibilities with her brother Roman. Sat at her dining table, she got no further than twenty pages, too easily distracted by the routines of Los Angeles life. So she took off for the source, returning to Tokyo and the Hyatt alone, and amid the songs drifting in from her iPod, gazing out at the circuit-board city, the slender story took shape.

Akin to *The Virgin Suicides*, the overarching tone is that of a memory of a life-changing event. The narrative is being recalled by either one of the characters. Or both. The film's viewpoint will pass between them, a metronomic movement linking two stalled lives, until their paths connect.

'I wanted the movie's structure to have all the different parts of a relationship condensed into a few days,' said Coppola. 'They meet, they break up.'[6] Such simplicity does her film a disservice. There is a powerful sense of something unfinished: we feel that they will never see each other again, but they have not broken up (were they ever together in that sense?) Among

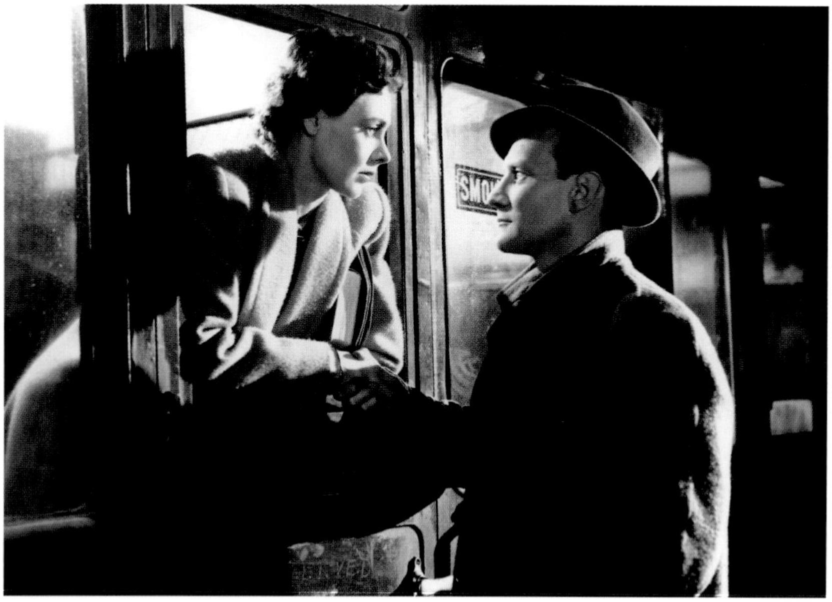

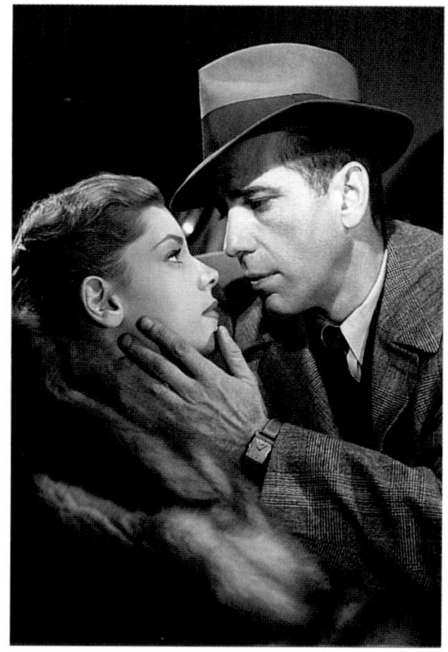

Above left and right: *Although such a modern film,* Lost in Translation *drew upon two black and white classics: the stymied romance of David Lean's* Brief Encounter *(1945) and the sizzle of* The Big Sleep *(1946).*

her inspirations was a combination of two distinctly different films: David Lean's brilliant *Brief Encounter* and Howard Hawks' sassy noir *The Big Sleep*. One offered a chaste love affair, the other a thrilling flirtation across an age gap.

Losing faith in his marriage (his wife sends habitual messages by fax or offers a disinterested voice at the end of the line – in fact, costume designer Nancy Steiner), Bob arrives in Tokyo to shoot his commercial. Staying at the same hotel is Charlotte's philosophy student, neglected in her recent marriage to an ambitious photographer (Giovanni Ribisi) distracted by his rock star assignment. They are each lost in their own way. Sleepless in the Hyatt's midnight bar they will find each other, save each other, spinning through a city as they fall in love, or something like love. Definitions are the sworn enemy.

'I wanted to react against so many films that are cold or cruel or cynical and make something with tender feelings,'[7] said Coppola. No further explanation was required.

The one face that never disappeared from her mind as she wrote was that runic moonscape belonging to Bill Murray. He was another wellspring: this recurring daydream of meeting him, in either kimono or tux, in the corridors of the Hyatt. It had to be him. His sensibility. That unpredictable flux of world-weariness, impishness, and charm. The only sane man in an insane universe. If Murray refused, she would give up on the film.

'I always loved *Groundhog Day* and *Tootsie*. Of course, *Rushmore*,'[8] she explained as the why-him questions poured in later. But this was an attempt to capture something more truthful in the Murray mood. 'I think he's really romantic, but not in a cheesy way,'[9] she concluded.

What is it about Bill? He hailed from Evanston, Illinois and via stand-up, improv, *Saturday Night Live*, *Ghostbusters*, and *Groundhog Day* reluctantly rose to comedy superstar. Fame bore down on him like gravity. Beginning with the depressed tycoon in Wes Anderson's *Rushmore*, he had entered a new phase of his career. Not exactly mature, but more nuanced. His genial melancholy spoke to the world.

Landing Murray took determination. He was essentially represented by an automated mailbox, his career a matter more of whim than strategy. It took a year of persistence: letters, calls, messages passed on by mutual friends, an entire weather front of persuasion. Then associate producer Mitch Glazer called to say he was sat right now with Murray in a restaurant, and she dropped everything and raced across Manhattan to make her pitch. Gripped by the same urgency that had won her *The Virgin Suicides*, she gave it everything: flirtation, compliments, a taste of the film she wanted to make; and by osmosis, or sheer desperation, he was won over.

There were no contracts, he looked her in the eye and promised to be there. She was sweating right up to the moment he landed at Narita International Airport. The whole $4 million production depended on him, a budget raised through a suite of foreign distributors (giving Coppola full creative control) already nonplussed by the scant, 70-page script, which to say the least was light on plot. Murray was on his way to his only Oscar nomination.

'This is the Bill Murray performance we've been waiting for: Saturday Night Live meets Chekhov,'[10] claimed *Slate's* David Edelstein.

At seventeen, younger than the part as written and still relatively unknown, the New York-born Johansson had featured in *The Horse Whisperer* and *Ghost World*, though it was little-seen indie sisterhood drama *Manny & Lo* that had caught

Below: *Sleepless in Tokyo – Charlotte (Scarlett Johansson) and Bob (Bill Murray) have their first meaningful encounter in the all-night bar of the hotel.*

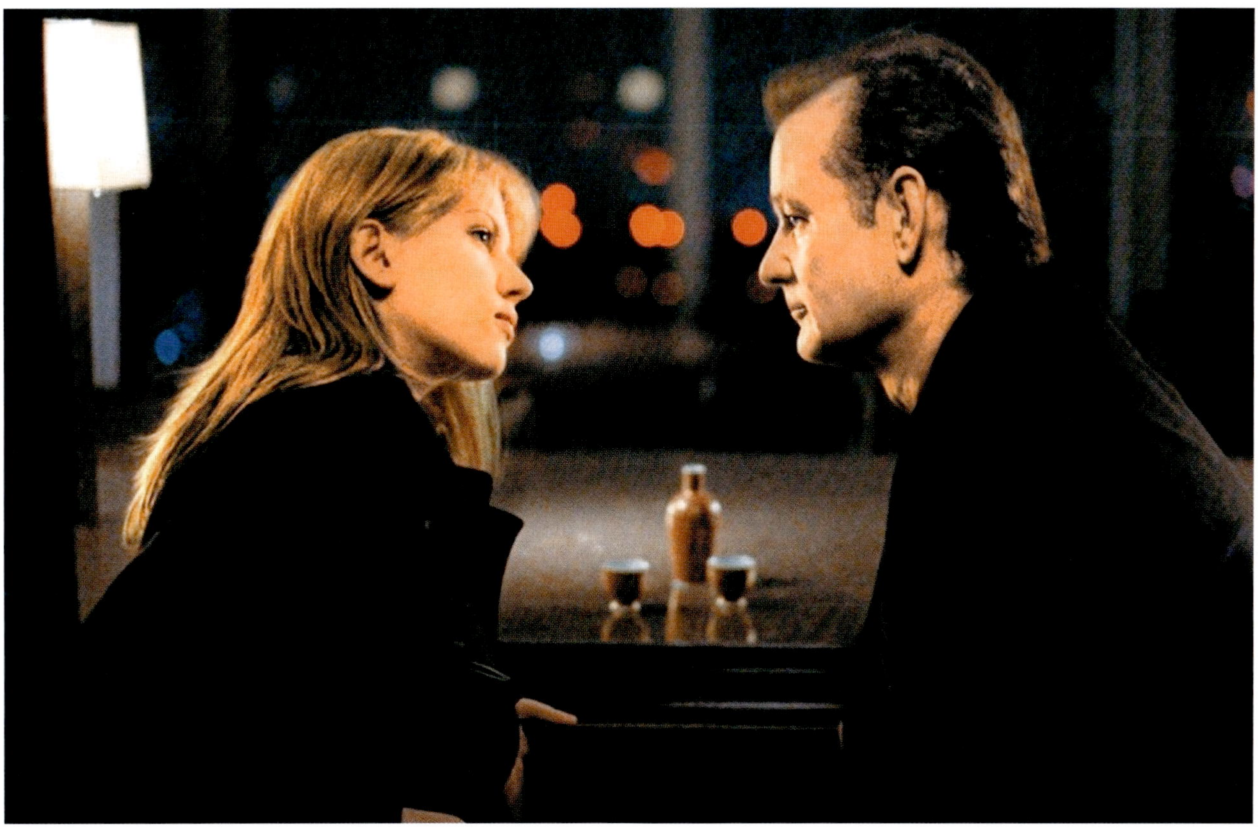

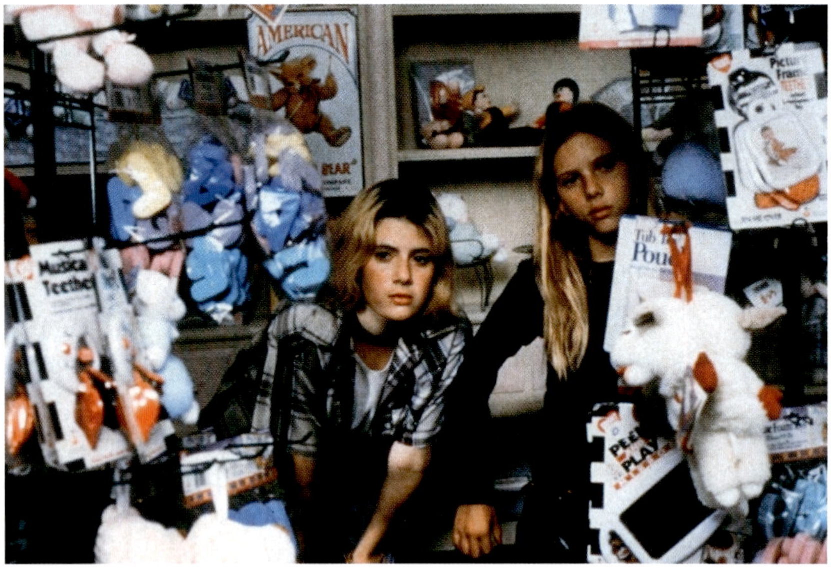

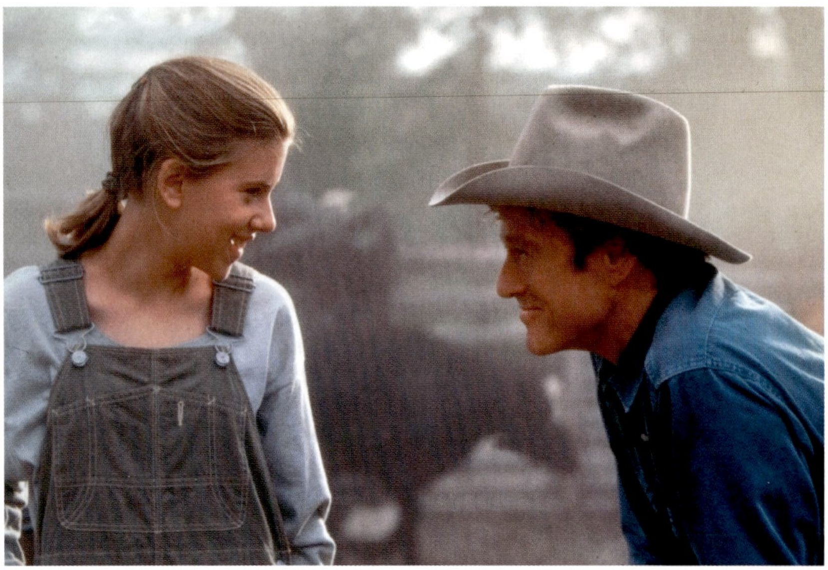

Top and above: *The rise of Scarlett Johansson – the young actress had already gained fame in indie comedy* Manny & Lo *(1996) and in* The Horse Whisperer *(1998) with Robert Redford.*

Coppola's attention. 'I was kind of thinking about Lauren Bacall and Humphrey Bogart in the back of my mind, and her voice reminded me of Lauren Bacall,'[11] she said. Bacall was nineteen when she starred in *To Have and Have Not*. Johansson was also at a similar transitional point in her life and career to where Kirsten Dunst has been in *The Virgin Suicides*, though Charlotte is that much older than Lux.

Coppola had worried that the character was too close to her own feelings of detachment. Then there was no source novel, she was the source: all the things on her mind in her twenties, on the shores of a breakdown, uncertain of her place in the world, rushing into a short-lived marriage with director Spike Jonze (slyly the model for Ribisi's shallow husband John). Reputedly, Jonze made *Her* as a riposte, pointedly including the voice of Johansson as the alluring AI and, by those minded to calculate, Rooney Mara as an avatar of Coppola. Asked for her thoughts, Coppola claimed ignorance: 'I know people really like that movie, but I haven't seen it. I don't know if I want to see Rooney Mara as me.'[12]

This surely is what draws so many fans to Coppola's flame, the idea that she too is complicated and a little lost. Charlotte was a 'culmination'[13] of things she had been through.

She cast Johansson after a single lunch; there was no need for an audition, she simply knew the actress was right. 'She's understated, not extroverted and hyper,'[14] and might have easily have added, *Like me*. It was others who noticed the physical resemblance.

'Sofia bleeds through the character,'[15] acknowledged Johansson: the quick ironic humour, the reserve, the unplaceable need, the pout.

It was a transitional film for the actress (into superstardom), but Johansson only ever felt the age difference with Charlotte when

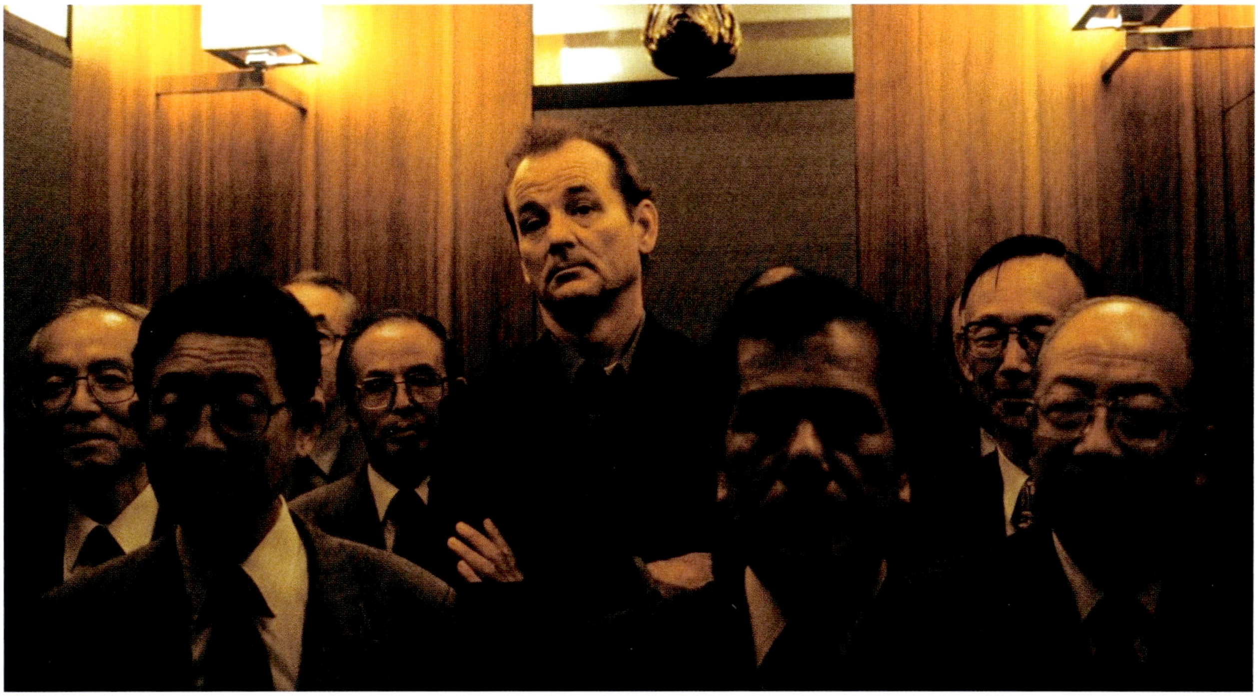

putting on her wedding band. 'Other than that, you think about it and it's like, "Five years here, five years there. No big deal."'[16] It's such a mature performance that she even shrinks the age gap with Murray. Then even Bob, admitted Coppola, was sort of herself.

They first set eyes on each other in the Hyatt elevator. Bob is hard to miss, towering over the Japanese men, so obviously out of place. Charlotte can only smile. 'Wordlessly, Coppola brings Bob and Charlotte together before they exchange a single line of dialogue,'[17] wrote academic Suzanne Ferriss. What is so beguiling is that the two characters become intensely aware of each other without articulating what they feel, something heightened by the director's freeform approach. Lines, gestures, glances, an entire language was improvised between the three of them. Half a page of script became a four-minute sequence. The whisper at the end was Murray's invention, born out of Bob's feelings.

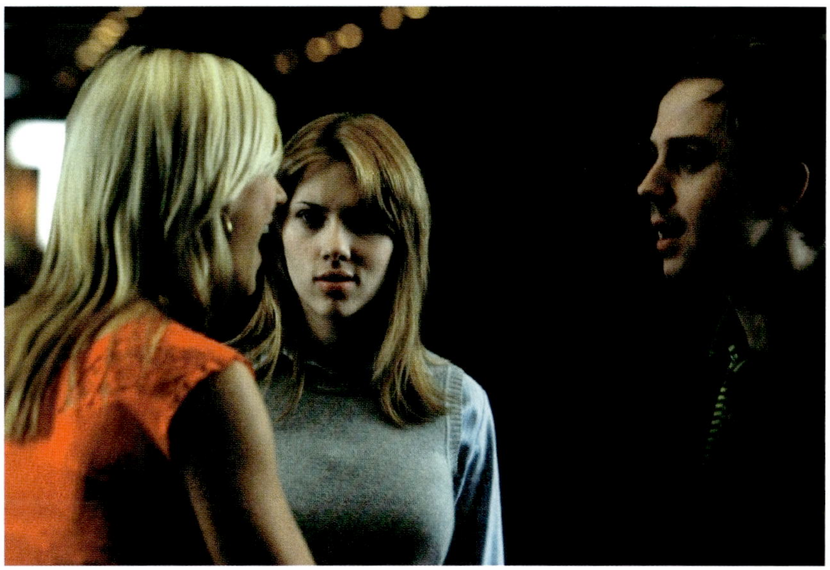

Top: *Odd one out – among* Lost in Translation*'s many iconic images. Bill Murray's Bob stands apart from the Japanese locals.*

Above: *Meanwhile, Charlotte (Johansson) finds herself disconnected from her marriage to John (Giovanni Ribisi).*

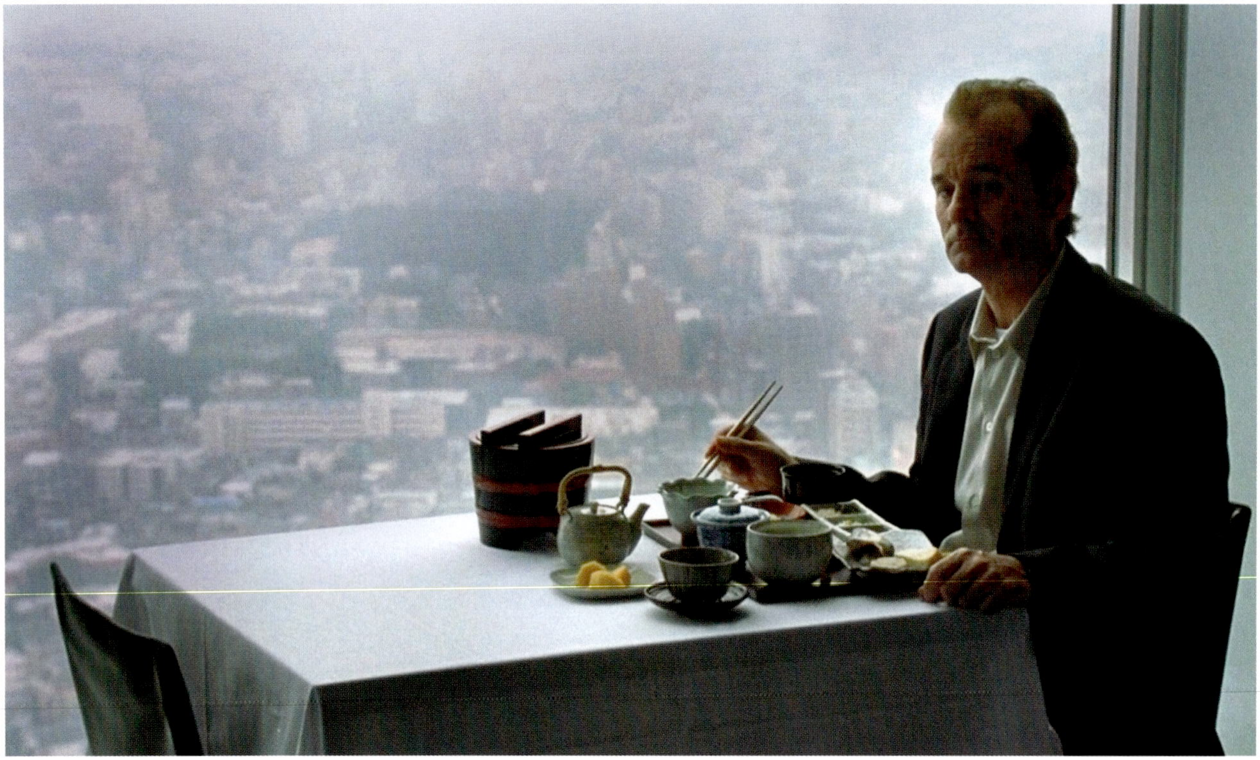

> "When the talk occurs between two people who could plausibly have sex together, it gathers a special charge.
> **ROGER EBERT**

Coppola never saw the film in clichéd terms, some doomed May-December romance. It was simply vital that her two leads were at 'opposite ends of their lives'[18] while confronting the same sense of alienation. She confessed to chaste but significant friendships she had had with older men. If an erotic charge is present in the film, it gets no further than a flirtation, an elusive longing. 'When the talk occurs between two people who could plausibly have sex together, it gathers a special charge,'[19] noticed Roger Ebert in the *Chicago Sun-Times*. The opening shot of Charlotte seen from behind, lying on the bed in sheer pink knickers, was based on Mario Sorrenti's photograph of Kate Moss, (which had adorned the cover of Coppola's treatment) and somehow expresses both sexuality and isolation.

If the script was an evocative sketch, she had the entire film mapped out in her head. Quite literally. She had plotted Bob and Charlotte's route through Tokyo's teeming metropolis months beforehand, providing sketches, photographs, and playlists, a mood board over a storyboard, her now-trademark blueprint for a vibe.

Beginning on 29 September 2000, the shoot lasted only twenty-seven days, with Coppola reacting to the sense of place even more than she had with *The Virgin Suicides*. Then the world around the characters is essentially non-fictional. This was almost reportage.

Within the slick, anonymous hotel, she wanted the fish-tank aura of jet lag, and drifting to the bar in the middle of the night. The nocturnal tones are almost hallucinatory. Then out onto the streets, to be engulfed by life. They had no permits as such. The local authorities were surprisingly lenient on the matter of permission; often

Opposite: *The loneliness of the long-distance traveller – framed in classic Coppola fashion, Bob (Bill Murray) takes a lunch for one high above Tokyo.*

Right: *Falling for one another – the question of sexual attraction hovers elusively in the air of* Lost in Translation.

Below: *Like Bob, Scarlett Johansson's Charlotte is consciously framed against the vast, bustling, uncaring urban environment. Only once they have met do they venture out into the city.*

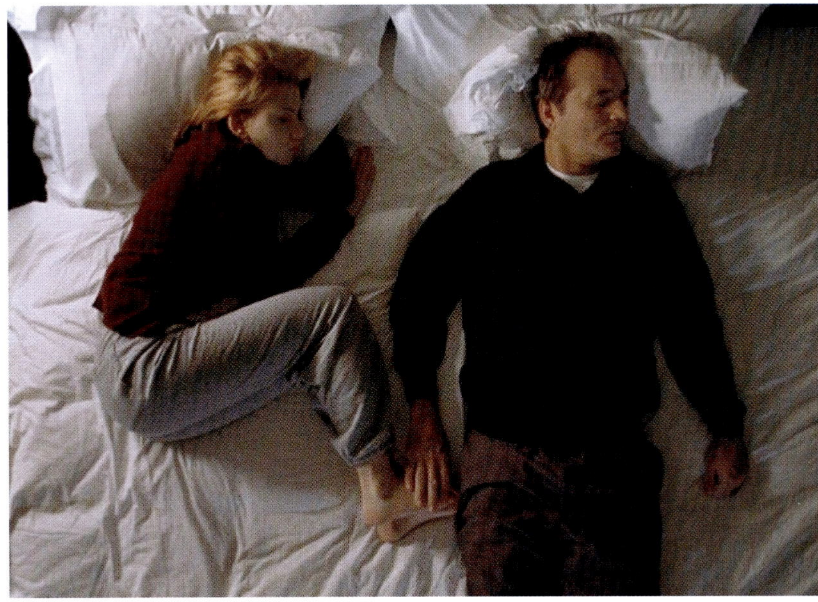

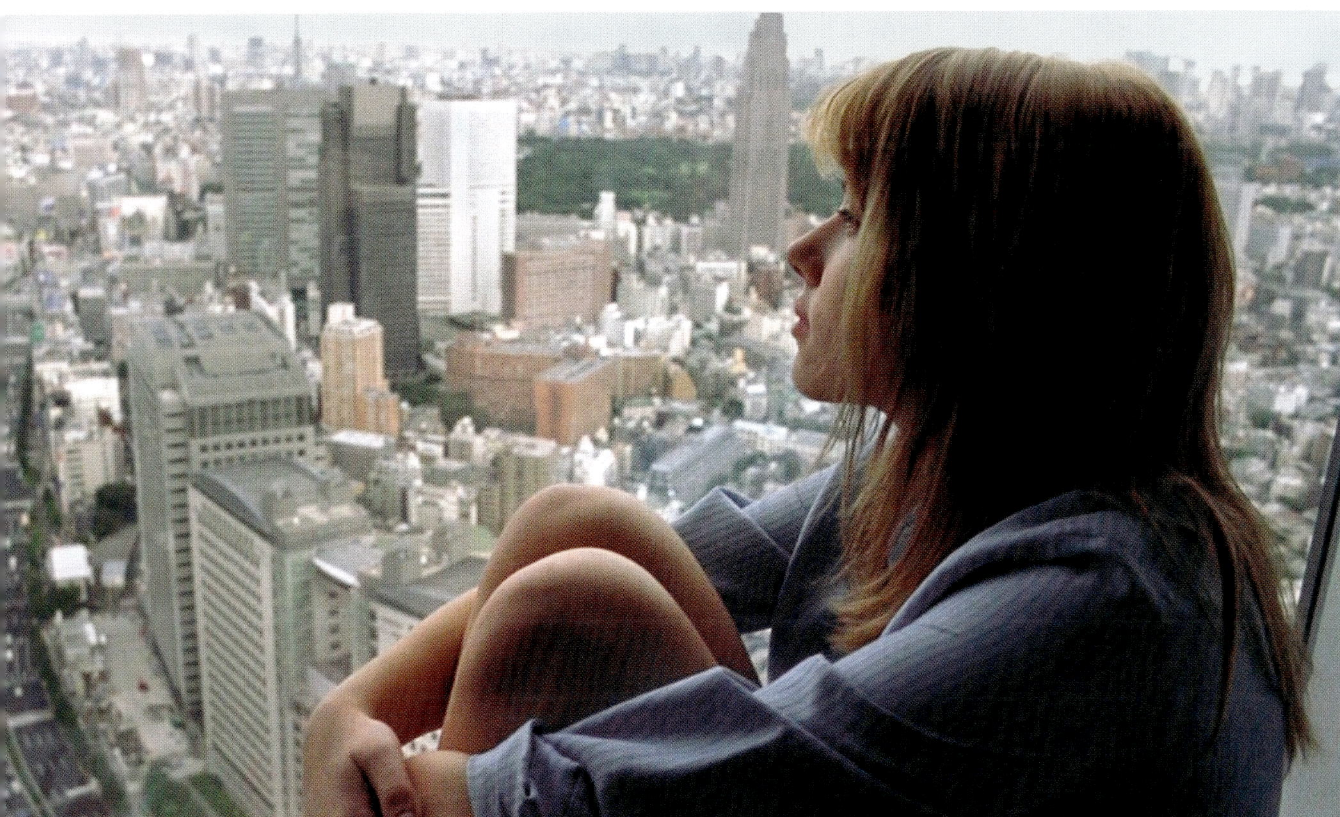

it was the uptight Americans who found themselves pressing for paperwork. The film demanded a guerilla-style filmmaking, flitting through Tokyo and Kyoto for six days a week, with a camera light enough to carry, zooming in on busy crossings from a nearby Starbucks or smuggled onto the subway to catch Johansson crammed in among real commuters.

'I wanted the film to look the way Tokyo looked to me when I visited,'[20] explained Coppola. She sat down with cinematographer Lance Acord (who had shot *Lick the Star*) weeks before and spoke of her scenes as snapshots, or memories, all these hypnotic longueurs unmoored from plot like Michelangelo Antonioni's neorealist *L'Avventura* or Fellini's *La Dolce Vita*, which the fictional duo watch together on hotel television. There are few close-ups, Coppola frames her characters in relation to spaces filled with other people. She likened her story to music, not built on dramatic scaffolding, but themes and variations. The tension came from the audience wondering what was going to happen between the two protagonists, like the mood Wong Kar-wai had created for *In the Mood for Love*.

The electric city provided its own lighting, the video-game glow of billboards and neon, the explosion of lightbulbs in a pachinko parlour, the ocean of commuters at Shibuya Crossing. Their film stock was light enough to absorb it all. It had to be on film, 35mm, not the current vogue for digital, she insisted. Film has the shimmer of memory, she said, or 'a love story.'[21] Texture is meaning.

Bob Reitzell returned to curate a soundtrack that would become its own success story (CD sales rocketed). The musical choices are as telling as a voiceover. Reitzell would send playlists to Coppola to sample, she still had the songs on her iPod that had charged her writing with emotion. Dream-pop synths mix with snarling guitars, Jesus and Mary Chain sharing the load with

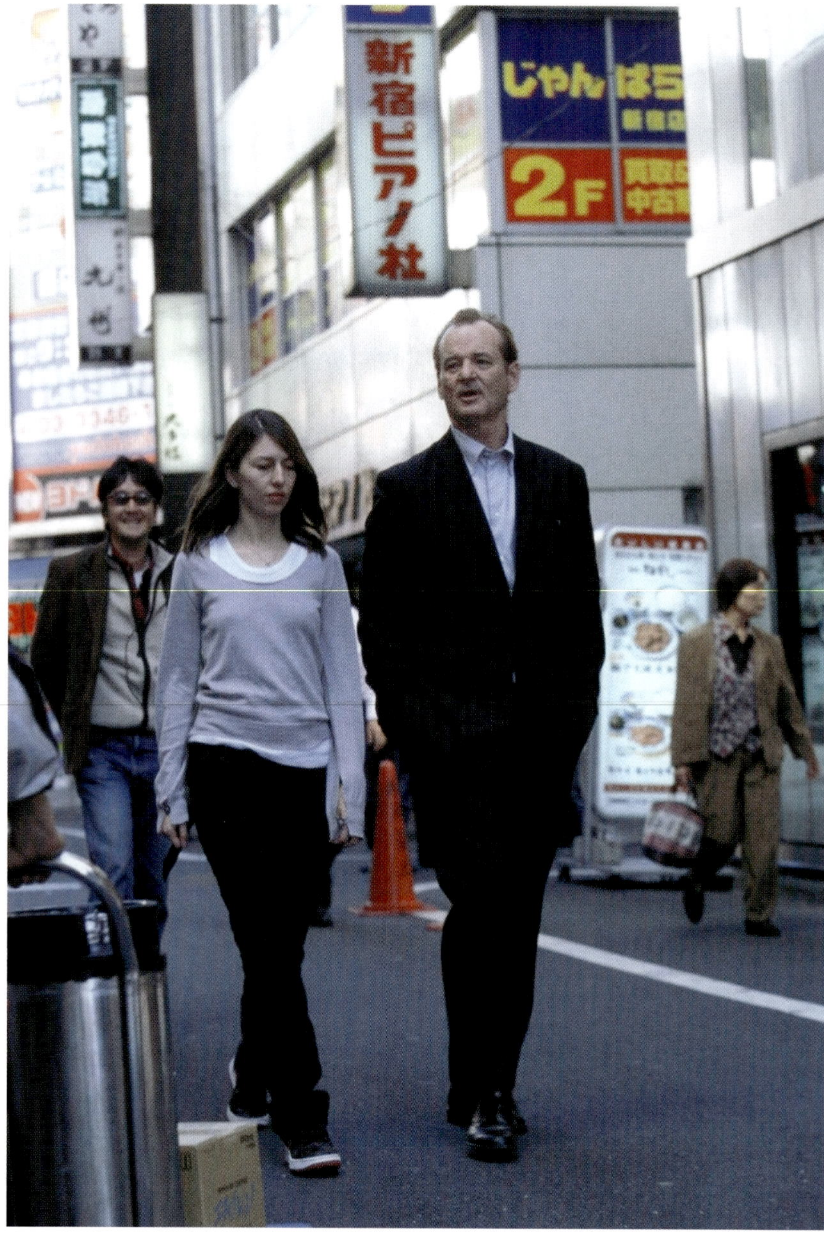

Above: *Sofia Coppola and muse Bill Murray in conference on the Tokyo streets. They would shoot guerrilla-style, often without permits, using the real city as a backdrop to fiction.*

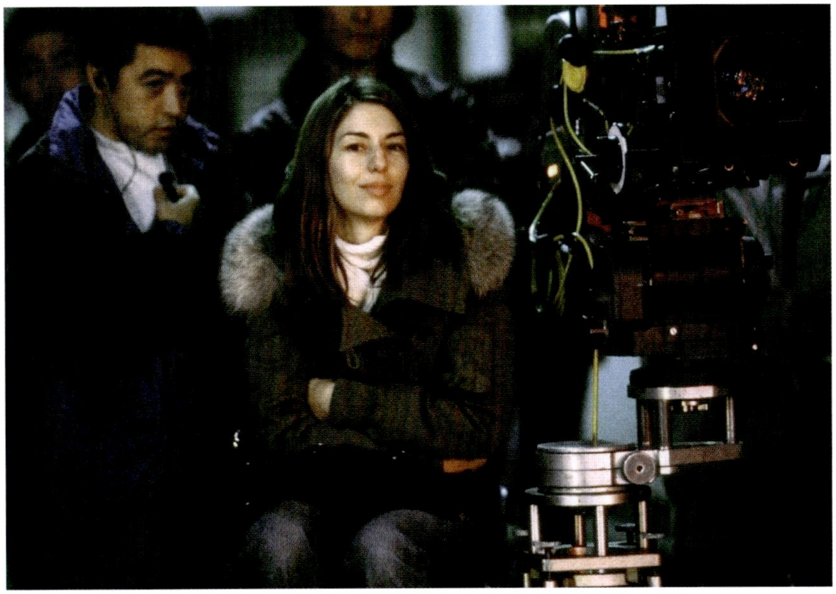

Left: *In her element – Coppola had the entire film literally mapped out in her head, with a route Bill and Charlotte would take through the city.*

Below: *The Murray whisperer – Coppola would instinctually know how to handle the star's mercurial nature. She is still the only director to land him a Best Actor nomination at the Academy Awards with* Lost in Translation.

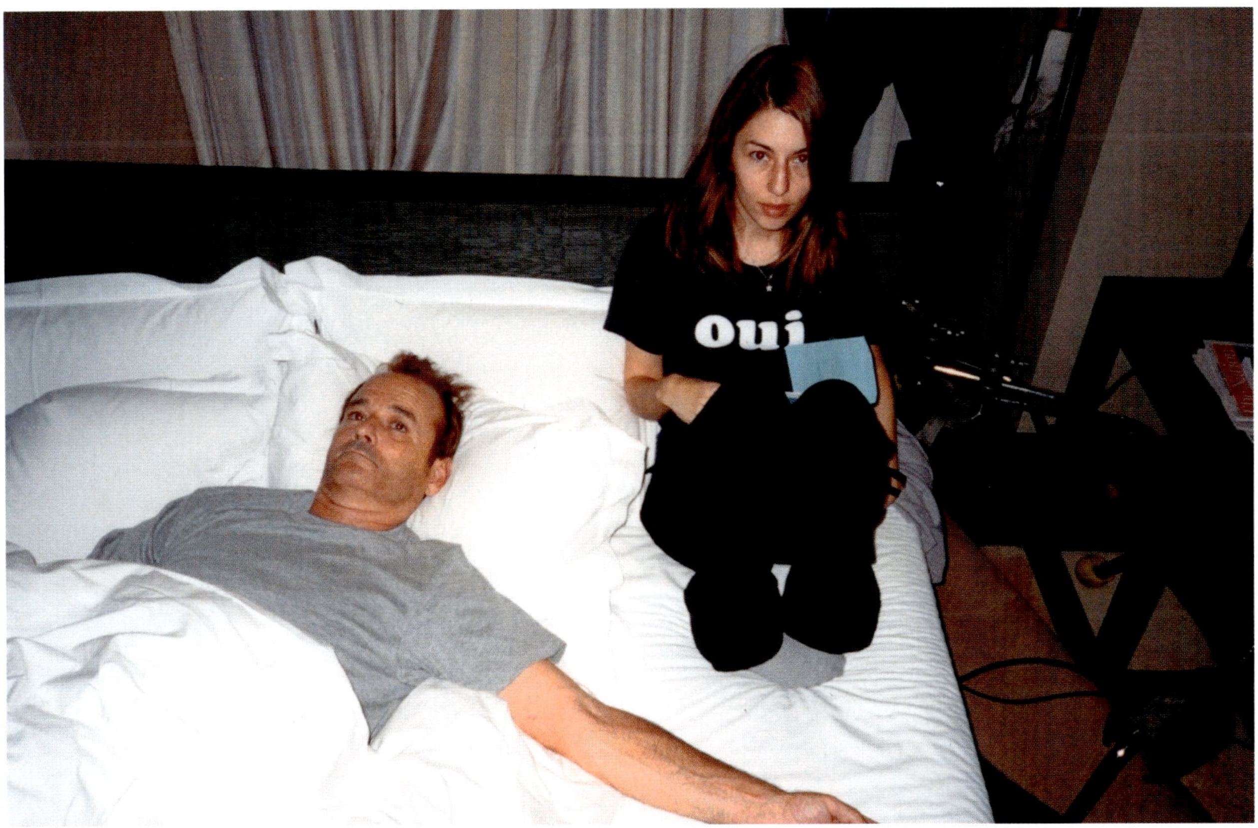

Right: *In the moment – one of Sofia Coppola's motivations for telling this story was the thought of filming Bill Murray doing karaoke. The sequence was almost entirely improvised from scratch.*

Below: *Coppola's intention was to cram an entire relationship between Charlotte (Scarlett Johansson) and Bob (Murray) into a few days – including the downs, as they share a fraught lunch.*

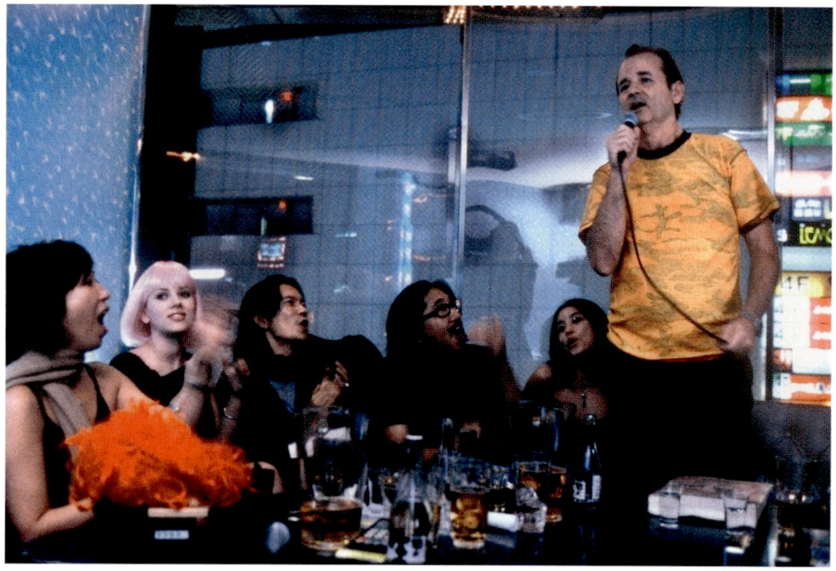

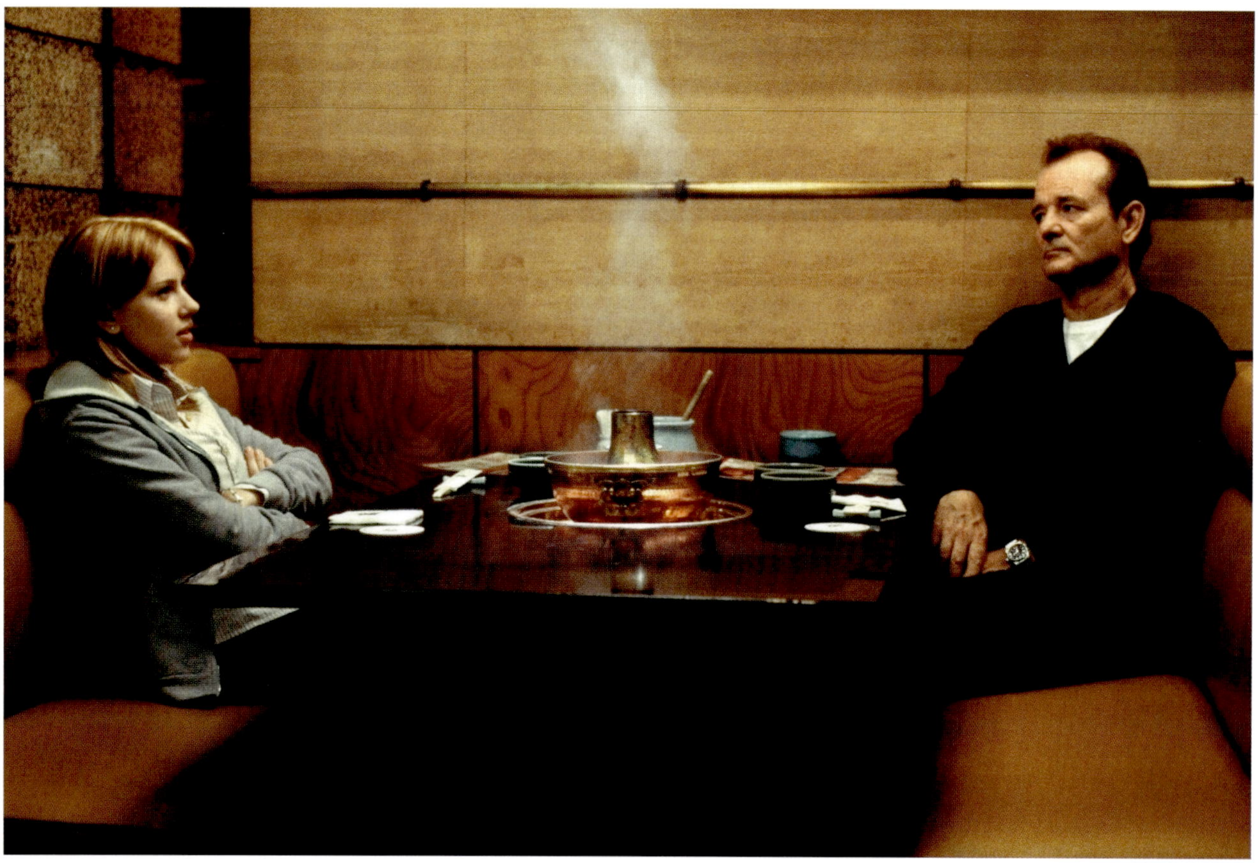

the floaty ambience of Air and Kevin Shields from My Bloody Valentine.

Overlapping with the music, Richard Beggs' sound design expands the sensory effect. *The New York Times'* Elvis Mitchell recalled how in the scene where Bob carries Charlotte to her room, 'the hotel corridor is dusted with aural density; the noise of air conditioners and fluorescent lights becomes a part of the milieu.'[22] Voices off-camera, public address systems, the soft clinking of the hotel bar, the old men gossiping in the sauna, and the sheer plenitude of the city streets serve to reinforce the characters' dislocation. And our sense of being there but not there at the same time.

How alike and unalike Coppola is to her New Brat contemporaries, the generation of hipster filmmakers whose fluctuating membership included Wes Anderson, Spike Jonze, Paul Thomas Anderson, Noah Baumbach, Todd Haynes, David Fincher, and Quentin Tarantino. They may share themes, draw from the same sources, but the likes of Anderson and Tarantino manipulate their worlds, entwining their plots, intersecting timelines, nesting stories within stories like Russian dolls. They advertise their cleverness. Coppola's enchantments lie closer to the looseness of life. She gives you her heart.

Take the karaoke scene (for instance), improvised in the moment. Effectively the camera is peering in on Murray, Johansson, and Charlie Brown, mostly in character, having a night out. Coppola let the actors sing what they wanted. Without fail, Brown launched into *God Save the Queen*. But for Murray, the director insisted on Roxy Music's *More Than This*. Maybe because of the romantic vibe, but mostly because she wanted to see him cope with the high note on the opening line (not well). The awkwardness is so beautifully human. We're not sure whether we are watching Murray or Bob, and not sure it matters.

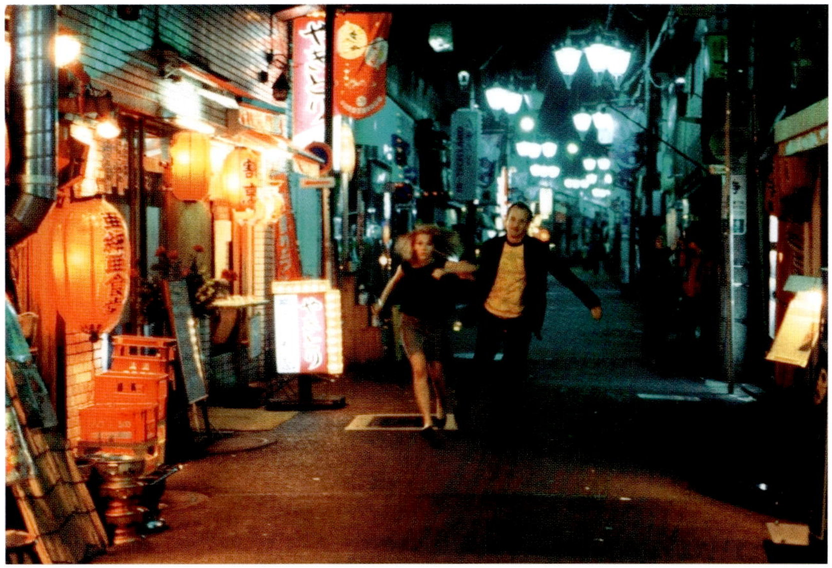

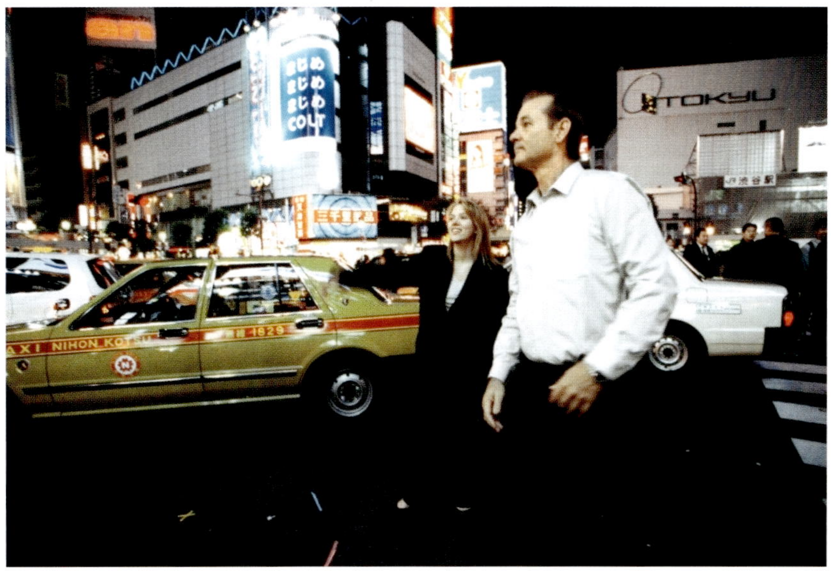

Top and above: *Released from the hotel, Charlotte (Johansson) and Bob (Murray) cut loose. Few films have captured the immediacy of a city seen by strangers like* Lost in Translation. *Cities by night became known as a Coppola forte.*

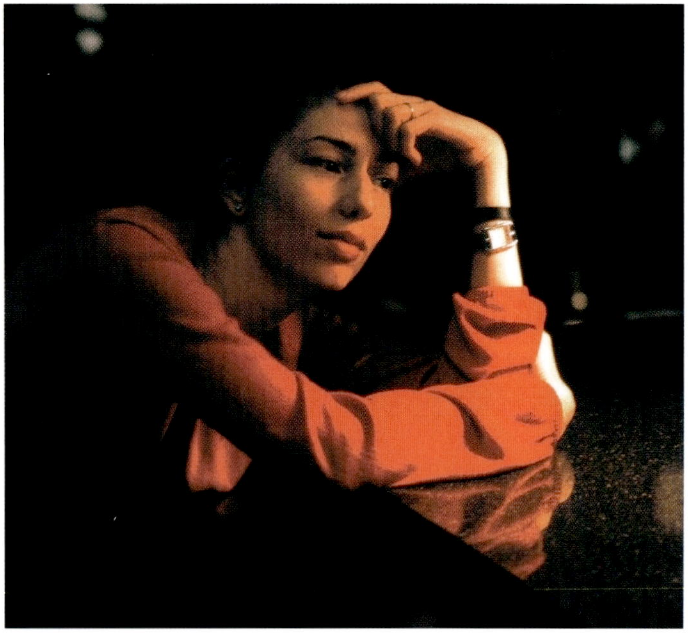

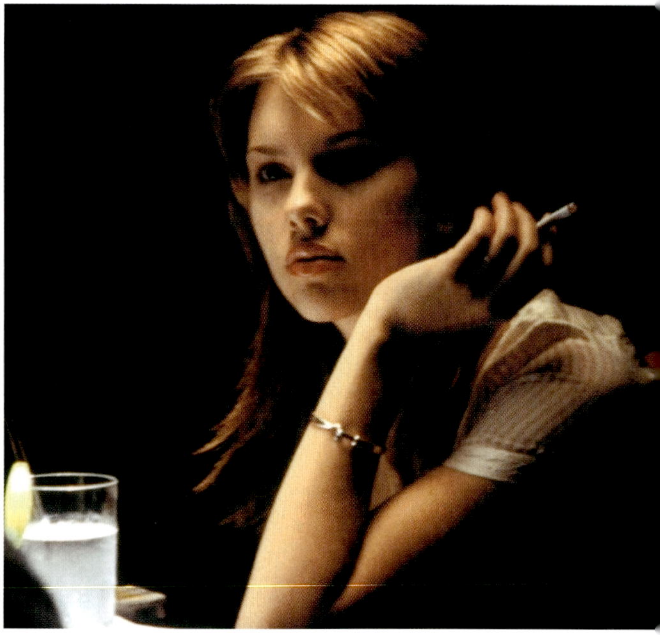

Above left and right: *Sofia Coppola was very open about the fact that Scarlett Johansson's Charlotte was in effect an alter ego for many of her personal experiences, including chaste relationships with older men.*

It was said that the comic films of thirties director Ernst Lubitsch were instantly recognizable because they possessed a *feel* unique to him. This intangible emanation was dubbed the Lubitsch Touch, impossible to pin down but unmistakeable all the same. By her second film the Coppola Touch was established: as light as breath, as loose as a dream, yet utterly authentic. She was a director 'with a cinematic language all her own,'[23] insisted Lisa Schwarzbaum in *Entertainment Weekly*.

Tipped off by the distributor's marketing department, Coppola would email her mother to report on the latest rave review. 'Did you know the *SF Chronicle* gave it a little man clapping, falling out of his chair! It's the best you can get!'[24]

Lost in Translation had been picked up by Focus for distribution in the USA – significantly, *after* Coppola had delivered her final cut – on its way to becoming a $120 million global sensation and the Coppola film by which her others will always be judged.

Time has confused the issue. In the modern era the film's reception is not quite so ecstatic. Accusations of cultural insensitivity dog Coppola's film, as they do Anderson's *Isle of Dogs* (which also happens to feature Murray and Johansson). But the chorus of naysayers tend to miss how the film is perfumed by its director's affection. In any case, her portrayal of Japan, the multiplicity of Tokyo in particular, is a world seen through the inexperienced eyes of this duo (and so alive compared to the stupor of the hotel). As Alice Lovejoy extolled in *Film Comment*, this is a film about transience. 'Delirious with exhaustion, set apart by language, culture, ethnicity, and time zone, the film's characters sense themselves in relief against the world around them.'[25]

This isn't a film about Japan, it is a film about two people in Japan. The country is refracted in the susurrations of their despair and elation. Any lapses into caricature, noted critic Carrie Rickey, are on account of Bob's myopia. 'Coppola makes the contrast between the hyperbole of American

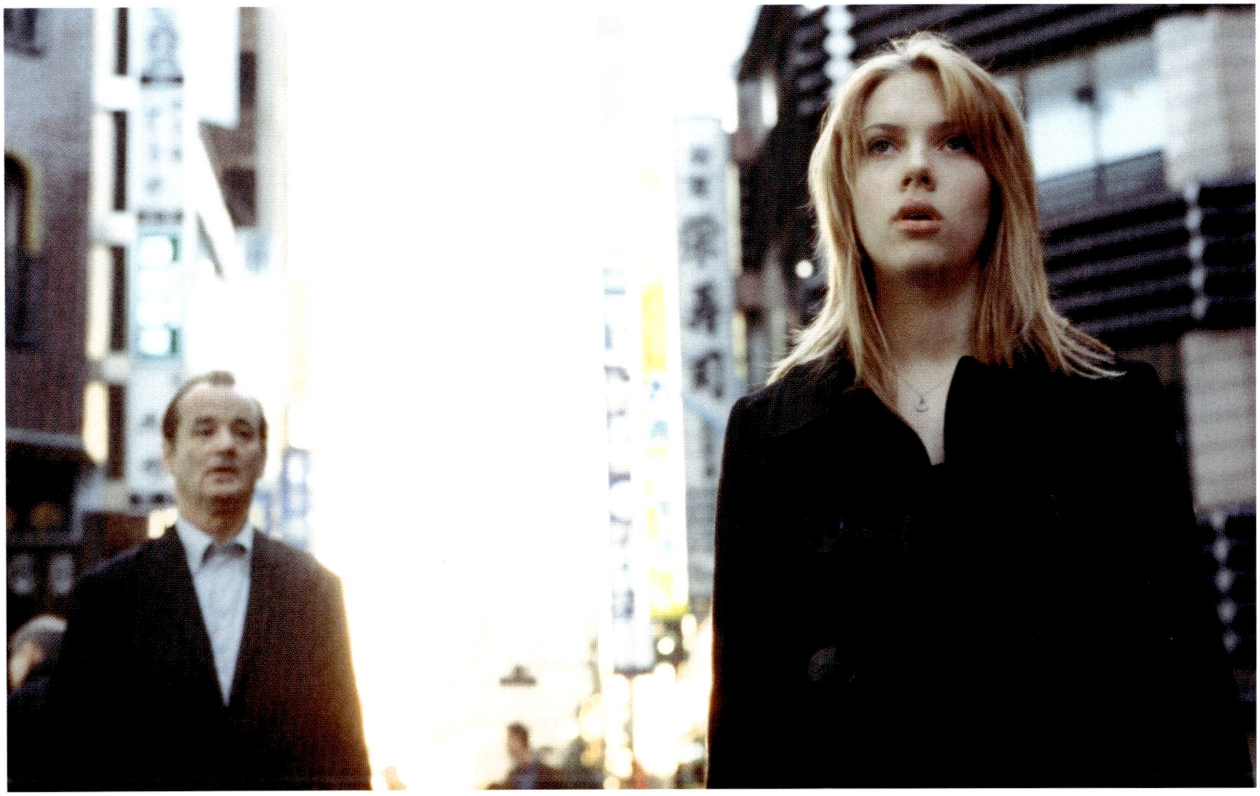

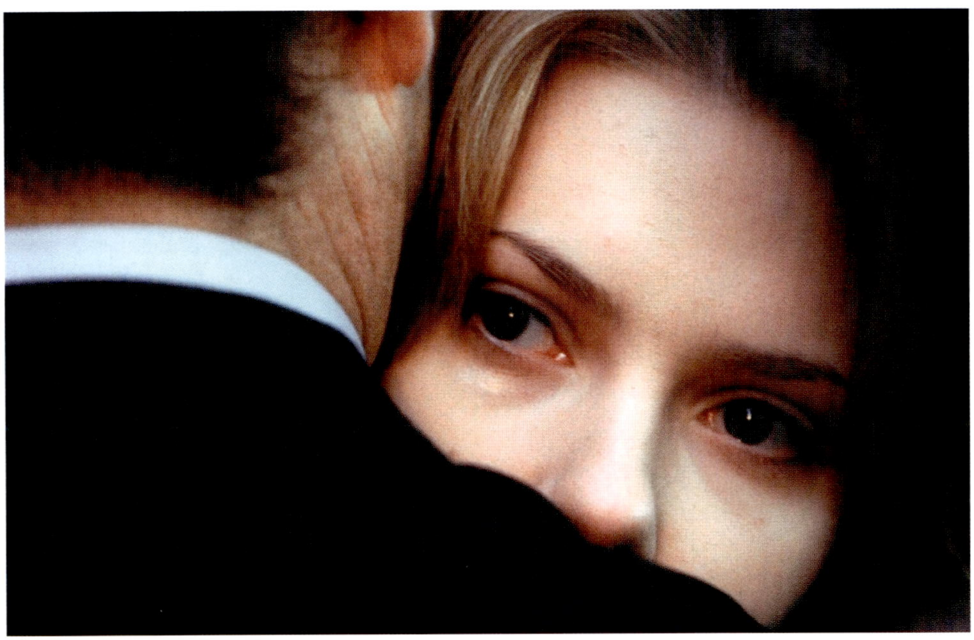

Above: *An ending for the ages – Bob (Bill Murray) tracks down Charlotte (Johansson) for the film's personal farewell. Breaking one of cinema's fundamental rules, the audience are kept in the dark over what he says.*

Left: *The whisper was ad-libbed by Murray, and whatever he may have said, the point is that not knowing what he says makes the moment more intimate. We can feel what he says.*

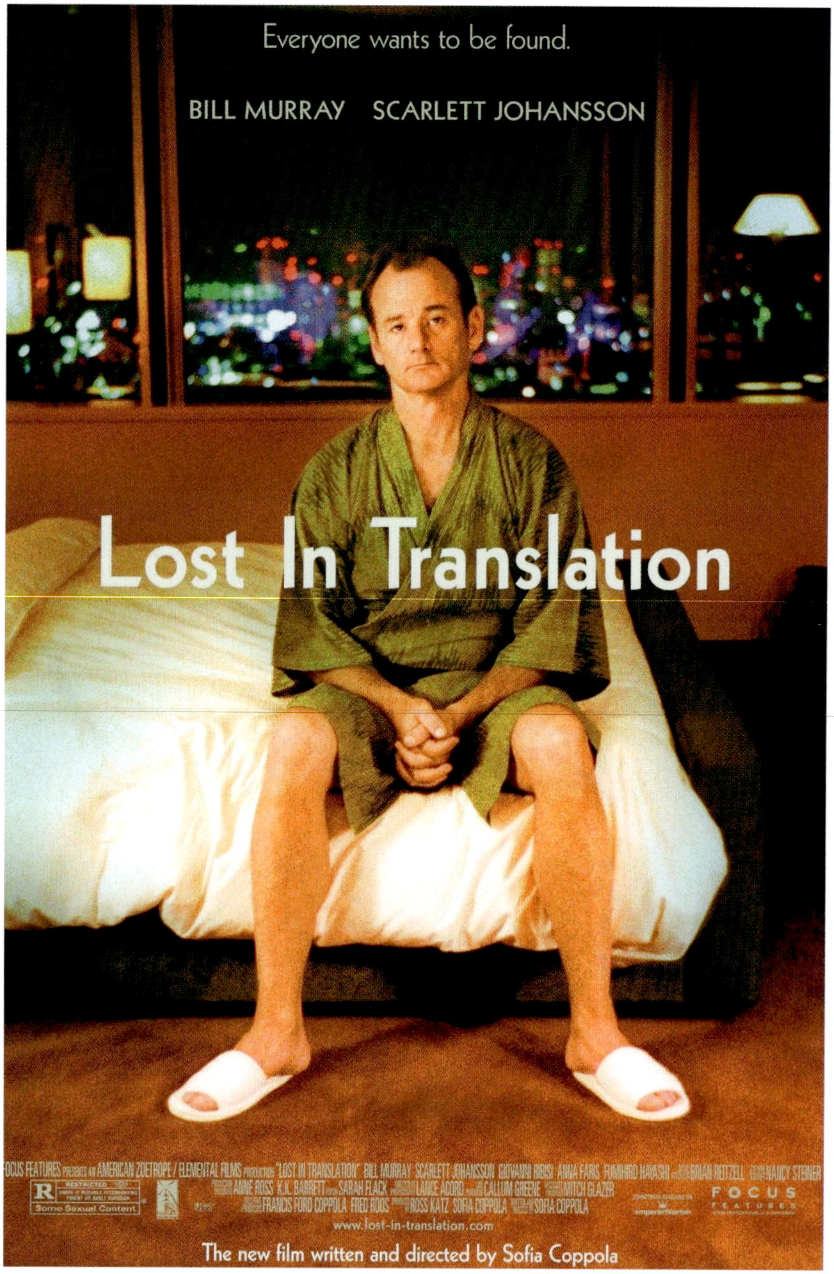

Above: *Where* The Virgin Suicides *grew into a cult,* Lost in Translation *became a sensation at the box office, recouping around twenty-four times its budget.*

commercialism and harmony of Japanese art as lyrical as a haiku.'[26]

Still, even Coppola's daughters were taken aback by the age gap when first shown the film. 'What's with that?'[27] they gawped. The family was actually in the Hyatt, having come back to Tokyo where Coppola's husband Thomas Mars and his band, Phoenix (who had, ironically, blessed the original soundtrack with the hit *Too Young*), had been offered a residency.

Coppola has been hesitant to confront any superimposed controversy. 'I was just doing my thing at the time it was made,'[28] she reflected on the film's 20th anniversary. Besides which, the story doesn't work otherwise. 'It's one of those unique, introverted gems, like *The Accidental Tourist* or *The Piano*, that either enfolds you with its generosity of spirit or leaves you cold,'[29] concluded Matt Brunson in *Creative Loafing Charlotte*. In other words, you can chose to be offended or enchanted.

And lest we forget, *Lost in Translation* took its young director all the way to the Academy Awards (another family trait). It gained four significant nods: Best Original Screenplay, Best Actor, Best Picture, and she was only the third woman in history to be nominated for Best Director. She would win for Original Screenplay. The lead-up to the ceremony was almost a parody of Bob's superstar treatment in Tokyo, and Coppola began to feel a similar detachment. There were ritzy dinners, live Q&As, hotel rooms filled with bouquets. Like a funeral parlour, she smirked to her mother. On the night, she presented an award with her father (awkwardly), but the world's eyes were entirely on her.

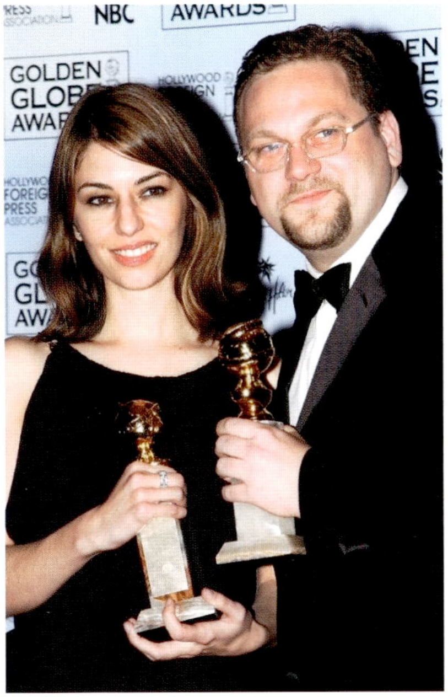

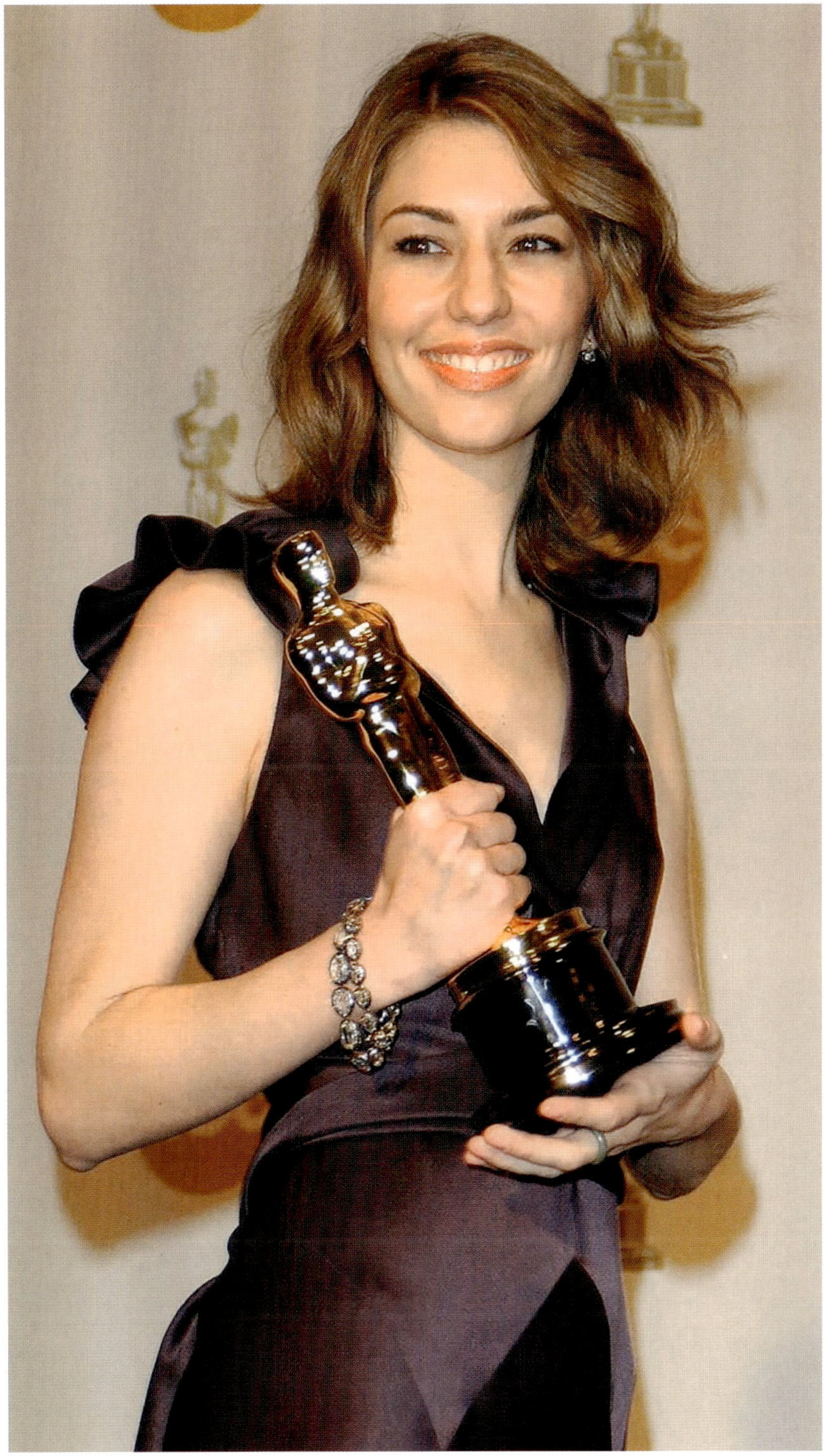

Above: *Sofia Coppola and producer Ross Katz celebrate winning three awards at the 2004 Golden Globes, among them Best Motion Picture – Musical or Comedy.* Lost in Translation *remains her most lauded film.*

Right: *Girl power – winning Best Original Screenplay at the Oscars for* Lost in Translation *made Sofia the most famous Coppola on the planet.*

LET HER EAT CAKE

Marie Antoinette (2006)

For her third film, she takes a chance, though it felt natural – a biopic of the notorious French queen as new wave period piece

For those listening closely, there is a constant whispering layered into the soundtrack. It might as well be high school. Everything about the new film is familiar and alien at once. The dresses are like walking bouquets, the teetering bouffants like whipped cream (trailing slipstreams of acrid hairspray on set), the place settings are dizzying, entire scenes are candlelit, aristocrat lackeys bow before smirking behind their fans, slaves to ritual, gadflies to gossip. This is the actual Versailles, the most palatial of palaces, the chintziest of hotels, where they have been given permission to film for one day a week. Which made things fraught for producer Ross Katz – there were priceless vases around every corner.

Sofia Coppola was Hollywood royalty, but the estate's administrators were equally impressed by how the script was attempting to climb inside the queen's head. Coppola's Marie Antoinette has the same faraway look as Lux in *The Virgin Suicides*, then she is being played by Kirsten Dunst. Her slippers are made by Manolo Blahnik (not to mention the powder-blue Converse), and she glides through a masquerade to the frosty post-punk of Siouxsie and the Banshees, the futurescape of the soundtrack echoing over the set. With all the masks, a smiling director dubbed it her superhero movie. There isn't a guillotine to be had. Matters of state are as encoded as recess. Coppola wanted teenagers to see her new movie.

Looking back, those first two films shaped how we perceive Coppola as a storyteller. One grew into a generational cult, the other anointed her as a singular voice. By 2006, she was all the rage. When Hollywood whispers mentioned the new 'Coppola' they were referring to Sofia. Could she live up to herself?

Which brings us to the problematic brilliance of *Marie Antoinette*. The headlines: Coppola's adaptation of Lady Antonia Fraser's revisionist biography of the French queen was heralded as a bold step, booed on its debut at Cannes, dismissed as gauche postmodernism by a cadre of critics (had Coppola lost her head?), left expectant audiences confounded on its release, and put the brakes on her career to the point where she contemplated downing tools for good. How could this unconventional dance with history be anything but a fascinating film?

Oppositet: *History restyled – Kirsten Dunst poses in flamboyant character as the teenage queen-to-be in Sofia Coppola's misunderstood biopic* Marie Antoinette.

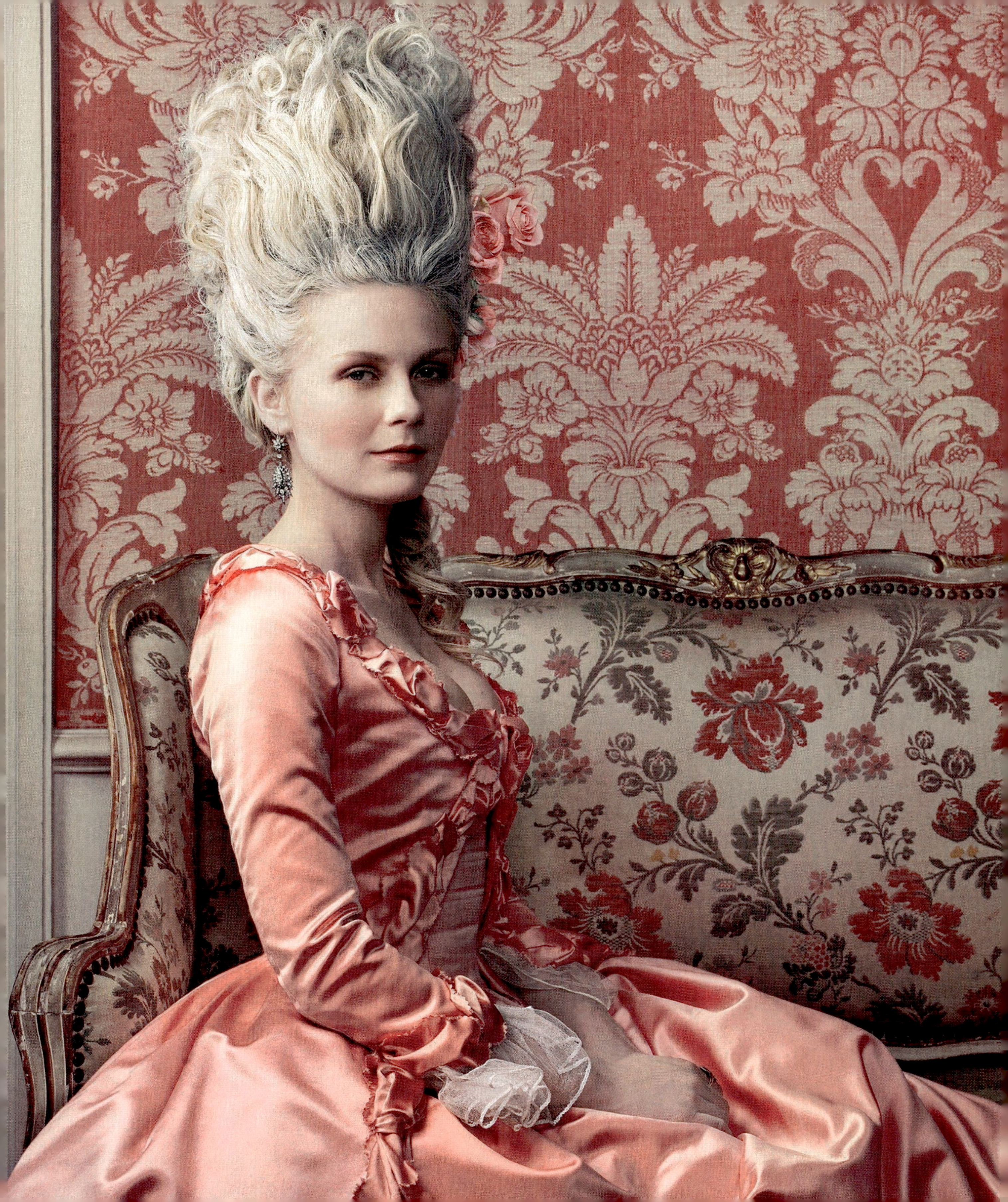

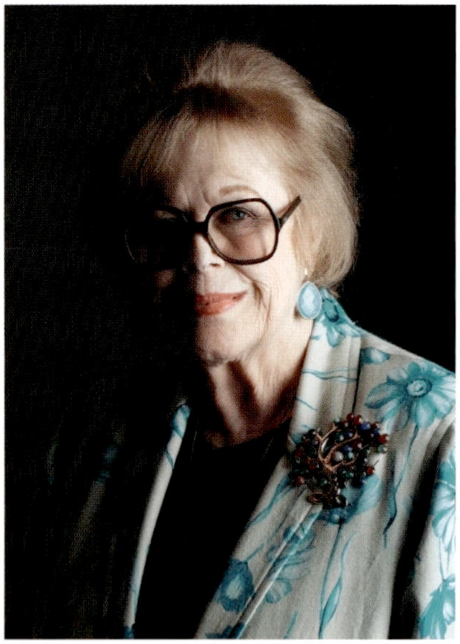

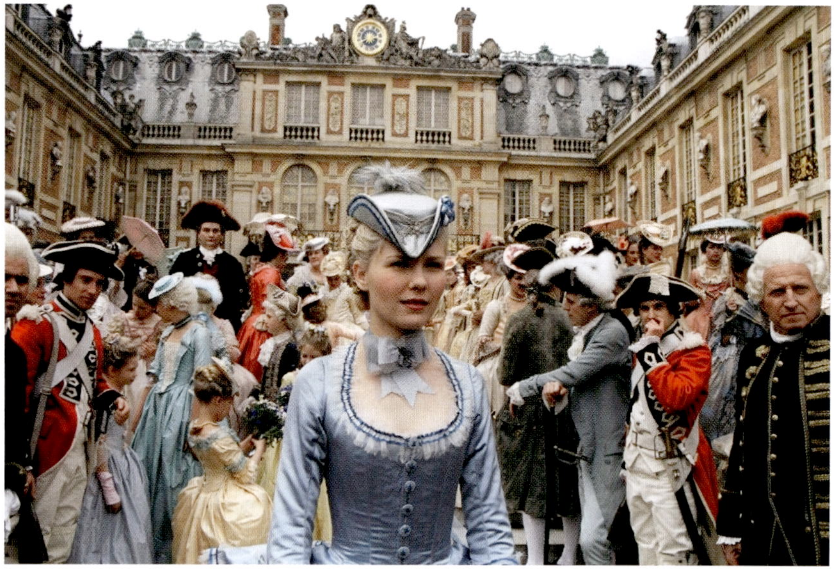

Above left: *Lady Antonia Fraser's revelatory biography* Marie Antoinette: The Journey *was a key inspiration, particularly in terms of Marie's daily life. In turn, Fraser would be an ardent supporter of the film.*

Above right: *Marie (Kirsten Dunst) arrives at the royal palace at Versailles, to begin a life as effectively the biggest celebrity in France.*

Since its tumultuous birth, her expensive so-called misstep has become regarded as an emphatic statement of intent.

It might be 1770 and nineteen ensuing years, and the (literally) glittering court of Versailles, but this is neither historical epic nor period drama in any conventional sense. This was the final stage, according to Coppola, of a trilogy of films following a girl's evolution. Each had a distinct inspiration: the first was a book impossible to resist; the second was a fictional extension of her own search for identity; the third repurposed history as a metaphor for the trials of young womanhood. They are connected across time and genre by Coppola's emotional subtext.

'In my three films, the heroines are young girls at a moment of transition who find themselves and become women,'[1] she explained. Marie had arrived at Versailles not even fourteen, barely a teenager, and Coppola saw a golden thread connecting her to the Lisbon girls supine in their bedrooms. The Austrian princess will find herself adrift in a dysfunctional marriage and alienated in her palatial surroundings with all their baffling rituals and rivalries, and the director could see the echo across time to Tokyo, the Hyatt, and troubled Charlotte.

Structurally, though it's not big on the scaffolding of plot, *Marie Antoinette* serves as its own inner trilogy: the journey of this princess, a bargaining chip in a favourable trans-European alliance, from lost girl to sexual awakening to motherhood and maturity (she lost her head at thirty-eight).

Her third film also held up a mirror to Coppola's evolution as a filmmaker. In *Marie Antoinette*, it is the ascendency of style that makes sense over expectations of historical probity. Beneath the ravishing tableaux runs a river of melancholy, those inescapable currents of Sofia Sadness.

The queen had slowly come into focus. Coppola had read Évelyne Lever's *Marie Antoinette: The Last Queen of France*, bought the rights (twice), before being swept away by Lady Antonia Fraser's *Marie Antoinette: The Journey*, which became her official guide to the French court. What was so unusual in Fraser's approach was her concentration on the spaces between recorded fact. What Coppola appreciated as 'the details of her

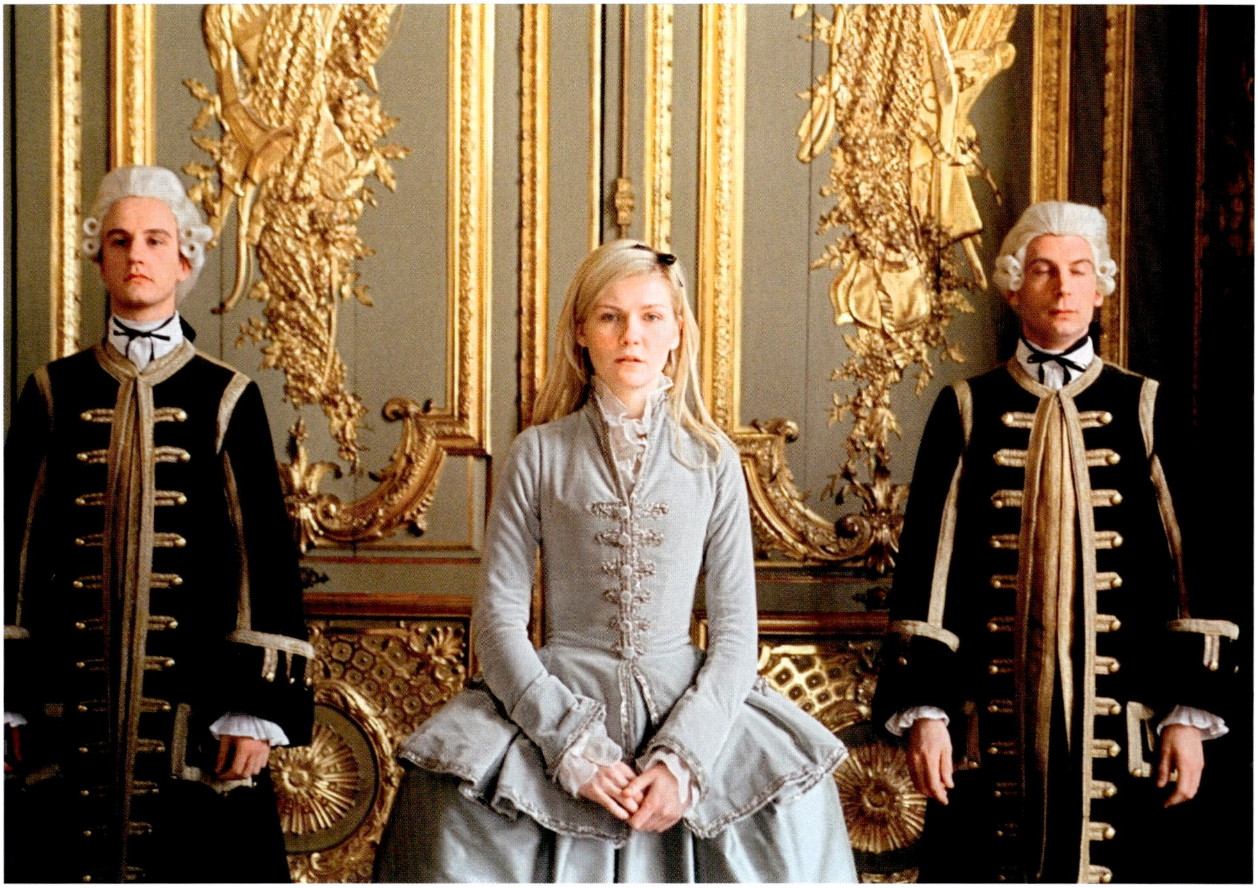

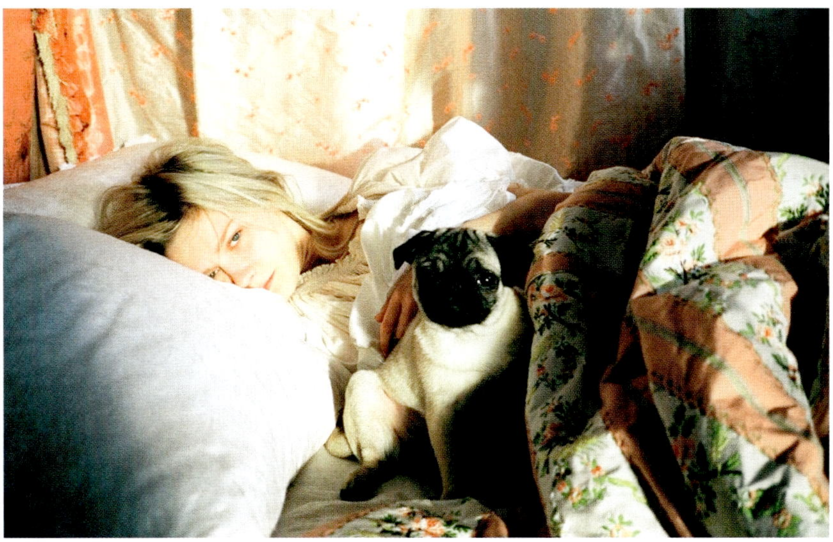

Above: *Sofia Coppola was at pains to remind the viewer that Austrian Marie (Dunst) was scarcely a teenager when she came to France. The film was designed to echo across time to her earlier studies in lost girls.*

Left: *When she arrived Marie was barely fourteen, and would have to grow up fast in a hermetic world of luxury and ritual.*

private existence.'[2] The letters she wrote, the way she actually bathed and dressed, how she spent her languid days. Fraser wrote with what *Vogue* called a 'radical sense of empathy,'[3] which doubles as a good description of how Coppola makes films. For her part, the filmmaker wanted to capture the way Fraser had created 'a pretty impressionistic portrait of her character.'[4]

It was a riposte to the stiff-limbed tradition of the biopic. 'I felt compelled to portray how her story had been misrepresented over time,' explained Coppola. 'I had this idea of how to interpret her life in a way that felt youthful and girly instead of academic.'[5]

She had been working on the adaptation alongside the script for *Lost in Translation*: when she got stuck on one, she moved to the other. At an unfixed point in 2002, overwhelmed by the list of potential characters and arcana of eighteenth century décor, her Tokyo dreamscape took precedence. Buoyed by the success of her second film, she returned to the book with renewed purpose and the backing of a studio for the first time. Her award-winning lustre landed her a deal at Sony, for a not inconsiderable $40 million (ten times what *Lost in Translation* had cost).

Amy Pascal, then co-chairman of Sony Pictures, described herself as a Coppola groupie. 'She's one-of-a-kind and when you decide that you're gonna make a movie like *Marie Antoinette* with a filmmaker like her, there's no point in curtailing their vision.'[6]

That vision was to include the least amount of realpolitik as possible, with the French Revolution only a distant murmur. This was about social dynamics, which in their own mysterious way were highly political. How did the world Marie was confronted with actually function? Moreover, Coppola wanted her story to be told entirely from the soon-to-be-queen's perspective. Sealed within the courtly chocolate box, she knew nothing of social unrest beyond the walls. She had no idea she was going to lose her head. Coppola's framework was precise: she would begin Marie's story when she arrives in Versailles and end when she leaves (just as *Lost in Translation* only lasts from Bob's arrival to his departure).

Fraser entirely approved of the approach and staunchly defended the film amid the backlash. Then she was another huge fan of *The Virgin Suicides*. This is the story of how Marie navigated her youth at Versailles, under the overwhelming glare of the court. 'I wanted to make the point that she and the people around her were teenagers,'[7] said Coppola. This is a portrait of all the frippery and decadence that filled her days; the jet lag of wealth. When the revolution comes to her doorstep, added Coppola, 'it's sorta like the party comes to an end and everyone has to go home.'[8]

Dunst's face had come to Coppola when she wrote the script, which helped bring Marie to life; a picture of the actress would adorn the cover of the script like a magazine cover. There was still that personal connection, the spiritual symbiosis they shared on *The Virgin Suicides*, and thanks to her genes Dunst had the perfect Germanic bone structure, ice-blue eyes, and coquettish smile. Thanks to her upbringing, she had the perfectly anachronistic valley-girl accent.

They met informally at the Chateau Marmont hotel in Los Angeles (implanting possibilities for a future film), where she handed Dunst the book and essentially the part.

Giving Marie a break was among the many sins accorded to Coppola's depiction. And Dunst plays her with a sympathetic immediacy. Like Charlotte in Tokyo, this new world is lost in translation: all the hierarchical absurdities and codified language; the recorded privilege of who

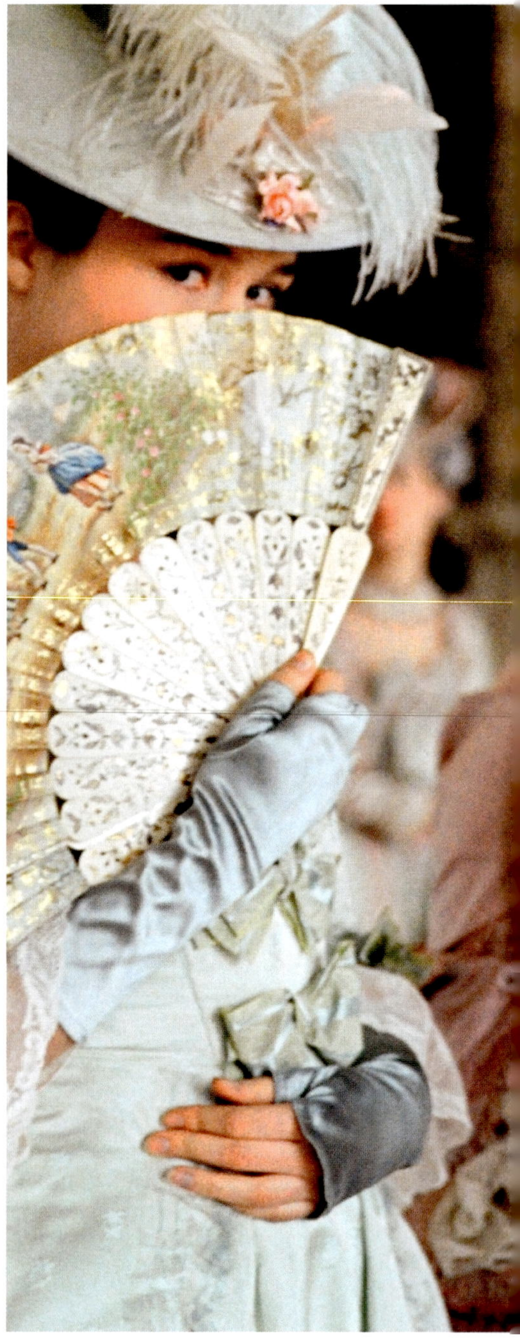

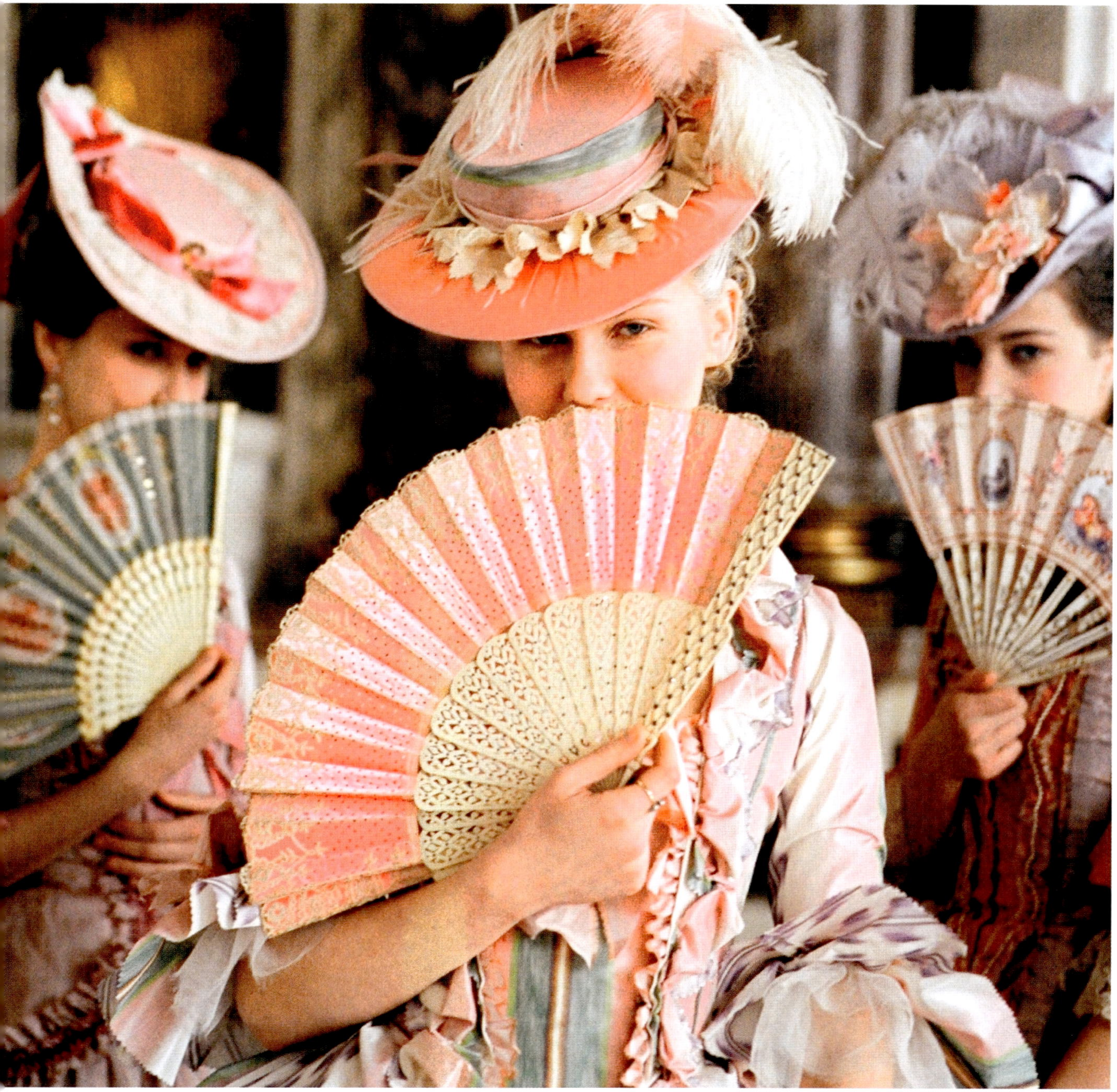

Above: *Every freeze-frame is a work of art – Marie Antoinette and her inner circle strike a pose. From the left: Mary Nighy, Io Bottoms, Kirsten Dunst, and Céline Sallette.*

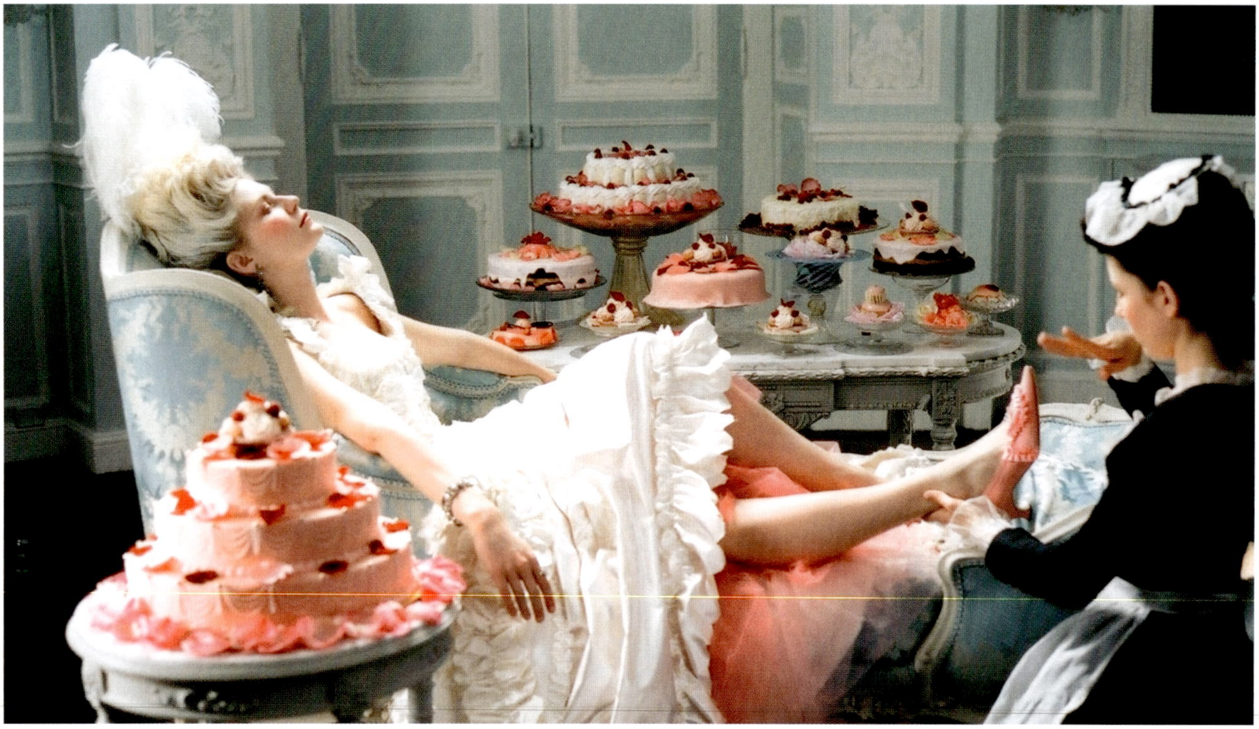

Above: *Pampering over the cracks – Kirsten Dunst's Marie inoculates her insecurity with the trappings of luxury.*

gets to dress the queen-in-waiting in the morning. 'Everyone at court has one goal,' Steve Coogan's Austrian Ambassador Mercy warns her, 'to get as high up as they can.'[9] It was a way of life.

Dunst's Marie is giggly, incredulous, and modern, relishing the absurdity as if it were all a game of fancy dress. 'She comes across as more alive, more at ease, more likeable than any young Hollywood actress…' applauded Jonathan Romney in the *Independent*. 'But we also get glimpses of a vulnerable, shattered sensibility.'[10]

The whole film is an act of reclamation. Marie's reputation was distorted by propaganda drummed up in libellous pamphlets. Something that 'still has a potency,'[11] noted Judy Davis, who brings a steely hauteur to the Comtesse de Noailles, font of court regulations. In any case, Marie was a polarizing figure in France before a frame had been shot, both icon and devil. Critics wondered if Coppola was still working through the critical mauling she had received for *The Godfather Part III* by empathizing with a queen who had got such terrible reviews. The opening shot of Marie lounging on a chaise longue, hemmed in by untouched gateaux and a maid at her feet, based on a fashion shoot by Guy Bourdin and set to Gang of Four's raucous *Natural's Not in It*, pronounces the decadent image history has made of her, which the film then sets about reconsidering.

Once she was over her wariness about an American playing Marie, Fraser fully approved of Dunst. 'Not only does she look absolutely beautiful and natural (that fabulous pink-and-white complexion, wide-apart blue eyes), but she's graceful,'[12] she wrote in her published diary. It was on record how graceful Marie was considered to be.

With Dunst as Marie, Coppola turned to her cousin to fill the powdered wig of her royal lummox of a husband. Los Angeles-born drummer-turned-actor Jason Schwartzman was the son of *Godfather* actress Talia Shire, Coppola's aunt (and he brings a whisper of Hollywood hierarchies). Coppola can lay claim to having pushed him to audition for his debut in Wes Anderson's *Rushmore*, and the preppy, self-aggrandizing Max Fischer surely informed her casting. The doltish heir Dauphin Louis-Auguste will find consummating his arranged marriage a tall order (it took until 1778 to plant the royal seed).

'Louis wouldn't sleep with her, so she wanted to go out and party – like someone in a bad marriage going shopping,' said Coppola. 'It just seemed like the same old story.'[13]

Bewildered by the proposition of playing a king (then Coppola wanted him bewildered), Schwartzman had to put on considerable weight for plump, indolent, painfully shy Louis, which he did by eating plates of donuts at 3 a.m. (Fraser described Louis as a 'fat slob'[14]). He was instructed, firmly, not to learn any French. All the cast were required to keep their natural accents (a mix of American, British, Italian, and indeed some French). Tying everyone down to some thespy Received Pronunciation would be too Masterpiece Theatre. The myriad accents reinforced the hotel scene of Versailles where everyone was on their way in or on their way out. It also allowed everyone to be natural. Or as close as they could get in a corset.

It was all so big, so busy, so demanding. There were thirty main characters, which Coppola cast on personality and vibe, for the collage of it all. Among them are Marianne Faithfull as Maria Theresa, Empress of Austria; Rip Torn (who took handling) as King Louis XV; Asia Argento as the king's scurrilous mistress (and mean girl) Madame du Barry; and the Australian Rose Byrne as Marie's BFF, the Duchesse de Polignac, who tries out an aristocratic British bray for comic relief.

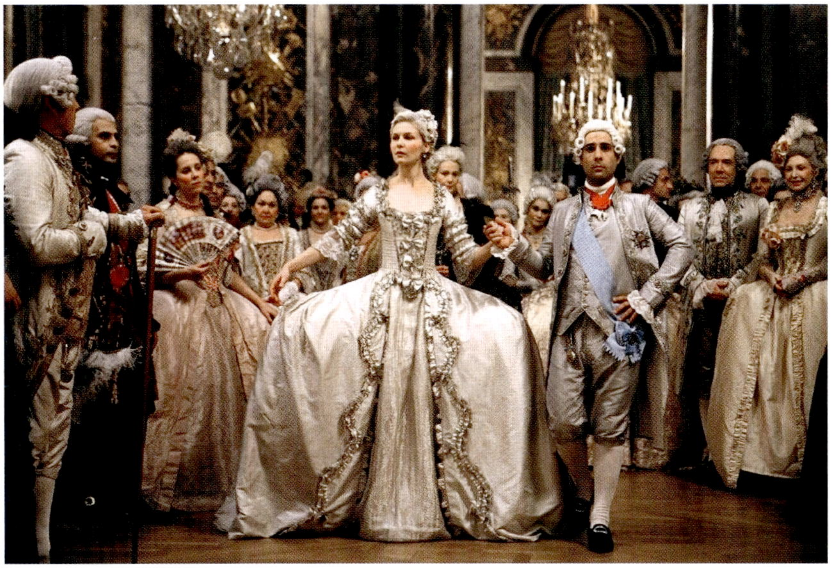

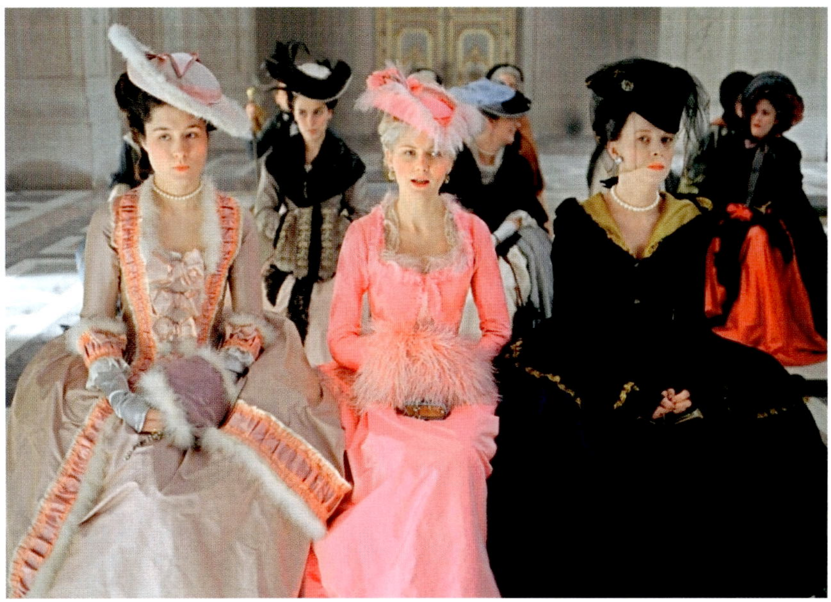

Top: *In every sense a costume drama – Marie (Dunst) and heir Louis-Auguste (Jason Schwartzman) parade the latest fashions, a scheme of looks devised by veteran designer Milena Canonero.*

Above: *Gossip girls – Princesse de Lamballe (Mary Nighy), Marie (Dunst), and the august Comtesse de Noailles (Judy Davis) form a close bond.*

Coppola had described the Duchesse to her as an uncorked bottle of champagne.

Over the spring of 2005, Coppola, cast, and crew were granted leave to shoot for twelve weeks at Versailles and in its manicured grounds. 'They were like, "This is your home,"'[15] she marvelled. Tourists would pass by and see girls in long gowns, powdered wigs and sunglasses smoking cigarettes and talking on their cell phones. Pedro Almodóvar, Wes Anderson, and, naturally, Francis Ford Coppola (again the executive producer) dropped by to take in the scene. They were effectively shooting on location, but the limitations of only having one day a week at the palace required a complex of other fully-dressed sites in and around Paris, including the Opéra national de Paris for the masquerade ball.

It couldn't look old, decreed the director. Everything was new when Marie arrived. So sets had to be built, including her gold and turquoise bedroom recreated with impeccable accuracy in the rundown Château de Millemont out in the countryside.

After the intimacy of *The Virgin Suicides* and the run-and-gun freedoms of *Lost in Translation*, the filmmaking itself had the aura of ceremony. Wine was served at lunch as was the rule with French productions. There were extras everywhere, scenes had to be choreographed, strategized, staged. Improvisation was almost impossible. Then Versailles was a kind of theatre. Marie had thought of herself as an actress.

This was the 'girliest'[16] of her sets, Coppola declared proudly, knowing the superficiality was a front for theme. All the gold and mirrors, all the taffeta, chintz and endless frill are stifling. 'The whole palate is costumes and cake,'[17] she laughed. It was meant to be too much (another of the volley of complaints), this ceaseless, Hollywood-like display of conspicuous consumption.

Marie Antoinette never actually said 'Let them eat cake.'[18] That was another jibe put about by the revolutionaries, but it stuck. So Coppola plays to the myth. Cake is the central motif, with a profusion of patisserie: biscuits, profiteroles, meringues to match the tottering hairstyles, and a paintbox of scene-stealing macarons. They had an entire cake department on hand, from the Parisian pastry house Ladurée (which blew up once the film was released). But rarely is anything consumed and we ache for a single, sugary taste.

They also had an on-set florist, Thierry Boutemy, who had flowers delivered once a week from Belgium. Coppola would stop to watch him make the arrangements.

'It's stylish, you know?'[19] commented veteran costume designer Milena Canonero, who had dressed *Barry Lyndon*, a touchstone for Coppola, and would win the Oscar just as she had done on Kubrick's period epic. The film needed to feel fashionable, insisted the director, these were eighteenth-century It girls. Design reflected psychology. The bone-sprung bodices spoke volumes – Dunst literally felt caged in.

Odile Gilbert, the most celebrated hair stylist in France according to *Marie Claire*, created a progression of looks for the leading lady, a girl's evolution mapped out in madly primped platinum blonde sculptures. Nobody would dare show their face at court without powdered hair.

'My attitude was, "How would Marie want a movie about her life to look?"'[20] said Coppola.

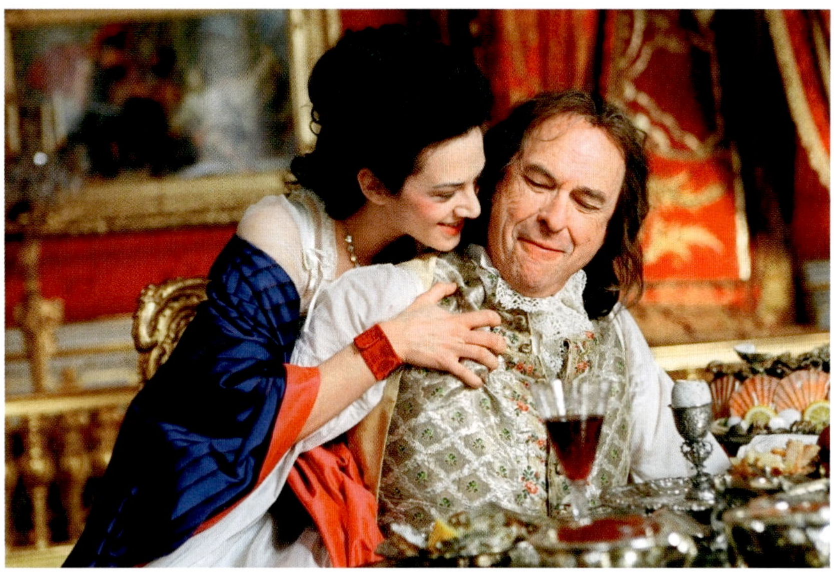

Right: *Asia Argento, another daughter of a famous director (Dario Argento), plays the scandalous Madame du Barry, mistress of Rip Torn's Louis XV.*

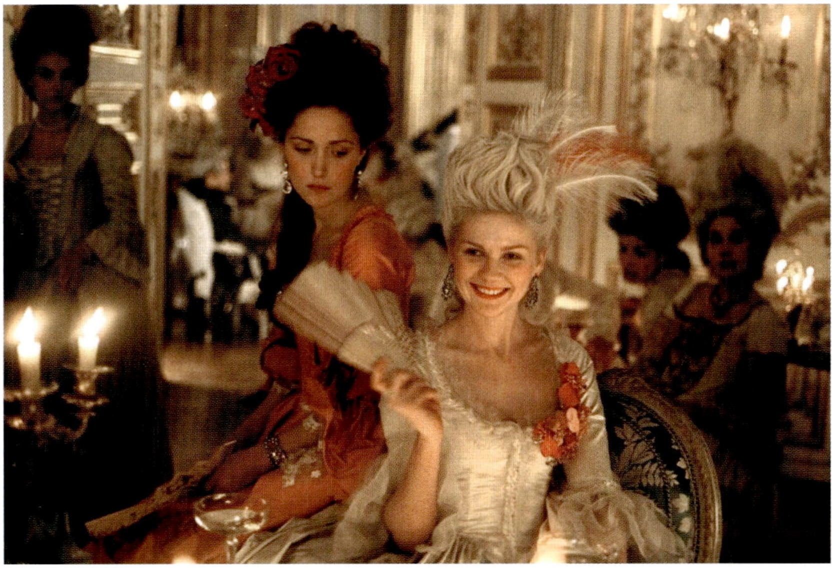

Left: *BFFs forever – the Duchesse de Polignac (Rose Byrne) and Marie Antoinette (Kirsten Dunst). Sofia Coppola wanted Versailles to insinuate all the hallmarks of an American high school.*

Below: *Thanks to her family name and humanizing intentions, Coppola was granted the incredibly rare opportunity to shoot inside and in the grounds of the actual Versailles. A fraught experience for the crew, terrified of damaging anything.*

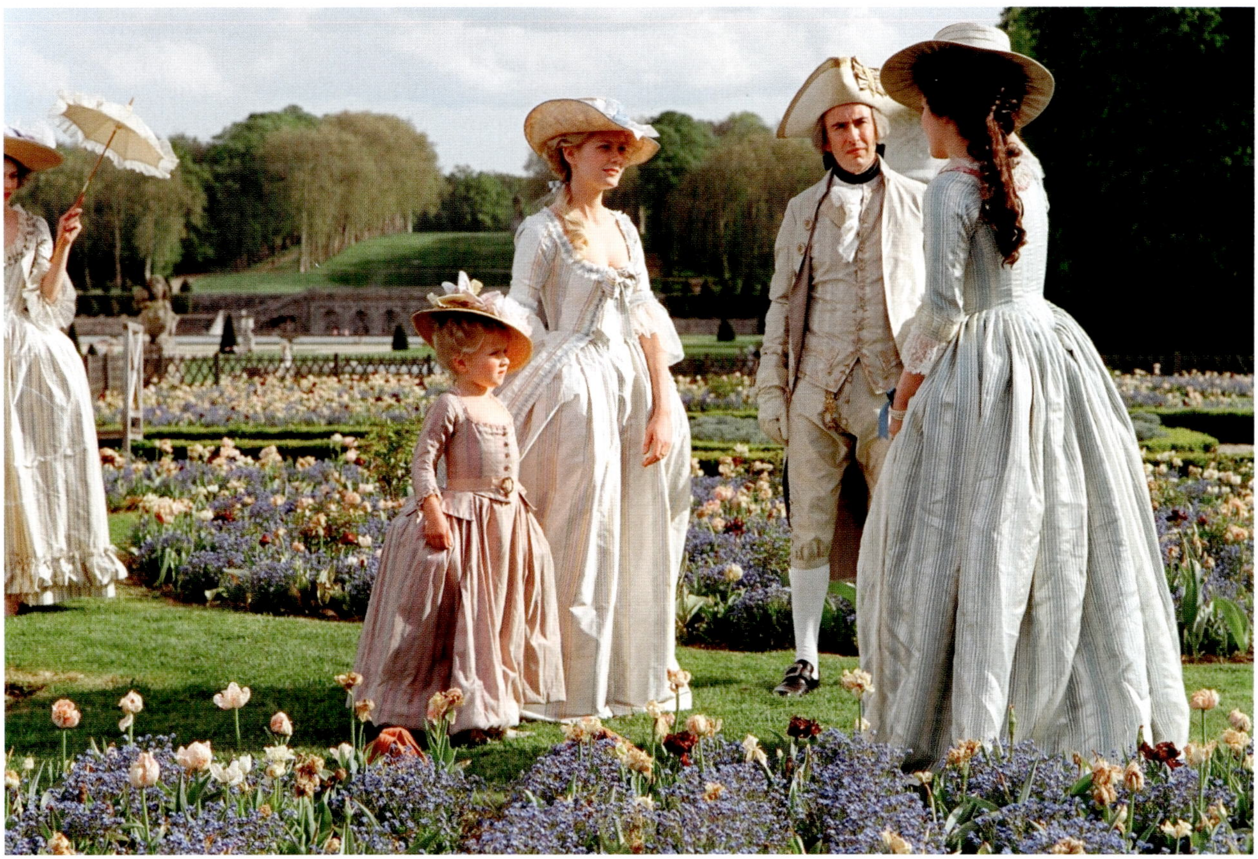

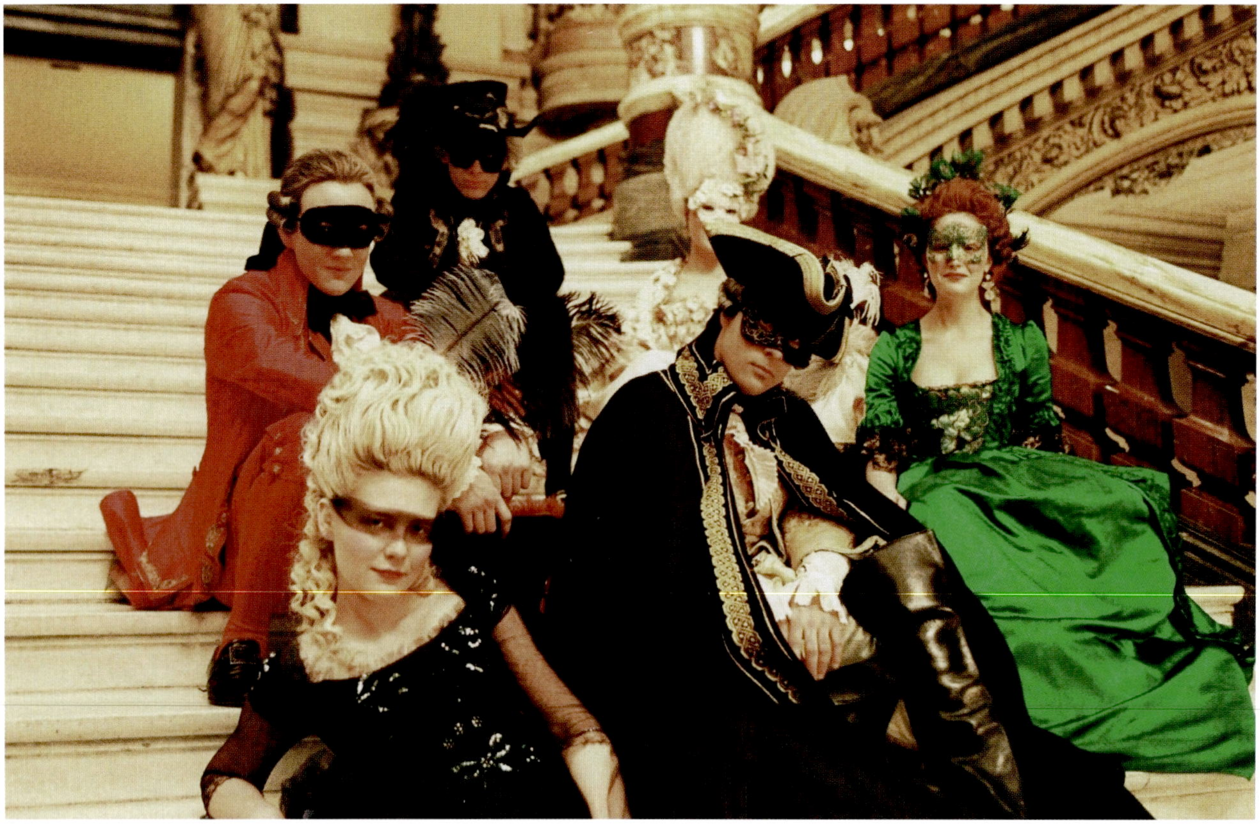

> I want it to be kind of irreverent, kind of how they were at the time. I mean, they're just doing what they want. They sort of have a little bit of a bratty attitude.
> ***SOFIA COPPOLA***

Long discussions were held on colour, there was to be no brown or beige, or dreaded sepia (QED: it must not recall the coffee-toned streets of *The Godfather*). She wanted high-key intensity, a sheen of pop primaries and soap-label pastels, history as bright as a candy store. We must also perceive a shift in mood with time. When Marie takes her entourage and daughter to lounge in Petit Trianon, the micro-château in the sweeping grounds, the look is more naturalistic to tune into her sexual awakening as she conducts a lavish affair with the dashing Swedish count Axel von Fersen (Jamie Dornan in his first film role), the Trip Fontaine of his day – a speculation portrayed as fact (more grumbles). Aswirl in montage, this was decadence as defence mechanism, a streak of adolescent self-indulgence.

'I want it to be kind of irreverent, kind of how they were at the time,' insisted Coppola. 'I mean, they're just doing what they want. They sort of have a little bit of a bratty attitude.'[21] Even the poster has a pink, punk-graffiti aesthetic.

By the closing chapters, as fate and history come calling (we hear the belligerent cries of the mob, gain a glimpse of unkempt bodies), shadows have literally gathered.

The Virgin Suicides had been naturalistic, if dreamy; *Lost in Translation* was spun within a city's electric shimmer and a reflection of real life. Where *Marie Antoinette* elaborates on her previous films is in its sense of play, all the conscious anachronisms for effect, the postmodern vernacular of inspirations worn like a label. Coppola would breezily cite Kubrick, Adam and the Ants, and the fashion

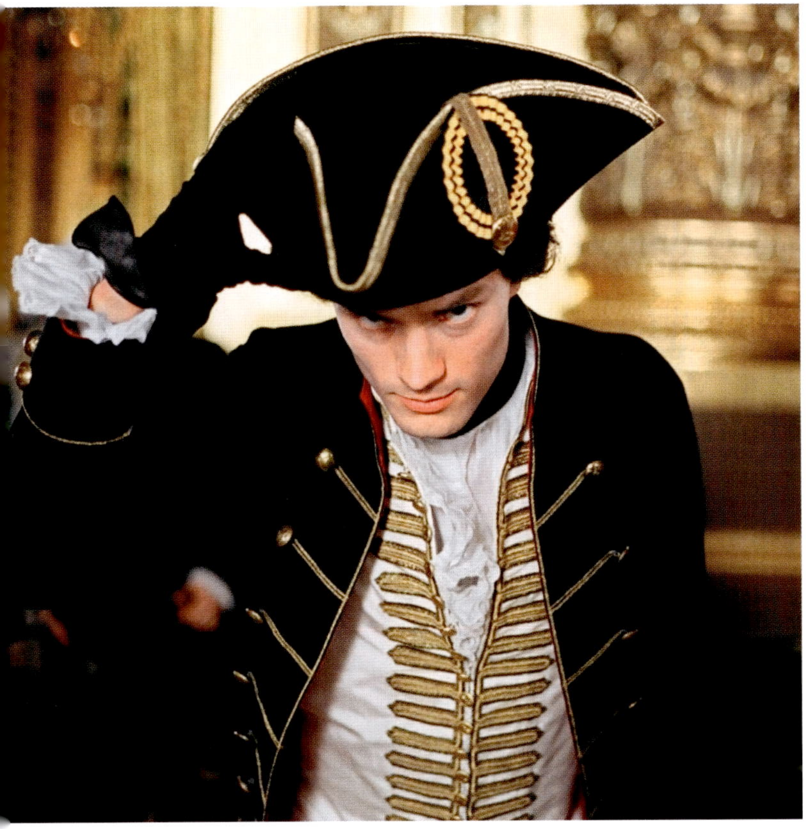

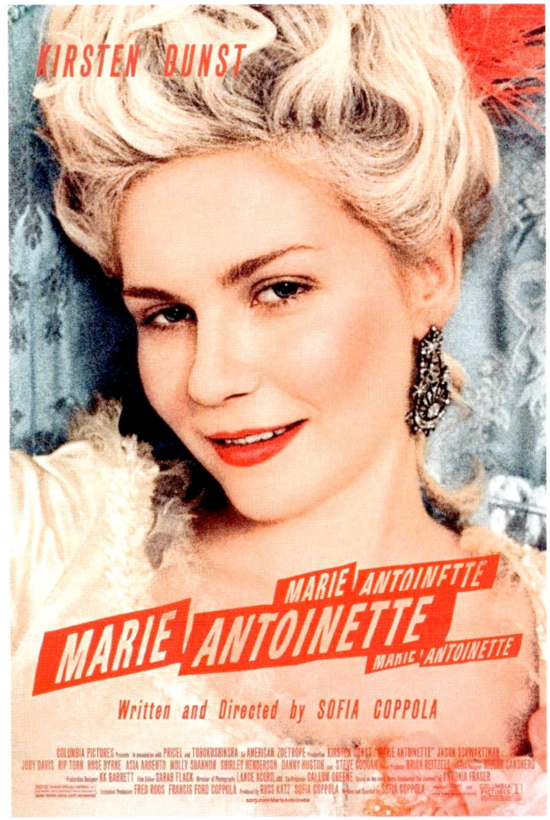

Opposite above: *Dancing with history – the masquerade sequence appropriated the way eighties pop videos appropriated (and exaggerated) the pomp of eighteenth-century high society.*

Above left: *A then unknown Jamie Dornan made his debut as Count Axel von Fersen, Marie's dashing lover.*

Above right: *Right through to the punk-inflected poster, the aesthetic was designed to send shockwaves through the fixtures of received history. Beneath her gentle exterior, Sofia Coppola loves to play provocateur.*

designer John Galliano, or Ken Russell's rock opera *Lisztomania*. And how she loved the glorious Mozart-biopic *Amadeus*, which strained the historical record with over-elaborate wigs and pop glamour.

As she wrote the script, she listened to two mixtapes, comprising over forty songs from her youth, and labelled 'Versailles Mix 1' and 'Versailles Mix 2.'[22] She had been thinking about all those Adam and the Ants videos she had grown up with and how the entire New Romantic scene in its pomp had recycled an eighteenth century aesthetic. Under the guidance of returning musical supervisor Brian Reitzell, Vivaldi's Concerto in G would share sonic space with Bow Wow Wow and The Cure – Robert Smith granting Coppola a cut-price rate on royalties in his admiration for what she was trying.

Critic Roger Ebert, a staunch defender of the film from the pages of the *Chicago Sun-Times*, deciphered what he called 'The Now upon the Then'[23] of *Marie Antoinette*. His point being that no one lives in the Then. In other words, Coppola wants us to feel a sense of Now in a period piece (almost) without breaking the illusion. We must be transported to Versailles in the present tense.

Even if by design, was it all too much?

Coppola is so good at dead time, life almost motionless, recalling the aromatic approach to film taken by European greats such as Antonioni, Visconti and Ophüls. Stretches pass without a word of dialogue. In a midsection given to airy montages of shopping, eating, affairs, portraits, and dalliances with her petting zoo, all the stuff that gave Marie a bad rap with historians,

Right: *Connections – while she was writing the script, Sofia Coppola (left) could picture no one else but Kirsten Dunst in the lead role. The connection with* The Virgin Suicides *was entirely deliberate.*

Below: *In terms of scale, location, and cast,* Marie Antoinette *remains the most ambitious project the director has ever mounted. But that would increase expectation too.*

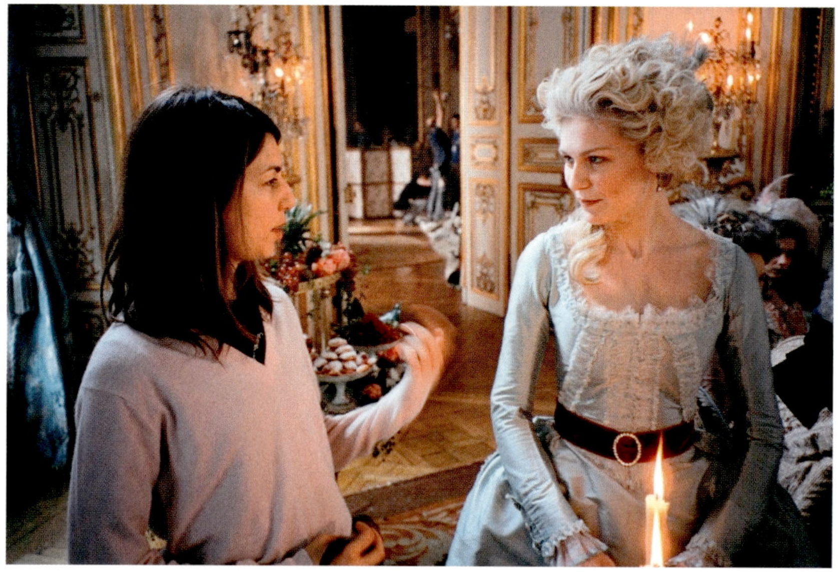

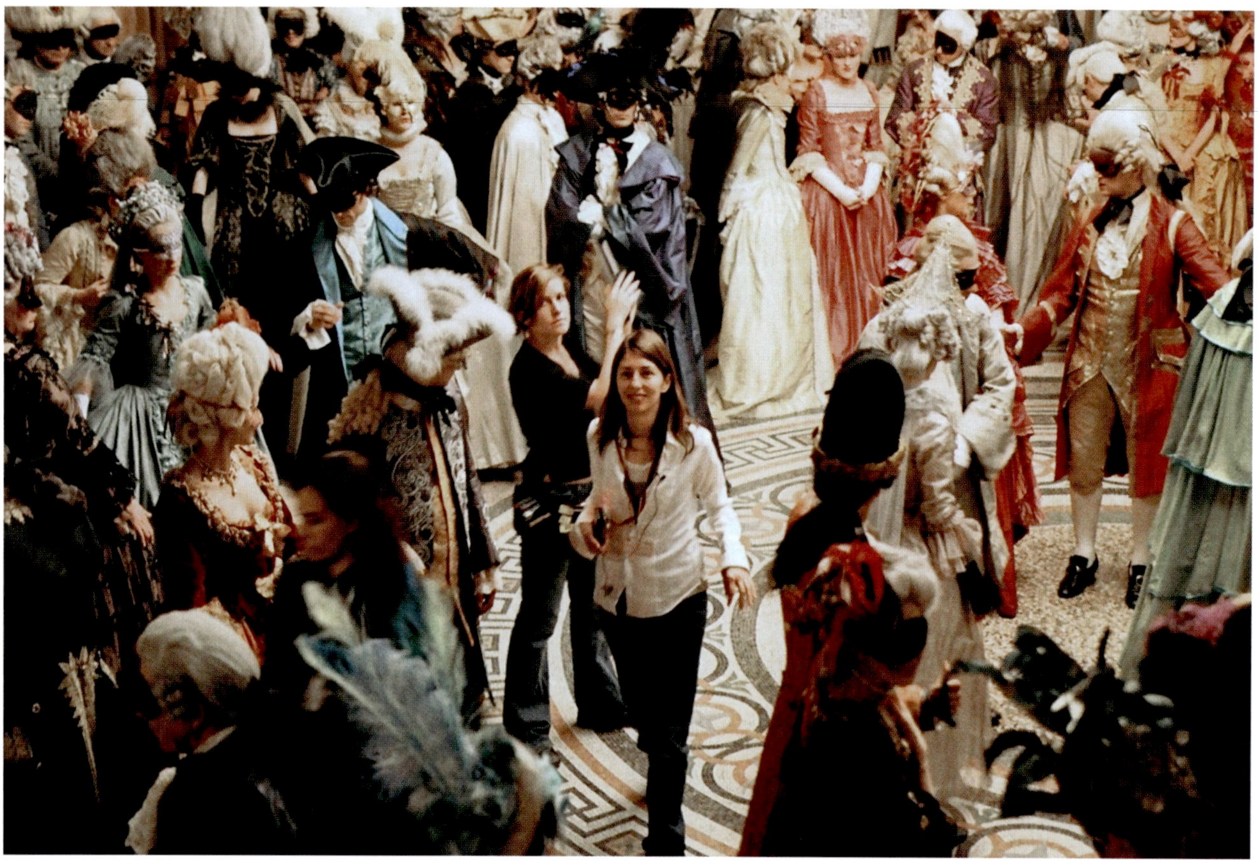

Below: *Crowning achievement – Coppola cast her own cousin Jason Schwartzman as the doltish Louis-Auguste, who becomes king. The actor was forbidden from attempting any kind of accent.*

the lack of substance begins to try our patience. But you wonder if that is partly the point – we feel Marie's boredom.

As a whole, what are we to read into the film's chic makeover of history? It is certainly a parable on celebrity: Marie is famous for being famous, objectified, and subject to the whims of fashion, hot one day, out the next, and by effect completely dehumanized. Was this as much Paris Hilton as Paris? History recycled.

Of course, a survey of life in a bubble bonds a queen's antechambers with the Lisbon sisters, entrapped in their rooms, and the soporific luxury enshrouding Bob and Charlotte. The theme will connect all her films, right through to the Graceland of *Priscilla*, just as Coppola's life has had its bubbles and hotels and listless summers. We are drawn back again to the realm of the autobiographical.

Her father had offered sage advice in the face of working for the studio machine: 'the more personal, the better it would be.'[24] She directed Danny Huston's performance as Marie's brother Joseph II toward memories she had of how her father and brothers would pace around her room fiddling with objects.

When she first wrote to Fraser, on pale-blue, personalized stationery, seeking the rights to make a film of her book, she claimed a close identification with the young queen 'coming from a strong family and fighting for her identity.'[25]

The calamitous response in Cannes is another myth. There were headlines about

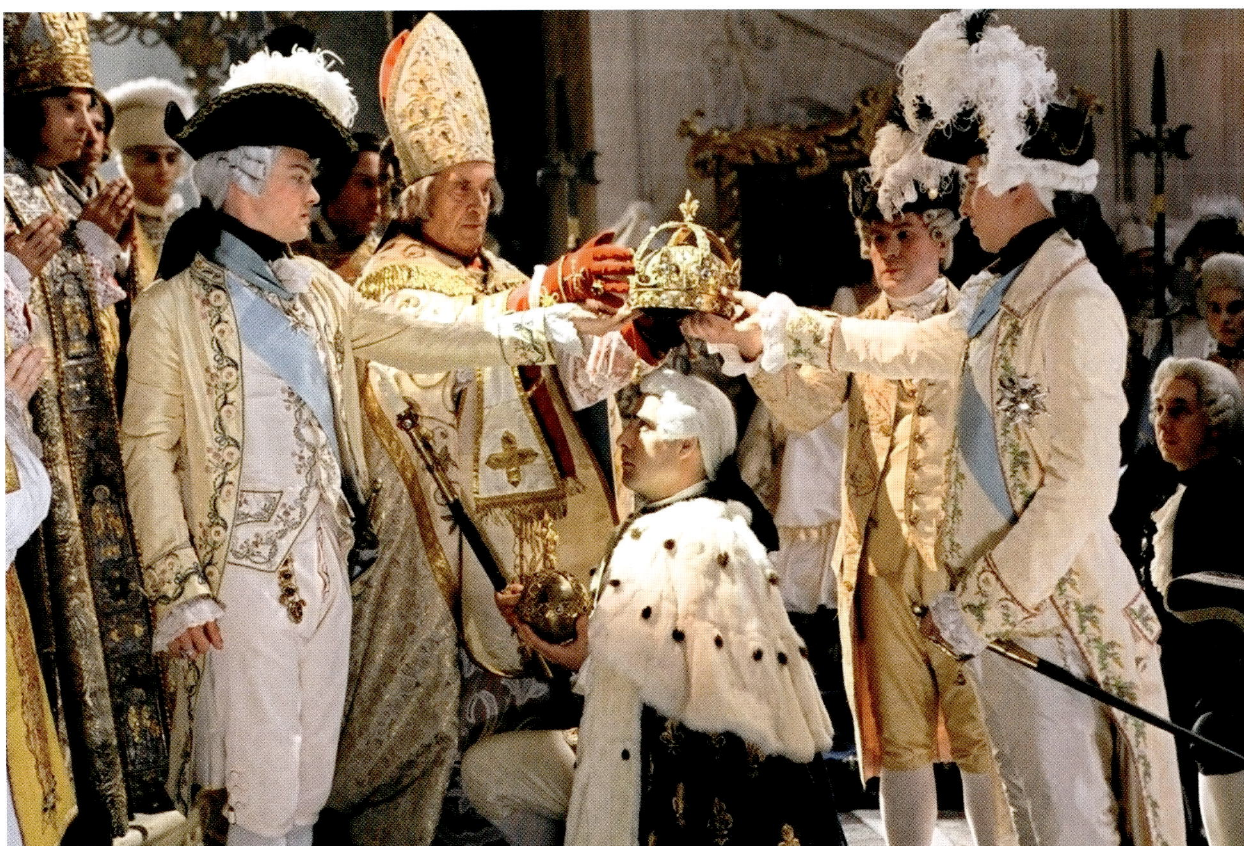

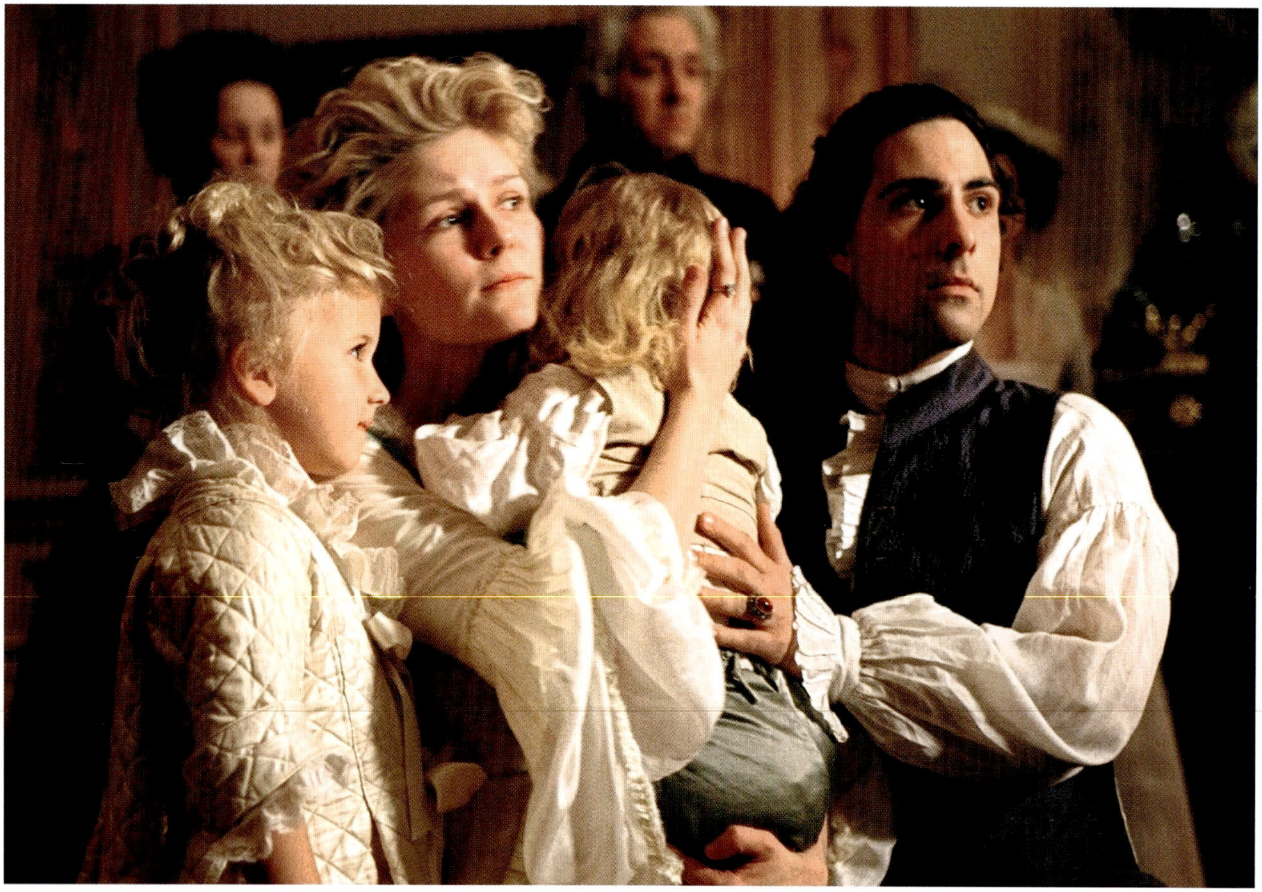

the film being met with a chorus of boos, but most of the critics who were at the screening can recall only one or two dissenting snorts, and boos were hardly unusual for the pontificating festival (a Versailles on the south coast). Only that became the news flash: Coppola derided for daring to show the queen in a generous light. And with a fetishistic thrill.

On its release in 2006, the film was (in hindsight) predictably polarizing. Proof that Coppola was impossible to ignore.

There were those vehemently against.

'An experience so rich and cloying that by the end you may feel that you've just cleared the whole pudding trolley,'[26] volleyed Anthony Quinn in the *Independent*.

People's Leah Rozen derided a depiction of 'the doomed 18th century French queen acting like a teenage flibbertigibbet.'[27]

In an elaborate opinion piece in the *New York Review of Books*, Daniel Mendelsohn concluded that the film 'ends up leaving out much that cannot be ignored.'[28] Wasn't the act of ignoring the unignorable a statement in itself?

'It's history written with truffles,'[29] scorned the *AV Club*. 'Fluffy,'[30] decried the *Irish Times*. 'Once again, she has given us a poor-little-rich-girl story,'[31] pouted Peter Bradshaw in the *Guardian*.

And there were those who were all for it.

Ian Freer in *Empire* celebrated, 'a sexy, witty, dynamic romp.'[32]

Above: *Fall of the House of Bourbon – Marie (Kirsten Dunst) and Louis (Jason Schwartzman) face the arrival of the Revolution. It is only at the very end that the big picture of history reasserts itself.*

Opposite: *Blending in – Dunst's Marie makes a floral statement. For once, the wallpaper was designed to overpower the actor.*

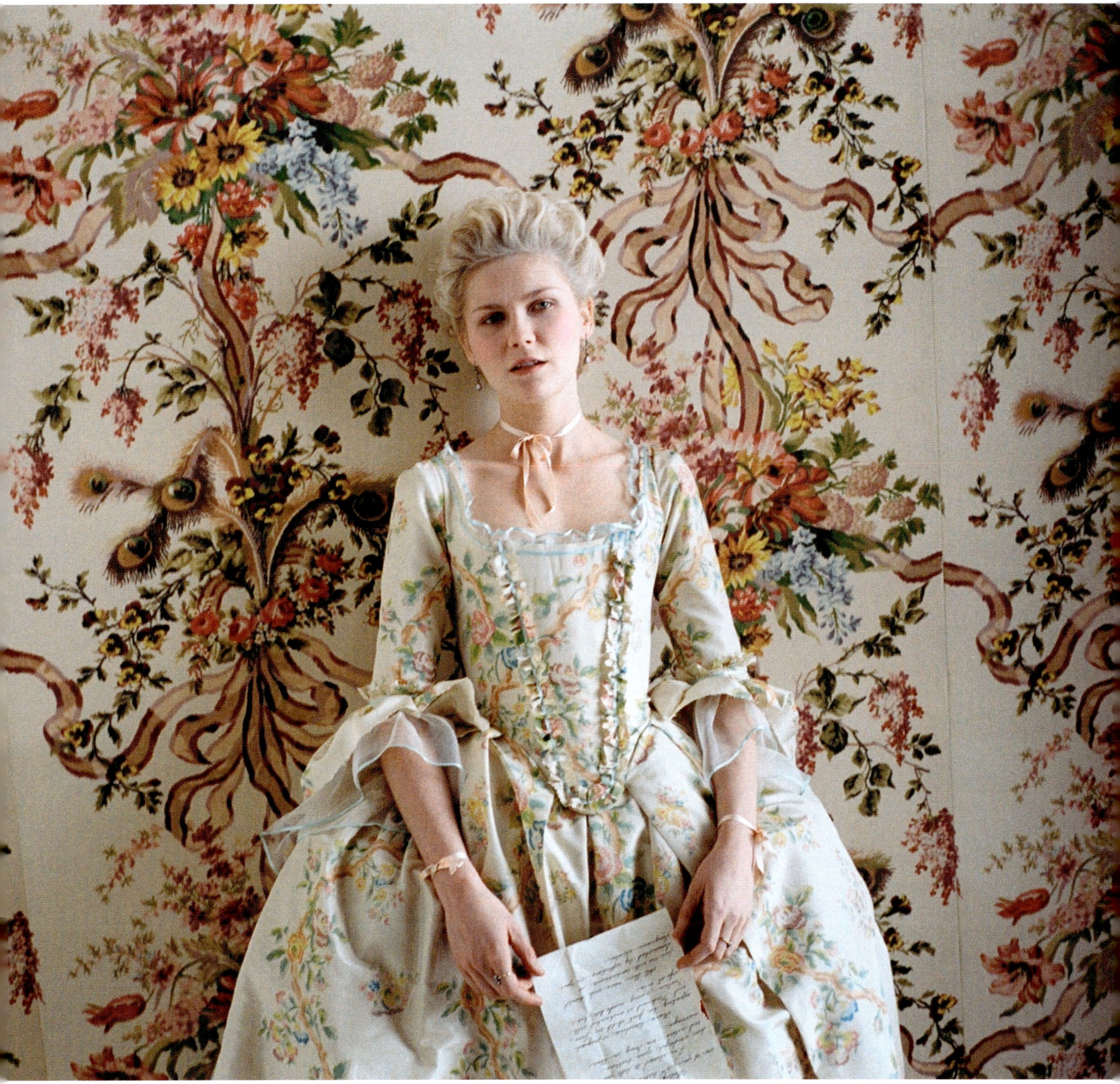

The Hollywood Reporter's Kirk Honeycutt saw a movie that 'slices through the cobwebs of history.'[33]

Roger Ebert took on the nay-sayers, noting how every criticism levelled at the film 'would alter its fragile magic and reduce its romantic and tragic poignancy.'[34] Which comes close to being entirely the point.

'It wasn't a hit,'[35] bemoaned Coppola. A total of $60 million worldwide (the $15m in America was a significantly poor return) amounted to an arthouse hit but a mainstream failure.

Could it be that *Marie Antoinette's* chic irony was simply ahead of its time? In its wake have come a procession of films and television shows flaunting their irony, such as *The Favourite, The Great, Bridgerton, The Grand Budapest Hotel,* even Quentin Tarantino's bloody reimagining of the Second World War for *Inglourious Basterds.* History with anachronistic trimmings has become its own genre. And Coppola's eighteenth-century teenage kicks have had their renaissance.

'*Marie Antoinette* still feels like something of a revelation, and is regarded as a cultural touchstone for so many filmmakers and designers,'[36] wrote Keaton Bell, reminiscing about the film in *Vogue* on its fifteenth birthday.

'Fifteen years on, it seems that the failure of imagination was not on Coppola's part but the world's,'[37] declared Katie Rife in *AV Club.*

Sensitive and flawed, beautiful and excessive, wacky and wise, *Marie Antoinette* is quite unlike anything else she has made – even period thriller *The Beguiled* is conservative by comparison (tonally, TV special *A Very Murray Christmas* comes closest). But it is still unmistakably a Coppola joint.

The ending, and she is so very good at endings, eschewing Marie's legendary encounter with the blade – that Ridley Scott opened his all-event *Napoleon* biopic with her beheading almost feels like an act of retaliation – is pure, evocative, layered Coppola.

'What are you looking at?' asks Louis, as they depart in the royal carriage, ejected from paradise, his wife gazing out at a rapturous sunset over the impeccable lawns. 'I'm saying goodbye,'[38] she replies.

The final vision of a trashed Versailles, where among the debris a bird has escaped its cage, is a devastating image of a transient world. The party's over.

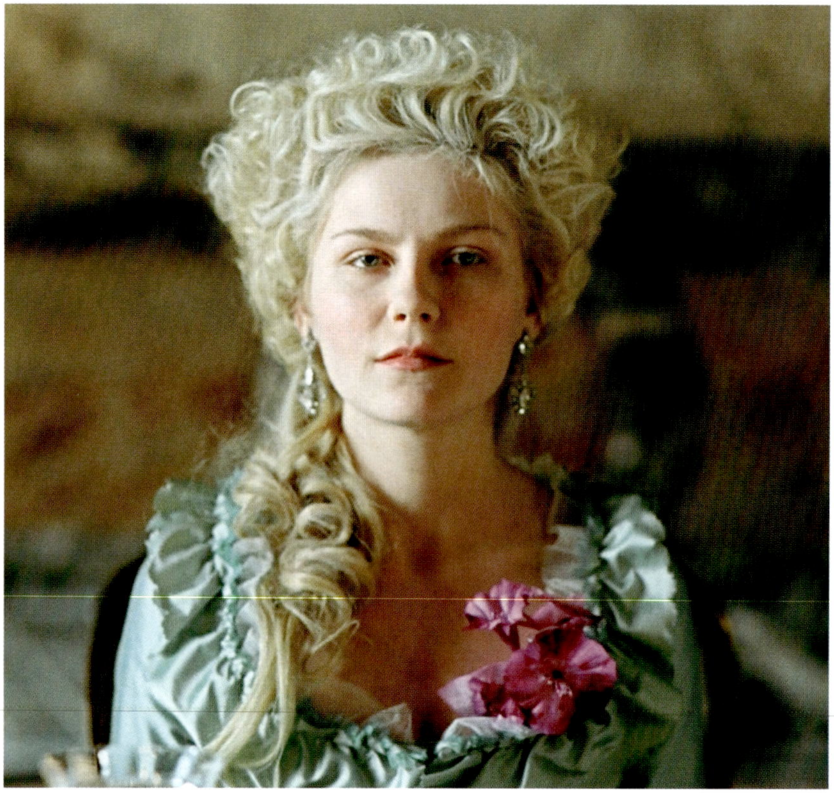

Above: *Amid the film's mixed reception, it is too easily forgotten how good Kirsten Dunst is in the lead role. She finds the listless spirit beneath the pomp and décor, and is one of the reasons the film is now regarded as a cultural touchstone.*

ROOM SERVICE

Every key setting in Coppola's world is a kind of hotel – and prison

1. The Lisbon Family Home, Detroit, in *The Virgin Suicides*
On the suburban outskirts of the city, the Lisbons' unremarkable house is the epicentre of the story. Coppola took the camera into the inner sanctums of the girls' bedrooms to imagine something both ordinary and mythic. It is also the venue of the quintet of death.

2. The Park Hyatt, Tokyo, in *Lost in Translation*
The defining location of her defining film, the hushed, hermetic world of the Hyatt never sleeps – it is both isolating and a place of solace, and saved up for use from Coppola's own experiences.

3. The Palace of Versailles, Paris, in *Marie Antoinette*
Flamboyant in style, rich in pastries, and shot in the gilded footsteps of history, Versailles is luxury bound by arcane rules. For Kirsten Dunst's Marie it is a place of exile: she is waited on hand and indeed foot, but never at home.

4. The Chateau Marmont, Los Angeles, in *Somewhere*
Coppola's second real-life hotel story centres on another flash from her own memory bank: the exclusive sun-drowsy LA hangout where she could figure out a film at leisure. It's the emblem of Hollywood living, neither one place or another.

5. Paris Hilton's Mansion, Los Angeles, in *The Bling Ring*
The very real, borrowed Hilton pad in the Mulholland Hills serves as an exhibition of ideal living for the titular celeb-drunk brats. It is another shining (indeed shiny) example of the fact that reality can give you every bit of art direction you need.

6. The Miss Martha Farnsworth Seminary for Young Ladies, Virginia, in *The Beguiled*
The film's only location, this faded southern mansion (and erstwhile school) is part haunted house, part asylum, and part sanctuary. In a fusion (interior and exterior) of two real antebellum houses, Coppola creates a kind of inverted Versailles where a man falls prey to temptation.

7. The Carlyle Hotel, New York, in *A Very Murray Christmas*
Another real hotel, another celebrity haunt, this old-school, swanky Manhattan joint is exactly where Bill Murray looks right at home – or pretends to at least. The TV special went in search of an ironic splendour, but landed on splendour.

8. Las Alamandas, Jalisco, Mexico in *On the Rocks*
After all the high-end New York cocktail bars, Coppola brings her film to its emotional climax on the windblown Pacific coast of Mexico and at another would-be luxury setting. It is, of course, anything but paradise in story terms. After the dazzle and fun of New York, within another hotel room, father and daughter will have their overdue confrontation.

9. Graceland, Memphis, in *Priscilla*
Another hotel in all but name. Designed to Elvis' kitsch specifications, Graceland becomes the archetypal vision of luxury as an isolating force. It is a palace of pure artifice. Fittingly, perhaps, it is the first time Coppola had to fake a central location. The pillared exterior and gates were built on location in Toronto, the rooms also nothing but sets. Then, in a sense, that is what they were.

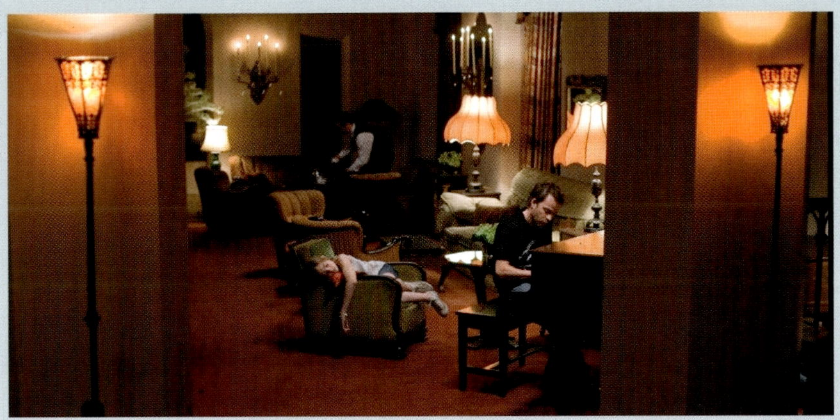

Left: *The ghostly lobby of the Chateau Marmont in* Somewhere.

HOTEL CALIFORNIA

Somewhere (2010)

Her fourth film returned her to the pleasures of an intimate production. It is about another hotel, but in her former home town of Los Angeles, and centred on a father and daughter

The gossip doing the rounds was that Sofia Coppola was done with filmmaking after the wounds of *Marie Antoinette*. If that was overstating the case, she did confess to feeling 'exhausted and discouraged,'[1] still so sensitive to the world (it's a key ingredient of the films and a Coppola trait). There had been a perceptible loss of momentum. Four years passed before she announced a new project, and it was hard to miss that this was a story about ambivalence, and about filmmaking too, or at least the side-effect known as celebrity, and about the city in which she had come of age, kind of hated, and missed dearly – Los Angeles.

She had also taken time out to have her first daughter, Romy. Nevertheless, she was more than ready for a change of pace, having been in that 'crazy macaroon world for so long.'[2] Something slower, less immediately complicated, a world she could ensnare with a single camera and tiny crew. She was also determined to tell a story from a male perspective, as she had plumbed Bob's dissatisfactions in *Lost in Translation*.

He was to be another movie star (though significantly younger than Bill Murray), whose face bears a memory of handsome and whose eyes betray nothing. His life would be based out of the famous Chateau Marmont hotel, that faux-French castle on Sunset, ersatz Versailles (though it leans more Alpine), where for decades stars had made it a point of pride to halt their transitory lives.

'During the *Lost in Translation* promo, I stayed at the Chateau Marmont for two weeks,' noted Coppola. 'Colin Farrell was staying there then, and I thought of him and a bunch of actors I've met when writing the character of Johnny Marco.'[3]

The seed of Farrell would bear fruit in *The Beguiled*, while it was Stephen Dorff, a friend of a friend, who became the most insistent presence in her imagination. Perhaps it was the hint of irony: Dorff's promising career had never gained the expected Farrell-like momentum. The Georgia-born actor had flourished young, starring in inspirational boxing drama *The Power of One* at eighteen, then Beatles biopic *Backbeat* (as lost Beatle Stuart Sutcliffe), but had sunk into slight, mostly villainous roles in the likes of *Blade*. Which was strange, because in person he always seemed so sweet.

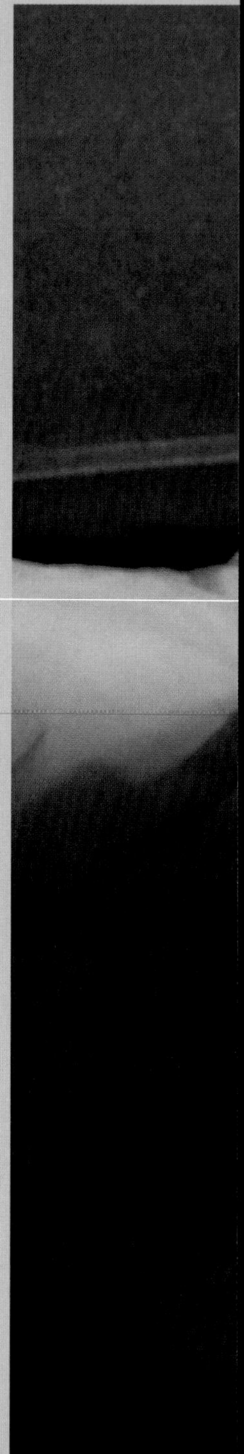

Opposite: *Cast adrift – Stephen Dorff as Johnny Marco, the Hollywood actor trapped in a spiritual funk and a hotel bedroom.*

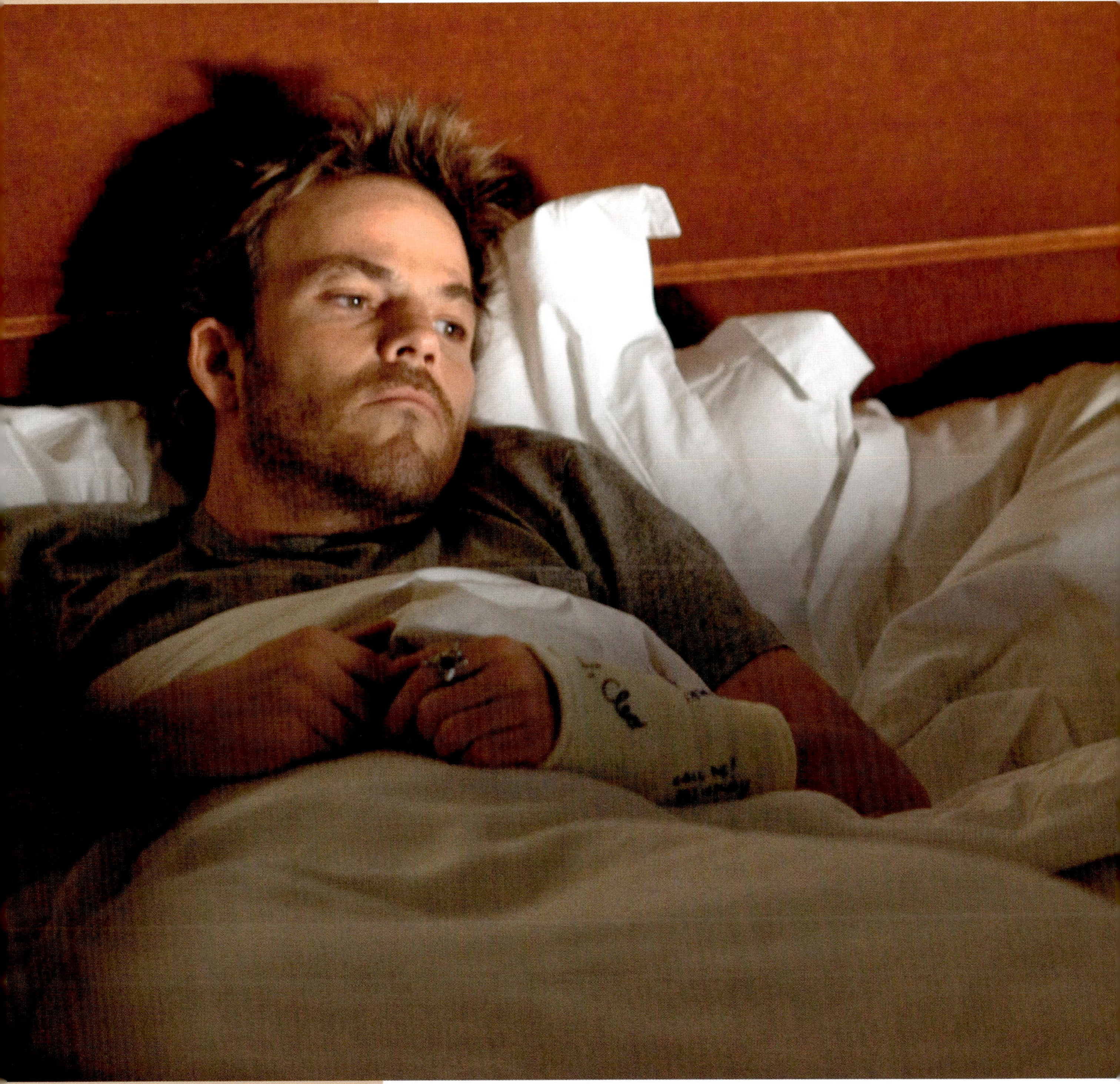

It was this essence, Coppola hoped, that would keep Johnny likeable when he could easily have become a drag for the audience.

Marooned in success, Johnny moves like an automaton through the routines of star machinery: premieres, award shows, press junkets, material filtered through Coppola's own experiences of film's ephemeral madhouse.

'Who is the real Johnny Marco?'[4] he is asked by a journalist during a stilted press conference, and he has no answer. That's the question being whispered throughout the film.

It was always so hard for Coppola to pin down an exact inspiration for her films, certainly compared to her peers with their recipe lists of references and projects waiting in the wings. It was more there were things she couldn't shake.

One was indeed a matter of scale. She had directed a Dior commercial in Paris with cinematographer Harris Savides, whose edgy naturalism had been prized by David Fincher, Ridley Scott, and Gus Van Sant. She and Savides got talking about their likes and dislikes when it came to the filmmaking process. She told him it was the simplicity of a small crew and a limited budget that she craved, the control. She hated doing coverage – all those different angles on the same event like math. She loved being able to let a scene unfold like life.

'I wanted to experiment with how simply we could make a film, with the least number of shots and amount of coverage,'[5] she said. Hired to shoot the film, Savides was in full agreement. Simplicity is an art.

So *Somewhere* was a conscious rejection of the exquisite maximalism of *Marie Antoinette*, all those costumes and extras, to return to the documentarian intimacy of *Lost in Translation*. The new movie would be independently funded for a slender budget of $7 million (it was an American Zoetrope production, with Focus Features distributing in the USA). With her brother Roman as producer, helping to gather a bijou crew of like minds, she retained full artistic control and happily worked (relatively) free from expectations.

Below: *Art imitating art – Sofia Coppola liked that Stephen Dorff brought the baggage of having shot to fame in his early career with such films as* The Power of One *(1992),* Backbeat *(1994), and* Blade *(1998).*

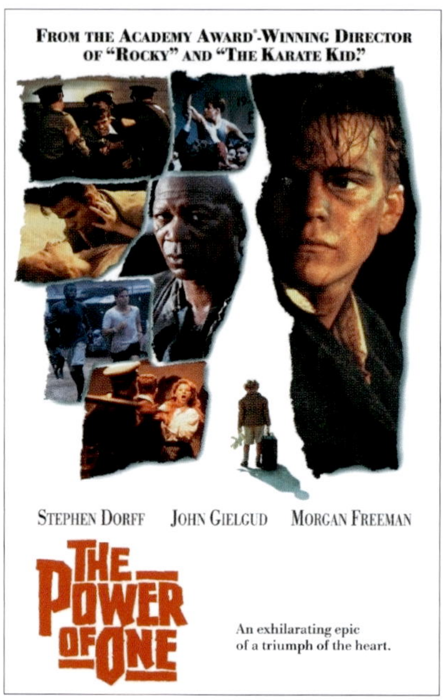

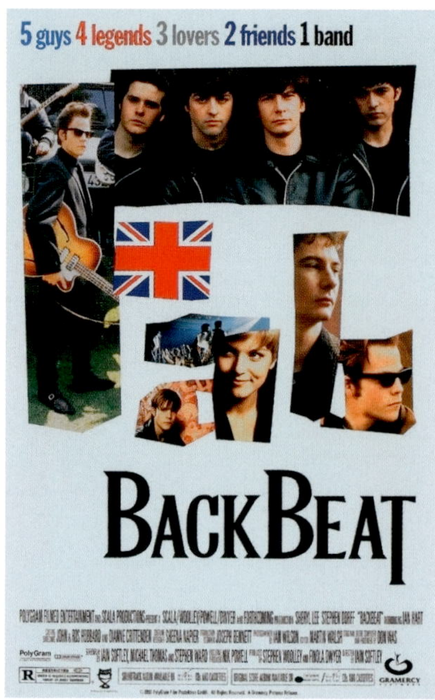

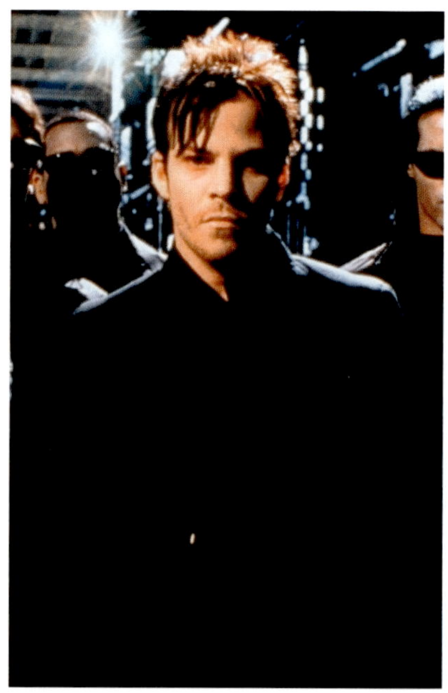

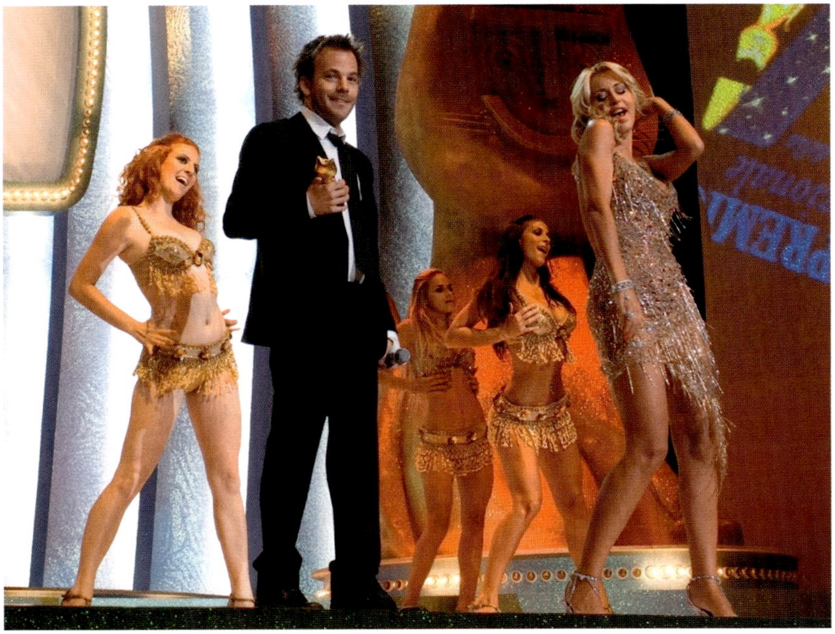

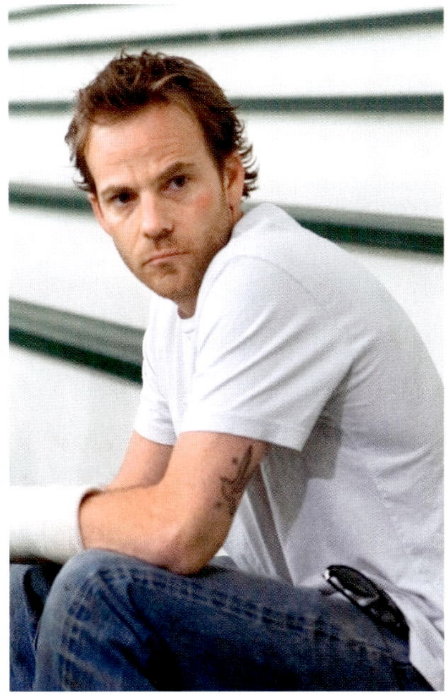

Above left: *Dorff's Johnny Marco turns on the charm onstage at the real Italian* Telegatto *awards – a ceremony Sofia Coppola had attended with her father when she was young.*

Above right: *Acting down – by managing to make the cosseted actor Johnny subtly likeable, Dorff succeeds in rendering his existential crisis somehow relatable.*

Another factor was dislocation. Coppola was now based in Paris with second husband (and regular collaborator), the musician Thomas Mars. An expat artistic community was blossoming in the city: Wes Anderson had crossed the Atlantic and her kingly cousin Jason Schwartzman was a regular, as was Roman. Among all the fetching architecture and wall-to-wall history, she found herself thinking about Los Angeles. Absence was having its natural effect. She realized she was pining for the sun-blasted sprawl she knew so well from her CalArts days; where, for all the money and sex and ambition, it was easy to come unstuck.

Worthy of note: *Somewhere* marks her second original screenplay, revealing an alternating pattern of adaptation and personal expression, while an overriding Sofia-mood prevailed. Art reflected life, life informed art.

She knew the Chateau Marmont, of course. She had stayed there on and off in the nineties, partied there, even held her twenty-second birthday bash around its aquamarine pool with Ethan Hawke and the Beastie Boys among the guests. How 'LA' her former life outwardly seemed, though she claimed to be more of an observer. The Chateau was a regular hang-out for the young and famous, almost a rite of passage.

With only sixty-three rooms, one bar, one restaurant, and what Coppola called its 'funky mismatched furniture,'[6] how opposite it is to the Park Hyatt in Tokyo: intimate, not in itself pretentious (that was a sell), but where you could bump into Benicio del Toro in the elevator (as the production did, slotting him into the movie). 'Some people go there to be seen, or hide out,'[7] mused Coppola. The staff know the guests by name, as they come to know the staff. The actual Ray, the parking lot guy, features in the movie, as does singing waiter Romulo Laki, doing his idiosyncratic take on Elvis's *Teddy Bear*, which he had once sung to a very young Sofia in the lobby.

'I think that hotel has a romantic and decadent feeling of history,'[8] she said. It was Hollywood myth, this storied presence under the mansion-littered hills. It was where Garbo hid from the glare of the cameras, where Jean Harlow managed a secret liaison with Clark Gable. Coppola's father was once keen to buy it, imagining an artistic community prospering a steep driveway up from the fumes of Sunset Boulevard, before being dissuaded by both his wife and a termite report.

And it was a place of strange death. Much of the hotel's complicated fame was still drawn from John Belushi's fatal overdose in one of the Chateau's cottages in 1982, and Coppola was actually staying at the hotel in 2004 when photographer Helmut Newton, one of her heroes, suffered a fatal heart attack after picking up his car from Ray.

'He was in a grey sweatsuit coming from the gym. I was excited to meet him because he was a hero of mine, and I was glad to thank him for a photo he had sent me,'[9] she recalled. When she returned to the hotel later, his car was crashed into the wall at the entrance surrounded by flowers, to which she pays tribute in the film.

In *Somewhere*, the Chateau exudes a bruised, morning-after aura to match Johnny's mood. By daylight you can see the stains on the carpet. This isn't exactly a flattering portrait, despite the fact they had lent Coppola the entire fifth floor for three weeks (that name once again smoothing the way). Dorff (a former resident) plied a bit of Method, living in the room above for the duration of the shoot.

So it's hotels and cities and psyches again, but in a radically different context. The *New Yorker's* Richard Brody (a Sofia convert) championed one of 'the most radical films ever made in Hollywood, if the root of the cinema is the conjuring of inner life through outer particulars.'[10] In stylistic terms, this is not so much the city enshrined in noir-ish lore from *Sunset Boulevard* or *The Long Goodbye*, or the spoiled grandeur of *Chinatown*, more the overripe cool of

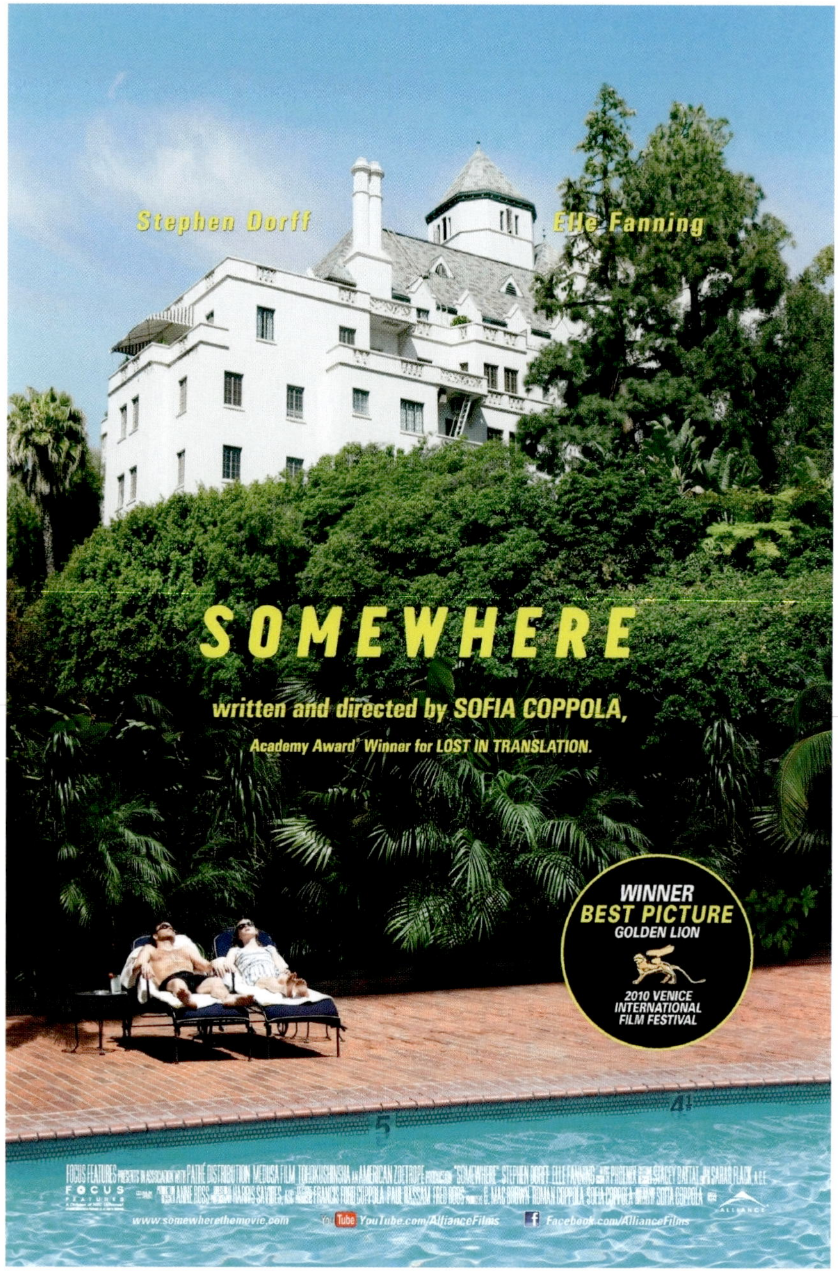

Above: *The celebrated poster for* Somewhere *reveals the poolside sanctuary of the famous Chateau Marmont on Sunset Strip, the hotel that inspired the film.*

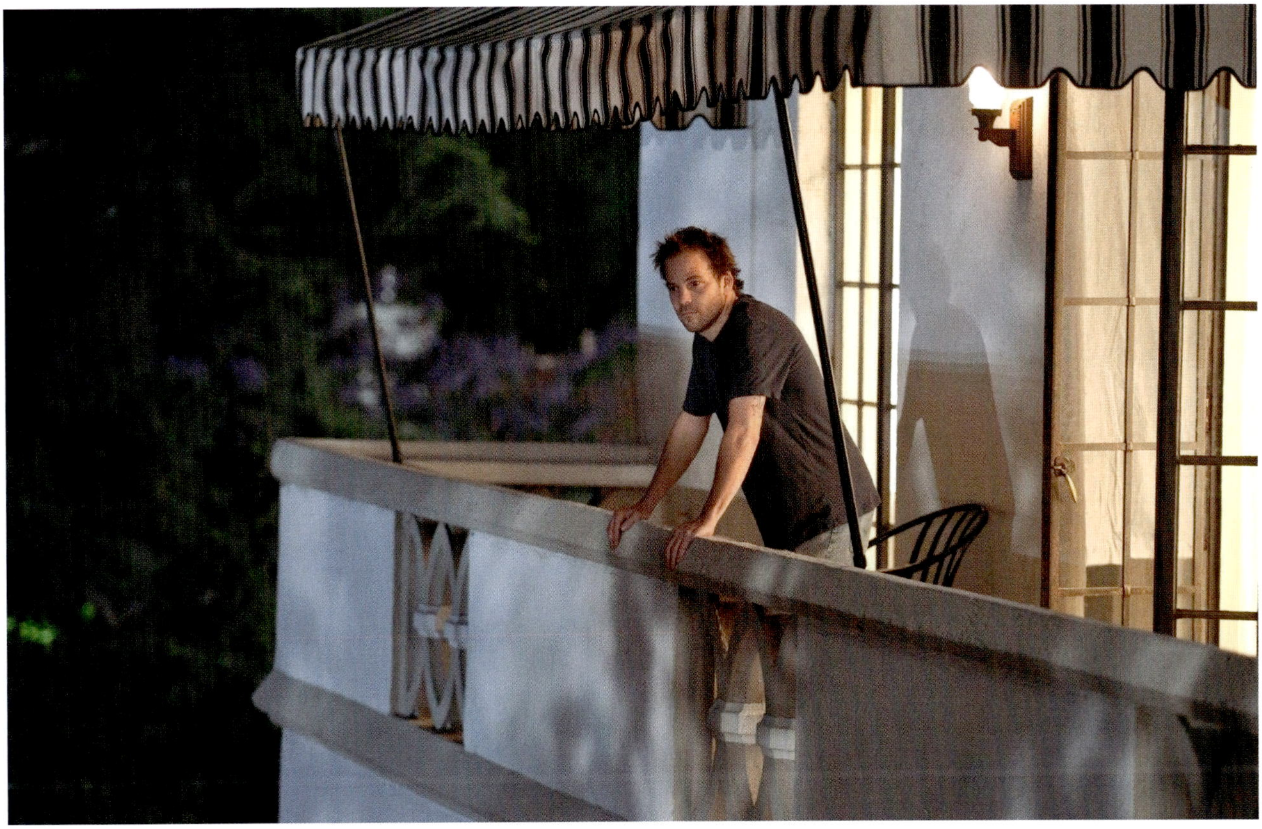

Shampoo and *American Gigolo*. Essentially, it looks like it really looks: hot and busy, with vacant sidewalks and heaving freeways, a low-rise cityscape mostly seen from the interior of Johnny's jet-black Ferrari. 'The very views of Los Angeles that we get from the car have a floating feeling,'[11] noted Brody.

'LA is like nowhere else,' said Coppola. 'I tried to capture the feeling of the place, the light, driving around...'[12]

This is the plot, such as it is: between promoting his new movie and preparing for the next, during Johnny's many idle hours, and without warning, he is left in charge of his eleven-year-old daughter Cleo (Elle Fanning), and for a brief, few weeks she awakens him from his torpor. It's a stirring more than a transformation. This isn't some miraculous wake-up call endorsed by the Hallmark Channel. He also falls down the stairs at the Chateau and (symbolically) breaks his arm. There's an ex-wife, an ex-girlfriend, a trip to Vegas and a flight to Milan as guests of the ebullient Telegatto awards (which were real – Coppola had once attended as her father's plus-one), but very little else. Apart, that is, from a series of mysterious text messages from an unknown number (An irritable ex? A rival? His conscience?) asking impertinent but incisive questions, such as 'What is your fucking problem?'

It's as close to abstraction as Coppola has come. If *Marie Antoinette* had drifted into daydream, this is a portrayal of a slump. It was like a challenge: how do you make a film about nothing while 'not making it totally boring?'[13] A laconic dare trialled by

Above: *Cities viewed by night – Johnny Marco (Stephen Dorff) takes in the view of Los Angeles from his balcony.* Somewhere *consciously recalls* Lost in Translation, *but context and character completely change the mood.*

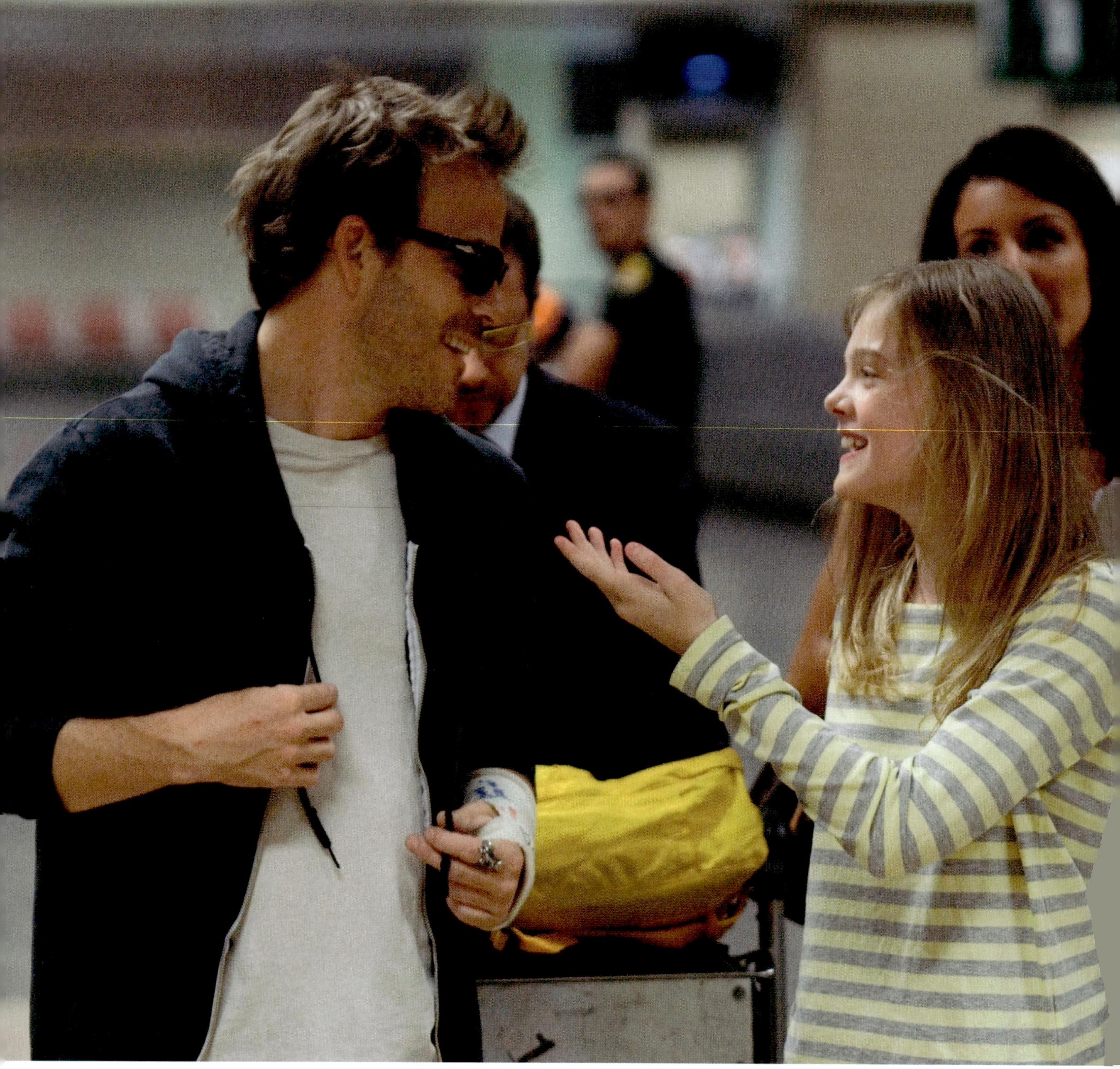

Opposite: *Wake-up call – the central cross-generational love story of* Somewhere *is between Johnny (Stephen Dorff) and his magnetic daughter Cleo (Elle Fanning). Commentators inevitably (and not without cause) drew comparisons to Sofia's relationship with her famous father.*

Below: *Encouraging the connection between her leads, Coppola encouraged the pair to bond off-camera, with Dorff actually picking up Fanning from school.*

Europeans like Federico Fellini and Chantal Akerman. Coppola used the same lenses as her father in *Rumble Fish* to make it feel more period than 2010. This is the morning after the riot of *Marie Antoinette*.

Turns of event, if you can consider them that, are never followed up on, cause has no outward effect. Plot points fade out leaving lingering question marks. More than ever, this is a collage of glimpses, moments, emotional fluctuations, and hints of what might be going on beneath Johnny's dumbstruck face.

Before the opening titles roll, we hear and then see that Ferrari doing laps at some parched, hinterland race track, just going round and round in circles. 'The Ferrari is a big part of his persona,'[14] said Coppola, noting how the virile growl of its engine is interwoven into the hubbub of Richard Beggs' ambient sound throughout, and even incorporated into the Phoenix score running beneath the titles. QED: he's going nowhere fast.

Besides *The Beguiled*, it is Coppola's darkest film, even if we cling to the belief that Johnny's trajectory is towards the light, from nowhere to somewhere. The director's explication of the title was that it was in the 'spirit'[15] of Californian Ed Ruscha's deadpan pop art, all that bold typography, one attention-grabbing word filling a canvas. The idea, she maintained, was 'that the main character needs to go somewhere else, but doesn't know exactly where.'[16] He is yearning for escape, a tide that pulls all of Coppola's protagonists, but why would you want to flee from paradise?

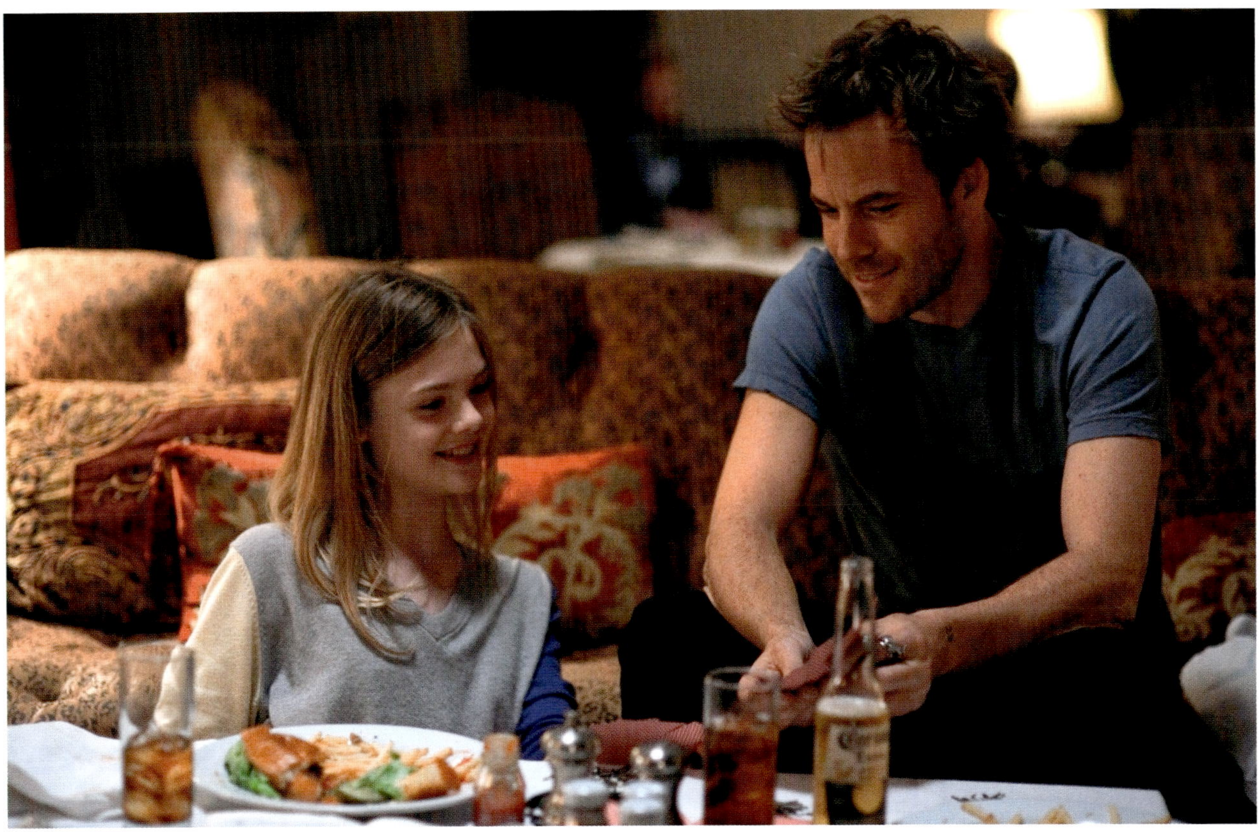

Johnny is devoid of the romantic essence of Bob and Charlotte, or the angelic longing of the Lisbon sisters (though he shares something of their lonely *ennui*), or even Marie Antoinette's exuberant boredom. To be frank, he's depressed. He's so passive, so nullified, he's almost mute. In the *Chicago-Sun Times*, Roger Ebert diagnosed anhedonia, the inability to feel pleasure. 'Johnny stares at the wall and the film stares back.'[17]

Coppola submerges us into his anaesthetized world. It's as if he's permanently jet-lagged. She experiments with the eerie sensation of real time on a movie screen. In an early scene, Johnny simply slugs beer and works his way down an entire cigarette. The oddest and funniest sequence, in the hollow, disarming way that the film has of being kind of amusing, finds the star lying on his bed as twin, blonde pole dancers Bambi and Cindy (the poles turn out to be portable, part of a dubious workout craze sweeping LA), hired for the occasion and dressed as candy stripers (student volunteers in hospitals, so a nurse vibe), go through their routine to 'My Hero' by Foo Fighters.

Bubbly, gung-ho twins Kristina and Karissa Shannon were stars of the Playboy Channel's reality show *The Girls Next Door*, and Coppola actually visited Hugh Hefner's famous mansion to watch them rehearse. It crossed her mind that she was 'having the full LA experience.'[18] But she shoots them without close-ups or cuts, just this long, unblinking, absurd shot to match Johnny's painkiller-washed eyes, lying there emasculated by his broken arm in a cast. We hear the squeak of their limbs, the routine is far from slick, and the whole scene is awkward rather than erotic. Coppola thought she had made it up (a sample of how low Johnny has sunk), only for Dorff to inform her that he had been to a bachelor party where that exact same thing had happened.

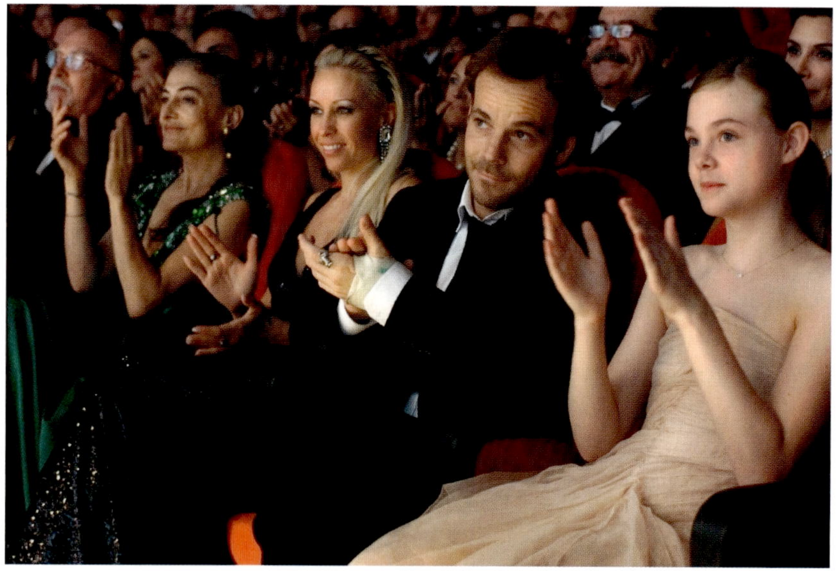

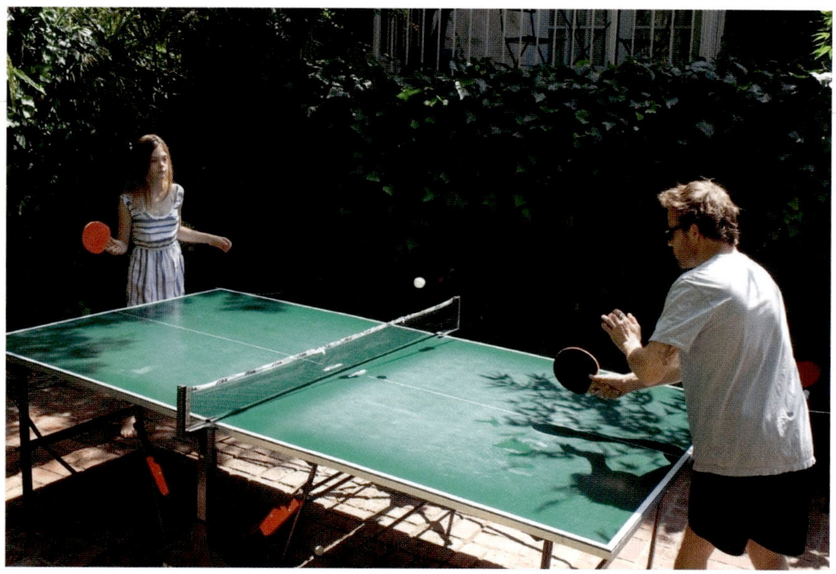

Top: *Johnny (Stephen Dorff) and Cleo (Elle Fanning) front row at an awards ceremony. In her own inimitable and highly personal way, Sofia Coppola was making a show-business satire with* Somewhere.

Above: *The bonding between Johnny and Cleo becomes the central thrust to the story. Will it be enough to lift him from his torpor?*

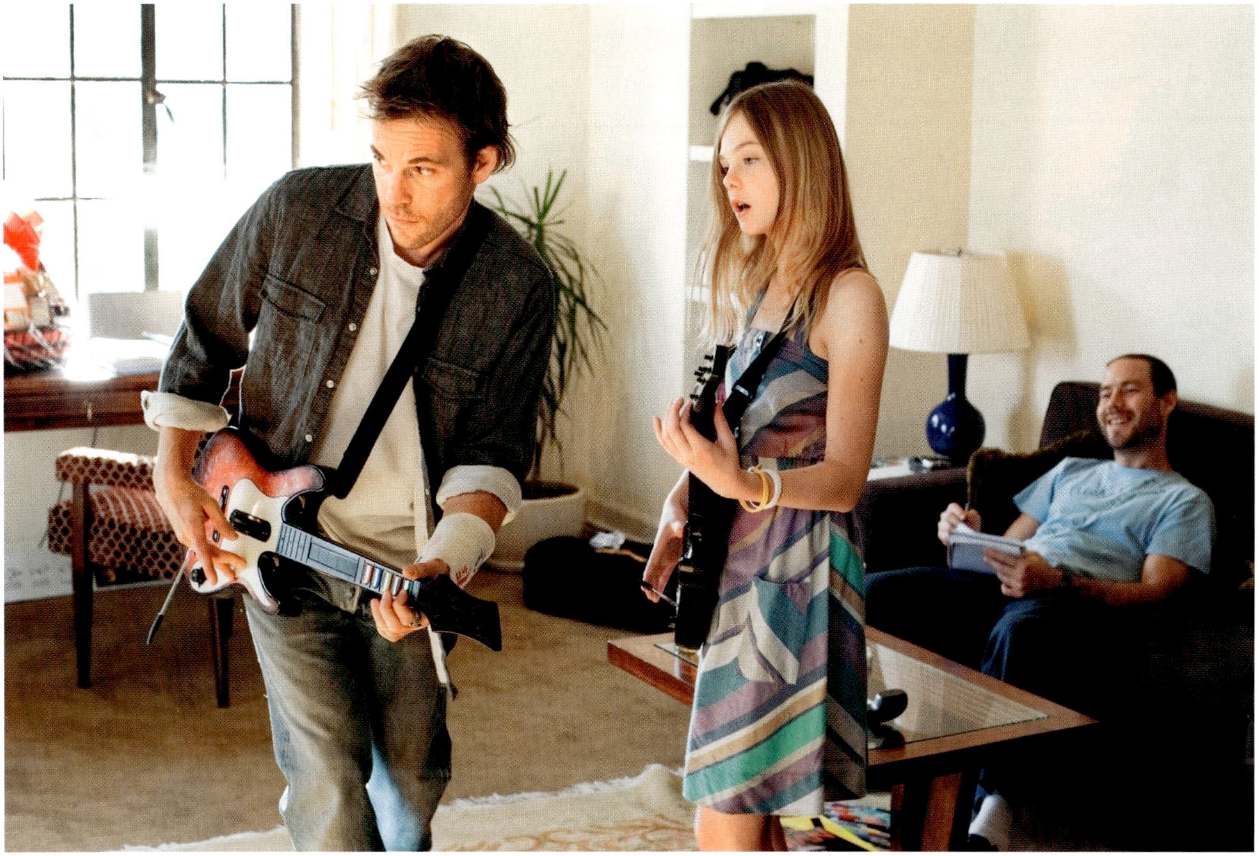

Above: *Guitar heroes – the effect Cleo (Fanning) has on Johnny (Dorff) – pictured with hanger-on Sammy (Chris Pontius) – essentially allows him to re-embrace his childhood.*

Irresistible girls come with ease and depart just as easily. Do we ever catch their names, does Johnny? It's noticeable that the first thing eleven-year-old Cleo does is mark down her identity in Sharpie (plus a girly heart) on his cast. She will be unforgettable. In contrast to the twins, Johnny is absorbed by his daughter's elegant, beautiful figure-skating routine (which Fanning learned by heart) to Gwen Stefani's 'Cool' – as Coppola saw it, 'the representation of something pure in his life.'[19] A scene that also acknowledged the influence of her father's short, hotel-based film *Life Without Zoë* (from the *New York Stories* triptych), which she had co-written as a teenager, in which the twelve-year-old heroine Zoë (Heather McComb) watches a female skater at Rockefeller Plaza.

It is also the image of a father realizing his daughter is about to become a teenager. In Coppola time, Cleo is about a year from the Lisbon phase, though she's too full of life to succumb to their fate.

Cleo needed to be a shot of adrenaline. Coppola had loved the vivacity of Jodie Foster in *Taxi Driver*, though obviously Cleo's character was far more innocent. She was based on a friend's daughter named Madison (the director unwilling to divulge more than a first name), who came down to the set. Producer Fred Roos had suggested the Georgia-born Fanning, younger sister of Dakota Fanning (*War of the Worlds*), who had already appeared in *Babel* and *The Curious Case of Benjamin Button*. As far as Coppola was concerned, out of all the girls she

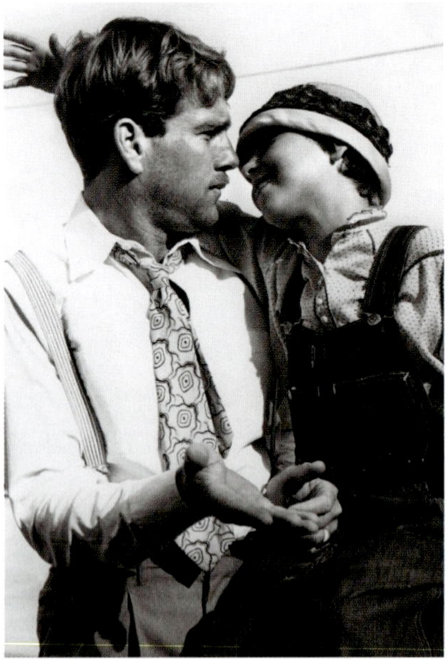

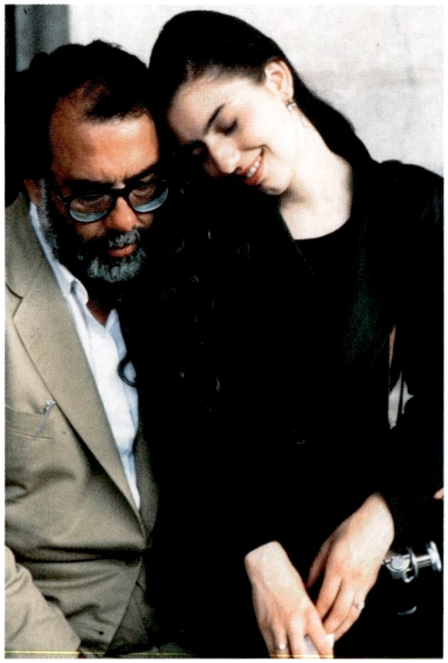

Far left and left: *Fathers and daughters is the movie's central theme, with Sofia Coppola referencing classics such as* Paper Moon *(1973, left), starring Ryan and Tatum O'Neal. And, of course, she drew on her relationship with her own father, Francis Ford Coppola.*

met, Fanning 'had the best smile and laugh.'[20] She brought life into the room. As with Kirsten Dunst, it was a matter of instinct.

For just over a month during the summer of 2009, Coppola went from the maximal to the minimal, shooting her fourth film with the laconic ease of a sketchbook. Savides kept a journey of the looping tracking shots, always ending up back where they started. They filmed in the Planet Hollywood Casino in Vegas (Coppola's father loved to write his scripts while staying in casinos, visiting the craps tables by night) and in Milan, but mainly slunk around the pool at the Chateau, where the production just became part of the scene.

Graphic designer Peter Miles created the iconic poster, as he had for *Lost in Translation* and *Marie Antoinette*. It captured the world of the film perfectly: a moment of bonding between father and daughter poolside at the Chateau, shades on, the clamour of LA held at bay by the palms. Connection mingles with decadence.

Or they crammed the camera and lights into Johnny's room, where we often find him under the sheets. There was a Bruce Weber photo of Matt Dillon in bed that inspired Johnny Marco's lifestyle. As well as John R. Hamilton's famous black-and-white of Clint Eastwood sitting up, on the phone, a breakfast perched on his lap.

Another touchstone was Peter Bogdanovich's *Paper Moon*, which partnered real father-daughter duo Ryan and Tatum O'Neal as a fictional con-man father and his might-be daughter, a film worthy of praise for not being 'too sappy,'[21] she thought.

'And, of course, when I was writing the part of his daughter, I was thinking of the adventures I'd been on that aren't usual for kids, like film festivals with my dad.'[22]

The final part of the *Somewhere* equation was parenthood. How telling it is that when Coppola becomes a mother she makes a film about fathers. It is here the theme of fathers and daughters emerges into the light. It had been in the air. How could it not be. She and her father shared an art? There are hints of something paternal between Bob and Charlotte in *Lost in Translation*, along with a million other things, and we see it in the soft befuddlement of James Woods as Mr. Lisbon in *The Virgin Suicides*, but it is *Somewhere* and far more overtly *On the Rocks* (from 2020) that had commentators pressing pencils to notebooks as they perceive a daughter turning her cinematic gaze toward a legendary father figure.

But that's not really the story.

Somewhere is only tangentially autobiographical. Johnny really isn't a cypher for her father; Cleo isn't really a version of Coppola. Which she reiterated *ad nauseam* on the kind of promotional treadmill parodied in the film. It's just that something unresolved is surfacing in *Somewhere*, a shimmer of memory and emotion around her childhood. She wanted to connect the film with real things. The absurd amount of spaghetti Johnny cooks himself at the end in an effort to be more self-reliant is a spoof of her father's love of commandeering the kitchen to deliver vats of pasta. Johnny and Cleo trying every ice cream on the room service menu at the palatial Hotel Principe Di Savoia in Milan (which genuinely has a private pool

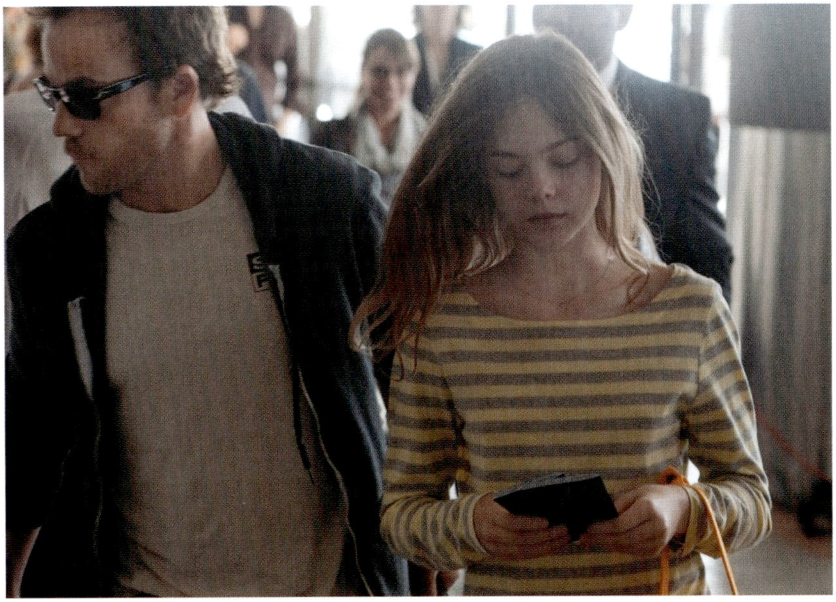

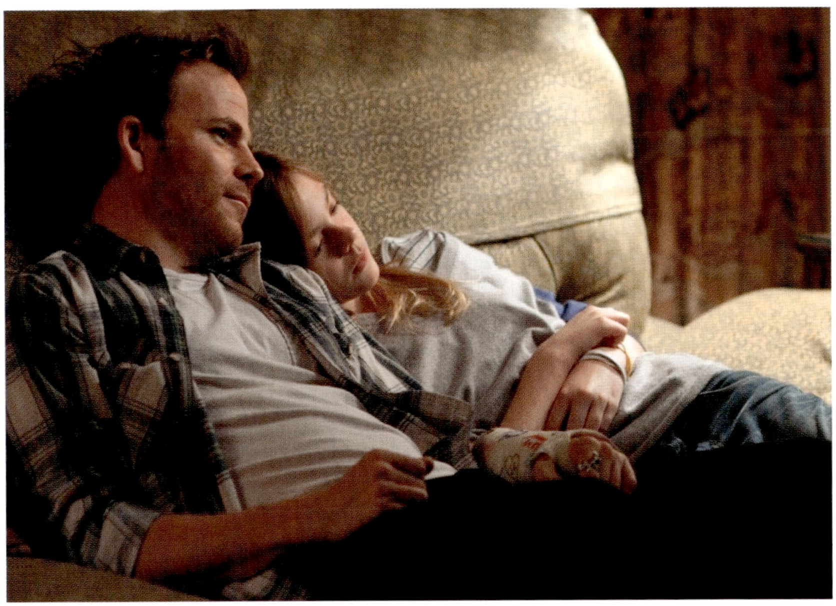

Top and above: *The abnormal normal – Johnny (Dorff) gives Cleo (Fanning) a taste of his conveyor-belt celebrity life. And the normal – Cleo introduces Johnny to the simple art of doing nothing.*

in the suite) recalled the time she had flu, and her father made her 'every ice-cream concoction he could come up with.'[23] And in the background of a party scene at the Chateau Marmont, Johnny's door never seemingly locked, a girl can be seen pouring from a bottle of 'Sofia', the sparkling rosé from the Coppola vineyard her father had named in his daughter's honour.

And here she was, directing with Romy on her lap, matching a famous photo of her sitting on her father's lap on the set of *The Godfather Part II.*

The tranquility of Coppola's set has never been so pronounced in the mood of the finished film. The script ran to only forty-three pages, without a line of dialogue for over fifteen minutes. For some critics it bordered on the inert. *Film Frenzy's* Matt Brunson, who had hailed *Lost in Translation* as a masterpiece, saw a director at a loss as to what to make, and choosing to 'simply film some navel-gazing ruminations that will mean little to anyone aside from herself.'[24] Was it all a matter of degree? Was hanging out at the Chateau an indulgence compared to the Hyatt? There were some beginning to question her loyalty to the privileged, something she would ironize in her next film.

With only a fleeting sense of the romantic pull of her earlier films, *Somewhere* struggled to find an audience, making only $15 million worldwide. There was a real danger her bandwidth was narrowing to the arthouse. It won the Golden Lion (best film) award at the sixty-seventh Venice Film Festival somewhat controversially, given that jury president Quentin Tarantino happened to be Coppola's ex and an LA native. He still considers it her best film. And there were plenty of critical supporters. 'It's a quiet experiment, a minimalist tone poem that does more with less than we're used to seeing,'[25] proposed local Kenneth Turan in the *Los Angeles Times.*

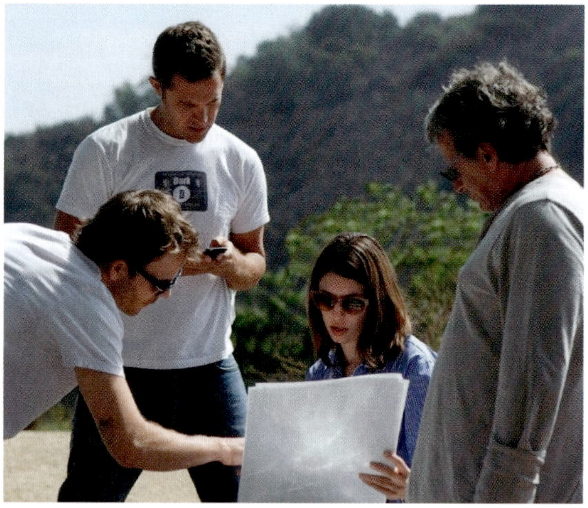

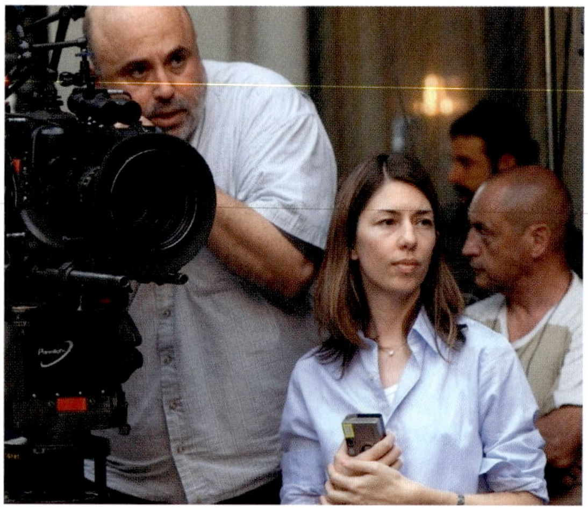

Top: *After the excess of* Marie Antoinette, *Sofia Coppola consciously sought to work with a limited crew on* Somewhere, *returning to the guerrilla approach of* Lost in Translation.

Above: *Coppola with cinematographer Harris Savides – often working with only a single camera gave the director the freedom to devise scenes on the spot.*

Right: *On the outskirts of Los Angeles, Coppola directs the film's final moments of Johnny setting out for a new life.*

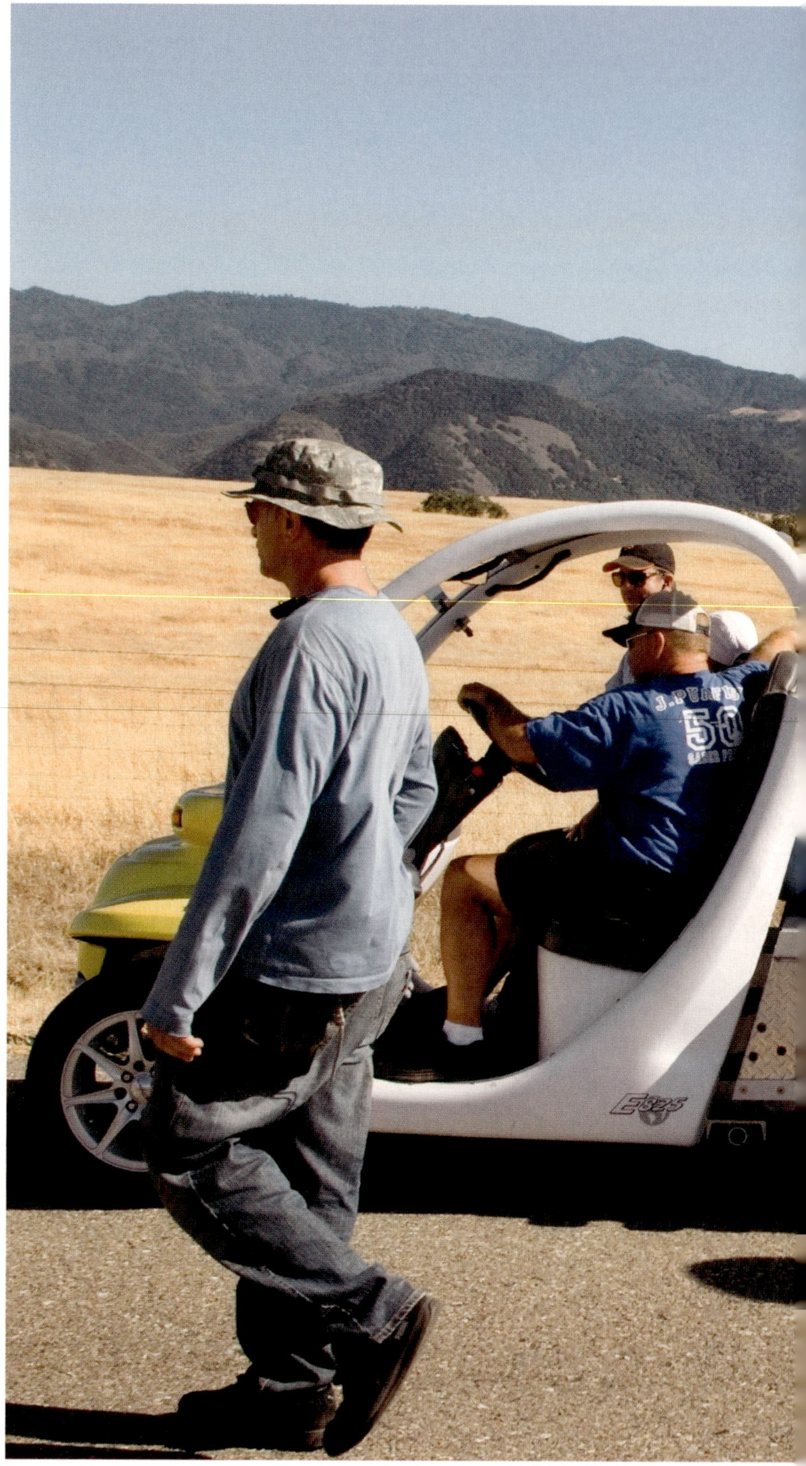

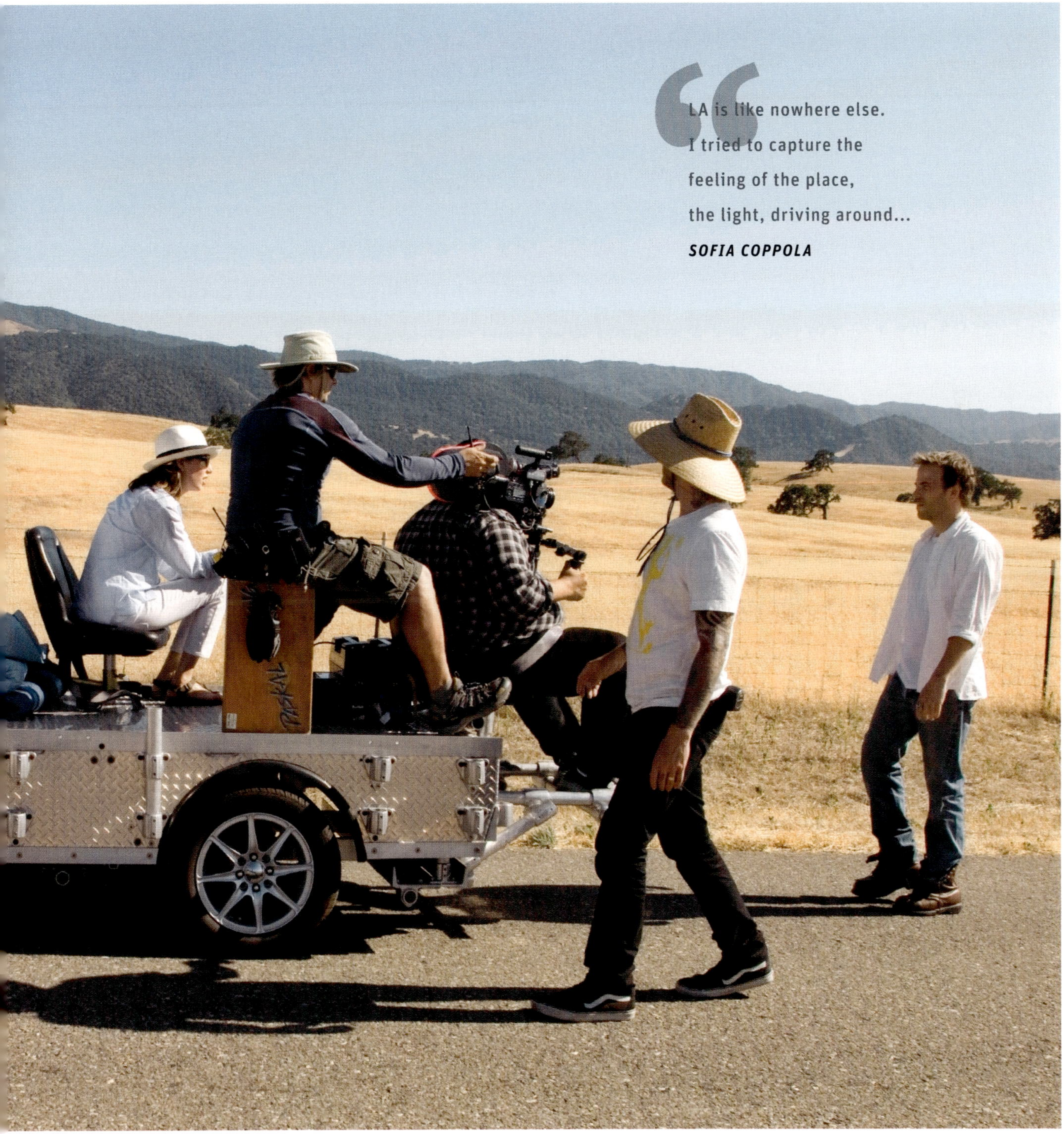

"LA is like nowhere else.
I tried to capture the
feeling of the place,
the light, driving around...

SOFIA COPPOLA

Right: *Johnny (Stephen Dorff) hits the road in his signature Ferrari, leaving the Chateau for what seems to be the last time.*

Below: *Coppola signs a copy of the film's poster. She had been disillusioned by the reception of* Marie Antoinette, *and* Somewhere *set the seal on the approach she would take throughout her subsequent career.*

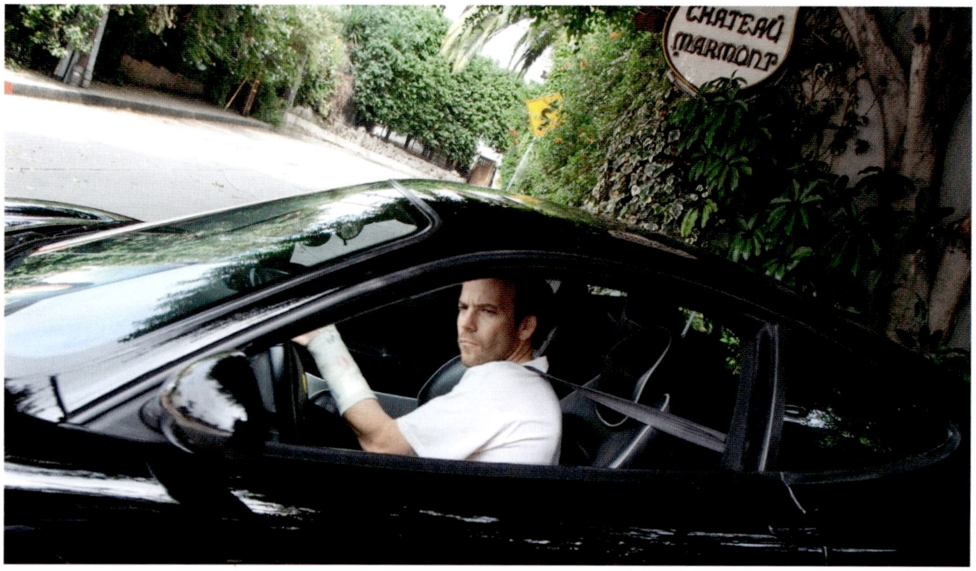

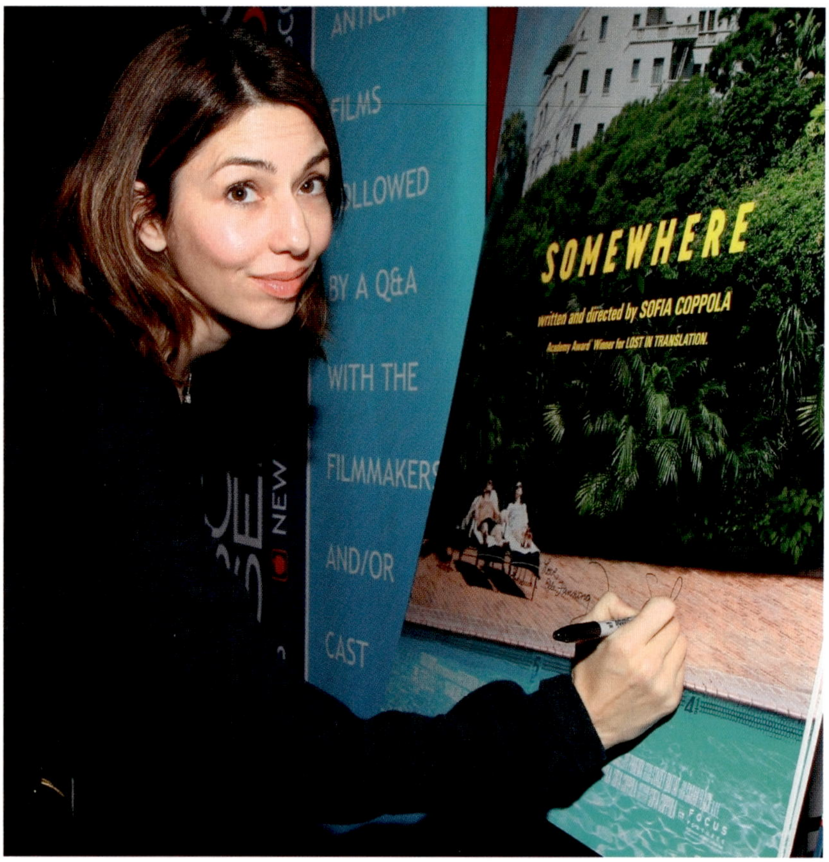

Somewhere is all gesture, all mood, all style, and as close to real life as Coppola has come, even if it's a rarefied life. 'I wanted the audience to be alone with this guy,' she explained. 'To get to know him.'[26] To think of this as minor Coppola is wrong, it could be her most challenging work. No one delivers empathy without sentiment as she does.

It is a familiar theme. 'I was thinking about the isolation that comes with success,'[27] she said. Her scarlet *Somewhere* notebook was emblazoned with 'Me. Me. Me'[28] in gold type. Her mood board was filled with pap shots of 'actor dudes'[29] lurching out of bars and clubs, or staring into space on chat shows. There is a sense of despair about the façade of stardom. Johnny's appeal to the opposite sex is down to an accident of fate and genetics, which he has no capacity to deal with.

If Coppola is luring us towards a point, it's that Johnny must find the answer within himself, as in her own way she did. His daughter isn't going to save him, neither is his ex-wife, nor any of the perks of his celebrity. Which brings us to the ending, that Coppola speciality. What are we to make of this?

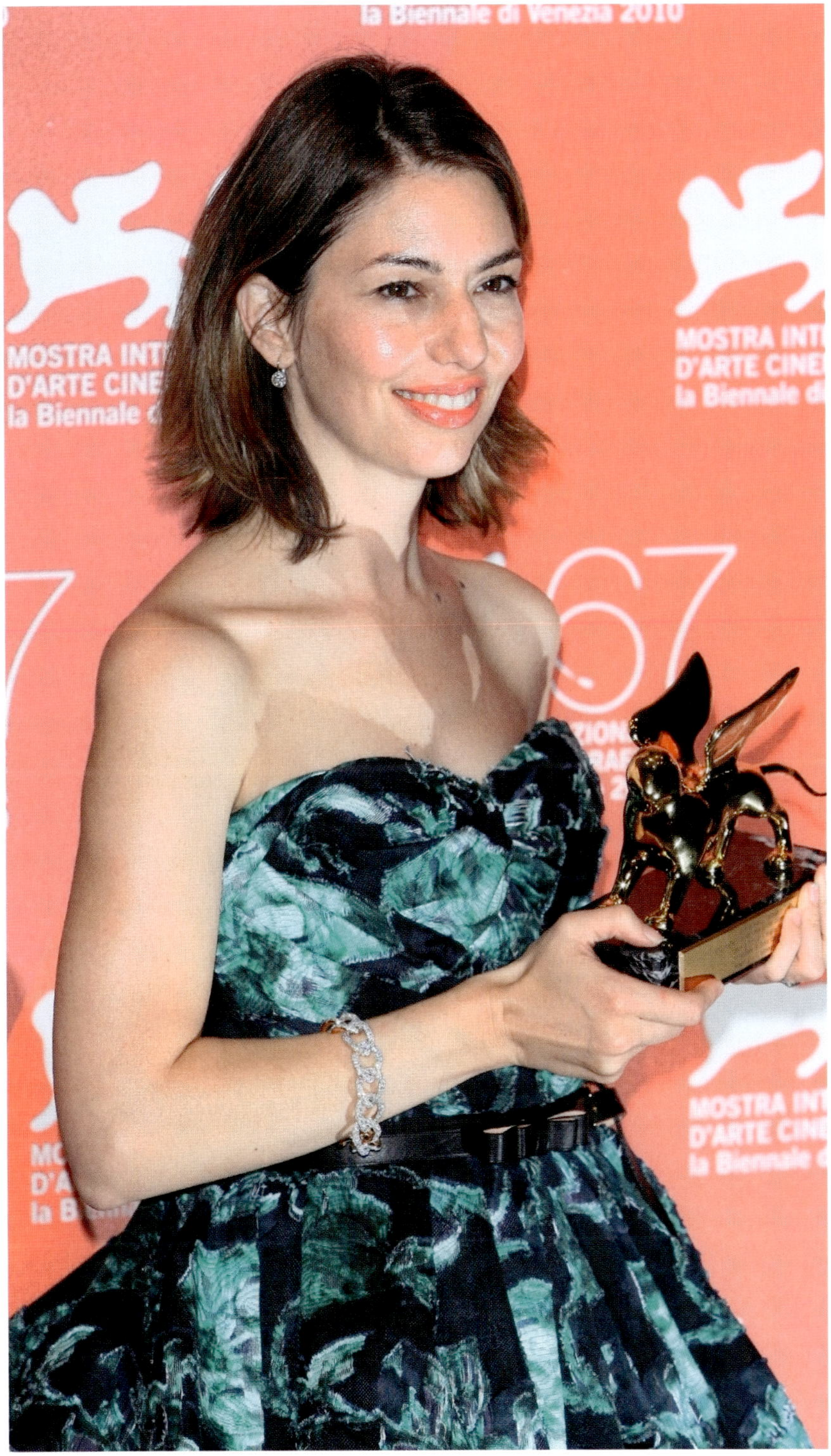

Johnny makes his way out of the Chateau. In Coppola's spiritual language, he has left the hotel. 'Shall we put your things in storage until you return?'[30] enquires the concierge. Johnny refuses the offer and gets into his waiting Ferrari. The camera tailgates his gleaming bubble along various freeways leading him out of the city, until finally he stops on a dry verge, stills that hungry engine, and gets out of the car, leaving the keys and a trilling alarm behind him. That virile car, sleek and anonymous, has been getting him nowhere. He's been going round in circles. So he walks away into an uncertain future, this faint smile forming on his lips, before the screen cuts to black and the music swells.

'It was important to see his expression,' said Coppola. 'I wanted the ending to be hopeful and optimistic, that he was starting a new phase.'[31] But she's happy for us to read it any way we want to.

Left: *While always a smaller film,* Somewhere *landed Coppola her next significant prize in the Golden Lion (for best film) at the 2010 Venice Film Festival.*

STEALING BEAUTY

The Bling Ring (2013)

Her fifth film presented a swerve into the brash, hyperkinetic true tale of Los Angeles teens on the take – yet beneath its moisturized skin was another meditation on wealth, dislocation, and cities by night

After the Tokyo Hyatt, after the Palace of Versailles and the Chateau Marmont, Sofia Coppola could now claim to have gained unprecedented access to Paris Hilton's shoe closet. The hotel heiress (there's an irony in there somewhere) and TMZ-stalked celebrity, famous for being rich and famous, proved surprisingly game. Stephen Dorff had introduced them at a party, but it was that Coppola name that once again opened (closet) doors: Hilton was a fan of her work (though perhaps less *au fait* with her father's filmography), granting her access not only to the Aladdin's Cave of said shoe closet, but to her entrance hall, bathroom, bedrooms, and fabled personal nightclub with glitter ball and stripper pole.

In interview, Coppola never failed to be profuse in her thanks to Hilton for contributing to the reality of her latest film. 'She's such a pop icon and has a sense of humour about herself,' she enthused, sounding not unlike her celebrity-obsessed protagonists. 'I think she was the first to really make herself into a brand. She's so dedicated to her style.'[1]

Coppola was more circumspect when it came to the question of whether Hilton didn't grasp, or didn't care to grasp, that the film wasn't exactly depicting her as an exemplar of modern culture. Coppola's rubbernecking camera takes in rooms crammed with Christian Louboutins, Gucci sunglasses, Louis Vuitton handbags, and pillows genuinely silkscreened with the starlet's pouting face. Even Marie Antoinette would blush.

Amid the numerous ironies fizzing within Coppola's fifth film, her crew had to sneak into Hilton's Hollywood Hills mega-crib under cover of night, 'because they don't allow filming in her neighbourhood.'[2]

The Bling Ring tells the true story (albeit with the perpetrators' names changed) of a quintet of bored Angelino teens from Calabasas, a well-off but anonymous upper-middle-class corner of the Valley, who hatch the idea of raiding the mansions of out-of-town B-listers – Paris, Lindsay Lohan, Rachel Bilson, Audrina Patridge, Orlando Bloom, Megan Fox – stockpiling more than three million dollars' worth of stolen clothing, jewellery, drugs, cash, a loaded firearm, and

Opposite: *Teenage kicks – the notorious fame-hungry quintet at the centre of Sofia Coppola's true-life crime story. As played by (from the left): Taissa Farmiga (Sam), Israel Broussard (Marc), Emma Watson (Nicki), Katie Chang (Rebecca), and Claire Julien (Chloe).*

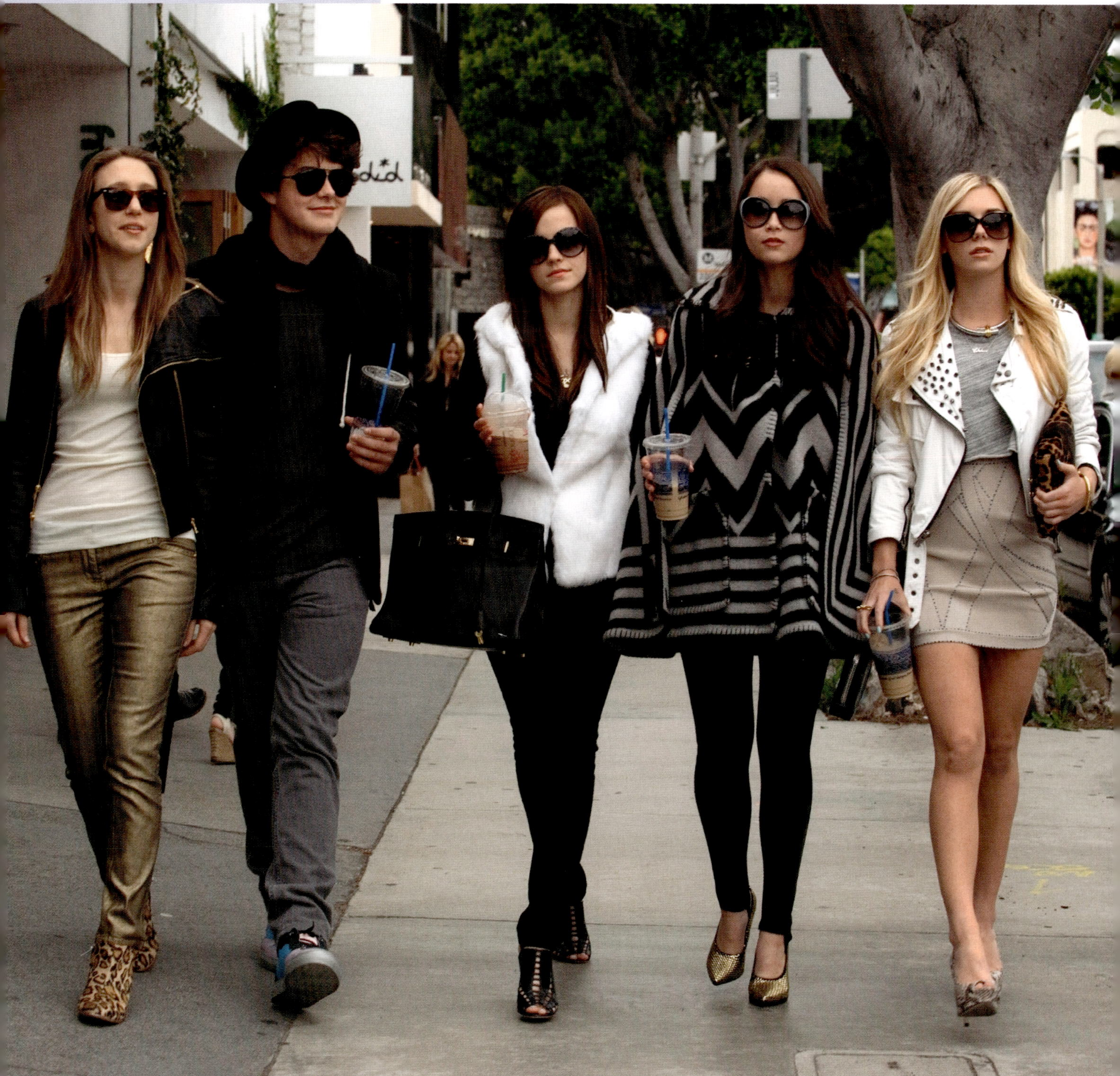

enough kicks to sustain a ten-month crime spree between 2008 to 2009. Okay, breathe.

This took a level of ingenious thinking. Using internet bulletin boards, they would figure out when the palatial digs would be unoccupied, work out a point of access, and guess (correctly) that their nominated celebs would be blithe enough to leave a key under the doormat. And in they waltzed.

As a film, *The Bling Ring* stops us in our tracks. It is a radical shift in style and energy that befits the subject, but shatters the Coppola mood. There's nothing autobiographical about it, apart from the geographical connection and, perhaps, a faint echo of her past as a fringe It girl. With *Somewhere* it completes a duet of LA stories about celebrity's sour enchantment, but this is the inside-out-take – a study in the corrosive pursuit of fame. These kids are among the many who can only crave invitations to party at the Chateau. On first viewing, it's like an 87-minute glitch in the dream state of the Coppola aesthetic.

And the *New Tork Times* commented: '*The Bling Ring* occupies a vertiginous middle ground between banality and transcendence.'[3] Which might be exactly the sweet spot she was aiming for.

The first-person viewpoint dissolves to dance between four girls and one boy and their nocturnal escapades: Katie Chang as

Below: *Marc (Israel Broussard), Chloe (Claire Julien), and Rebecca (Katie Chang) plot their next heist on the Indian Hills High School steps. With an exception made for Emma Watson, Sofia Coppola deliberately and thematically cast unknowns in the central roles.*

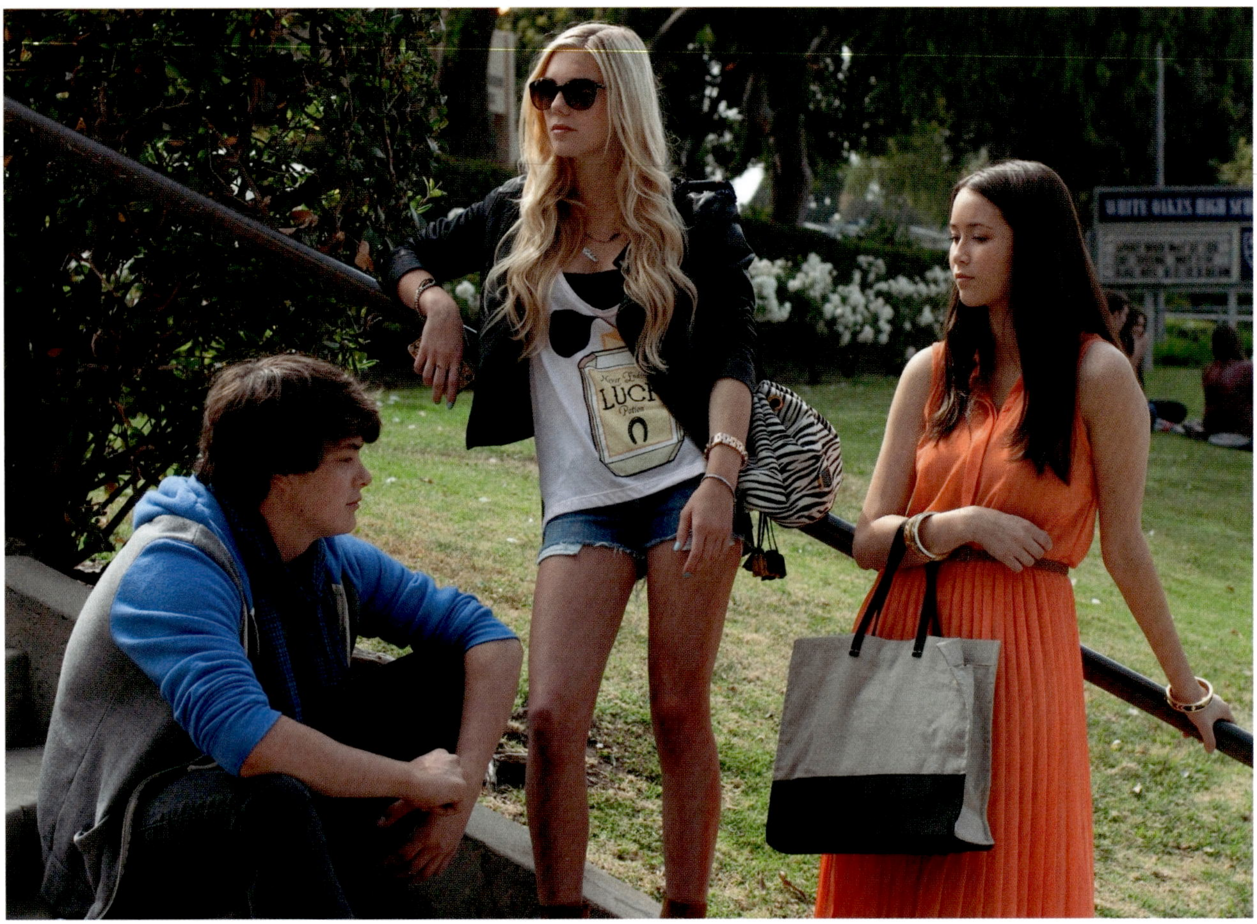

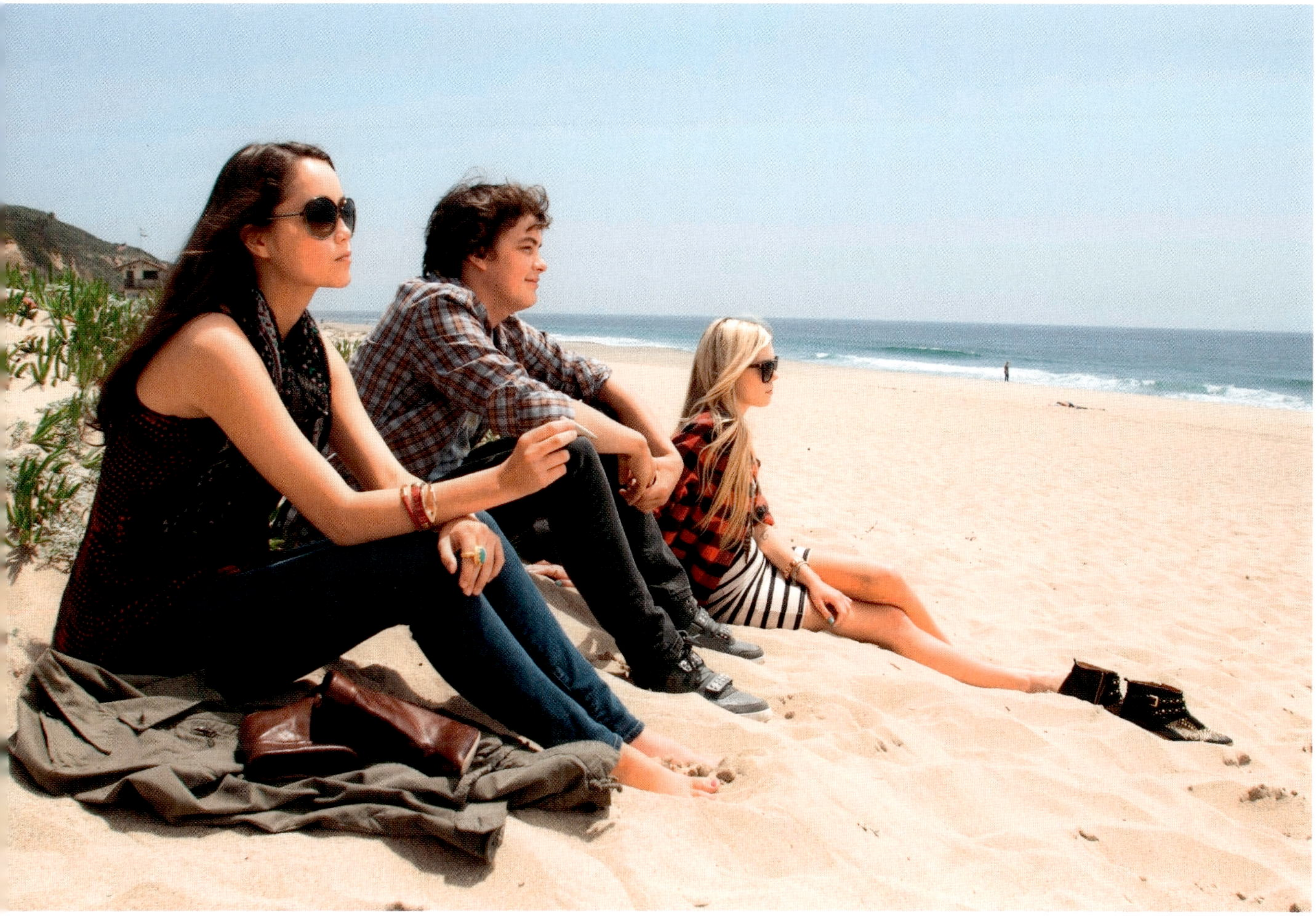

Above: *Life's a beach – BFFs (or not) Rebecca (Chang) and Marc (Broussard) soak up the Californian sunshine with Chloe (Julien).*

icy Rebecca, Israel Broussard as twitchy Marc, Emma Watson as bubble-headed narcissist Nicki (who would have done just fine at Versailles), Claire Julien as giddy Chloe, and Taissa Farmiga as Sam, Nicki's BFF, the one who got away with it.

Coppola has become the cool, distant observer of mice in a luxury maze. In one fabulous, very un-Sofia shot (thus far), devised by cinematographer Harris Savides, the locked-off camera zooms in slowly from a distance, taking in the whole of Patridge's glass-flanked modernist home as the tiny figures of Marc and Rebecca flit from room to room. It's like watching a video game.

The Bling Ring is a turning point. Over the horizon there is a marked (if relative) shift toward plot-driven stories and a broader palate, as if, with *Somewhere*, Coppola had got something out of her system. But wasn't her magic based on the belief that character *was* plot? The growing intensity from film to film – handheld camera invading the actors' personal space, the enclosure of ambient sound, and all those unfinished thoughts – allowed us to see ourselves in the characters.

'Remember Scarlett [Johansson] perched in the window ledge in *Lost in Translation*, looking out over Tokyo? You project your feelings on her. That's what

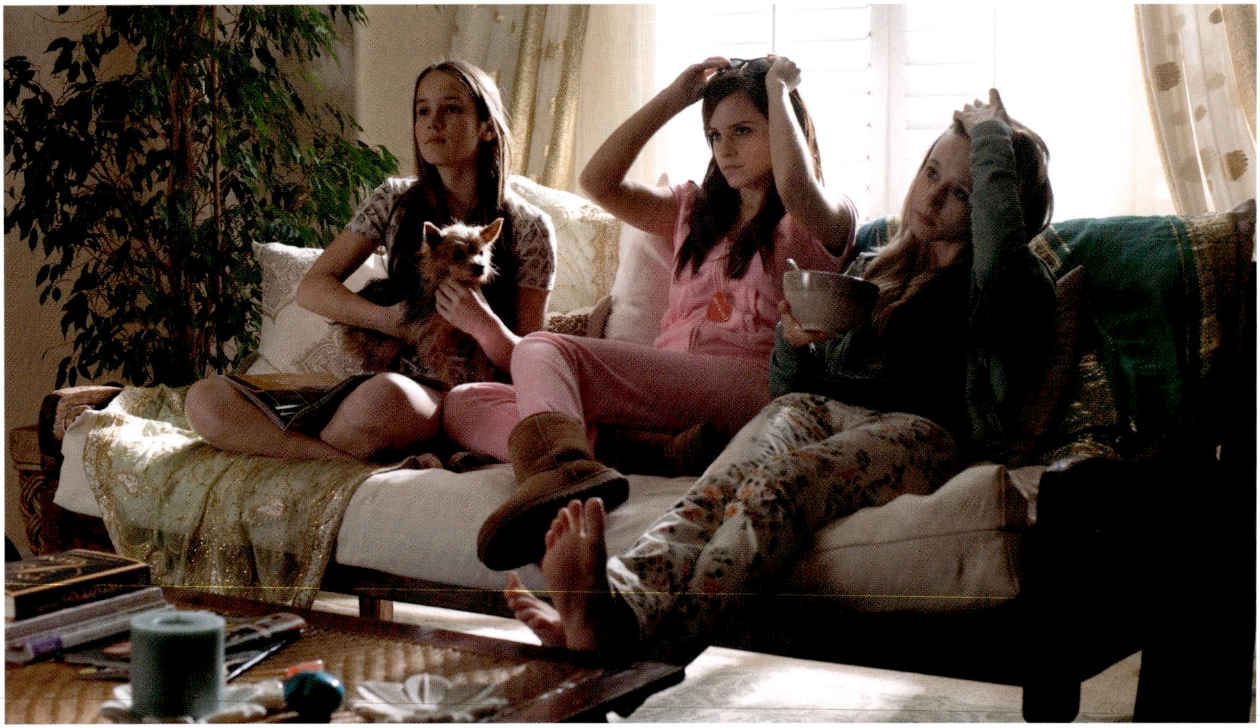

I'm going for,' she explained. 'I want the visual ways to tell the story rather than have the characters talk…'[4]

On set, she spoke of states of mind rather than story. In this scene you're just tired out after all the partying. Right now, you're desperate to get out from the hotel, to see the streets.

Proudly watching his daughter mature into a major filmmaker, Francis Ford Coppola found a suitable metaphor in the family's lucrative venture in viniculture. 'Sofia has what we call in the wine industry *"terroir."* This means, all you need to do is see a few moments of film, and you know she made it.'[5]

They were such different filmmakers when it came to the philosophy of postproduction. 'He moves things all over the place; I stick to the script,'[6] she laughed. The father finds the movie in the edit suite; the daughter finds her movie in the sound mix, where you can make the audience feel as if they are really there.

We didn't go to see the new Sofia Coppola in order to watch a film so much as float in it. Her work occupied its own pocket of the space-time continuum. Could that soothing, trancelike passage of events survive the shockwave of having to get somewhere? *The Bling Ring* has three discernible, though intercut acts: the arrival of Marc at Indian Hills High School, falling in with Rebecca and her wild-partying clique, then summoning up the chutzpah to rob the rich to give to themselves, before the inevitable arrest and downfall.

Compared to the drowsiness of *Somewhere, The Bling Ring* could be an action movie; Coppola even stages a car crash, when one of her doped-up mean girls runs a stop sign. The gorgeous night skies of LA, the glittering metropolis reaching into infinity like a fluorescent ocean, recall the

Above: *Middle-class malaise – sisters Emily and Nicki (Georgia Rock and Emma Watson), along with adopted sibling Sam (Taissa Farmiga), try to concentrate on some home schooling.*

Opposite: *Sam (Farmiga) and Nicki (Emma Watson). Sofia Coppola homed in on the central contradiction of the characters, or the central act – they were air-headed teens with the cunning and chutzpah to orchestrate a crime spree.*

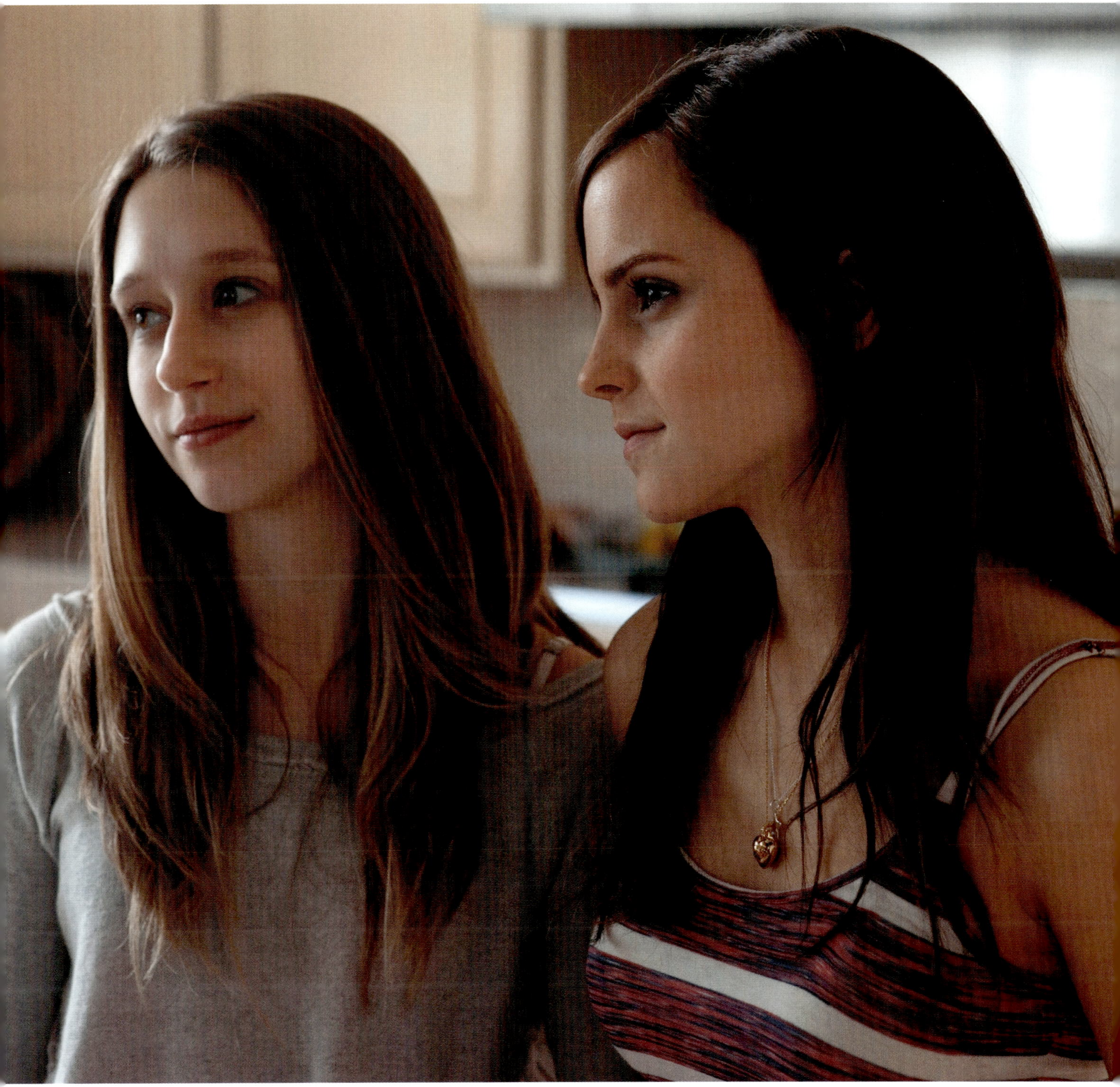

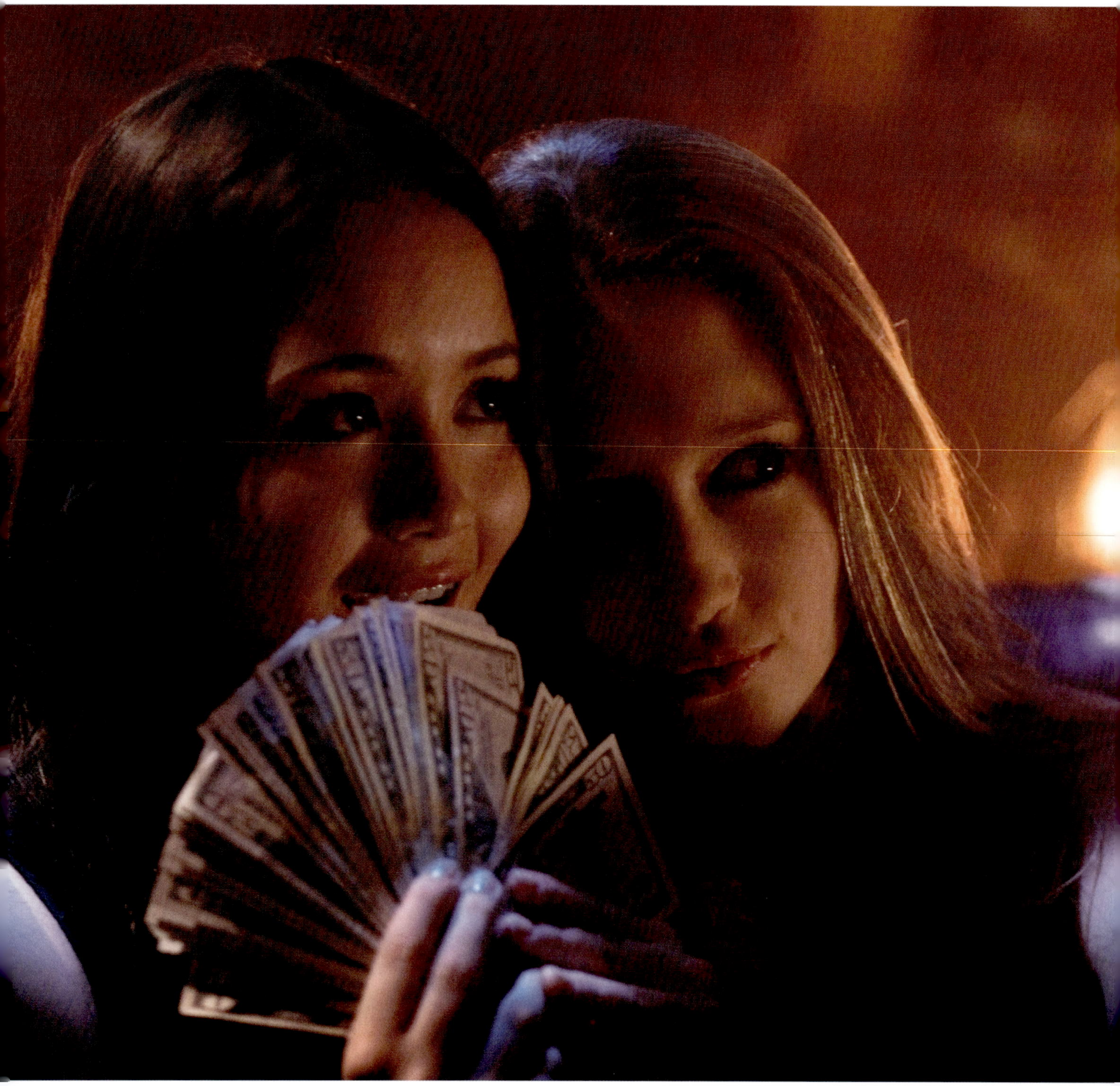

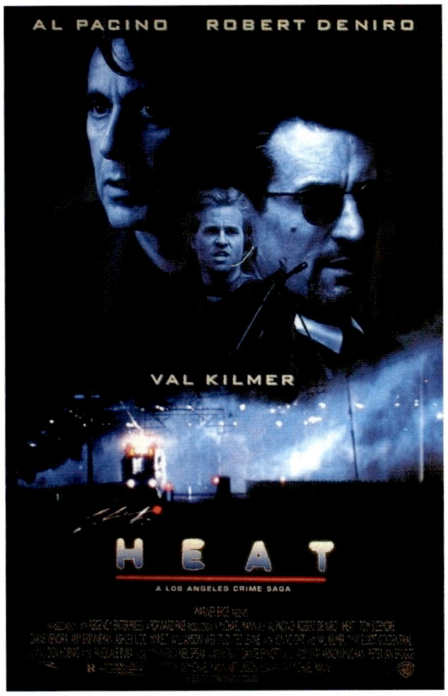

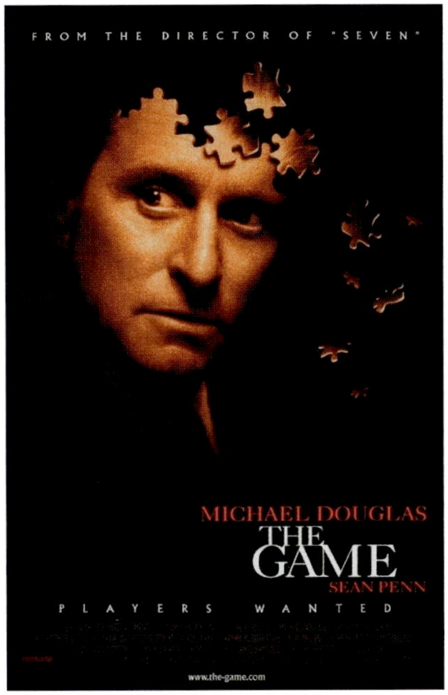

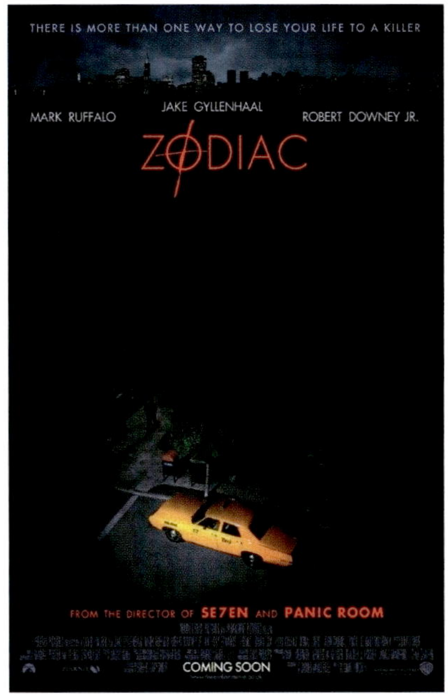

Above: *In her own, film-literate way, and through the experience of cinematographer Harris Savides (who had worked with David Fincher), Sofia Coppola was channelling modern crime classics such as* Heat *(1995),* The Game *(1997), and* Zodiac *(2007).*

Opposite: *The dark side of youth – Rebecca (Katie Chang) and Sam (Taissa Farmiga) experience the illicit thrill of their actions as well as the quick rewards.*

mythic backdrop to Michael Mann's great LA noir *Heat*. Likewise, Coppola's crooks have their codes and hierarchies, and bonds that tie them together (at any rate, while the going is good). Savides replayed some of the gritty, surveillance-style shots he deployed with David Fincher in *The Game* and *Zodiac*. In its frenetic way, it is Coppola's one and only crime film, though *On the Rocks* flirts with the private-eye genre.

Dubbed the 'Bling Ring'[7] by a gleeful media, the teens have a parasocial relationship with their targets that is oddly dysfunctional. They are obsessed with their hedonism and style, all the high-end brands that accrete around lavish lives. More than even for the material gain, they hunger for the ceaseless attention, to be snapped by the paparazzi or caught in the grainy video footage of online tabloid TMZ. Effectively this is an attempt at transformation, lame caterpillars to pop butterflies: they want to *become* their targets by slipping into their clothes and trying on their scents. But are quite happy to rip them off to do so.

This is more anthropological study than character piece, closer than ever to documentary, even if Coppola's subjects are having trouble living in the real world. There is no need for the ironic embroidery of *Marie Antoinette*, the meta is built in.

Unsurprisingly, for a while Coppola had no intention of directing *The Bling Ring*. She had simply caught the article in a copy of *Vanity Fair* she had picked up for a flight. 'I was surprised no one was making it,'[8] she said, and sought out the rights for Zoetrope, the family production company; maybe she would stay on as producer.

Written by Nancy Jo Sales, 'The Suspects Wore Louboutins' brought to light the startling tale of seven high schoolers so enamoured with the fast-track celebrity of the moment they set out to steal their lives. In an ironic feedback loop, the crucial five, Alexis Neiers, Nick Prugo, Courtney Ames, Diana Tamayo, and alleged ringleader Rachel Lee (who has never been interviewed) achieved their goal of becoming household names. After all, what was the point of doing this, if like they weren't found out? Though they were in denial when it came to the consequences of their actions.

Coppola was more than aware of the growing commotion of online voyeurism, having relocated to New York from Paris with her family, setting up an office nearby in which to try and write. It was here the idea of *The Bling Ring* kept bugging her... There are times when intellectual curiosity can be enough, and the dare of trying on new clothes as a director.

'I was in the mood to do something obnoxious and faster, and something kind of in bad taste,' she admitted. 'And the story seemed to say so much about what's happening in our culture today.'[9]

She loved the immediacy of it. Go back ten years and these events would be unintelligible – this was a story about right now. Coppola saw the hysteria of these teens as a passing wave, never suspecting how her film foretold a selfie-saturated future of Instagram and TikTok, when the mania of online culture would become a cultural standard. 'I didn't realize it was just the start of a huge shift in the way things would be.'[10]

With an $8 million, independently-raised budget (via a triad of American, French and German money), she roused her inner circle to a different challenge: Roman Coppola as producer and second-unit director, Savides behind the camera (later replaced by Christopher Blauvelt due to ill health; Savides passed away before the film came out), Richard Beggs for the immersive soundscape (LA's chittering night), and Brian Reitzell to provide the almost-diegetic needle drops, tracks he and Coppola figured the characters would be into. They sing along to M.I.A.'s 'Bad Girls' on the car radio.

From March to April 2012 the lightweight production scampered across Los Angeles, from Zuma Beach to Los Feliz Oaks (for celebrity mansions as marbled as hotel lobbies) to the disused Sybil Brand Institute for Women (for the jail scenes). Compared to *Somewhere*, this is a more detailed depiction of LA's hazy class structure, where jewel-encrusted neo-celebrity translates as royalty. In Calabasas, Coppola sought out the most oppressively beige homes she could find, capturing them in the hard, glaring, Californian daylight. There is none of the gauzy dreamlike grace of Grosse Pointe in *The Virgin Suicides*, this is teens life as a eulogy to monotony.

It was the first time she had used digital cameras, liking how they felt more 'immediate.'[11] She was consciously sampling the pop mania of reality television, editing out of chronological order as the story careers from police interviews to nightclubs to malls to the beach, almost a parody of John Hughes' glossy teen romances of the eighties. Costume designer Stacey Battat made it a mission that none of the young cast wear the same clothes twice.

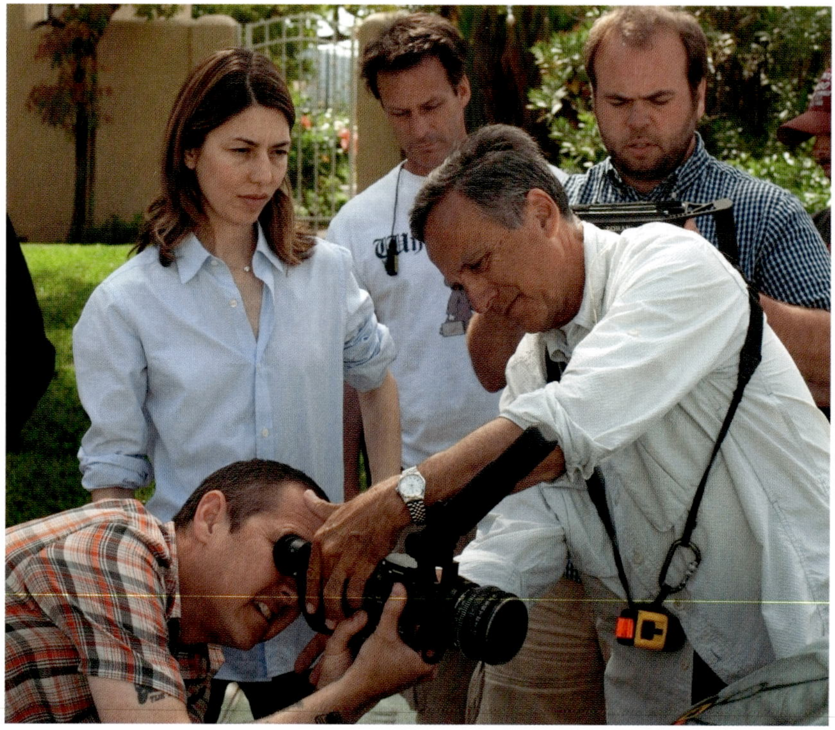

Above: *While working with her usual lo-fi methodology (there is an air of documentary to the film),* The Bling Ring *was Sofia Coppola consciously stepping outside of her comfort zone.*

Opposite: *The film was shot in the literal footsteps of the original crimes. In a sense, it is the inverted LA story to* Somewhere, *about those on the outside of the hotel walls trying to break in.*

It's the ultimate in-joke: a director often accused of style over content embraces a bacchanal of superficiality. Except that neither of those facts rings true. This is a film about how superficiality became a kind of psychosis; the uncalculating frenzy under the accessorized exterior, a search for the discontent beneath the style. Watch how the camera gradually closes in from wide shots to tighter set-ups. Coppola claimed it consciously lacked the beauty of her earlier films, but that is not entirely true, there is still a fairy-tale glow, LA can't help it.

The Bling Ring is insistent and sharp-tongued, and Coppola's least satisfying film. She was trying to make something hip and popular (and popcorn) and a critique of such values. Is it all too real? Sales gave her access to the full transcripts of her interviews. Coppola met two of the actual kids, Neiers and Prugo, as well as Brett Goodkin, the detective in charge of the case. Prugo told her that one of the girls had wanted to steal Paris Hilton's Chihuahua, which the director put into the movie. You couldn't make up something like that.

In the wake of the film, Neiers went on record with her dismay at her portrayal in the guise of Watson's (arguably) vacuous Nicki, determined the film was way off the mark: 'That's the thing that's so frustrating when you have someone that's as brilliant as Sofia Coppola and as wonderful an actor as Emma Watson working on a movie together.

> I was in the mood to do something obnoxious and faster, and something kind of in bad taste...
>
> **SOFIA COPPOLA**

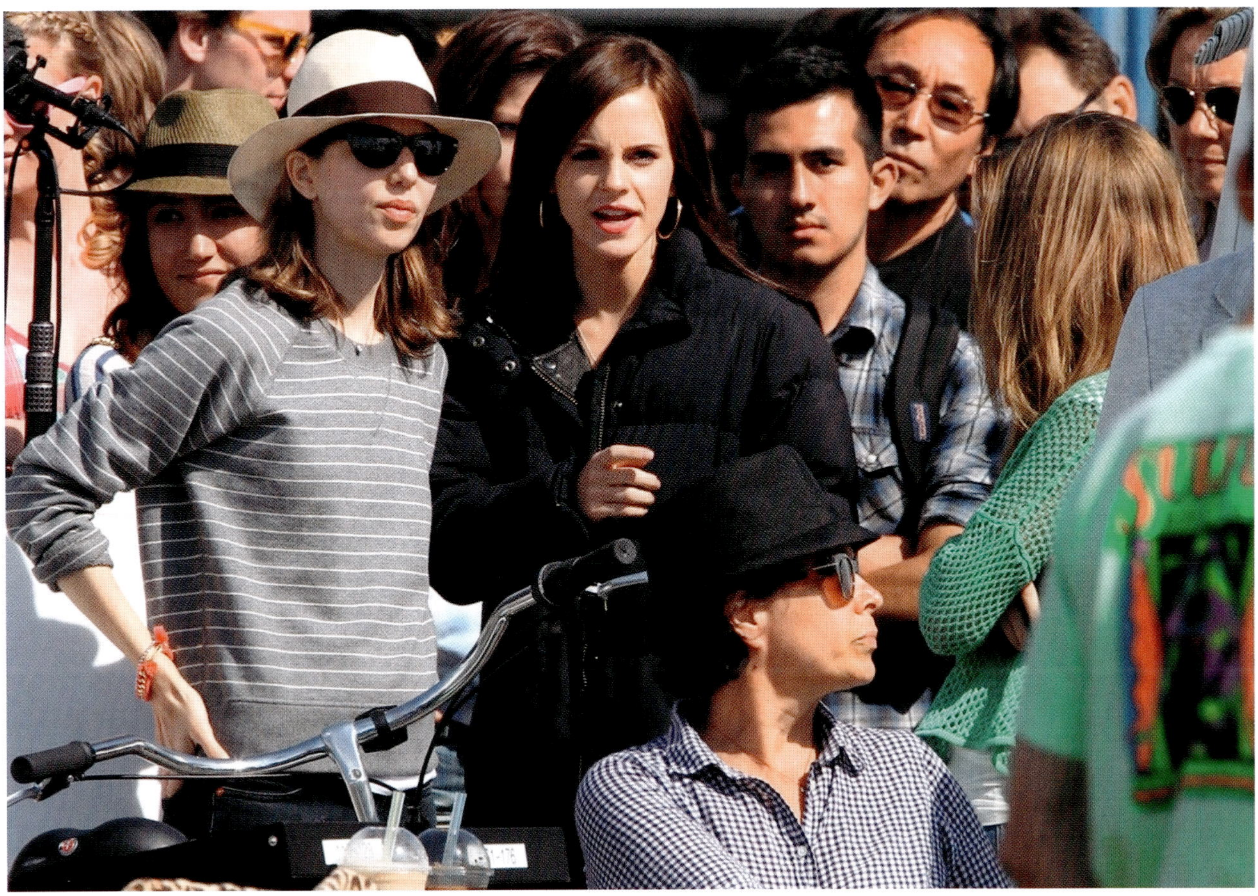

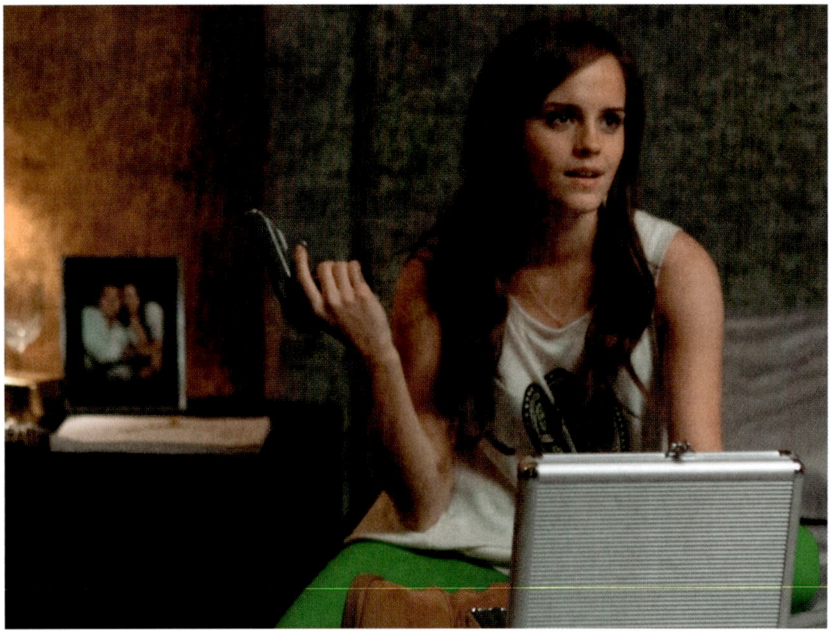

Left: *There was an inherent irony in casting Harry Potter alumna Emma Watson, but it was her incredible Valley Girl accent that nailed it. Watson hits the perfect comic pitch as Nicki.*

Opposite: *The inner sanctum – Nicki (Watson) appraises her glittery finds in Paris Hilton's mansion. A very real setting of questionable taste.*

You have this opportunity to do something really great and to dig deeper and to look at the complexities, but it's just lazy.'[12]

It turned out that Neiers and her sister were already mining their notoriety for the 2010 Netflix docuseries *Pretty Wild*. Moreover, their story had already been made into a forgettable Lifetime TV movie from 2011, also called *The Bling Ring*, starring an as-of-yet undiscovered Austin Butler and Sydney Sweeney, as well as Jennifer Grey, from the more innocent age of *Dirty Dancing*. 'I am glad that film came and went, but it was everything I wouldn't want my film to be,'[13] responded Coppola, having watched five minutes of her rival.

She wasn't entirely neutral. On one level, she recognized that she was channelling her 'oak tree'[14] mother Eleanor, who had such a disdain for Hollywood (as a culture), in all its self-regarding madness.

The reason names were changed was not out of respect for the innocent, but to make sure the guilty didn't benefit from another shot of fame. She had intended to cast five unknowns to maintain the façade of reality. The ostensible leads, Chang and Broussard, had been instinctual picks, in Chang's case walking into the room with an air of insouciant entitlement fully formed (and fully adopted). Farmiga, as the brattish, reckless Sam, was the younger sister of actress Vera Farmiga and would go on to a buoyant career in horror. Julien, as the pretty, punky Chloe, was the daughter of cinematographer Wally Pfister.

Watson was different. After years of playing brainy Hermione Granger in the *Harry Potter* films, she was indeed a major celebrity, which added a more risky irony to the mix. A generation later, she might have fallen prey to these kids' larcenous pursuits. Her presence might easily have broken the film's fictional spell (pun partially intended).

It was just that producer Fred Roos (who handled casting) and Coppola were won over by how adept and eager Watson proved at transforming into this airheaded party girl, at once wholly absurd yet believable. Much of the film's humour rests on Watson's perfectly pitched Valley Girl whine, with a trace of Anna Faris as the featherbrained starlet in *Lost in Translation* (Coppola certainly has it in her to be barbed). And the fact we do register it's Watson. Nicki's excuses reach poetic heights of self-delusion, disavowing her avaricious crimes in proportion to the increasing magnitude of her sunglasses, until she resembles a petulant stick insect.

'I'm a firm believer in karma and I think this situation was attracted into my life as a huge learning lesson for me to grow and expand as a spiritual human being,'[15] she babbles to the assembled TV crews, lines taken verbatim from her interview with Sales. 'Thank you for respecting my privacy,'[16] she concludes, signalling the exact opposite.

Watson had never experienced such freedom as an actress. The script was more of a guide, leaving room for the relationships and heady blather to be found in rehearsal, where Coppola stored up ideas for the shoot. The director employed her brand of mild, blurring-the-edges Method, encouraging

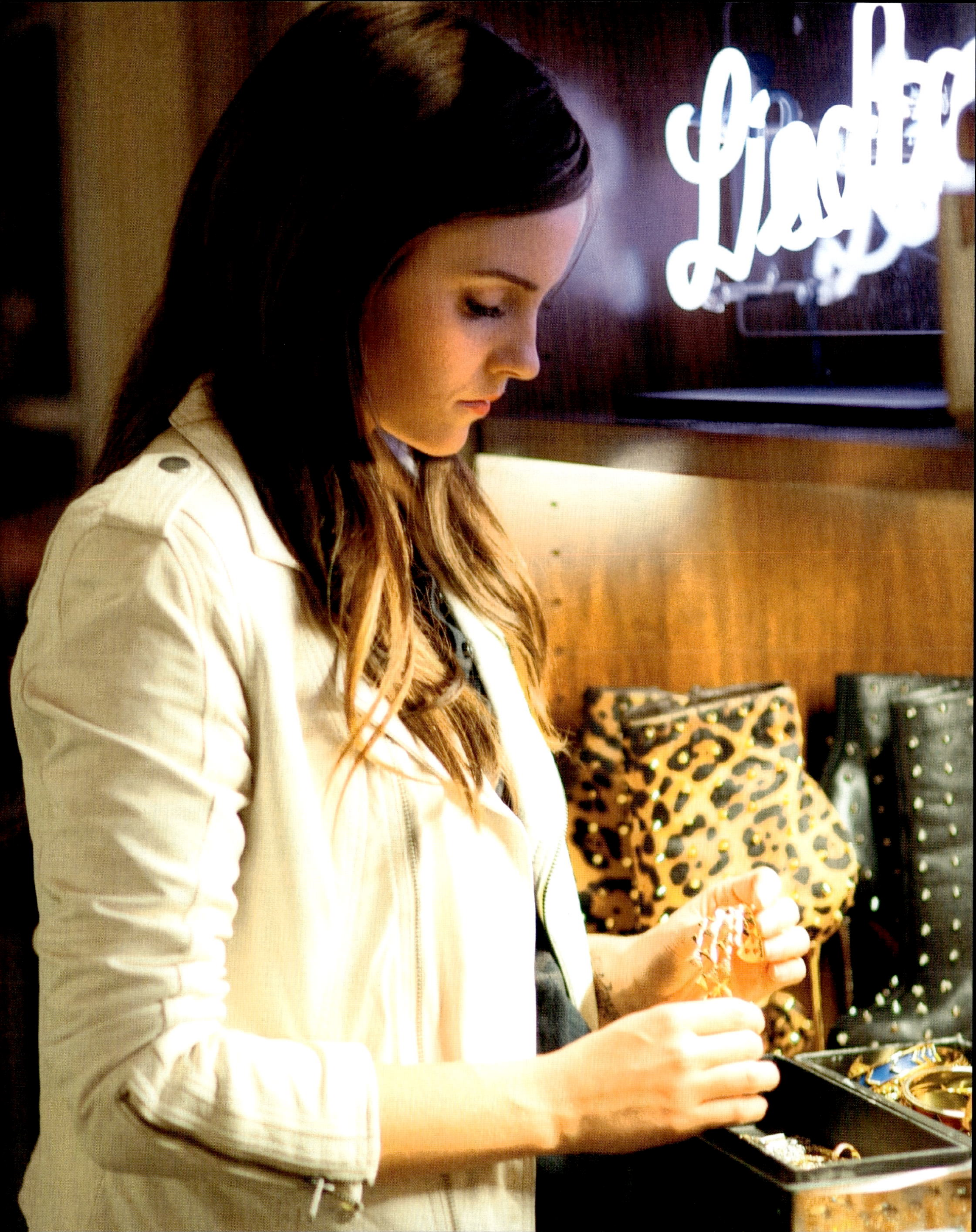

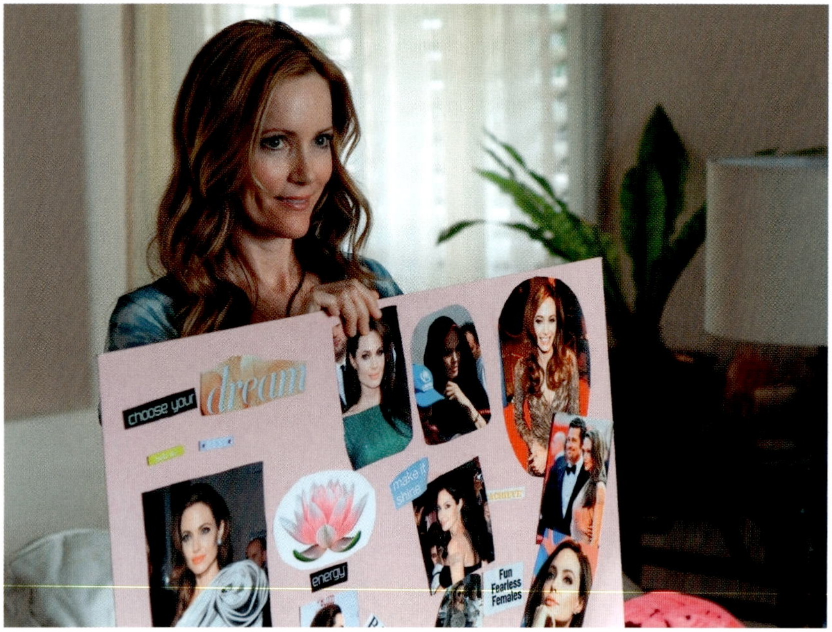

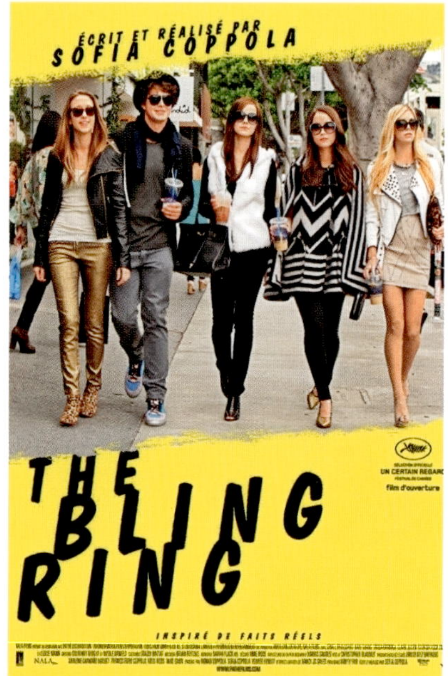

her young actors to become the characters, inseparable on set, with a full complement of inside jokes.

Just as the Lisbon actresses had been left to lounge around and Stephen Dorff was tasked with picking up Elle Fanning from school while preparing for *Somewhere*, Coppola sent her actors out as a group to shopping malls and nightclubs. 'That way, during the club scenes when they are partying, they're really partying,'[17] she said. Slow-motion shots of the gang, post-heists, euphoric on the dance floor, have the forget-yourself ecstasy of the *Marie Antoinette* montages. *The Bling Ring* could be read as *The Virgin Suicides* through the looking-glass – this gaggle of listless teens given way too much freedom.

'I wanted to see it through their point of view,' insisted Coppola, 'to understand how they got so into it.'[18] She wanted to capture the fun of it all.

Of course, she had mapped out the film's sensibility on her own mood boards, a patchwork of gossip mags, celebrity shoots, glossy adverts, Marilyn Monroe promoting Chanel. Life smearing into art, Coppola used Facebook photographs from Julien's actual nights on the LA scene as reference material, and pressed her young cast to create collages that summed up their characters, some of which appear on their bedroom walls.

'What you remember about her films are the microclimates of feeling and longing,'[19] proposed Carrie Rickey in the *Directors Guild of America Quarterly*. As Coppola herself put it, 'My movies are not about being, but becoming.'[20] Like the boys yearning for the Lisbon sisters in *The Virgin Suicides*, the Bling Ringers covet the sanctums of these minor celebrities like a forbidden paradise. All her characters are lost in translation. We begin to wonder if *The Bling Ring* is such a radical departure after all. Kirsten Dunst even cameos as herself.

As with the decadence of Versailles in *Marie Antoinette*, Coppola goes in for a full accounting of the era's splurge of consumerism and therapeutic need for new things, channelling her own background in

Above left: *Leslie Mann as Nicki's misguided mom Laurie – with a Angelina Jolie celebrity mood board Emma Watson had made in preparation for the role.*

Above right: The Bling Ring *was an attempt by Sofia Coppola at populism, and tends to divide her fans. But the more you look, the less of a departure it seems.*

Opposite: *Fatal flaw – Chloe (Claire Julien), Rebecca (Katie Chang), Marc (Israel Broussard), and Nicki (Emma Watson) celebrate their latest heist. Taking selfies while wearing stolen gear!*

fashion and photography, an ambassador for many of the brands being lusted over in her film. Yet more irony.

They do finally get their comeuppance. Or most of them: Sam was never caught on the CCTV supplied as evidence by their glitzy victims, and gets away clean. What they never counted on was that bragging about their stolen bling online was probably not a good idea, and in the final act the stoic LAPD come knocking on their doors with search warrants to be greeted by the stupefied faces of their parents, so telling in their anonymity. Only Leslie Mann as Nicki's vacant mother Laurie is given significant screen time, and is played for laughs, home schooling her inattentive brood in the latest New Age pap with the same nasal whine as her daughter.

To conclude, then, *The Bling Ring* does fit the bill: teenage panic, social satire, cityscapes. And it really doesn't: visually frenetic, fever-pitched, dwelling in the shallows, inspired by a determination to break with Coppola's own conventions. The film took her back to the Cannes Film Festival (that fountainhead of celebrity) where she got a warmer reception compared to the open hostility met by *Marie Antoinette*. In 2013 she was viewed as an established director offering her latest work, not the upstart catching a lift on her father's tailcoats.

By its release on 14 June 2013, however, the reviews were more polarized than even for *Marie Antoinette*. Where was the becalmed, thoughtful Sofia we knew and loved? The problem is the Bling Ring are not the mythical incarnations of *The Virgin Suicides*, but the subjects of a tangy study in brat-pack excess, and thus hard to like. In *The Observer,* Catherine Shoard called it 'a shallow film about shallow people.'[21] Audiences never really warmed to the film: it scraped just over $20 million worldwide, a moderate return for a title that projected mainstream potential. There has been little sense of any re-evaluation going on; the world has overtaken *The Bling Ring*.

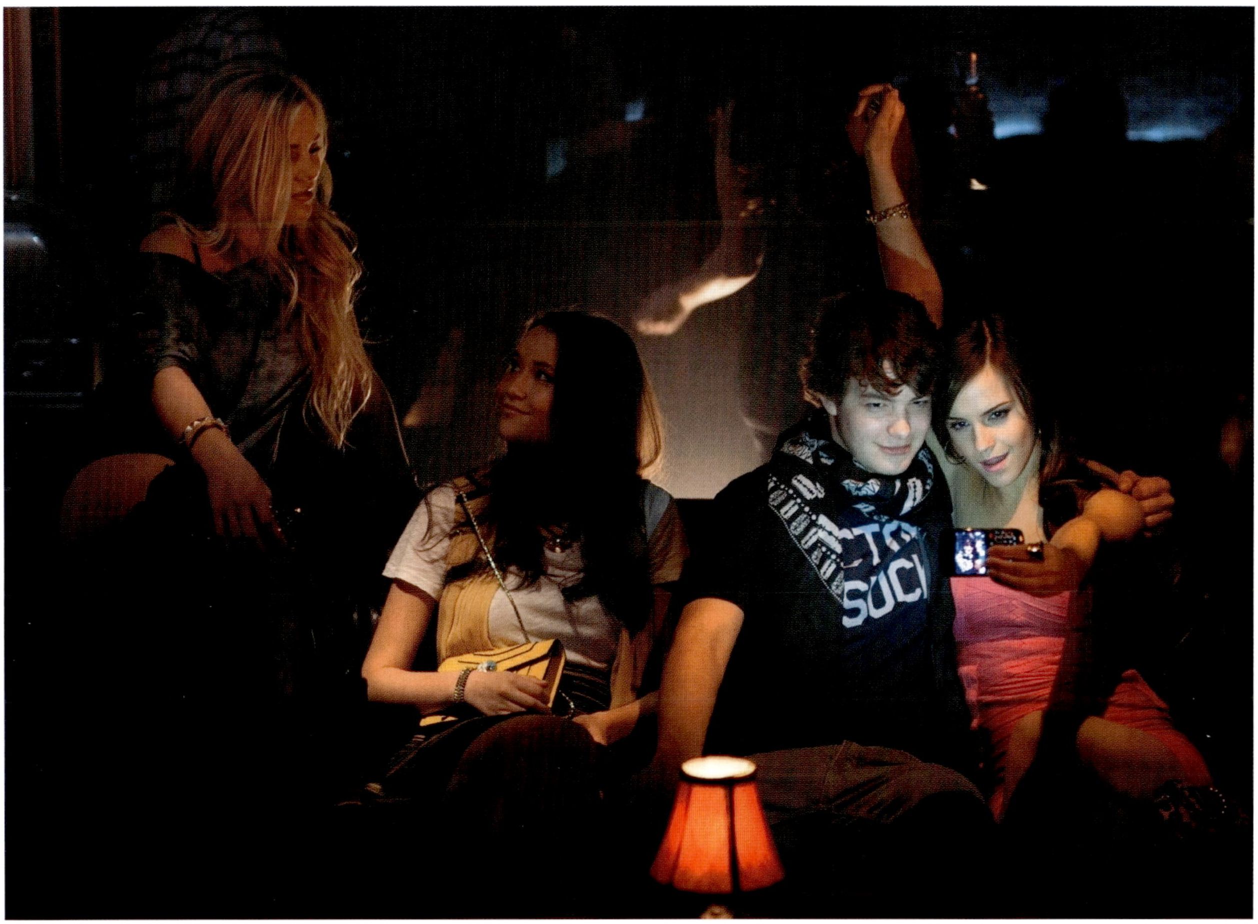

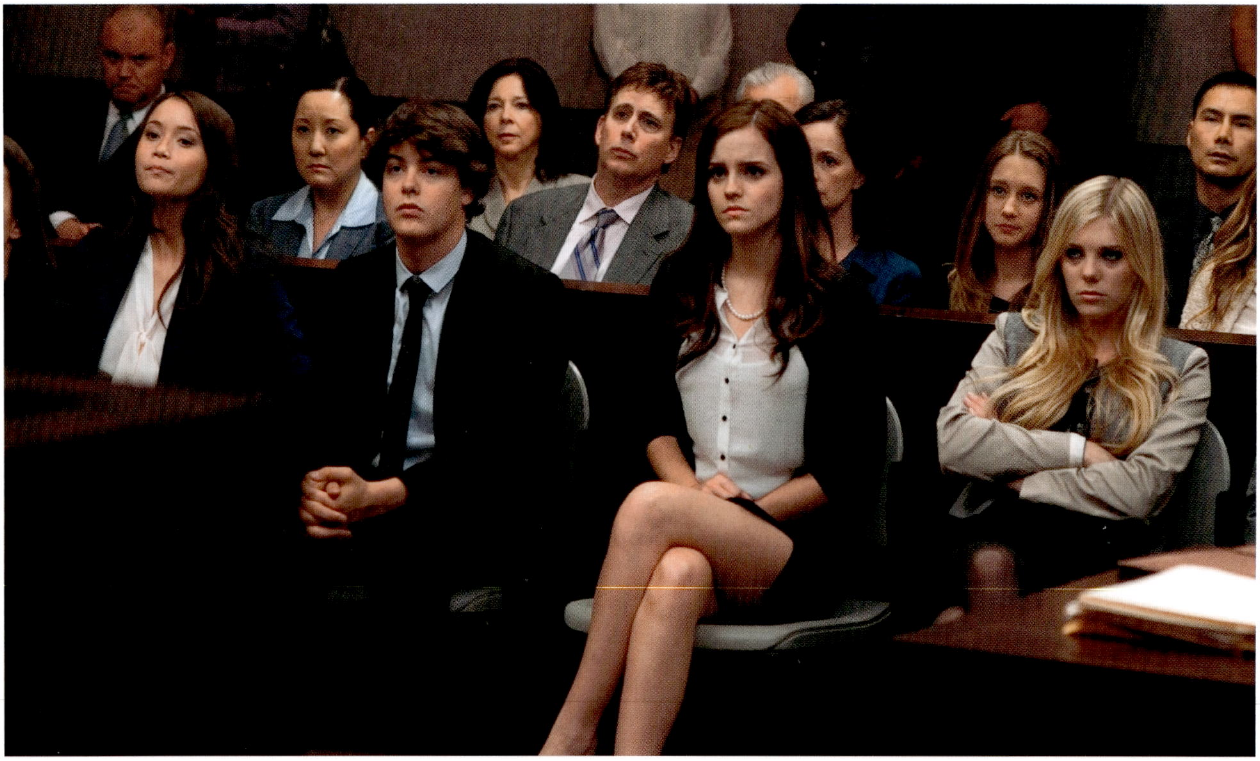

Above: *The comeuppance – Rebecca (Katie Chang), Marc (Israel Broussard), Nicki (Emma Watson), and Chloe (Claire Julien) face the music. But even court offered a kind of celebrity.*

Right: *If there is a Sofia Coppola type in the film then it is Broussard's Marc – who finally recognizes what he has lost.*

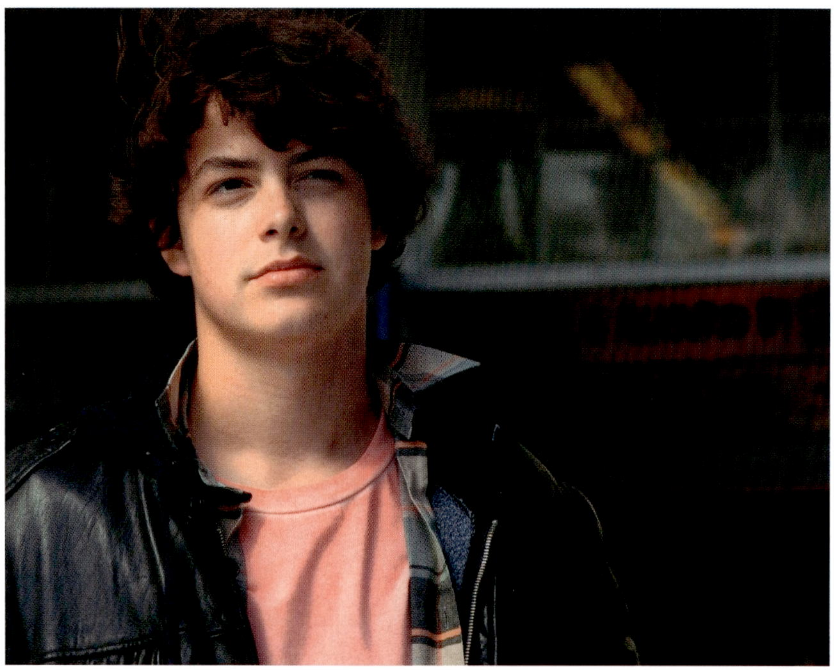

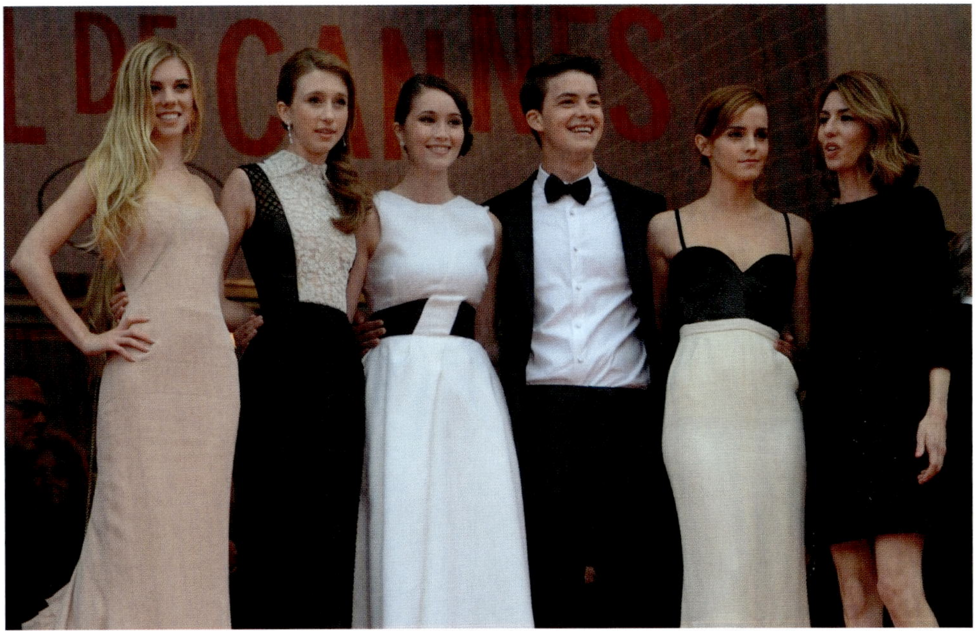

Left: *Fame squared – stars Julien, Farmiga, Chang, Broussard, and Watson take a bow with Sofia Coppola at the Cannes Film Festival. Exactly the kind of exposure the original Bling Ring would have savoured.*

Recalling a recent work of one of her father's old set, Martin Scorsese's *The Wolf of Wall Street*, in which American greed plays as pure, hyperbolic farce, Coppola also refuses to pass judgment on her shrill subjects. '*The Bling Ring* embraces the material, visual and aesthetic culture of the garish late aughts not to rebuke it but simply to perceive it,'[22] contended Hafsah Abbasi in *Paste*.

'Judgment, as far as Coppola is concerned, can be taken for granted,' wrote Stuart Klawans, praising the film in *The Nation*. 'Laughter is a given, and attempts at understanding would be just so many exercises in social stereotyping.'[23]

Maybe so. But something is lost this time. By keeping her distance, we never truly come to understand the characters, or feel them in that Coppola way. At the end of *Lost in Translation*, it is as if we have known Bob and Charlotte our entire lives. Rebecca, Marc, Nicki, Sam, and Chloe evaporate from our minds as the credits roll.

There are only tantalizing moments when the film cuts through the celebrity static and detects genuine loneliness, and only in the case of Broussard's Marc, through whose doe-eyes the story is nominally told. Hints at a need to be accepted as he gets caught in the magnetic, manipulative hold of the enigmatic Rebecca. Among Coppola's handwritten notes is a familiar description: 'closeted, secret life, outcast, good kid, misfit at home, lonely and vulnerable.'[24] The swift glance Marc gives Rebecca, beside him in court, face frozen, eyes locked into the distance, speaks of a friendship shattered by their arrest, if it existed at all. Was it only in the giddy high of breaking and entering that they were drawn together? Is Paris Hilton's closet their Tokyo? It is to Marc Coppola grants her signature shot: gazing out of the window of the prison bus, designer clothes traded for an orange boilersuit, and finally our senses stir.

Yet it is Nicki, the most unnerving character, who is given the last word. She is being interviewed yet again, released after thirty days in prison, and still bleating about her innocence. How much of this is an act remains elusive. Maybe she never really knew. It turns out, the irony curving to infinity, she was locked up at the exact same time and in the exact same jail as Lindsay Lohan (incarcerated for violating probation after DUI charges). Nicki winces in recollection, as if sucking on a lemon, her eyes rolling heavenwards. 'She got to keep her extensions in.'[25] It remains Coppola's most divisive film.

SOME ENCHANTED EVENINGS

A Very Murray Christmas (2015) and other pursuits

With Bill Murray as host, she experiments with a cozy television Christmas Special as an ironic intermezzo between features, one of many extracurricular projects

Here we come to an interlude among the flow of feature films, and with it a Hollywood-sized regret – Sofia Coppola's *The Little Mermaid*, the film that got away. If *The Bling Ring* had noticeably drifted toward the mainstream, this was the whirlpool of a blockbuster – or whatever a Coppola-styled blockbuster might look and feel like. You can see the appeal: Hans Christian Andersen tells the tale of a lonely mermaid princess who washes up on alien shores, tail magically exchanged for legs, and has to cope with love and rejection. Or *Lost in Transformation*.

Announced in 2014, the project was set up at Universal through versatile production house Working Title, who were behind *Four Weddings and a Funeral* and (encouragingly) Coen brothers curios like *Fargo* and *The Big Lebowski*. The potential budget was never made public, but the entire outlay on *Somewhere* would barely have covered catering. To play aquatic heroine Ariel, Coppola was thinking of Maya Hawke, who shared the blessing and burden of a famous lineage, being the daughter of Ethan Hawke and Uma Thurman.

'I wanted to shoot it really underwater, which would have been a nightmare,' recalled the director, and it is hard to picture Coppola in wet suit and designer goggles like a svelte James Cameron. 'But underwater photography is so beautiful.'[1]

A year of work went into *The Little Mermaid*: location scouting, casting, scripts, while the ritual of mood boards evolved into elaborate special effects tests – this was a very different fish for the director. But it wasn't the fabric of filmmaking that brought the project to a premature end so much as a philosophical awakening.

Coppola just wasn't in her element.

After another meeting ground down her spirit with batty talk of how to appeal to thirty-five-year-old males (with *The Little Mermaid*?), she faced up to the inevitable. Universal wanted to make an entirely different film. She had naïvely thought she could still go her own way. Was she heeding her father's legacy, all his legendary turmoil at the studio forge? There are just too many people to please, when she only wanted to please herself. She accepted she wasn't a good fit, but was wounded nonetheless – she had loved the idea.

Opposite: *Showtime – Bill Murray (as Bill Murray) lights up a dream sequence in Sofia Coppola's 2015 made-for-television curio* A Very Murray Christmas.

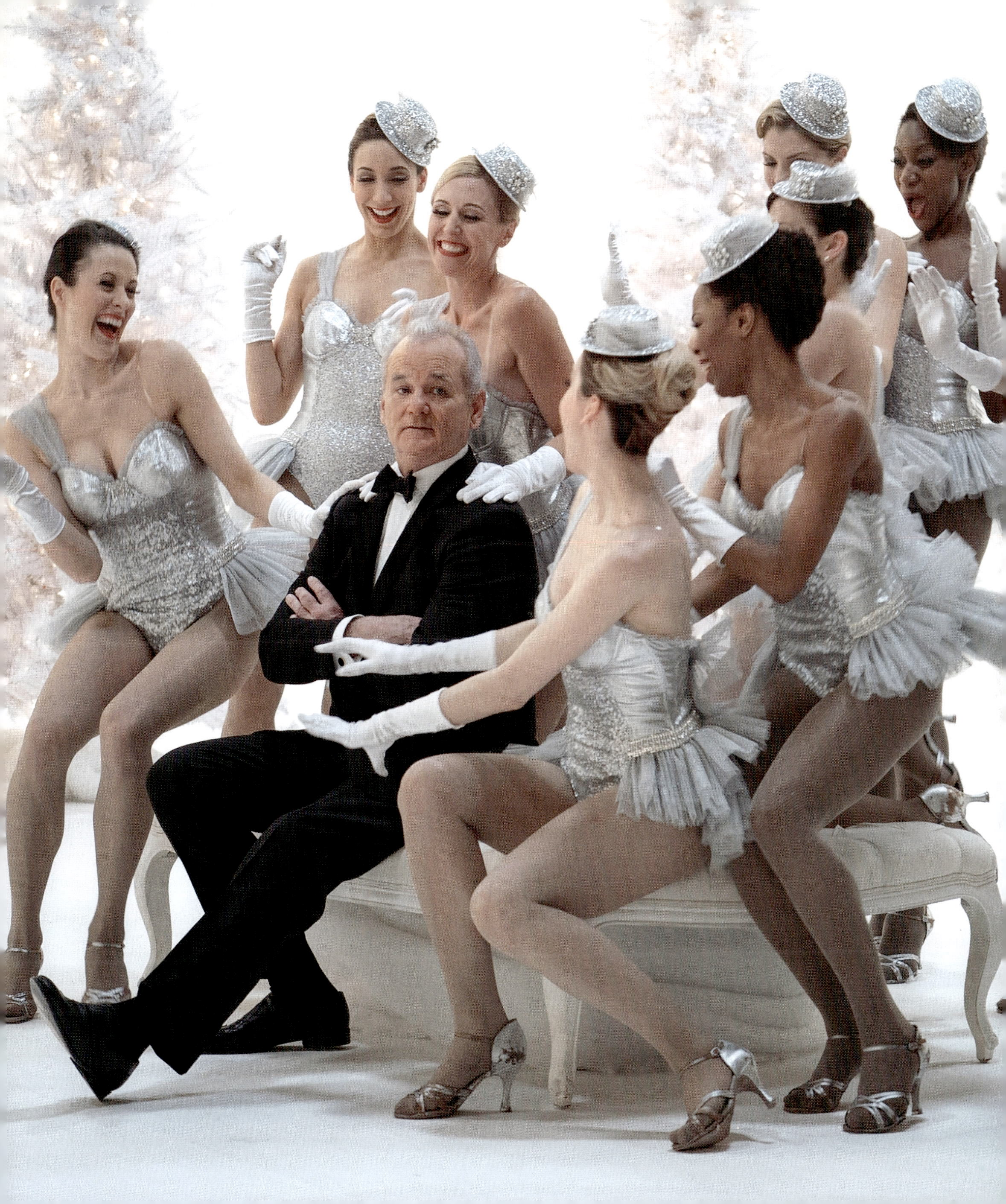

'It wasn't the Disney version, it was actually the original fairy tale, which is much darker,' she explained. 'I thought it would be fun to do a fairy tale, I've always loved fairy tales, so I was curious about doing that.'[2]

In any director's career projects run aground. There was also a brief period when she contemplated the offer of *The Twilight Saga: Breaking Dawn – Part 2*, but only briefly. However, the case of *The Little Mermaid* is instructive in a number of ways. Its loss influenced the immediacy (and zaniness) of what came next, but also fixed the compass of her career. There was never going to be a Sofia Coppola who dabbled from time to time in studio material. An acknowledgement accompanied by a sense of loss: for *The Little Mermaid* we will never get to see (a film as ethereal and haunting as *The Virgin Suicides*), and for the influence she might have brought to bear on the mainstream. And it was also accompanied by a sense of relief. Ever since, Coppola has stuck to her own, distinctive path, with comparatively modest budgets, but the freedom to express herself.

As an aside and somewhat modern badge of honour, satirical website *Funny or Die* created a mock trailer for 'Sofia Coppola's *The Little Mermaid*.'[3] This mainly involves airheaded mermaid AnnaSophia Robb and slacker boyf Evan Peters hanging out by the pool at the Shellteau Marmont. 'I don't know what it is, but there's something fishy about you,'[4] he muses, then smokes underwater.

Meanwhile, Coppola was quite ready to send herself up. Over barely four and half, heavily improvised days, no more than a swig of production, she cleansed her spirit with *A Very Murray Christmas*. Made for Netflix, this was a television special with the charming aura of something thrown together off the cuff, which is pretty much the case. Since it is about something thrown together off the cuff. To be exact, this is a one-hour Christmas Special that tells the story of a one-hour Christmas Special – a powder-puff comedy, undoubted indulgence, and wild departure much closer to home.

From a certain angle, it was sticking to the thematic rules: hotels, cities, alienation, family ties, and Bill Murray. The comic ruse was largely inspired by how much she loved to watch spirit animal and nonchalant muse Murray sing. Coppola had an image of the *Lost in Translation* star in Bemelmans Bar, the cocktail lounge of New York's Carlyle Hotel, crooning beside a grand piano, bourbon in hand and once more attired in a tuxedo (how she loved him in a tux too).

The full story is that Murray and Mitch Glazer, who had produced *Lost in Translation*, had already been working on an ironic variation of a Christmas Special with the streaming giant, but when Coppola became interested it took flight. The second of three collaborations with the star, *A Very Murray Christmas* was already on her to-do list before *The Little Mermaid* drifted away.

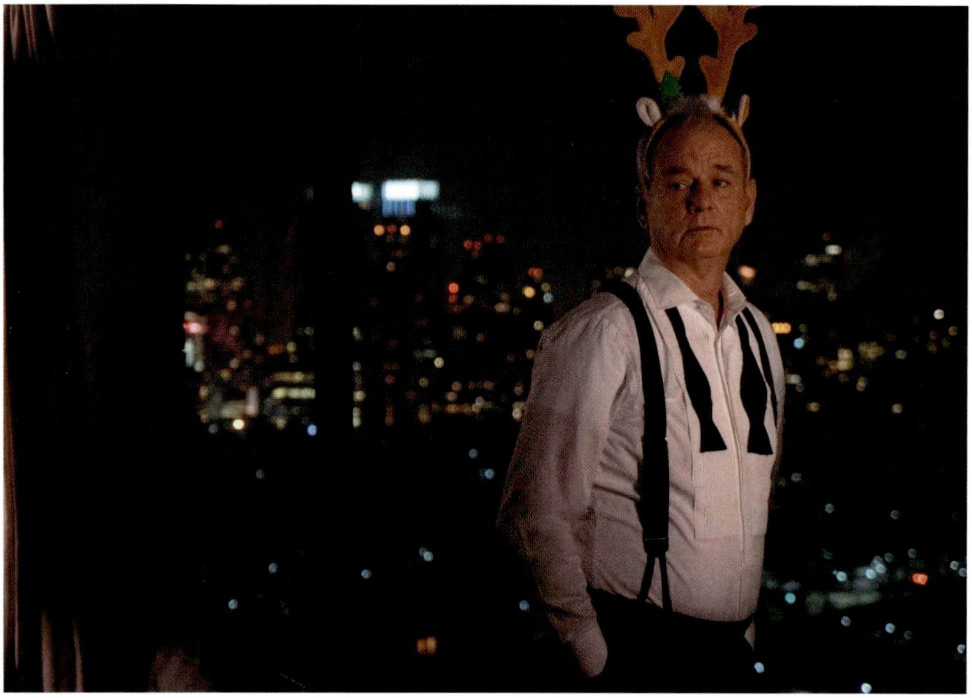

Left: *Seasonal grumblings – with* A Very Murray Christmas, *Sofia Coppola was knowingly playing with her own imagery, shooting a sullen Bill Murray in a hotel room with New York beyond.*

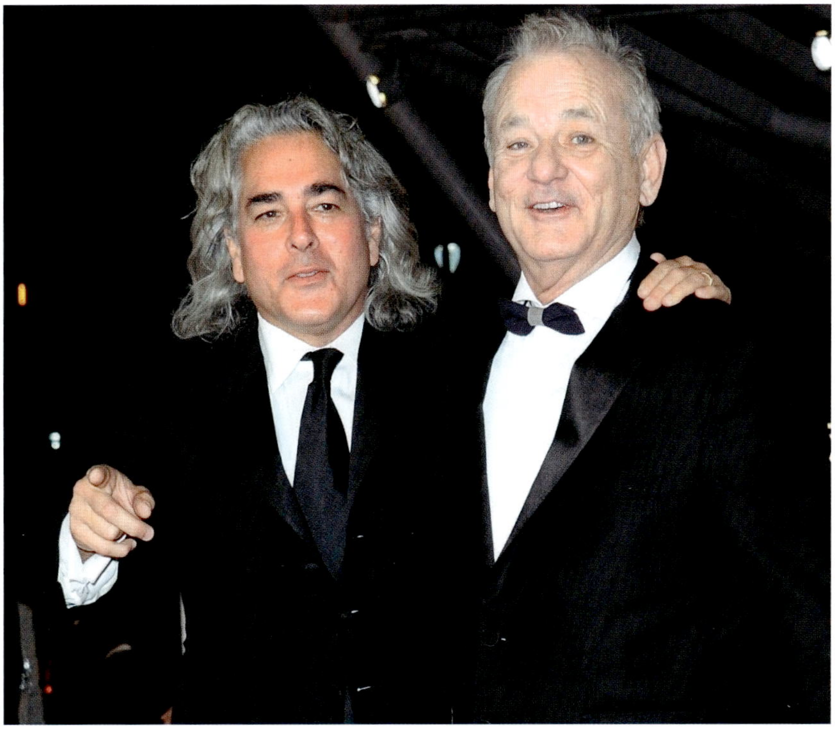

Left: *Producer Mitch Glazer (who had worked on* Lost in Translation*) and Murray had already been planning an ironic take on a Christmas Special before Coppola became involved.*

Below: *The classic Christmas Special combo – the unlikeliest of duets, as David Bowie sung 'The Little Drummer Boy' with American favourite Bing Crosby. The glittering city backdrop would not have gone unnoticed by Coppola.*

Coppola was emulating a very specific form of cultural strangeness – the hermetic world of the Christmas or Holiday Special that thrived on American television throughout the sixties, seventies, and eighties, but has never really gone away. There was a randomness to Christmas Specials that had always intrigued her. They never had much of a story to offer, simply a certain breed of host – such as Dean Martin, his incongruous tan bordering on leather; or Bing Crosby, America's avuncular emcee – pretending they were at home, in front of a *de rigueur* crackling fire, as various guests dropped by to duet. This is how Crosby came to perform 'The Little Drummer Boy' with David Bowie of all people, the standout collaboration of *Bing Crosby's Merrie Olde Christmas*. There had also been more ironically inflected, modern iterations: the 2013 combo at the heart of *Lady Gaga & The Muppets' Holiday Spectacular* speaks for itself.

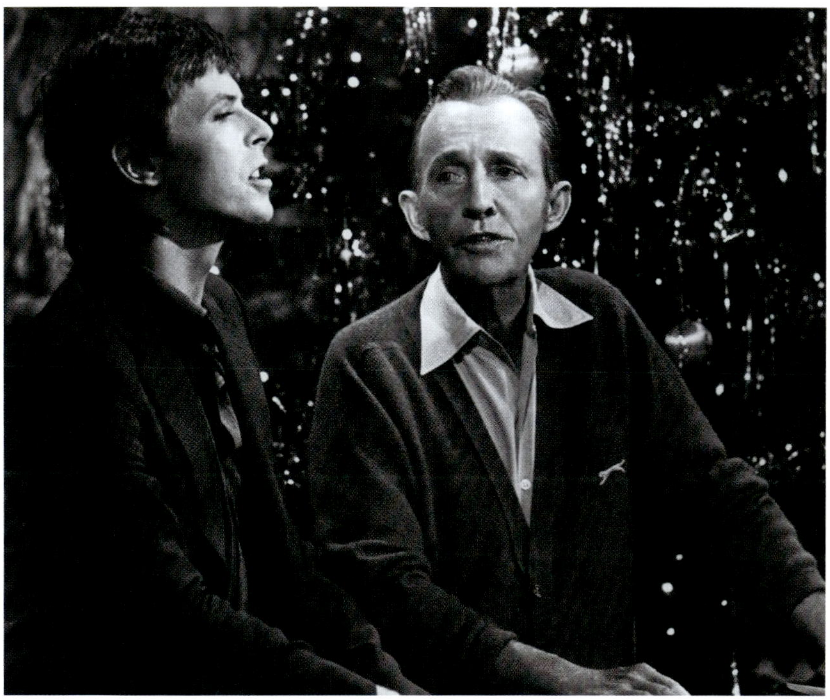

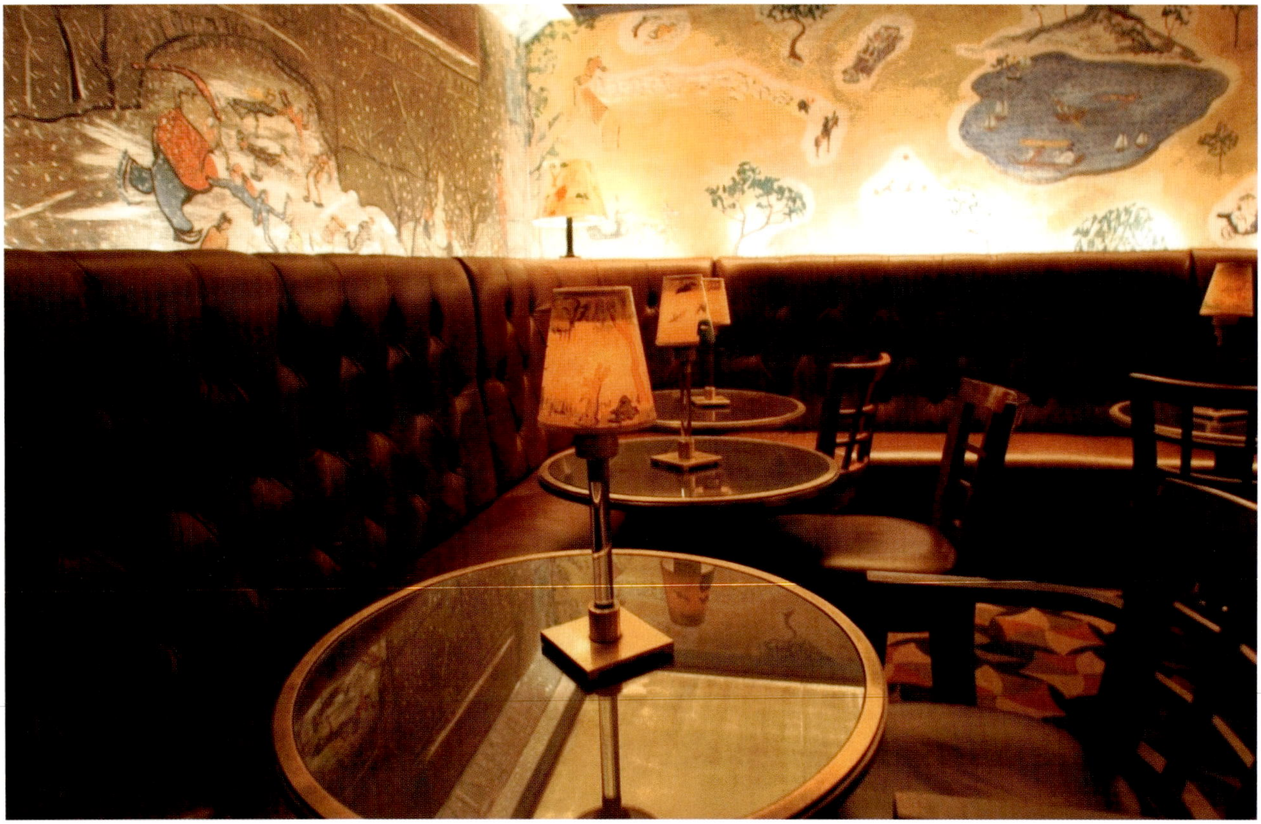

Above: *The interior of the famous Bemelmans Bar at the Carlyle Hotel – a setting for* A Very Murray Christmas, On the Rocks, *and for Sofia Coppola's own social life.*

What Coppola sought was 'the nonlinear, no-logic, anything-can-happen feel,'[5] where songs just popped up out of nowhere. To put things more simply, she wanted 'to do something joyful.'[6]

She couldn't help but be stirred by the city. This was a fairy tale of New York, the gleaming metropolis where her father was born and raised, the original gateway to America. For that matter, it was where she had been born, her mother rushed into hospital as her father toiled on *The Godfather.* And it was now the place she called home. 'Uptown New York feels very Christmasy to me with the decorations and traditions,'[7] she said.

A Very Murray Christmas was possessed by a nostalgia for bygone eras. Which included her own: the television film (the exact mode here is hard to define; it's sort of a hazy shade of a fiction) opens in undeniable Coppola mood, with Murray gazing out at a snow-globe New York from his suite at the Carlyle, that disconsolate face, as softly cratered as the Moon, reflected back at him in the glass.

The Art Deco Carlyle Hotel was different again to the sleek modernity of the Park Hyatt or the laidback groove of the Chateau Marmont. Opened in 1930, it was old-school Manhattan, regularly frequented by intellectuals and upmarket celebrities. As well as having access to one suite, Coppola was granted leave to shoot in Bemelmans Bar, the famous piano room lined with Ludwig Bemelmans murals, which has played host to John F. Kennedy and Tom Cruise – yet more sacred ground cleared for her serene productions. She knew it socially, loved its untroubled atmosphere, and would feature the venue heavily in her next film but one, *On the Rocks* (also with Murray, not coincidentally).

In time-honoured tradition, the plot is little more than a coat hanger for songs, in-jokes, and the soft gleam of celebrity, beginning with an approximate Bill Murray (Murray) having second thoughts about the Christmas Special he's agreed to host. Such misgivings stem from the New York blizzard that has stalled the planned studio-based extravaganza; the realization that Christmas Specials are a foolish endeavour anyway; and that he's come down with a bad case of the Christmas blues. Given this is Murray channelling Murray, how upbeat he's ever been is questionable. 'God hates me,'[8] he informs his diligent producers (Amy Poehler and Julie White), while wearing a pair of comedy antlers. He will finally be cajoled into his jacket and down to the hotel bar to make the best of things, where a miscellany of guests come and go despite the weather outside being frightful.

Before pen was put to paper, Coppola had sat down with Murray to brainstorm their televised party, the key question being whom they might invite. Given the limited production schedule and the fact it was a bit of a whimsical gas (requiring all involved not to take themselves seriously), the guest list was a cross-generational tangle of Murray's Rolodex and Coppola's inner circle, with a lot of favours being called in.

Comedian Chris Rock was Coppola's idea but Murray's contact (they duet on 'Do You

Below: *Bill Murray duets with Chris Rock in* A Very Murray Christmas *– Coppola enjoyed mixing Murray with very different energies. The quality of singing wasn't necessarily a priority.*

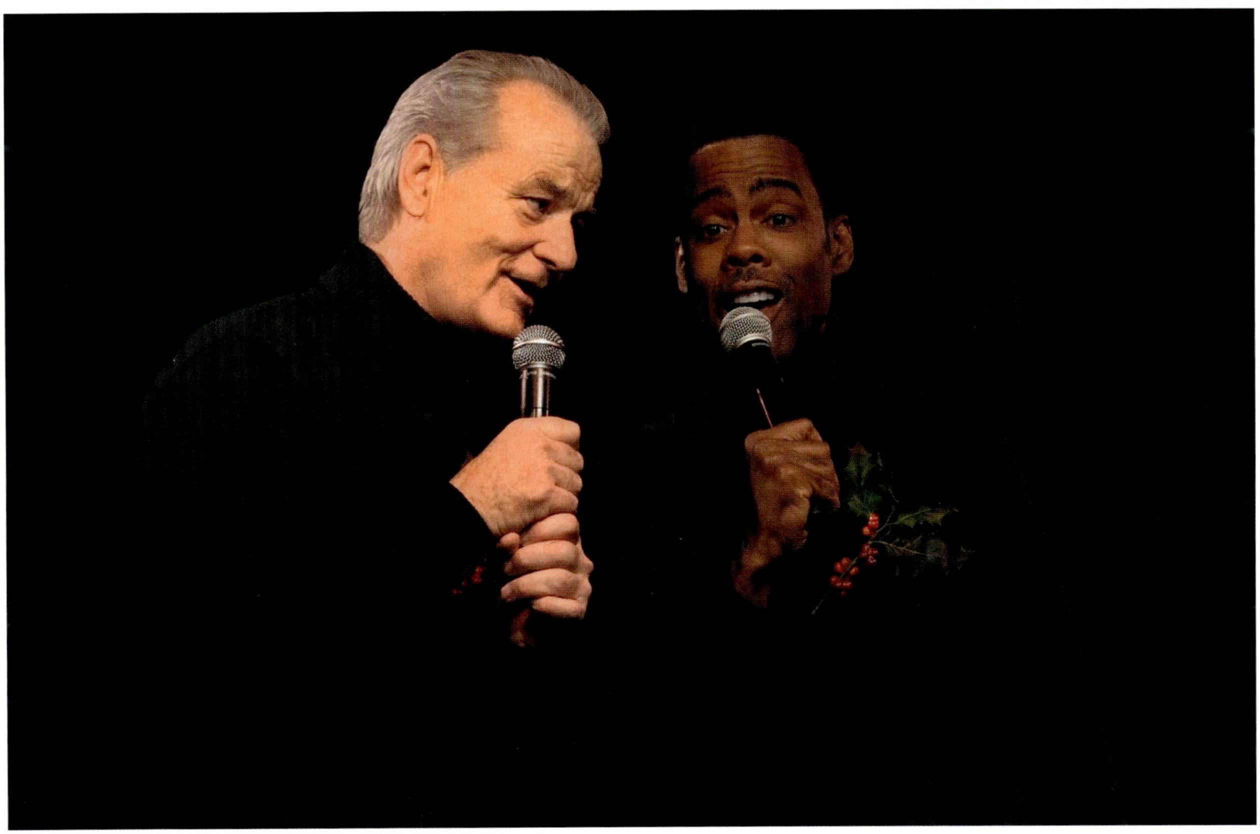

Hear What I Hear?' in turtlenecks), as was David Johansen, formerly of the New York Dolls and assaying the Ghost of Christmas Past in Murray's Dickens remix *Scrooged*. Another friend, George Clooney, was a last minute replacement for rapper Rick Ross (who had agreed then stopped returning calls), and soldiers his way through 'Santa Claus Wants Some Lovin'' with Murray, Miley Cyrus, and a chorus line of dancing girls in silver dresses in what is effectively a dream sequence.

Coppola had applied her persuasive charms to land bestie Rashida Jones (who first met Coppola when she played Charlotte during the early read-throughs of *Lost in Translation*) and cousin Jason Schwartzman, who play an engaged couple having second thoughts; Maya Rudolph (a natural at this game) as a real lounge singer; and Coppola's husband Thomas Mars along with his entire band, Phoenix, gamely dressed as French waiters.

Art was imitating art, with the musical numbers being recorded live (excluding the dream sequence). This is Murray, as Murray, performing in Bemelmans. Coppola had shot music videos, and there were those karaoke moments in *Lost in Translation*, but she had never done musical numbers per se. If not quite the open water of *The Little Mermaid*, this was fast-paced, experimental stuff, including the use of multiple cameras for the first time, while maintaining a slightly shambolic, muddling-through energy.

A production assistant had been posted at the doorway to the bar as they hustled to get their shots, and this being Bemelmans, one of the hotel guests dissuaded from grabbing a drink was Paul McCartney. What a duet with Murray that might have made, but by the time Coppola had hurried to the door, the great Macca had moved on.

Paul Shaffer, bandleader on *Late Show with David Letterman*, was brought in to orchestrate and perform (in person) the

Below: *The guest list of* A Very Murray Christmas *featured friends and contacts of both Sofia Coppola and Bill Murray. Back row, from the left: Jenny Lewis, Maya Rudolph, Rashida Jones, Jason Schwartzman, and Dimitri Dimitrov. Front row: Paul Shaffer (who orchestrated the music) and Bill Murray.*

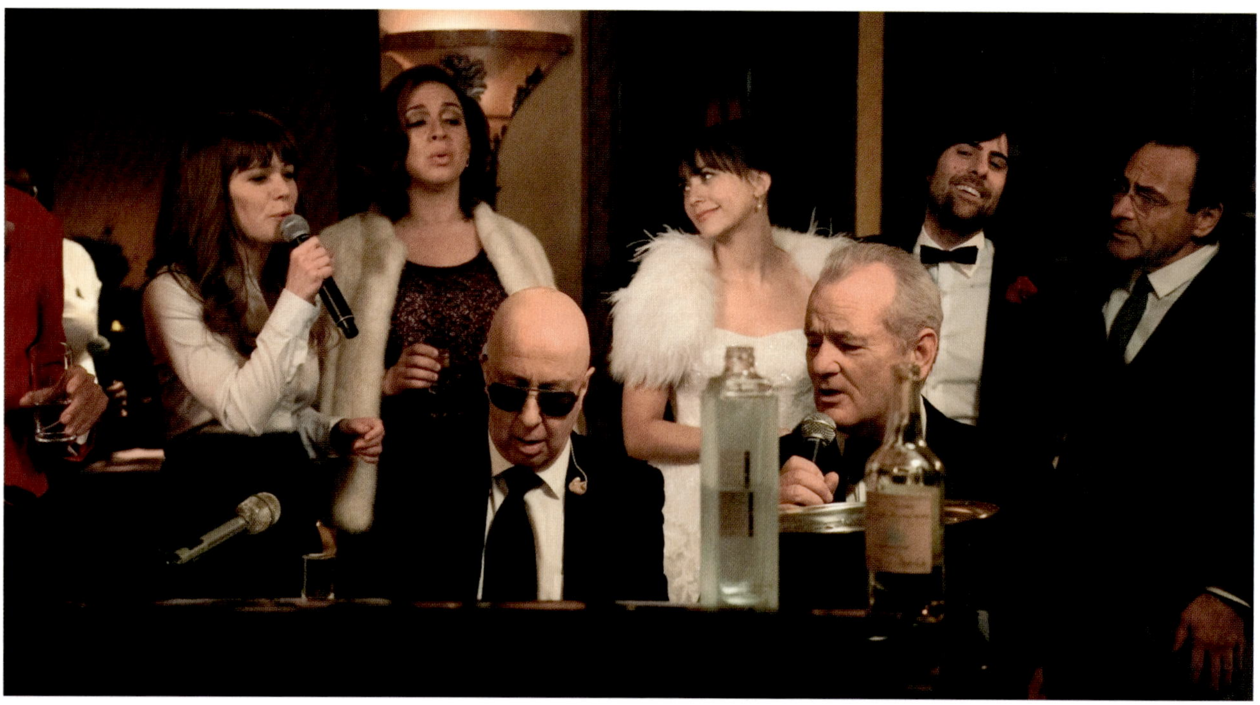

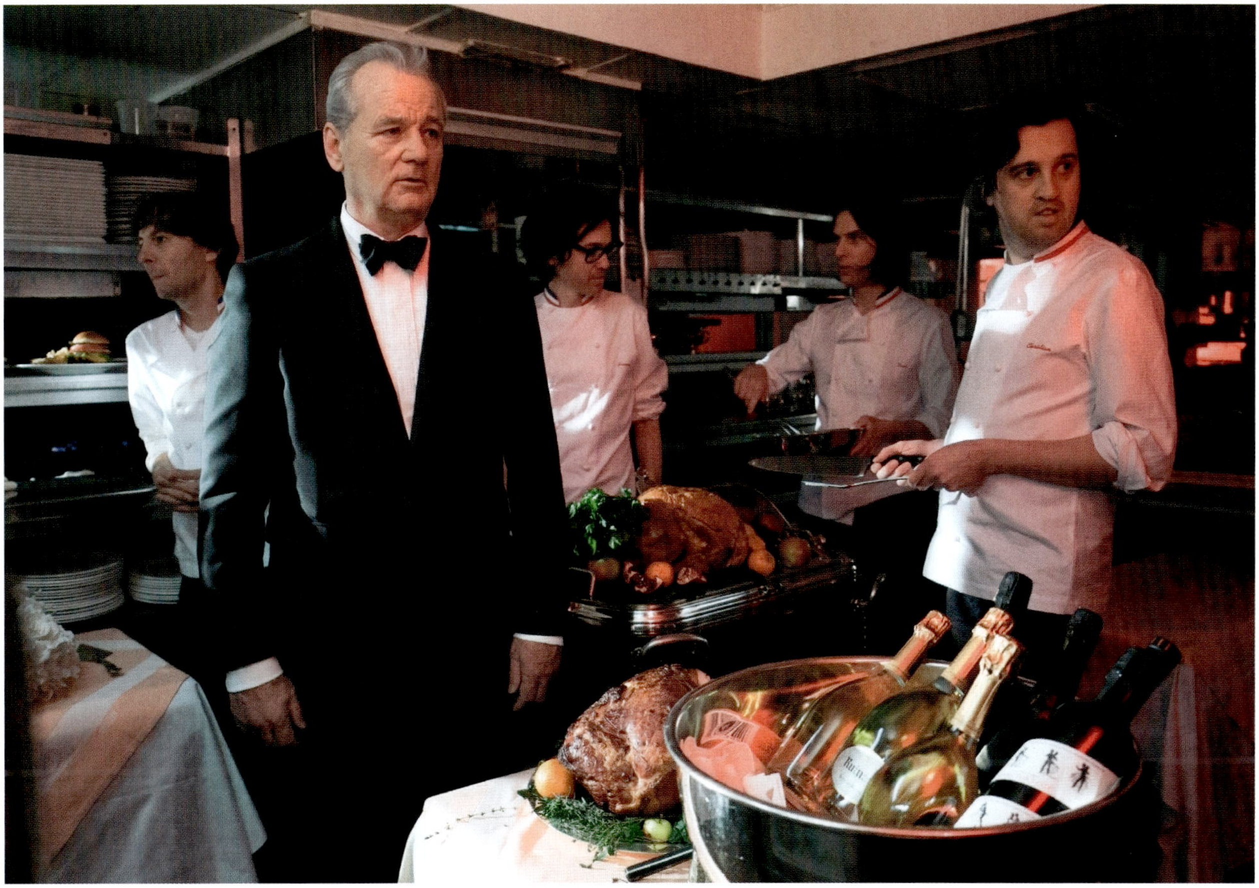

Above: *Getting in with the in-jokes – Murray hangs out with the kitchen staff, played by the French band Phoenix, including Coppola's husband Thomas Mars (left).*

music. A good choice, given Shaffer knew what it meant to deal with the flurry of television. Moreover, seasoned by years on *Saturday Night Live*, the comedy show on which Murray had prototyped his current vibe through his Nick the Lounge Singer persona, Shaffer was also well-versed in divining the star's unusual flavour.

'I think that Billy himself really wanted to try to create [a genuine holiday special], doing it in his own way, of course, and playing off it and commenting on it and all,' he surmised. 'But still, doing one, doing a Christmas special, you know? I think it's coming from a very noble place.'[9]

The way Coppola used music was turned inside out. On her movies, right from the writing stage, the chosen songs set the atmosphere, as elemental as lighting and costumes. Here the music wasn't playing inside the heads and hearts of the characters or the director, but right there in the snowbound bar. Yet the Christmas tunes were still setting a mood, a tricky mix she defined as 'playful and sincere.'[10] The best Christmas songs are the sad ones. The season is infused with melancholy.

So what are we to make of it all? Does *A Very Murray Christmas* even count as a Coppola movie? There is a charming, haphazard, self-aware quality, a hint of life true to her style. In keeping with the karaoke magic of old, delivery of the songs ranges from the professional (Cyrus) to

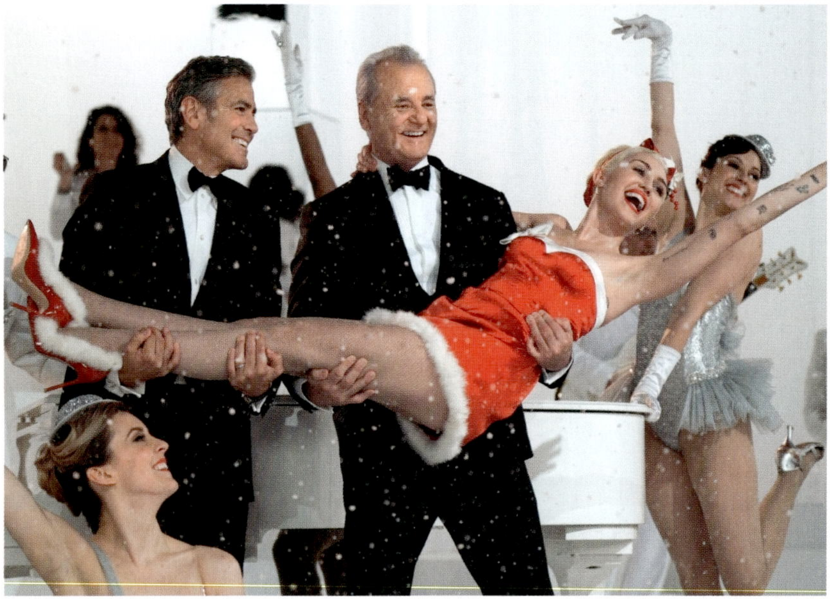

Above and right: *Fulfilling Sofia Coppola's long-held desire to mount a full Hollywood musical number, Bill Murray is joined, in a dream sequence, by George Clooney and Miley Cyrus. It is the only section of* A Very Murray Christmas *filmed on a soundstage (in Queens).*

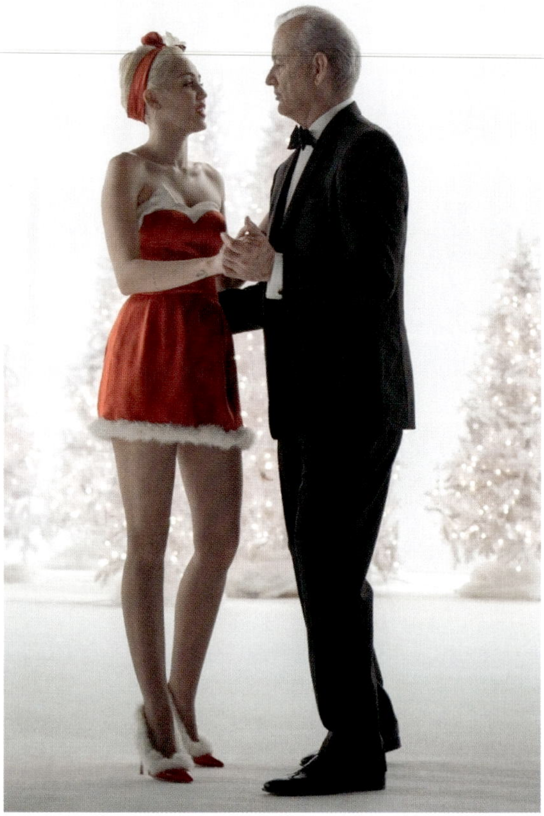

the knowingly ragged (Clooney, Rock, Schwartzman), with Murray's gruff charisma lighting the way. But the rules are vague, the guests (sometimes themselves, sometimes not) and their dilemmas remain sketchy at best. At less than an hour long, it's more of a whimsical diversion in the canon.

'Every element of *Very Murray Christmas* lazily asserts that this is a minor effort from the celebrated filmmaker,' decided Chris Stanton in *Paste*, 'but that looseness inadvertently allows Coppola to flit from one of her fixations to the next, turning the whole exercise into a guided tour of Coppola-isms.'[11]

Coppola wants to avoid being kitsch. Which is a challenge, given this is about the kitschiest format known to humanity. The resulting tone is odd – a heartfelt parody. It's not laugh-out-loud funny, more observationally wry. It is indeed another mood piece. Put it this way, it's an unusual cocktail, and an acquired taste.

While Coppola's feature film output remains comparatively (and admirably) small, her restless imagination leads her into other art forms. She has been dubbed a 'transmedia audiovisual stylist,'[12] which might allude to the fact her oeuvre contains work as photographer, fashion designer, model, skincare brand ambassador, board member of art galleries, and producer of films alongside the day job. Which recalls both the multiplicity of her early career and a family inheritance. Father, mother, brother, and extended Coppola relations have diversified into everything from wine to comparative literature.

What concerns us here is visual material. Let us take it category by category.

First, Coppola's music videos. Having escaped the nest for the alternative scene of nineties Los Angeles, she had become part of Sonic Youth's circle (it was where she met first husband Spike Jonze), starring in their video for 'Mildred Pierce.' This led her to directing various videos (while still not considering herself in any meaningful sense a director). Given how her movies are soaked in music, these reveal an aesthetic in embryonic form. They are mood boards for the films to come.

She began in 1993 with Walt Mink's 'Shine.' Filmed on the sprawling, sun-kissed lawns and poolside at the Coppola Estate in Napa Valley, the alt-rock band play as ethereal young girls lounge and swim. Even the flowing editing hints at *The Virgin Suicides* and *Somewhere*. It was followed in 1996 with 'This Here Giraffe' by The Flaming Lips, made in a flickering, home-movie style, including messy bedrooms and a smiling Leslie Hayman, who would later be cast as one of the Lisbon sisters.

Alongside her filmmaking (having acknowledged she was now a director), she directed the video for Air's 'Playground Love,' the signature track from *The Virgin Suicides*. Scenes from the film are mixed with the unusually surreal sight of Lux's discarded gum doing the singing (not from the film), as well as the meta-note of Coppola herself on set during the school dance sequence (with the aura of a heavily staged moment). This idea of videos as extensions of her films was incorporated in Kevin Shields' 'City Girl' from *Lost in Translation*, which plays against a travelogue of Tokyo, using both cuts from the film and unused footage, including the lovely moment of Scarlett Johansson turning a quizzical look directly into the lens before smiling.

In 2003, when asked to pitch for the stand-alone video for The White Stripes' Burt Bacharach cover 'I Just Don't Know What to Do with Myself', Coppola had replied 'I don't know – how about Kate Moss doing a pole dance?'[13] And that is exactly what we get, in intense black and white. There is an immediate through line to the pole-dancers in *Somewhere*, but the mood

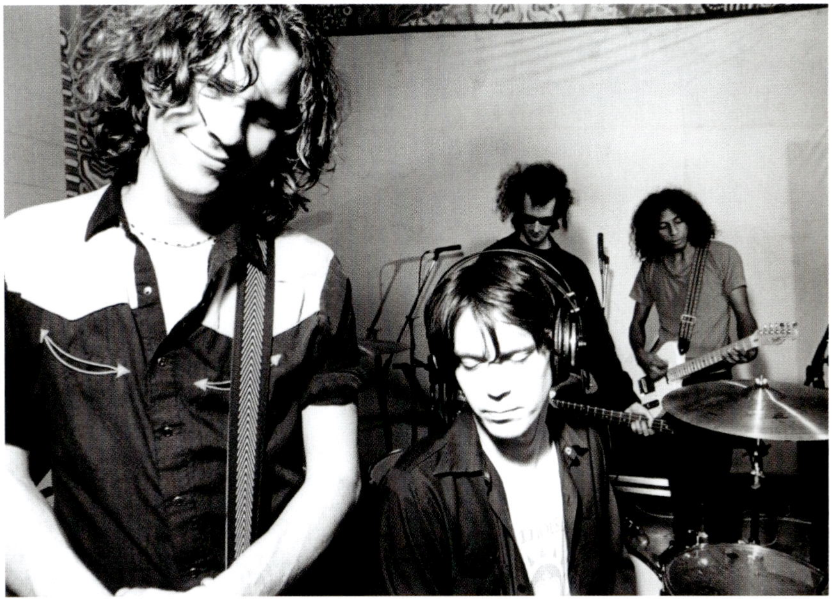

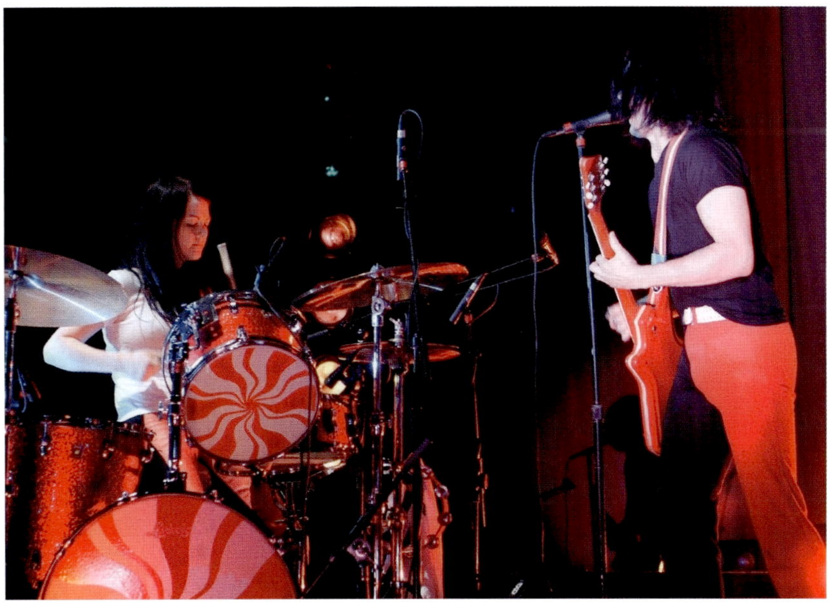

Top: *Earning her visual stripes – Coppola's directing talents were honed by making videos for such cutting-edge bands as The Flaming Lips (top) in 1996, and The White Stripes (above) in 2003. She would maintain a powerful imaginative link with contemporary music throughout her filmmaking.*

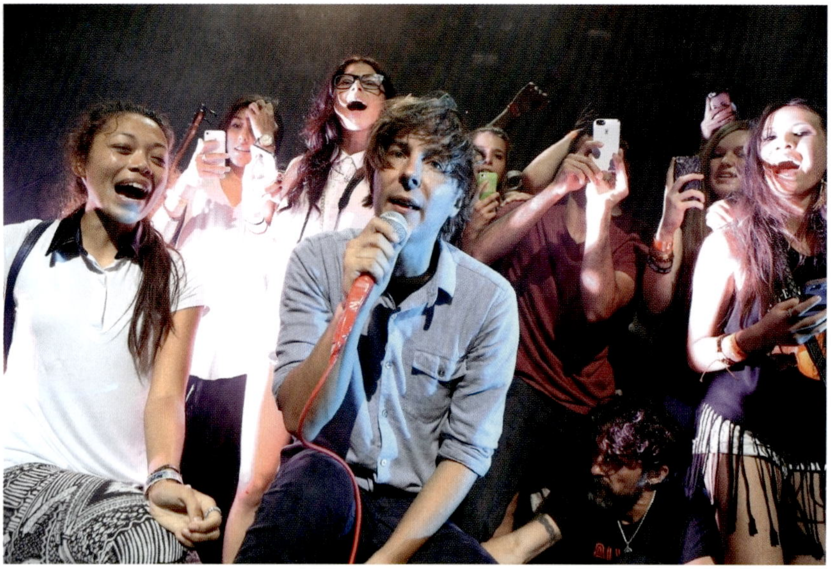

> I wanted the video to be about the girls losing it over the band, and that feeling you have when you think a band is romantic. I always like the idea of longing.
>
> **SOFIA COPPOLA**

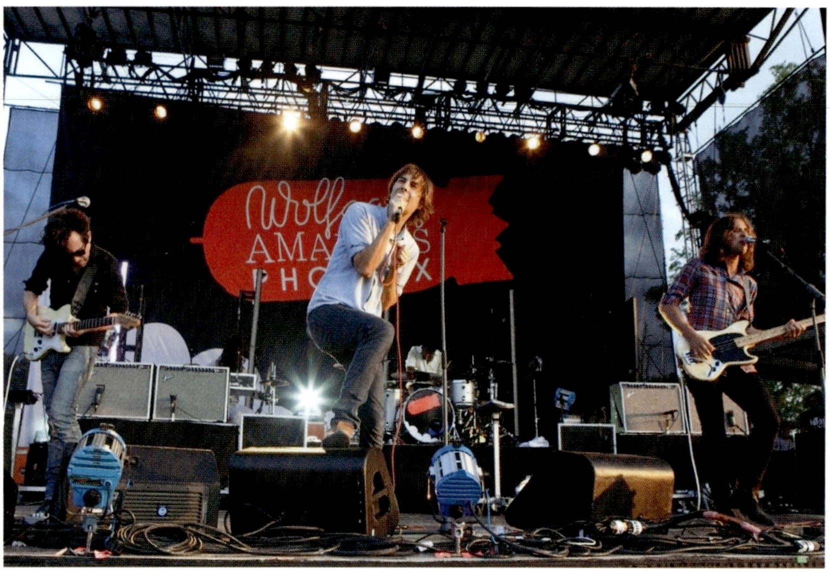

Top and above: *The potent live presence of French rockers Phoenix, led by vocalist Thomas Mars, who married Sofia Coppola in 2011 (they had met in 1999). Phoenix have served as musical collaborators throughout her career, including on* Lost in Translation, Marie Antoinette, *and* Priscilla.

couldn't be more contrasting: beautiful, captivating, erotic, but almost sculptural.

Then in 2013, she directed another chiaroscuro video, arguably her most haunting, this time for Phoenix and the song 'Chloroform.' Inspired by weeping images from Joseph Sterling's book of photography *The Age of Adolescence*, Coppola's camera leaves the silhouetted band behind for close-ups of beautiful girls in the crowd all overcome by emotion as they listen to the song.

'I wanted the video to be about the girls losing it over the band, and that feeling you have when you think a band is romantic,'[14] she explained. It was about fantasy and music, and points us to the painful allure of celebrity within *Priscilla*. 'I always like the idea of longing,'[15] she added.

Aligned with her love of high-end fashion, Coppola has shot commercials for a number of exclusive brands. To cynics this spoke of the world of rarefied privilege which Coppola inhabited, but it is as much about an ethos and art form as wearing expensive clothes. There is an ambience that flows back and forth with her films – what writer

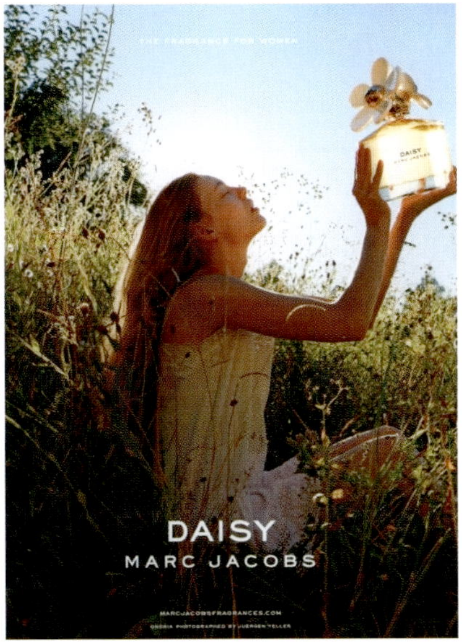

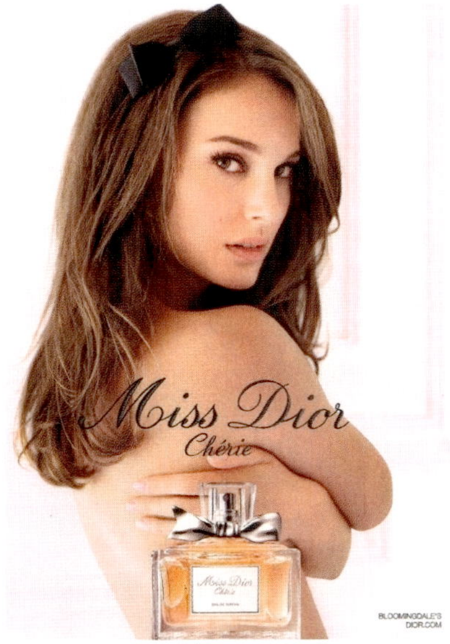

Left: *Always in style – Coppola would foster deep ties with the fashion industry, particularly with Marc Jacobs, who would translate her imagery (and use her directing skills) to create campaigns.*

Below: *Beyond their creative collaborations, Coppola and Jacobs have been close friends for decades.*

Hannah Strong terms 'the Sofia Factor.'[16] These films-in-miniature include those for Dior (among them the *Marie Antoinette* pastels of the Natalie Portman ad for Miss Dior Chérie), Calvin Klein underwear (featuring Rashida Jones and Kirsten Dunst), and H&M (to the soulful tones of Coppola regulars Roxy Music).

Meeting in the nineties, Coppola developed a collaborative friendship with designer Marc Jacobs that has lasted for decades. She has been written about as his muse, becoming the face of his 'Marc Jacobs perfume' in 2001. In turn, the designer would homage the growing cult around *The Virgin Suicides* with his dream-girl campaign for the later fragrance Daisy. In 2013, Coppola would make her own contribution to the ongoing Daisy commercials with bucolic images of young women in natural settings, a tribute to Peter Weir's period mystery *Picnic at Hanging Rock*.

Premiering at the Venice Film Festival in 2025, *Marc by Sofia* is (at the time of writing) Coppola's latest film. It is also her first documentary, though exactly how objective she could or wanted to be is open to question

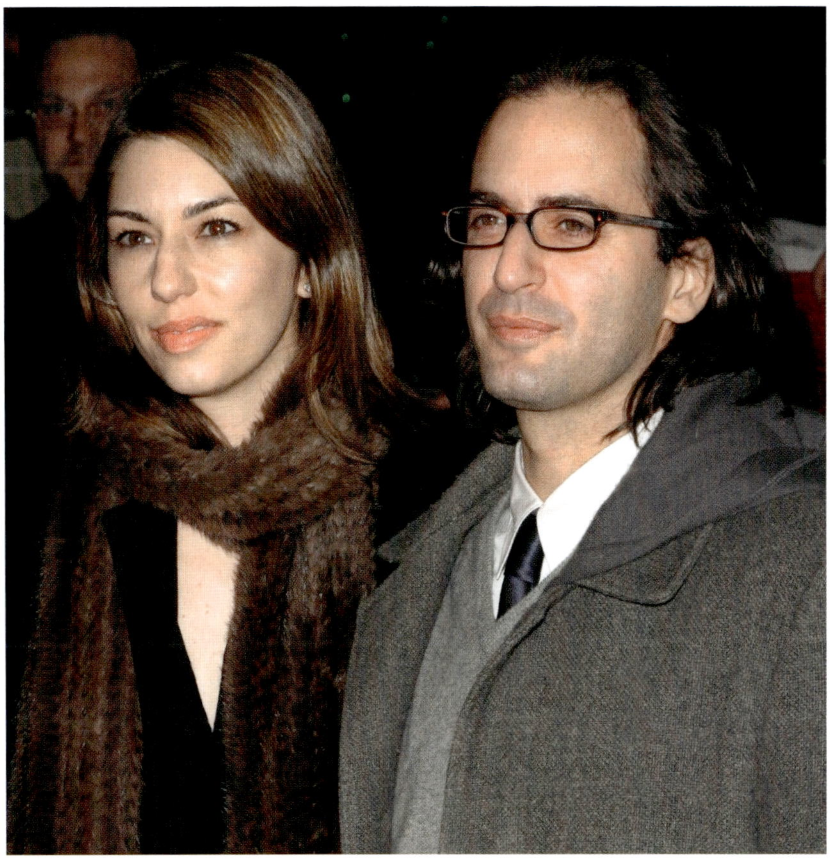

Right and below: *Sofia Coppola's first documentary (made in 2025) was a profile of Marc Jacobs,* Marc by Sofia. *It explored their long friendship, as well as the creative world of the designer.*

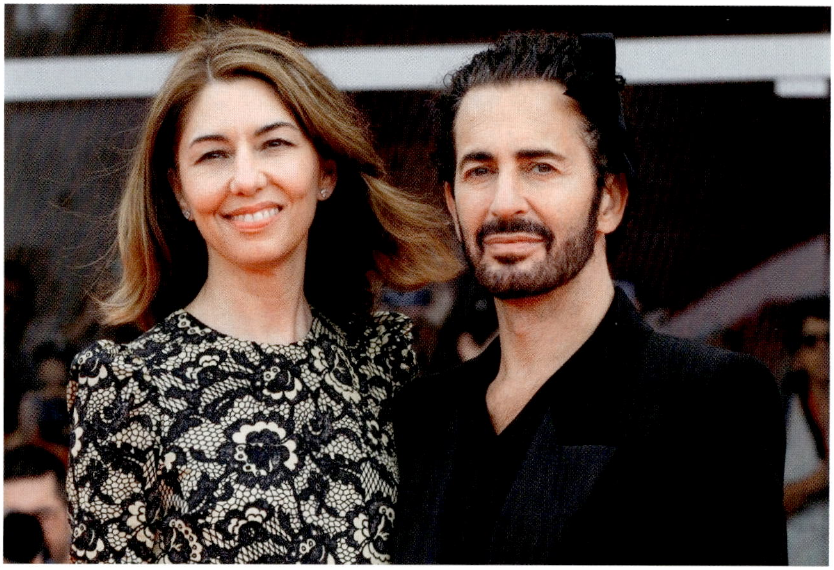

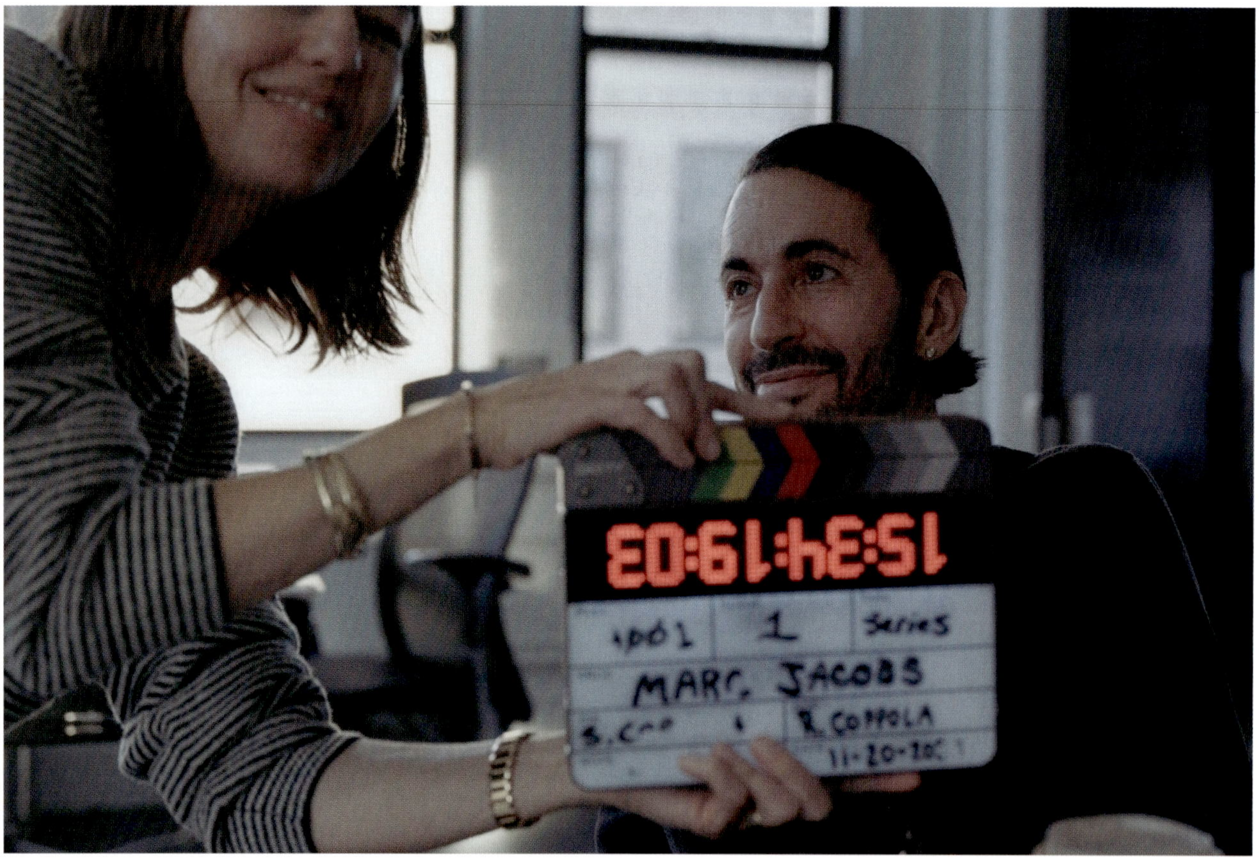

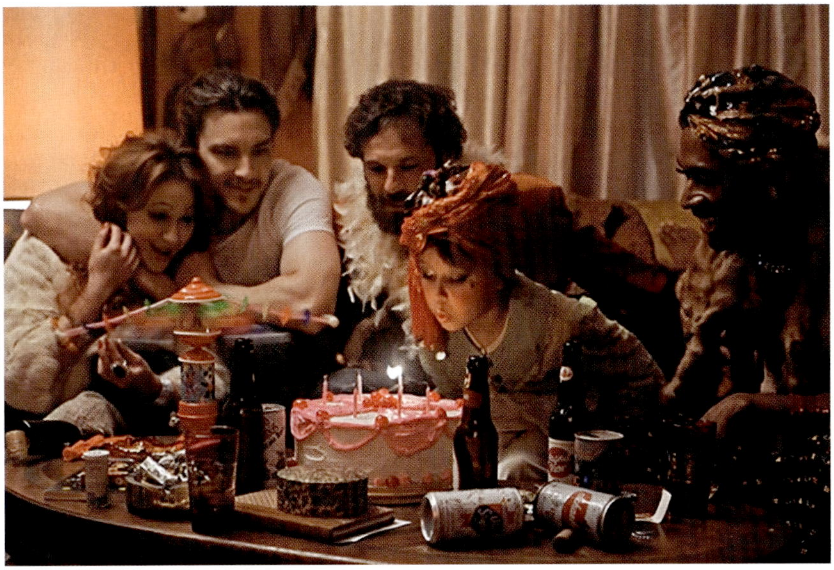

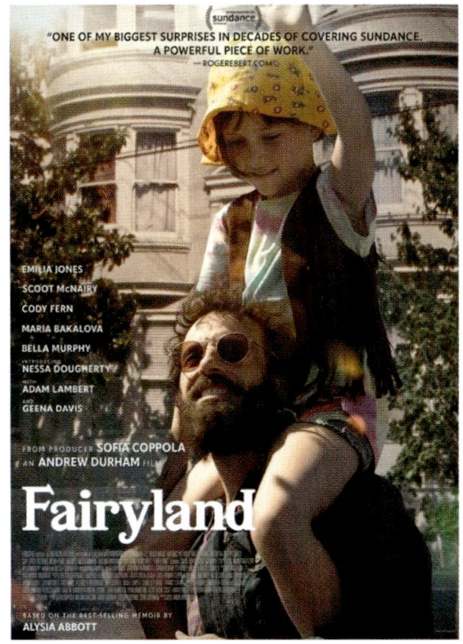

Above left and right: *Through the family production company American Zoetrope, Coppola served as producer on Andrew Durham's drama* Fairyland *in 2023. The film shared many of her own recurring themes: loneliness, coming of age, eccentric fathers.*

in this survey of his life and career. As one of Jacobs' best friends, she leans towards the affectionate. She had had her qualms at first. 'But I kept thinking about how much fun it would be to follow this collection, popping in throughout the process.'[17]

The narrative structure tracks the weeks leading to a major Jacobs launch in 2024, while charting his career, his inspirations, his perfectionism, and their friendship (Coppola occasionally slipping in front of the camera). What works is how the film dispenses with the formality and penetration of documentary for a more impressionistic, naturally Coppola mode bordering on collage. Close-ups of models applying eye lashes, the filigree texture of fabrics, flitting through his archives to a pop soundtrack. In truth, we learn less about 'Marc', and more about 'Sofia's' connection to his work.

'It's a bauble of a film, but also so distinctly Sofia Coppola's style that it's a must-see for anyone interested in the aesthetics of her career,'[18] wrote Caryn James in *The Hollywood Reporter.*

With her father taking a back seat, relatively speaking, family production company American Zoetrope is now run by Roman Coppola, with his sister's considerable input. She has helped develop films alongside her own. For instance, *Palo Alto* (2013) and *The Last Showgirl* (2024) from her cousin Gia Coppola; and romantic comedy *Paris Can Wait*, directed by her mother Eleanor in 2016.

Coppola served as producer on *Fairyland* in 2023, directed by Andrew Durham and starring Scoot McNairy. We can see the thematic connection: the emotional story recounts a young girl's memories of growing up with a gay single father in San Francisco's Haight-Ashbury district through the seventies and AIDS-struck eighties.

In 2016, Coppola took to the stage, directing a new version of Giuseppe Verdi's *La Traviata* for the Italian state broadcaster. Which was a slightly ironic move given the last time she had spent a night at the opera (in public), at the climax of *The Godfather Part III*, she had been shot dead. In this case, however, she was applying her creativity behind the scenes of the Teatro dell'Opera di Roma, across fifteen sold-out evenings.

Right and below: *Grand gestures – the 2016 production of* La Traviata, *directed by Sofia Coppola at the Teatro dell'Opera di Roma, starred Antonio Poli as Alfredo and Francesca Dotto as Violetta (right), with costumes designed by Valentino.*

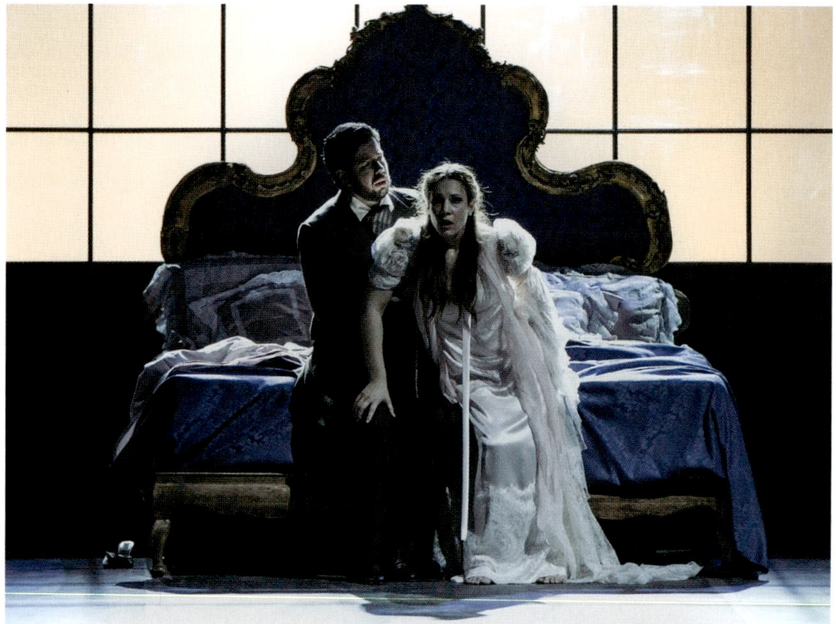

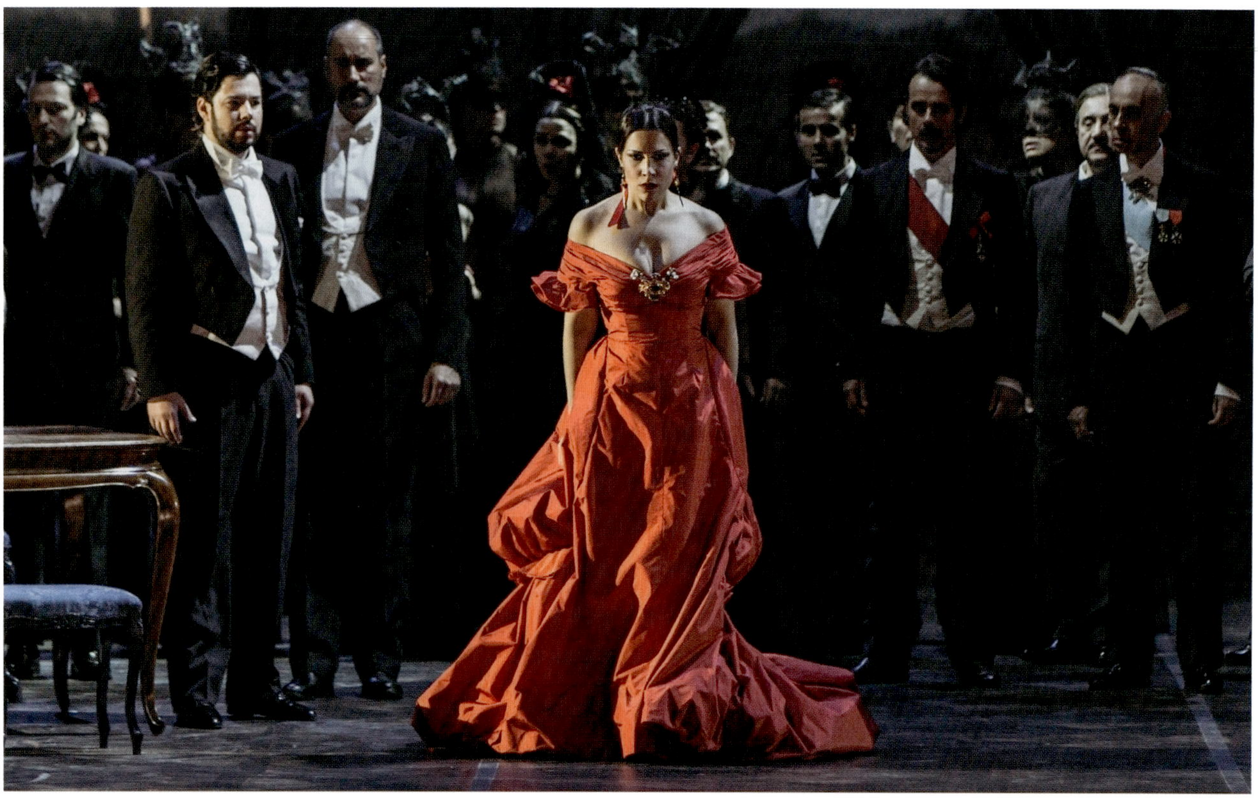

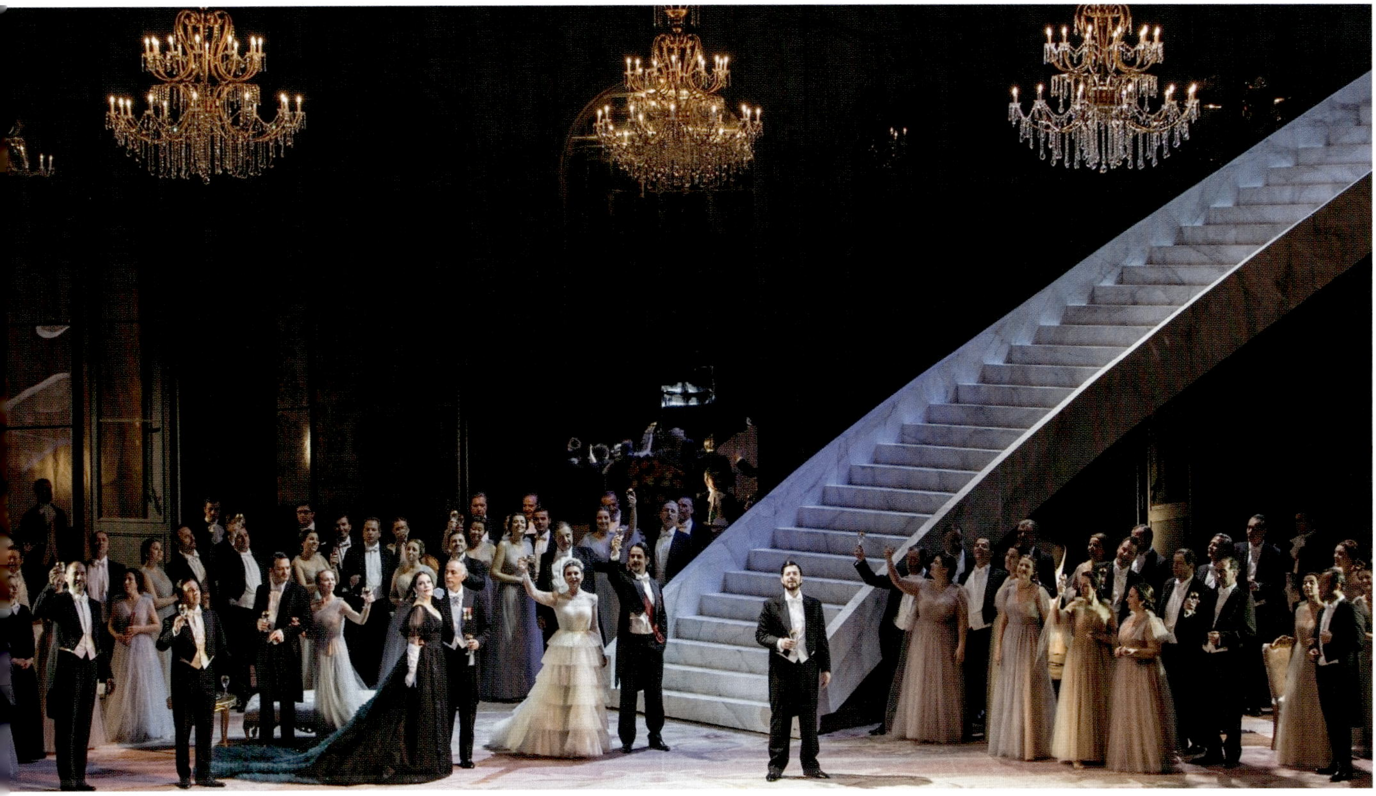

Above: *With the stage sets designed by Nathan Crowley,* La Traviata *returned Coppola to the maximal stylings of Marie Antoinette, but with none of the irony. Opera, she might also have said, was in her blood.*

Coppola hadn't planned on opera, it was simply that she had been invited to direct by the team at Valentino (who were providing the costumes) and 'couldn't say no.'[19] Released from the camera's thirst for reality, grandiosity was the order of the day. The chance to mix extravagant sets, the work of English production designer and friend Nathan Crowley (who had done Batman movies with Christopher Nolan), and elaborate costumes like a living painting.

The production was filmed by French cinematographer Philippe Le Sourd (establishing a relationship that would continue across her next three films), and released into cinema worldwide. Akin to *A Very Murray Christmas* and *Marc by Sofia*, completists consider it canon. But it is hard to judge on cinematic terms. This is an opera, performed before the footlights.

A long way from the quietude of her early films, the tale of forbidden love across the strata of a restrictive Parisian society, centred on fallen heroine Violetta (Francesca Dotto), does summon an air of romantic tragedy we might construe as Coppola-like. There are certainly hints of *Marie Antoinette* in the sumptuous colours. In its madcap, minor-key way *A Very Murray Christmas* might have whetted her appetite for some full-throated song. Signally a continuing expansion of the Coppola palate and range, *La Traviata* was released on the eve of her next film, which itself could be viewed as operatic.

AN UNCIVIL WAR

The Beguiled (2017)

Her sixth feature film offered a daring move into genre, be it Western or period piece or even horror, but there was still no doubting who was behind the camera

The subway was leaving for Coney Island when Sofia Coppola received the news. She had only recently returned to the comforts of New York and family after a third sojourn at the Cannes Film Festival to bang the drum on behalf of her latest film and ascend the treacherous, red-carpeted steps of the Palais for the official screening, alongside her radiant cast, including Nicole Kidman, Kirsten Dunst, and Elle Fanning. In her wake was a warm response to the $10.5 million American Civil War drama *The Beguiled*.

Times had changed. Coppola had barely made it to the Cannes photo call when word reached her that the first tweet was 'really pro.'[1] The next, she was informed, was 'a badass one.'[2] Praised as a radical change in approach, the movie was making the critics laugh as she hoped it might; they were also catching all the coded glances the camera had carefully sought out on set, the intimate language of rivalry that would seed violence and death. *The Beguiled* was charged material.

As *Time's* Stephanie Zacharek assessed the movie, 'It's essentially unlike any other Sofia Coppola film, a serene, supple picture that hits more than a few notes of despair.'[3]

Nevertheless, Coppola had no expectations of competing for the major prizes. Lacking her father's sense of entitlement, she was pleased enough to have launched her new film unscathed. Thus she had happily returned to the relative anonymity of New York, the exhaustion of explaining herself done with for now. The film would be officially released two months later on 30 June 2017.

So it was she was taking her daughters for a day out to the sea front amusement park when the first call came through from Focus Features, Universal's artier-inclined arm behind *The Beguiled*, announcing that she had won an award. 'They didn't say what prize, they just said it was a prize,'[4] she recalled.

Surfacing at Coney Island, her phone rang again. This time it was Thierry Frémaux, august head of the festival, who informed her that she was the recipient of the Best Director prize. The significance was huge both in terms of her own reputation and the industry at large. It was fifty-six

Right: *Identity crisis – in* The Beguiled, *Elle Fanning features as the strong-willed Alicia, who is awakening to the idea of her own sexual allure.*

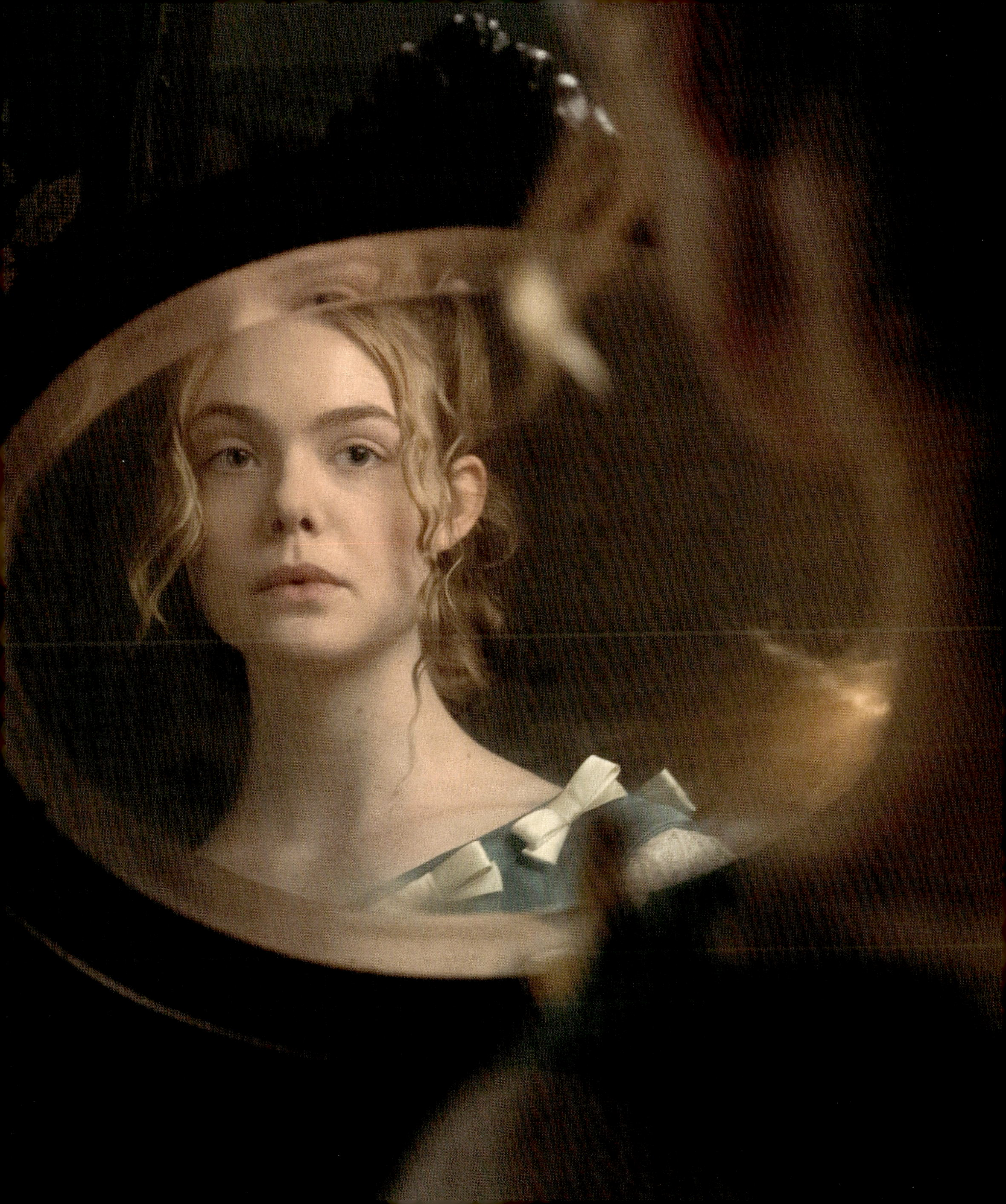

Right: *In 1961, the Russian Yuliya Solntseva was the first female to win Best Director at the Cannes Film Festival...*

Far right: *... and it would take until 2017 for another woman to receive that award – Sofia Coppola, for her exotic genre piece* The Beguiled.

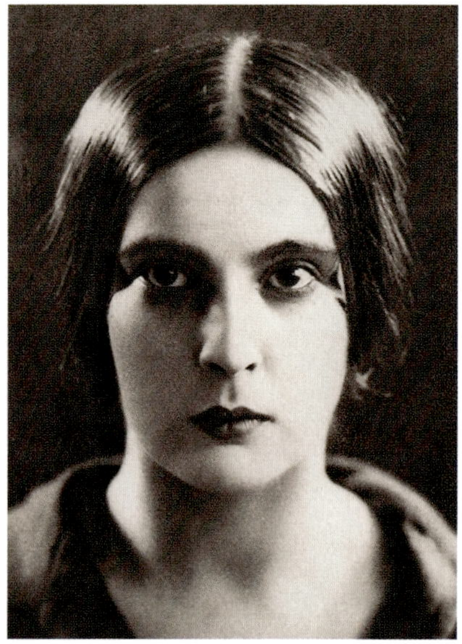

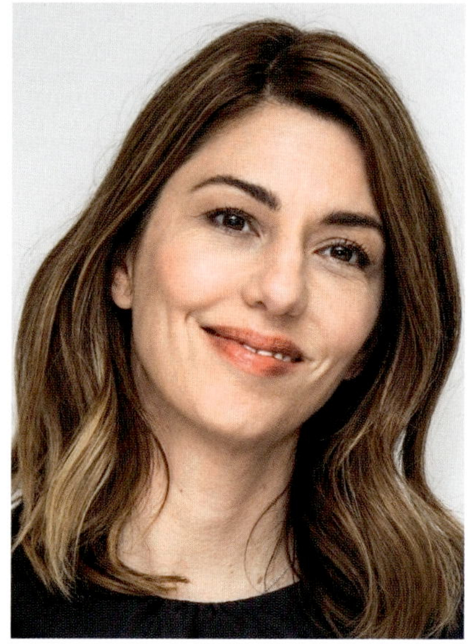

years since the only other female winner, Yuliya Solntseva, director of *Chronicle of Flaming Years* in 1961.

But history would have to wait as phone reception wavered and her daughters jostled for her attention, and the award-winning director spent the day among Coney Island's ageing rollercoasters.

It might not be in her nature to storm any ramparts, but Coppola was well aware that she remained a rarity as a working female director, pursuing a vision that could be considered female (if labels had to be applied). 'I just think, half the world is female, so I just make what I want to see, and I feel there are other women out there that want to see a point of view closer to theirs.'[5]

Speaking at the Cannes press conference, Kidman was vociferous about consciously choosing to work with female directors, and had some stark figures to hand: only 4.2 percent of feature films in 2016 were directed by women; or one in every twenty-four productions. Out of nineteen films competing in the main thread of the 2017 festival, only three were directed by women.

When it was first announced, *The Beguiled* had caused a stir. A Western? Well, not quite. The genre at work here is elusive. A remake of a heated Clint Eastwood-Don Siegel picture of 1971 that had not exactly stood the test of time? Well, it was going to be drawn from the same novel by Thomas P. Cullinan, but was effectively an alternative adaptation, using the same story but reorienting the focus – telling it differently. A plush period melodrama to be made with stunt men (a first for Coppola) and elements of horror even? Well yes, on both counts.

'I would never want to remake someone else's film,'[6] insisted Coppola again and again. It was just such a curious story, all these different women cut off from the world. There are echoes of *The Virgin Suicides*: girls at windows, men arriving at the door, a torrent of upholstery and sexual awakening, that aura of memory. Only the desperate results are not suicide but murder. Likewise Coppola shifts the story to a female perspective, where the Siegel film was strictly seen from the unwholesome perspective of Union solder Corporal McBurney, played by Eastwood at the height of his fame.

The set-up is deceptively simple. In 1864 Virginia, three years into the Civil War (a chorus of distant cannons lingers in the air), a wounded Union deserter (Colin Farrell as the new McBurney) is found at the gates of the Miss Martha Farnsworth Seminary for Young Ladies. Miss Farnsworth herself (Kidman), a rigid governess, orders him to be taken in and cared for, but not without a presentiment of the disturbance he will bring to the stultified regime still in place beneath her roof. All the local men have long since departed (and, in Coppola's telling, the slaves too), leaving a fragile balance among those left behind, including Dunst's teacher Edwina and Fanning's intemperate Alicia, eldest of the five remaining students – the two actresses a conscious reminder of Coppola's intricate past. The civility that is maintained will prove a thin veneer across more primal urges.

The idea had come by chance: Anne Ross, her regular production designer, had suggested she go back and watch the original. There might be something there, she said, only half joking. Coppola and Ross had been friends for decades, all the

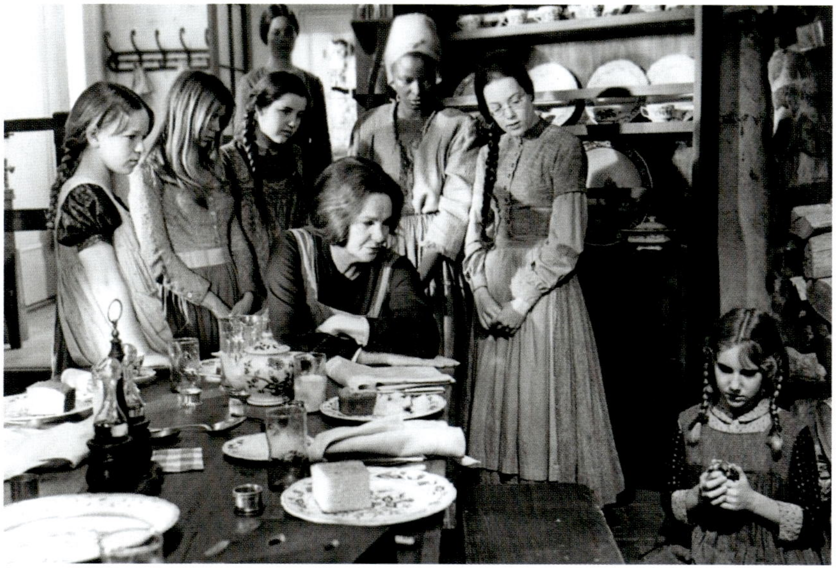

Left: *The original version of* The Beguiled *(1971), directed by Don Siegel, featured Geraldine Page as Miss Farnsworth, the role Nicole Kidman would take in Sofia Coppola's readaptation of the book in 2017.*

Below: *The pale ladies – Coppola's female cast for* The Beguiled. *From the left: Kirsten Dunst (Edwina), Angourie Rice (Jane), Emma Howard (Emily), Nicole Kidman (Miss Farnsworth), Elle Fanning (Alicia, in the chair), Addison Riecke (Marie), and Oona Laurence (Amy).*

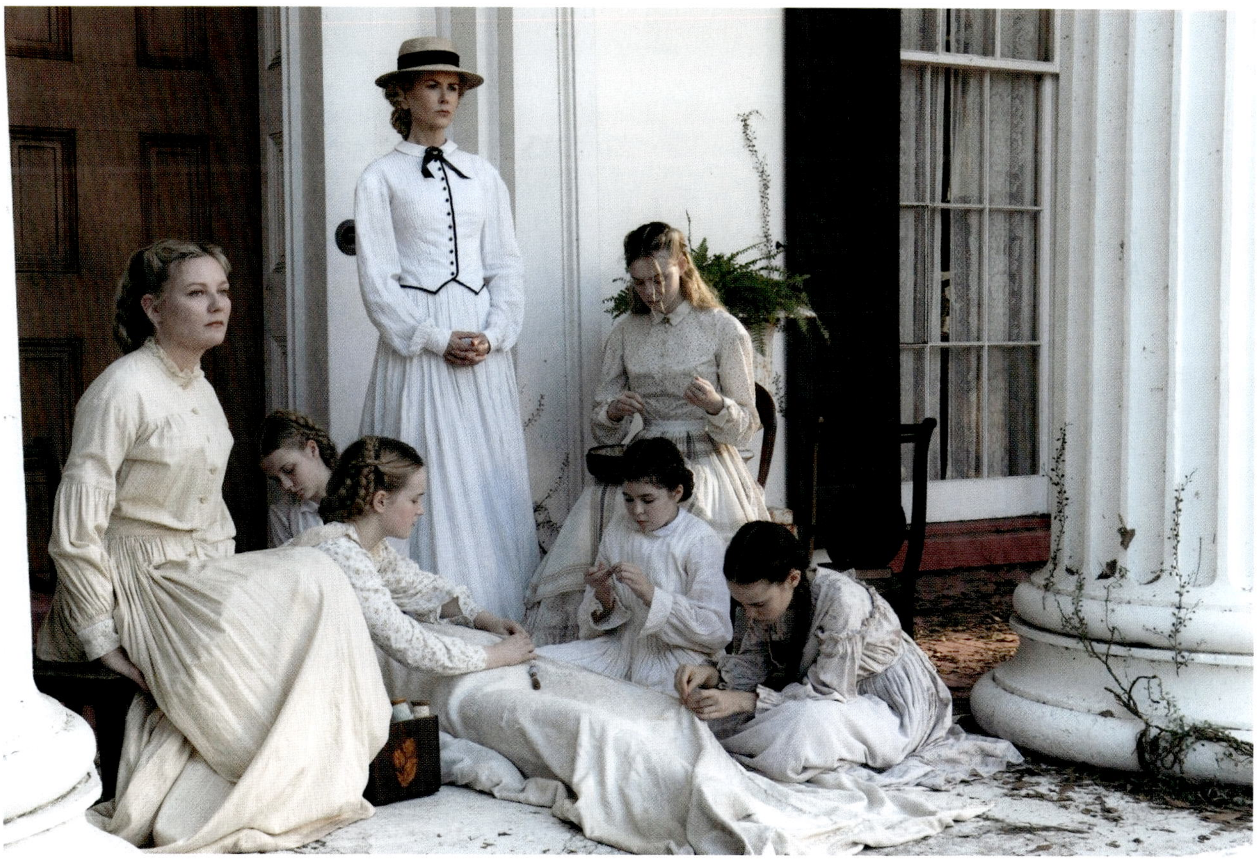

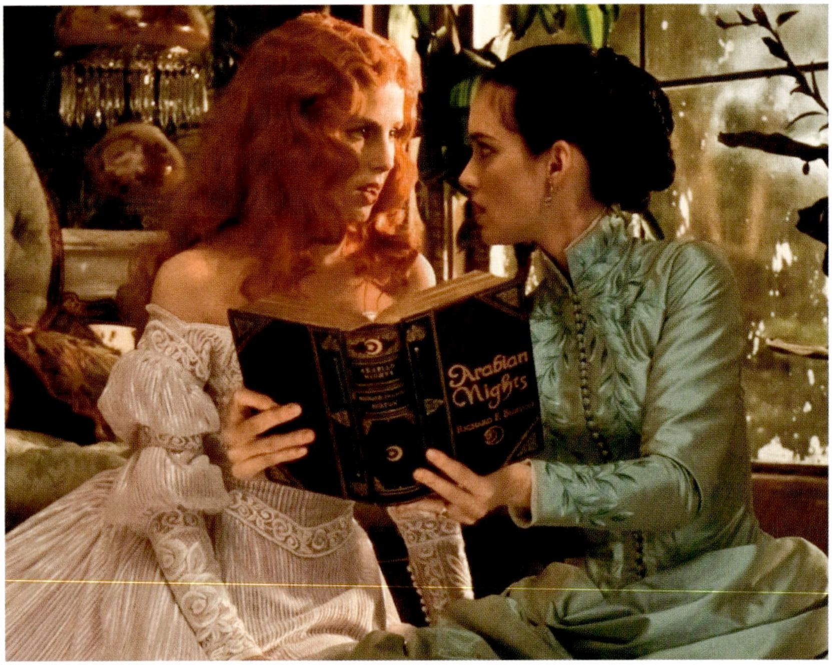

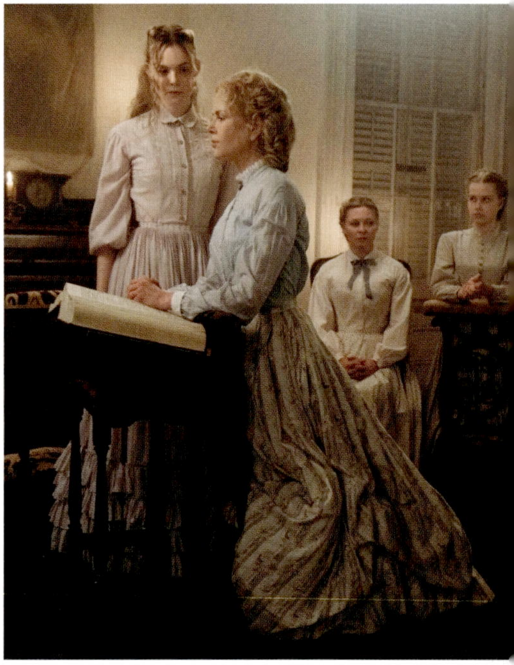

Above left: *In 1992, Francis Ford Coppola would try his own take on the gothic with a florid adaptation,* Bram Stoker's Dracula, *which featured Sadie Frost (left) and Winona Ryder (right)...*

Above right: *...Sofia Coppola's venture into the genre,* The Beguiled, *is far more subtle, though not without its heated passions running beneath the surface.*

way back, in fact, to when the designer had served as an assistant on the more palpitating gothic fevers of Francis Ford Coppola's take on *Bram Stoker's Dracula*. They had then both crewed on Lucas Reiner's zany time-travel comedy *The Spirit of '76*, where Sofia had been hired to do the costumes. With design integral even at the writing stage of Coppola's projects, Ross comes onboard at their very inception, providing her own set of mood boards. They know how to communicate with one another. How to suggest ideas.

So Coppola rewatched Siegel's film and in turn tracked down a copy of the original novel, a pulp title from 1966. The book offered something different again, each chapter was from a different character's perspective, but quality-wise it wasn't really worth reading. The Ohio-born Cullinan was a playwright primarily, but pivoted to novels with a Civil War theme, interested in the potential for evil that lurked beneath notions of civility – America was a society that had gone to war with itself. Staying in the Italian countryside, a long way from New York and the 'professional writing world,'[7] she slowly went through the book, marking up the passages that stirred up images, while her children swam outside in the sunshine.

The Eastwood movie, to her mind, was more feverish, even weird, this macho nightmare it was impossible to forget. McBurney was a wounded rooster in a henhouse. It may be the most charismatically unpleasant role the star ever entertained. Both Eastwood and Siegel had fought to keep the book's *Grand Guignol*, leg-lopping finale.

Coppola wanted to see McBurney through the eyes of these abandoned women and then fill her film with what she could add from 'imagination and life and stuff.'[8] Even if she had grown up in a very different era, this was her gift. Real emotion was her primary palate. However, there were to be none of the postmodern games of *Marie Antoinette*: the surface should remain purely period, with an aroma of the now roused by the novel's predicament. Steve Erickson of the *Nashville Scene* wasn't the only critic to discern 'a feminist spin on the narrative.'[9]

Beneath her choices lay that unconscious cycle of adaptations and original material. After *A Very Murray Christmas*, which was almost made up on the spot, this was a story that spoke to both filmmaking and literary tradition.

It had been an odd turn of events, but typically Hollywood, that her new film would be backed by the same studio with which she hadn't seen eye to eye over *The Little Mermaid* – and even that she was venturing down the studio path again at all. This was mostly a matter of expediency: Universal held the rights. The project was also put together under the mantle of Focus Features, ostensibly the studio's independent arm (an oxymoron that speaks of how compartmentalized the industry's thinking can be), happy to be in the Sofia business. For further clarity, Focus had previously financed the loosey-goosey charms of *Somewhere* (though may have been quietly pleased that *The Beguiled* resembled a movie), so there was good history as well as bad. To conclude then, it was a studio film, but everyone could pretend otherwise.

As its Cannes debut revealed, this was a fascinating switch into genre: not strictly a Western, more of a Southern Gothic, offering a chance to play with all these traditional motifs. The edginess of *The Bling Ring* was flowering into something more pungent – a new side to the older Coppola, where the dreaminess slips into nightmare. There was, she sensed, a fascinating question at the heart of the story. What happened to these Southern women, raised to cater for men, when the men went away to war and in

Below left: *Clint Eastwood, as Union soldier McBurney, gets a shave from the slave Hallie (Mae Mercer) in the 1971* The Beguiled. *The character of Hallie would be controversially swerved in Coppola's version.*

Below right: *In the 1971 take, McBurney plies his charms on Edwina (Elizabeth Hartman), the school teacher played by Kirsten Dunst in Coppola's reimagining.*

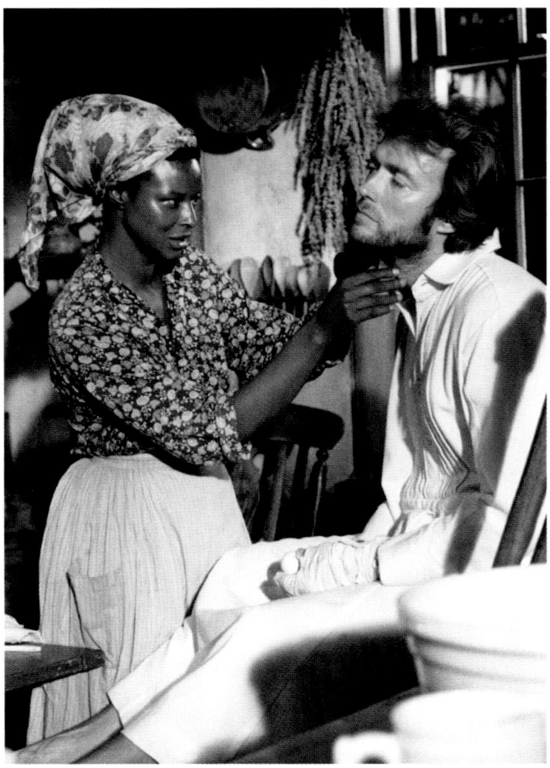

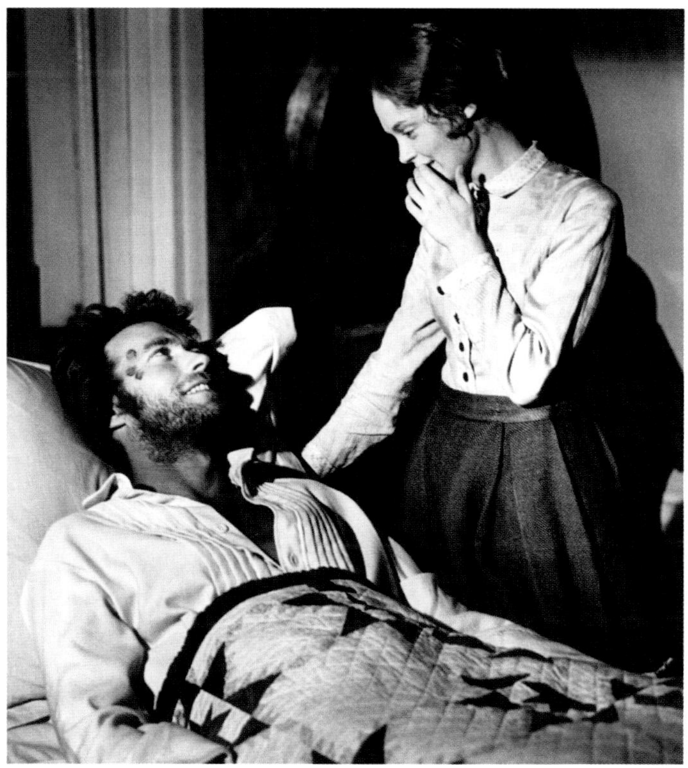

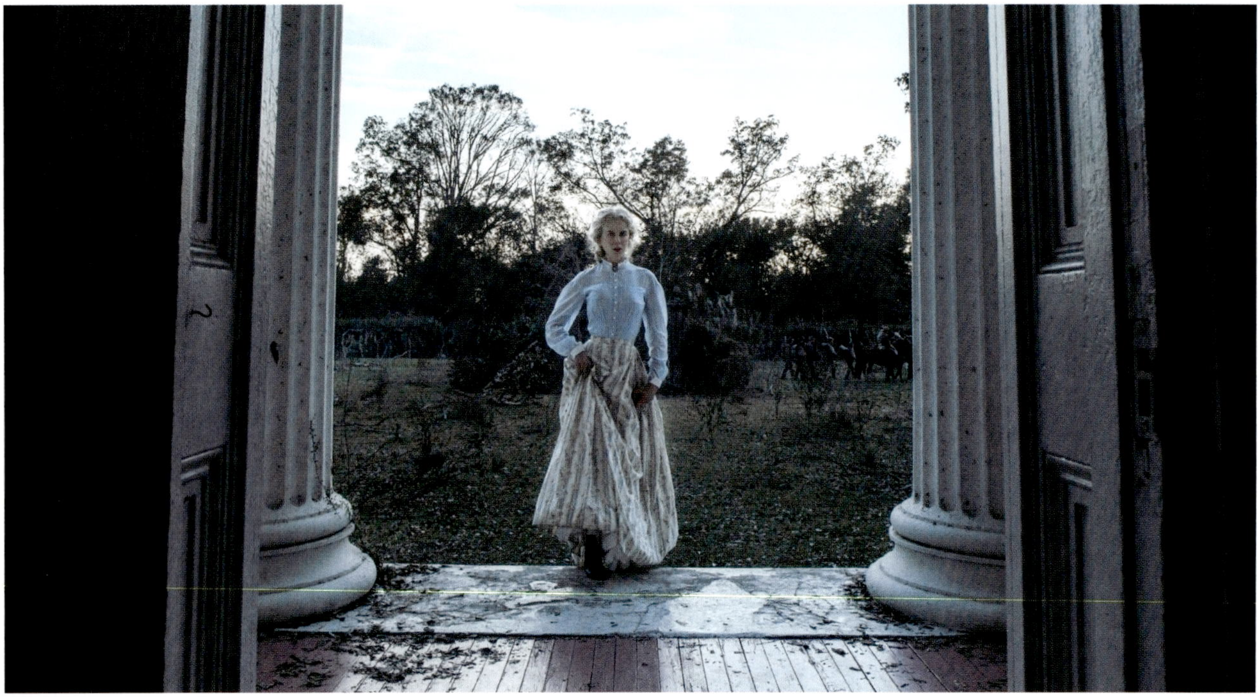

many cases never returned? How might they evolve in their absence? A world of porcelain convention was cracking under the pressure, and with this intruder in their midst liable to shatter entirely.

There was so much going on beneath the surface: all this 'non-verbal communication'[10] between these women with their staunch hierarchies. And with this alien creature, this man with his festering wounds. Everything was so over-the-top, with the possibility for delicious melodrama. 'Southern women were an exaggeration of femininity and how women should act,'[11] she said. It was all about performance: the barely concealed scorn, the frozen smiles, the serrated comments.

The exteriors were found at an 1846 Greek-revival in Napoleonville, Louisiana, a former plantation transformed by subtle means into a state of neglect, as if nature was reclaiming the land. Everything had to be a little overripe. Spanish moss hung across the cypress trees like discarded clothing. More than ever, atmosphere was critical, the heat rising out from the earth and into these women. The tone, she said, 'came a lot from the location.'[12] The score by Phoenix is sparse and classical, a twist on Monteverdi's *Magnificat*. For the first time there had been no soundtrack to accompany the writing, only the murmur of the Italian countryside. Sensory effects are integral to the film: birdsong, wind, and that distant rumour of cannon fire. There needed to be a sense of arrested time and arrested passion.

The Beguiled is closer to the natural world than any of Coppola's previous films. The camera peers through branches, with long shots of tiny figures framed against trees or the phallic pillars of the house. It's as if someone else is watching.

The interiors were shot in one of the oldest houses in New Orleans, owned curiously enough by the actress Jennifer Coolidge. They tested candlelight and

Above: *It's all in the framing – Sofia Coppola deliberately poses her characters against the rigid fixtures of the old house, the place in which they are all trapped.*

Opposite: *Table talk – the scant pupils and teachers share their (authentically) candlelit mealtimes, a chance for Coppola to reveal the fragile social hierarchies that already exist within the house.*

> You want to follow the emotional state of the characters in a visual way... The film starts off in this lacy, pastel, soft world, but then the softness goes away and it gets darker...
> **SOFIA COPPOLA**

filmed authentically within the dancing shadows of the era, a marked contrast to the period looks of *The Virgin Suicides* (gauzy and perfumed) and *Marie Antoinette* (pretty in postmodern pink). Claustrophobia was key, the feeling that these walls are closing in. The sense of place is impeccable. Despite the distant and ultimately violent new milieu, Coppola's preoccupations are satisfyingly in evidence: female identity, male encounters, and a metaphorical hotel suffocating its clientele.

'You want to follow the emotional state of the characters in a visual way,'[13] noted Coppola. She and Ross had looked closely at Peter Weir's *Picnic at Hanging Rock* (a regular touchstone) as well as Roman Polanski's 1979 Thomas Hardy adaptation *Tess*, for the lacy delicacy of the costumes, this veil of femininity. She read books on nineteenth-century etiquette, deducing they would wear no makeup or bare any flesh, and studied materials in the Met costume archive, seeing how the dresses would have faded from being repeatedly washed. They were cut off from the world, these women, and wouldn't have had a lot. They themselves were faded, colourless, ghosts haunting this remote place. Historical realism was intermingled with otherworldliness.

With cinematographer Philippe Le Sourd, she studied photographs and paintings from the era. The look and design maps a shift deeper and deeper into the gothic. 'The film starts off in this lacy, pastel, soft world,' explained Coppola, 'but then the softness goes away and it gets darker...'[14] John Singer Sargent's paintings offered women in white dresses against black backgrounds.

The ensemble of seven females itself charts a journey from girlhood into womanhood, capturing Coppola's thematic arc in a single film: Kidman (forty-nine), Dunst (thirty-five), Fanning (eighteen),

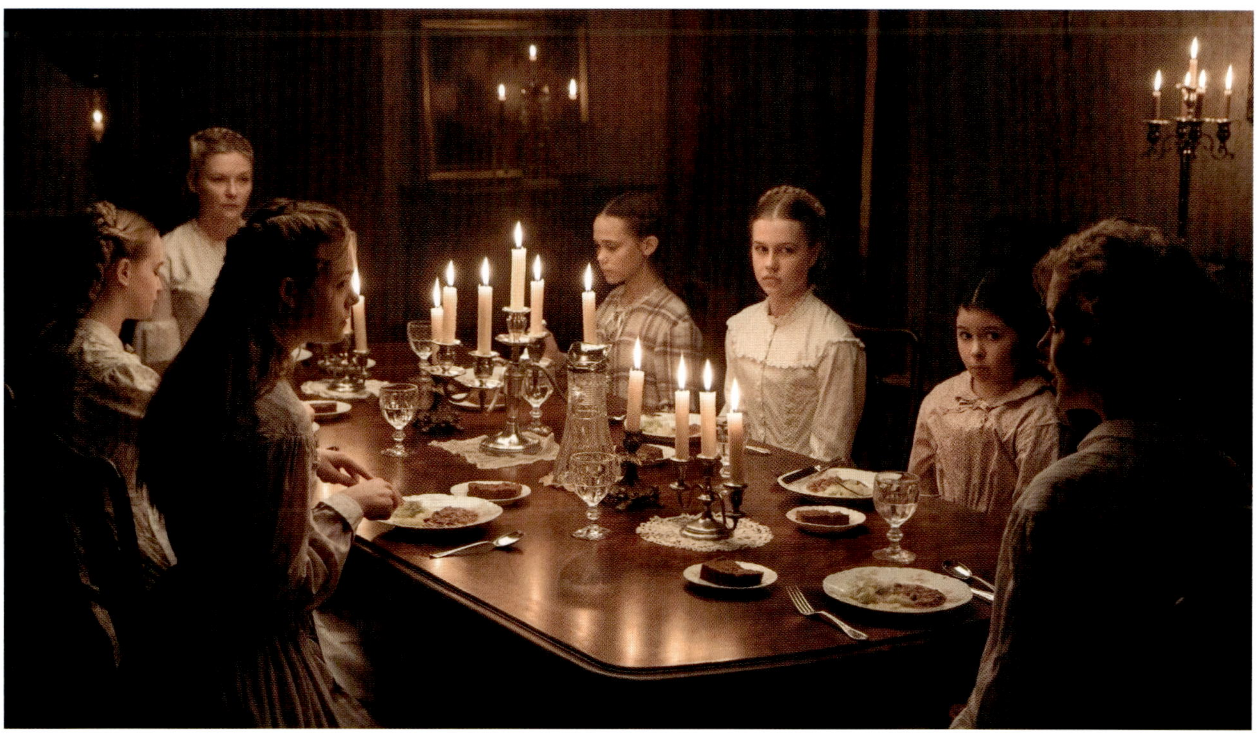

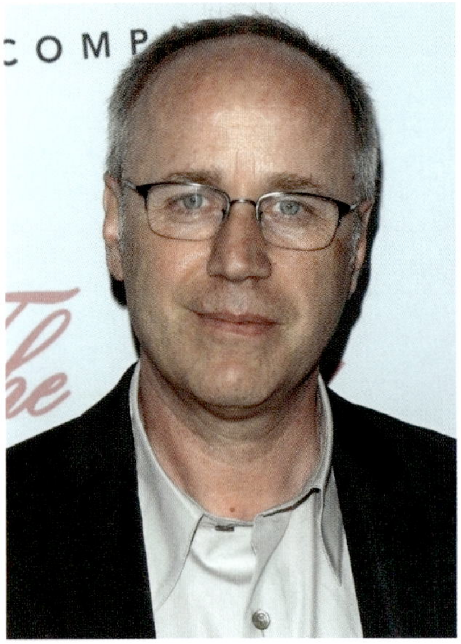

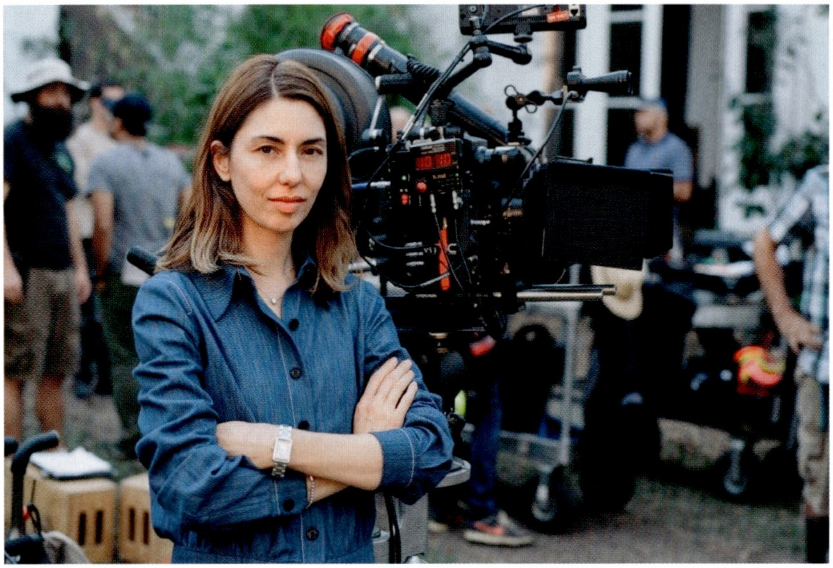

Above left: *Cinematographer Philippe Le Sourd works wonders with the limited light sources of the period, giving the film a sense of unease, even of the otherworldly.*

Above right: *Sofia Coppola posing on the set of* The Beguiled *in Napoleonville, Louisiana. The film – plot-driven, genre-leaning, period, and murderously intentioned – was a thrilling challenge to her typical approach.*

Oona Laurence (fourteen), Angourie Rice (sixteen), Emma Howard (sixteen), and Addison Riecke (thirteen). The director enjoyed the fact that Dunst and Fanning were naturally inhabiting older characters, and also working against the flow of their personalities (and previous Coppola roles). Dunst, she noted, 'plays a really repressed character and is not like that at all.'[15]

Edwina is an outsider herself. 'She is a little bit of a town girl,'[16] as Martha dismissively addresses her at the dinner table, code for more worldly, less classy, the kind who would don an unseemly shoulder-baring gown for dinner with their new guest. For Edwina, McBurney simply presents the possibility of escape from the time-lapsed South. Whereas Fanning's Alicia, according to Coppola, is 'vain and self-absorbed,'[17] closer to the character's depiction in the book: a young girl awakening to the effect her looks have on a man. They all respond to this brooding catalyst as if in their collective need and loneliness they had conjured him up like the Devil.

Coppola is interested in how these women interact with each other. In changing the perspective from male to female, they lose the mystique of book and 1971 film (and the mythologizing of *The Virgin Suicides* and Marc in *The Bling Ring*) and become human. She saw the story as fundamentally about how they are 'being torn between what they should do, and their desires.'[18] Instincts as shrill as the gasping needs of *The Bling Ring*.

Martha is the first of Coppola's female protagonists to be a fully grown woman (a breed of distant mother notwithstanding: Kathleen Turner as Mrs Lisbon, Marianne Faithfull as Empress Maria Theresa, Leslie Mann as new-age goof Laurie Moore). She had pictured Kidman from the moment she started writing, going backstage in London to hand her the finished script: the celebrated Australian actress had worked with Kubrick, won an Oscar for *The Hours*, and listed films as diverse as *Moulin Rouge, Dogville,* and *Paddington* in her résumé: she was currently appearing in *Photograph 51* in the West End. Kidman loved what she read, but keen to sample the fabled harmonics of a Coppola set, hadn't needed much persuading.

What impressed Kidman the most was how a director with such a strong vision

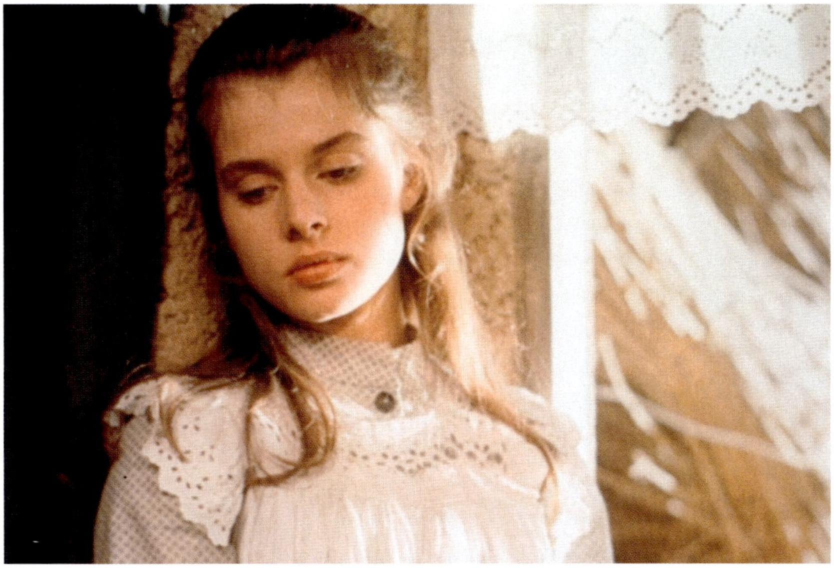

Left: *Nastassja Kinski in Roman Polanski's Tess (1979), one of the key inspirations for the lacy, textured look of* The Beguiled.

Below: *Kirsten Dunst as the lovelorn Edwina in* The Beguiled. *Having Dunst return in an older guise was a deliberate ploy, positioning the film within the context of Coppola's explorations of womanhood.*

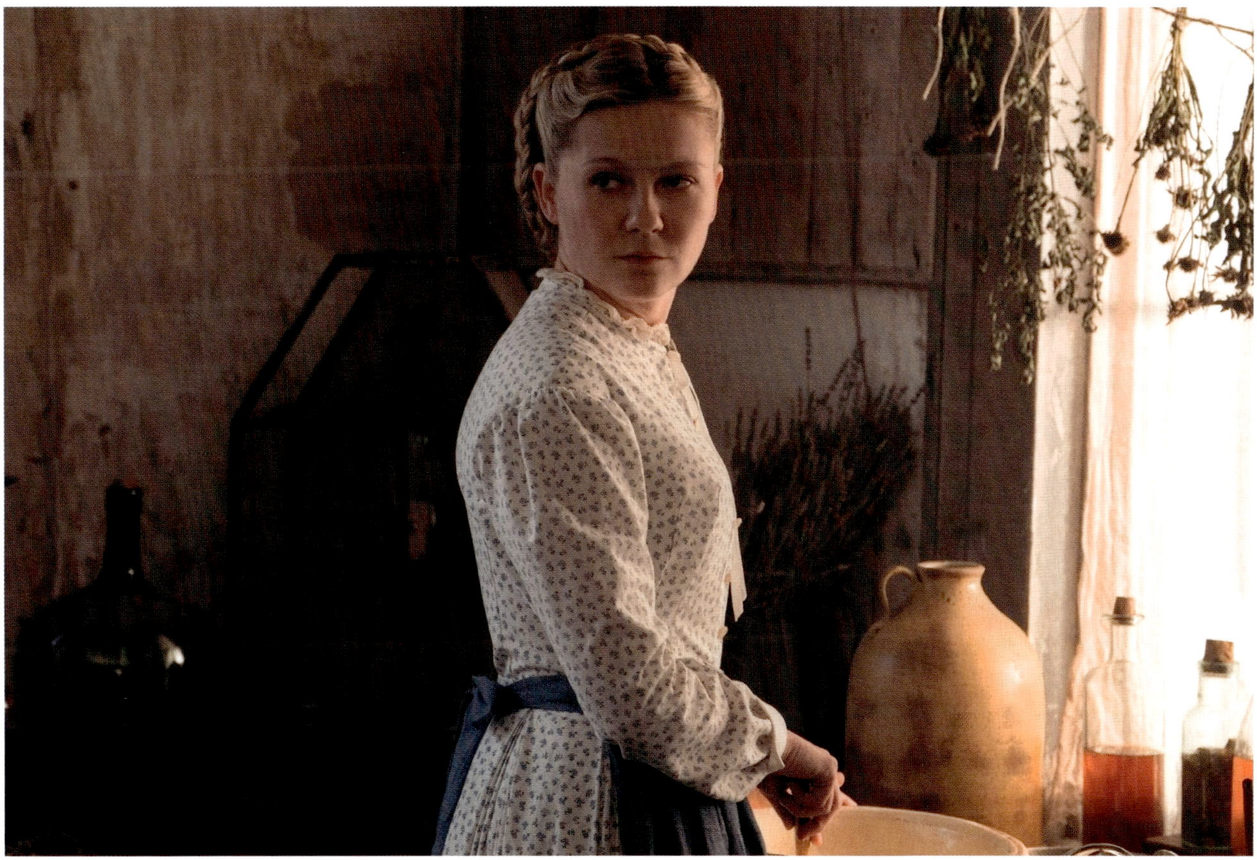

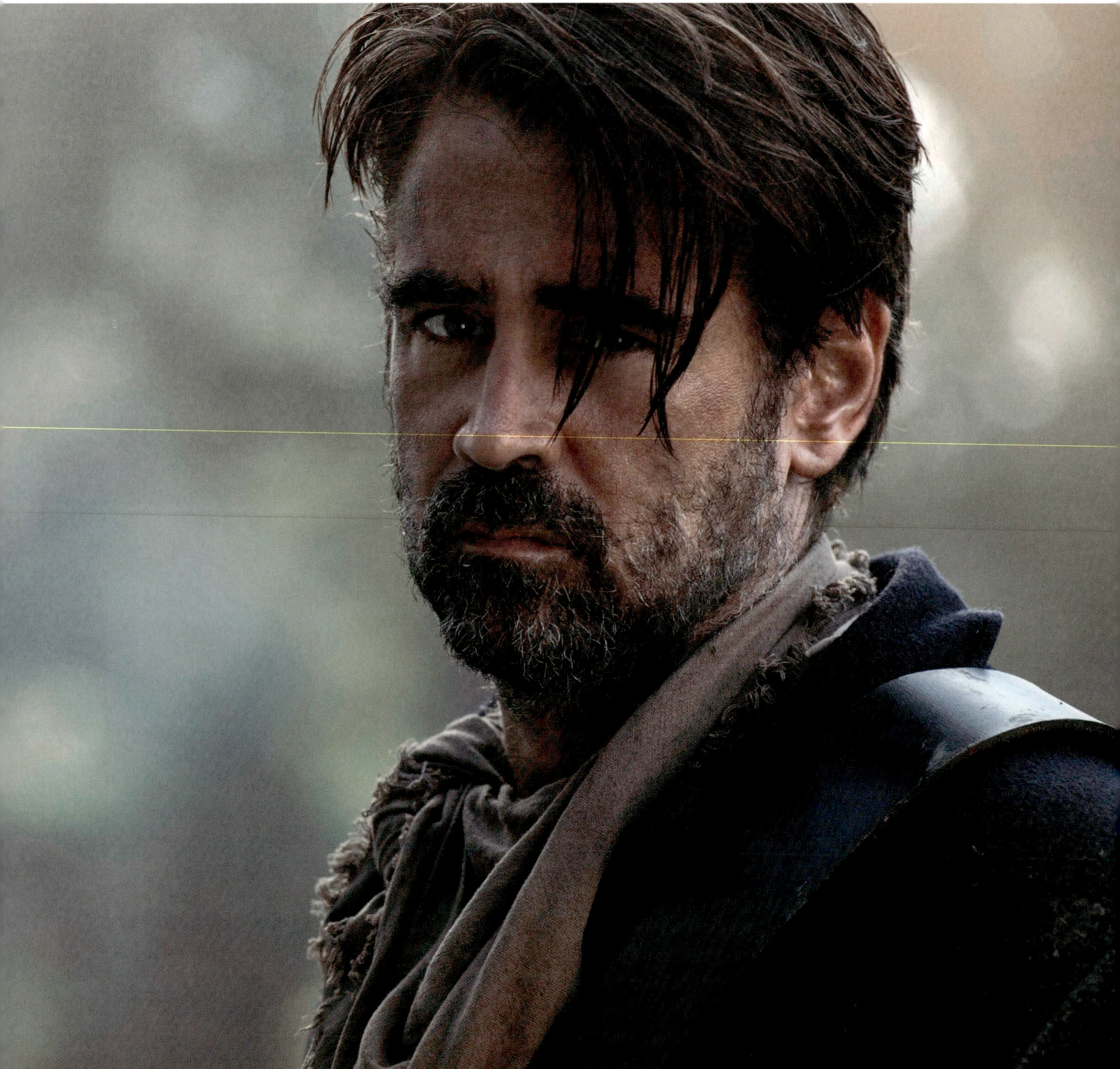

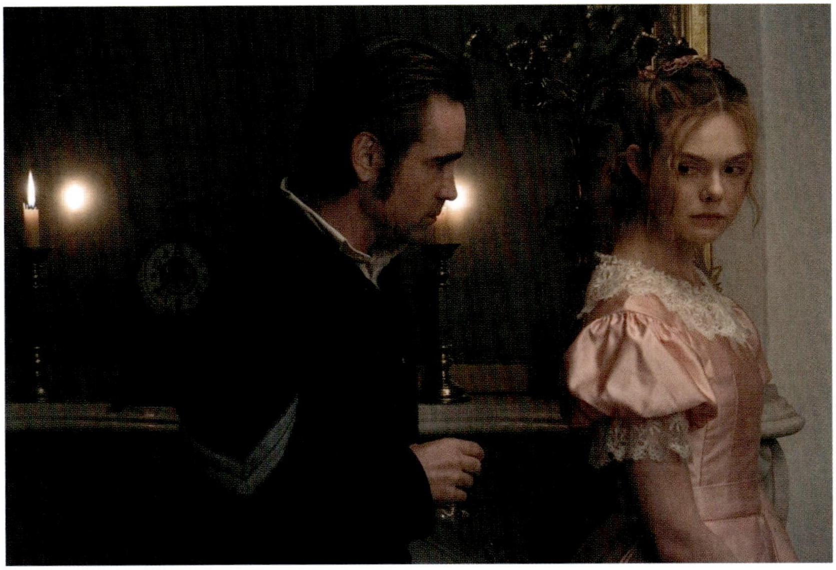

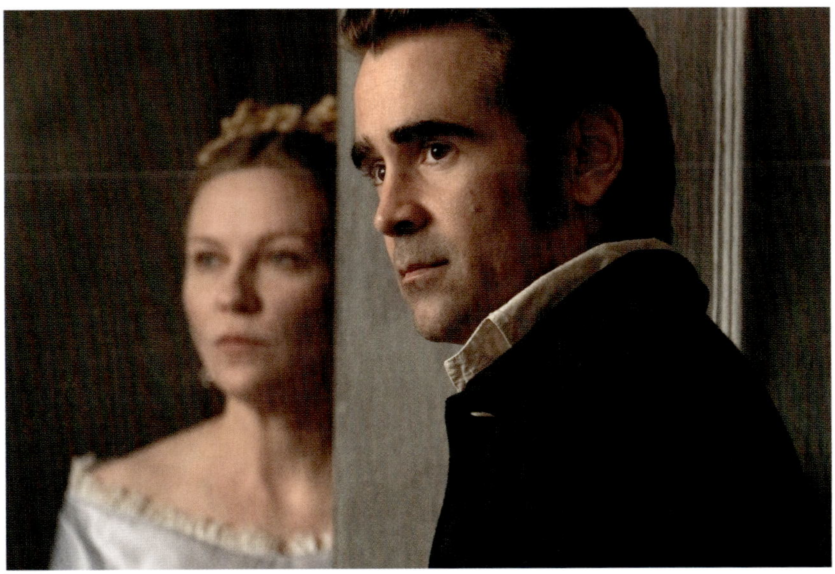

Opposite: *A rooster in the hen house – Colin Farrell takes over from Clint Eastwood as McBurney, on the one hand the Devil in their midst, on the other a desperate opportunist simply trying to survive.*

Top: *McBurney will work his charms (and be worked upon) as he targets both the sexually awakening Alicia (Elle Fanning)...*

Above: *... and the more worldly Edwina (Kirsten Dunst), who is looking for a way back to civilization from this isolated house.*

for what she wanted could remain so demure and elegant. It was all analogous, she thought: there was 'an elegance'[19] to the filmmaking and the atmosphere on set. 'You just sort of want to do anything to make her happy,'[20] she said. Coppola had mastered the Zen art of getting exactly what she wanted by non-aggression; Bill Murray christened her the 'Velvet Hammer.'[21] There is, we suspect, a hint of Coppola in Martha, keeping her composure (just about) amid riptides of emotion.

Farrell thrived in what he called the 'immense lack of tension'[22] on set, watching his director assemble her shots almost by osmosis. Between set-ups beneath the humid Napoleonville sun, the cast would sit around a picnic table just as the actors had lounged on the suburban lawns of *The Virgin Suicides*. It was such a counterpoint to what was going on in front of the camera. When they came to shoot the darker elements of the story, things may have become more serious, more focused emotionally, but the sense of camaraderie was never lost.

Known for his charismatic and frequently loquacious presence in *Miami Vice, Minority Report,* and *In Bruges*, and another eager to work with Coppola, Farrell revelled in the hot-blooded subtext, slowly exposing the rogue beneath McBurney's charm, a dark naturalism aided by a rare chance to retain his Dublin accent. 'In the book he was an Irish immigrant so I like that Colin keeps his accent and he's more exotic to them, just to really contrast how feminine they are,'[23] explained Coppola. Farrell saw McBurney as a survivor, this dirt-poor, immigrant man helplessly conscripted into the army who 'loses himself'[24] in this almost hallucinatory environment. Coppola wanted him morally complex, a figure both manipulative and mysterious. His sincerity is a moveable feast.

We have never sampled such a vulpine creature in Coppola's world before (Johnny in *Somewhere* can barely summon a facial expression). With black, flowing locks, heavy brows, and fierce sideburns, McBurney has the aura of Heathcliff about him, or a werewolf, a herald for the mercurial Elvis to come in *Priscilla*.

McBurney will draw both Edwina and Alicia to his flame, and even stir dormant feelings in Martha, setting them off against each other. Things reach a feverish head when he's caught in bed with Alicia and in the confusion takes a fall down the stairs, badly breaking an already injured leg. Assessing the damage, Martha decrees that they must, for mercy's sake, amputate. 'Edwina, bring me the anatomy book,'[25] she snaps, not without a hint of relish. These are ghoulish currents delivered with the same Coppola concentration on texture. Martha's blood-stained nightgown a splash of horrific imagery in the inky, chittering night, before the scene cuts to the morning after, leaving the sawing to our fertile imaginations. It is a film more concerned with aftermaths.

However we read the necessity of Martha's actions – medical emergency or romantic vengeance – no one is missing the emasculation metaphor. It also marks the turning point. Tensions rapidly evolve within the Seminary walls. McBurney becomes less the blue-belly Yankee enemy as the battle lines are drawn between the North and South of the sexes. Farrell put it more simply: 'It was just that he was a man.'[26]

McBurney turns savage, a one-legged Mr Hyde thrashing around in his locked room, the camera lingering on the key. The power has shifted. Time to pick some unsavoury mushrooms.

So *The Beguiled* is Coppola moving within a more established storytelling mode. Cause and effect, the building of tension to dramatic crescendos. No one had ever described her as visceral before. Yet there was no doubting who was behind the camera.

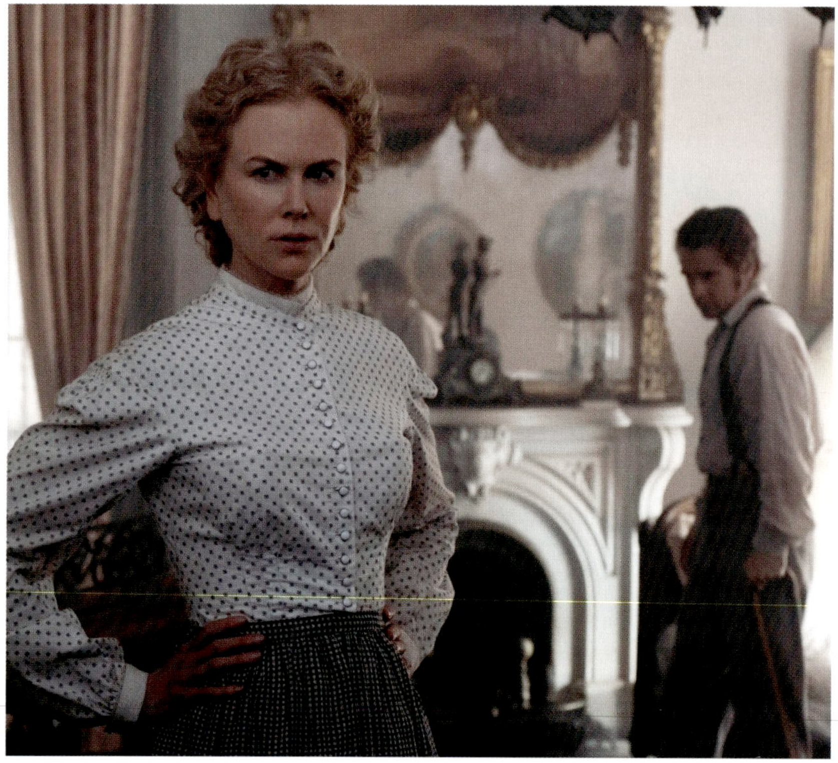

'The camera in her version of *The Beguiled* expresses and inhabits the women's isolation...' noted Ryan Gilbey in the *New Statesman,* 'while her delicate touch as a director keeps the mood frisky even at its most fraught.'[27]

J. Hoberman, in the *New York Review of Books*, praised a film 'more contemplative and psychologically complex'[28] than the original.

In the *New York Times*, A.O. Scott saw a film that was 'less a hothouse flower than a bonsai garden, a work of cool, exquisite artifice that evokes wildness on a small, controlled scale.'[29]

'She's so tasteful and keeps it classy,'[30] reported Fanning on the finished film.

In other words, Coppola was having her cake and eating it. These are gothic conventions delivered in her own gilded handwriting. Here too lay the rub. Was it all too tasteful? In her natural poise

Above and opposite: *The Civil War becomes a battle of the sexes – Miss Farnsworth, a forthright Southern lady (Nicole Kidman), will wrestle with her own desires as she attempts to deal with this dark, disruptive force in her seminary.*

and restraint, had Coppola tempered the swampy weirdness of the Eastwood flick? Her version never feels as outrageous as the 1971 picture, where McBurney's presence unlocks flashbacks to Martha's incestuous relationship with her brother.

'*The Beguiled* '71 gluts,' wrote Melissa Anderson regretfully in the *Village Voice*, 'Coppola's film tamps down and reduces.'[31] Could she simply not bring herself to depict the pivotal operation?

All of which raised a further question. Did we even want Coppola to roughen up her tranquil mood with hacksaws and poisoned soup? In enlarging her spectrum, was there the chance she would lose what made her special?

The studio marketing department, at least, could vouchsafe a classic piece of prestige Hollywood filmmaking with movie stars, an elegant period setting, even the hallmarks of genre, and a discernible plot. While not the leap *The Little Mermaid* might have presented, they are both fairy tales in their own way. This was a sought-after broadening of her appeal, and *The Beguiled* performed admirably if unremarkably, making $27 million worldwide.

What no one was expecting was a backlash.

In the lead-up to the film's release, a sense of outrage (stoked by a media in which newsworthiness was increasingly equated with potential outrage) mounted over the fact Coppola had, in effect, whitewashed the film by writing out the slave character Hallie, played by Mae Mercer in the 1971 version. The director had been in London doing press, and it seemed as if every interview was about the race issue. 'Usually, I would just ignore what people were saying, but my ten-year-old-daughter heard us talking, and was like, "Are people going to think we're racist?" I was like, "Oh my God, this has gotten out of control."'[32]

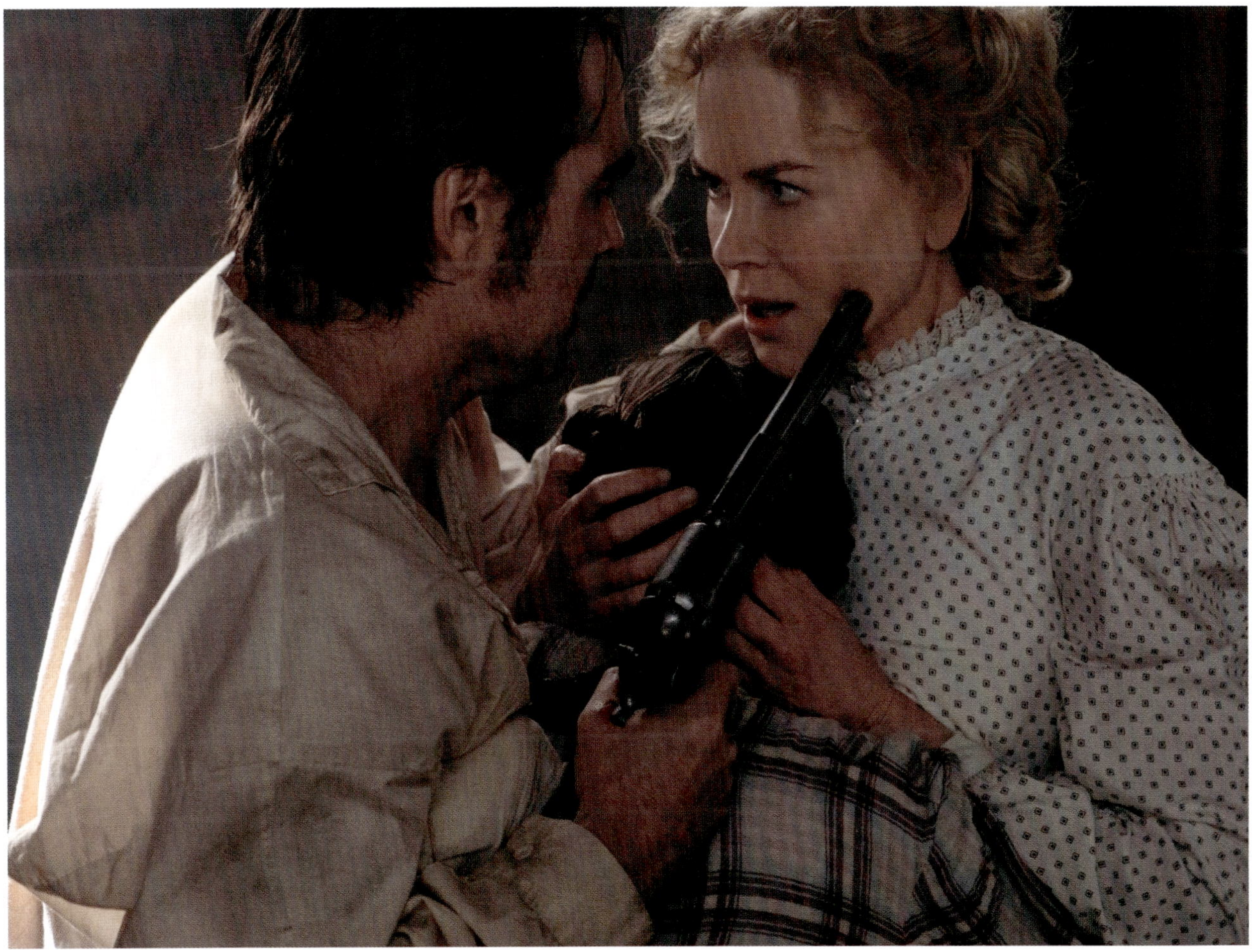

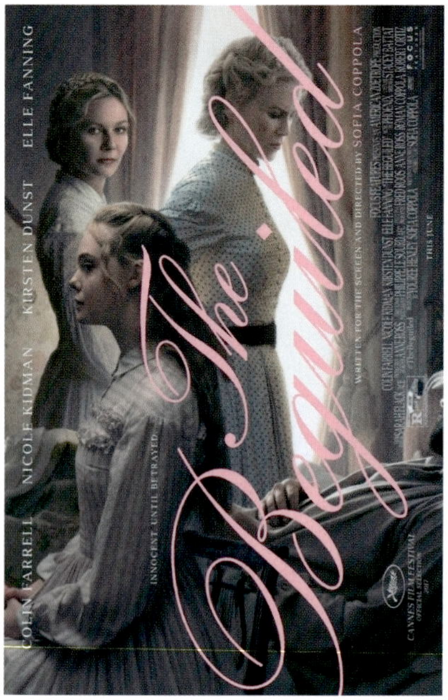

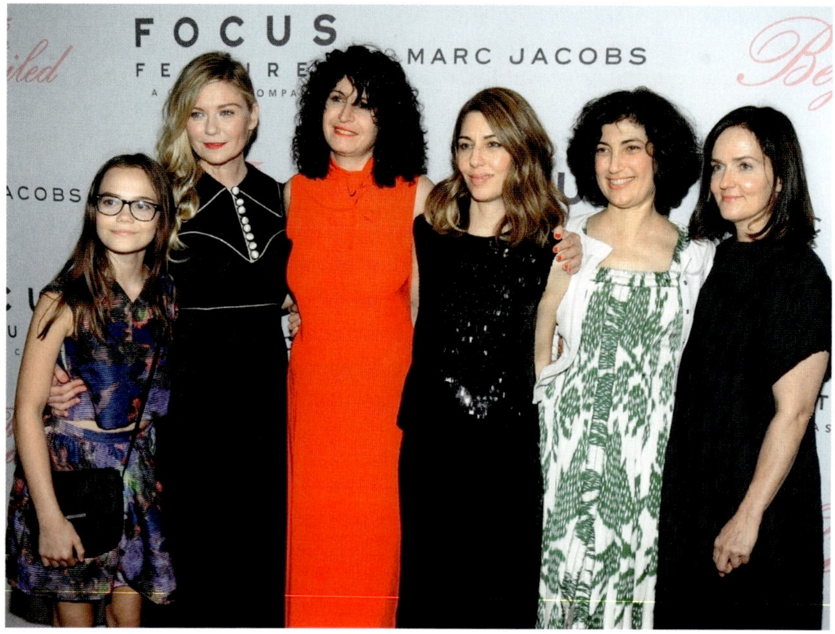

Above left: The Beguiled *is another of those films that could only have been made by Sofia Coppola – something that becomes ever clearer with repeated watching.*

Above right: *Actresses Oona Laurence and Kirsten Dunst join moderator Tamara Jenkins, director Coppola, editor Sarah Flack, and production designer Anne Ross at the New York premiere in 2017.*

Looking back on the short-lived scandal from the vantage point of 2025, she maintained that she had made a purely artistic choice. 'You have to go with your heart, and what you feel right about.'[33] She had been more than aware that she was dealing with a loaded historical moment, but she wanted to speak about this one group of women. 'This was such a particular situation,' she insisted. 'I felt like this tradition of film, with the token servant character, is not something that I want to continue.'[34]

Then this was the director who took the revolution out of *Marie Antoinette*. Coppola isn't a political filmmaker in the broad sense. She prefers to locate something subtly (always subtly) relevant in the cultural worlds in which her characters are embedded: the isolation of wealth, the clamour of fame, social position, and the experience of women. Despite its period setting and deviant comedy, *The Beguiled* was fated to stir up some very modern debate. This is the story of a group of insulated women taking matters into their own hands when a troublesome male presence falls into their company, bringing the toxic to toxic masculinity.

However, as Coppola biographer Hannah Strong noted, 'there's something less triumphant and more devastating about *The Beguiled* and its paradise lost…'[35] The storyteller does not relish their vengeance – still the only murder committed in a Coppola film. These women remain relics trapped in their bygone antebellum, abandoned by the world like the lost Lisbon girls of *The Virgin Suicides*.

GENERATION PERPLEXED

Sofia's fellow filmmakers who have majored in dislocation and angst

Roman Coppola
Though his directing career has been far more sporadic, Coppola's brother Roman has carved out a surreal branch of the family trade with psychedelic, Paris-set, sixties-filmmaking romp *CQ* (look out for the in-jokes on dad), seventies, California-set relationship comedy (with added Bill Murray) *A Glimpse Inside the Mind of Charles Swan III*, and episodes of classical music series *Mozart in the Jungle*. There are familiar hints of tortured artists and otherworldly settings.

Spike Jonze
Coppola's first husband brought an innovative, genre-bending flourish to nineties filmmaking with the likes of *Being John Malkovich* and *Where the Wild Things Are*. For all their whimsical traits, his films have an abiding melancholy. The soft AI-themed sci-fi of *Her* is seen as a riposte to Coppola's barbed references in *Lost in Translation*.

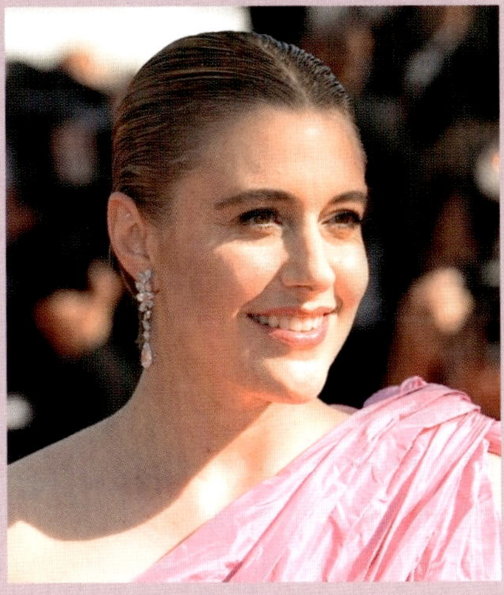

Quentin Tarantino
Coppola's ex-boyfriend needs little introduction. He is the grandstanding *enfant terrible* who shook up indie cinema with the violent, ironic, prolix grooves of *Reservoir Dogs, Pulp Fiction, Inglourious Basterds* et al. Yet there is something reflective and poised in a set of work devoted to character. The sense of city and mood in *Once Upon a Time in Hollywood* surely pays homage to Coppola.

Wes Anderson
A close friend, Wes Anderson (a frequent collaborator with Roman) is both a kindred spirit (and Murray fan) and the exact opposite to Coppola. Such elaborate comedy dramas as *Rushmore, The Royal Tenenbaums,* and *The Grand Budapest Hotel* are as aesthetically pleasing as her work, but made to measure. If Coppola hides within the folds of her films, he makes his presence felt.

Greta Gerwig
Gerwig and Coppola have much in common. *Lady Bird* and *Little Women* lean toward female coming-of-age stories, parent-child narratives, and the pull of nostalgia. Though Gerwig is less of a stickler for style, ranging from social realism to the camp theatrics of *Barbie*.

Left: *Greta Gerwig, director of* Lady Bird *(2017).*

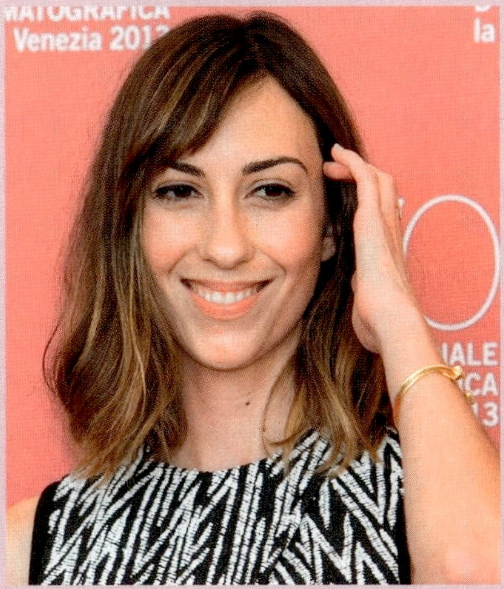

Above: *Gia Coppola, director of* Palo Alto *(2013).*

Gia Coppola
Coppola's niece, and fellow style icon, Gia has made her name with three searching, inventive indies: *Palo Alto, Mainstream,* and *The Last Showgirl.* Films that explore self-expression and the need for connection. And she has a real feel for Californian locations.

Noah Baumbach
New York native Baumbach charts the emotional travails of his articulate, flawed characters, often at a moment of transition in their lives. However, his films, including *The Squid and the Whale, Marriage Story* (with Scarlett Johansson), and *Jay Kelly*, offer a symphony of awkwardness.

Paul Thomas Anderson
Epic in scope, uncompromising in its delivery, Anderson's work charts American life through intense characters and elaborate settings. While more storm-tossed, the likes of *Boogie Nights, Magnolia*, and *There Will Be Blood* share with Coppola that need to get as close as possible to their chosen subjects.

THE ODD COUPLE

On the Rocks (2020)

Her seventh film is vintage Coppola, with a mismatched couple adrift in a luminous city. Indeed, that is Bill Murray alongside Rashida Jones. Only this is New York, they are father and daughter, and busily playing detective

They say familiarity breeds content. Before our eyes is another modern city by night. A jeweller's display of neon, diamond-bright windows, and hot taillights viewed from a passing car. A young woman is sat beside an older man, who has the beguiling face of Bill Murray, a little more weathered, but still caught somewhere indefinably between amusement and frown. His hair is now a penumbra of silver. Lips pursed disapprovingly, his pretty passenger is brunette and looks more than a little like Sofia Coppola, but is in truth her close friend, actress Rashida Jones. She is playing Laura, exasperated daughter to Murray's bon vivant Felix, and in a madcap flight across town they might be having the time of their life.

'There are worse sins than allowing a director to coast smoothly through her favourite moves,'[1] appreciated Donald Clarke in the *Irish Times*. He's not wrong. We are in the embrace of another wonderful film, featherlight and ocean-deep. And there is no missing the fact that we are being asked to compare and contrast it with *Lost in Translation*, which is still considered her masterpiece. Like the sip of sake or a New York Martini, only later do you realize how much it's moved you.

Yet there is something new at work. Coppola's latest has the vigour of a detective story. The double act on the trail of suspected wrongdoing. Time-honoured clichés enriched by the impression that they are not the point.

Laura and Felix are slaloming through the monied avenues of Midtown Manhattan in a temperamental scarlet Alfa Romeo. Paging all Freudians: this is the very 1959 model of Giulietta Spider that Coppola's father bought after winning a screenwriting competition, playing the big shot in his early Hollywood days. His daughter casts cars as an extension of personality; she thinks it might be a Californian thing. In *Lost in Translation*, Bob travels in taxis, swept along by alien currents. In *Somewhere*, Johnny's horsepowered Ferrari is always going round in circles. Felix's boisterous Alfa is all looks and noise, whirring like a lawnmower, and completely unreliable when it draws to a halt. There isn't time or indeed an available window for Laura to lean against and be drawn into reverie in that most iconic of all

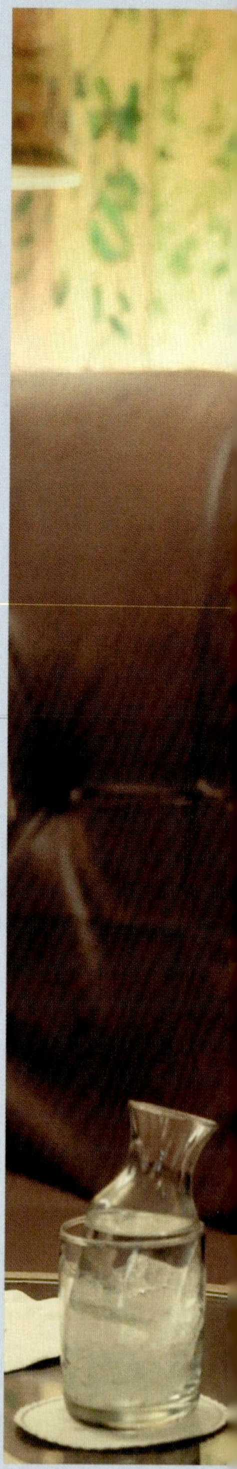

Right: *Daddy issues – Felix (Bill Murray) and his daughter Laura (Rashida Jones) take a pitstop during their helter-skelter pursuit of her husband's improbable infidelity in* On the Rocks *(2020).*

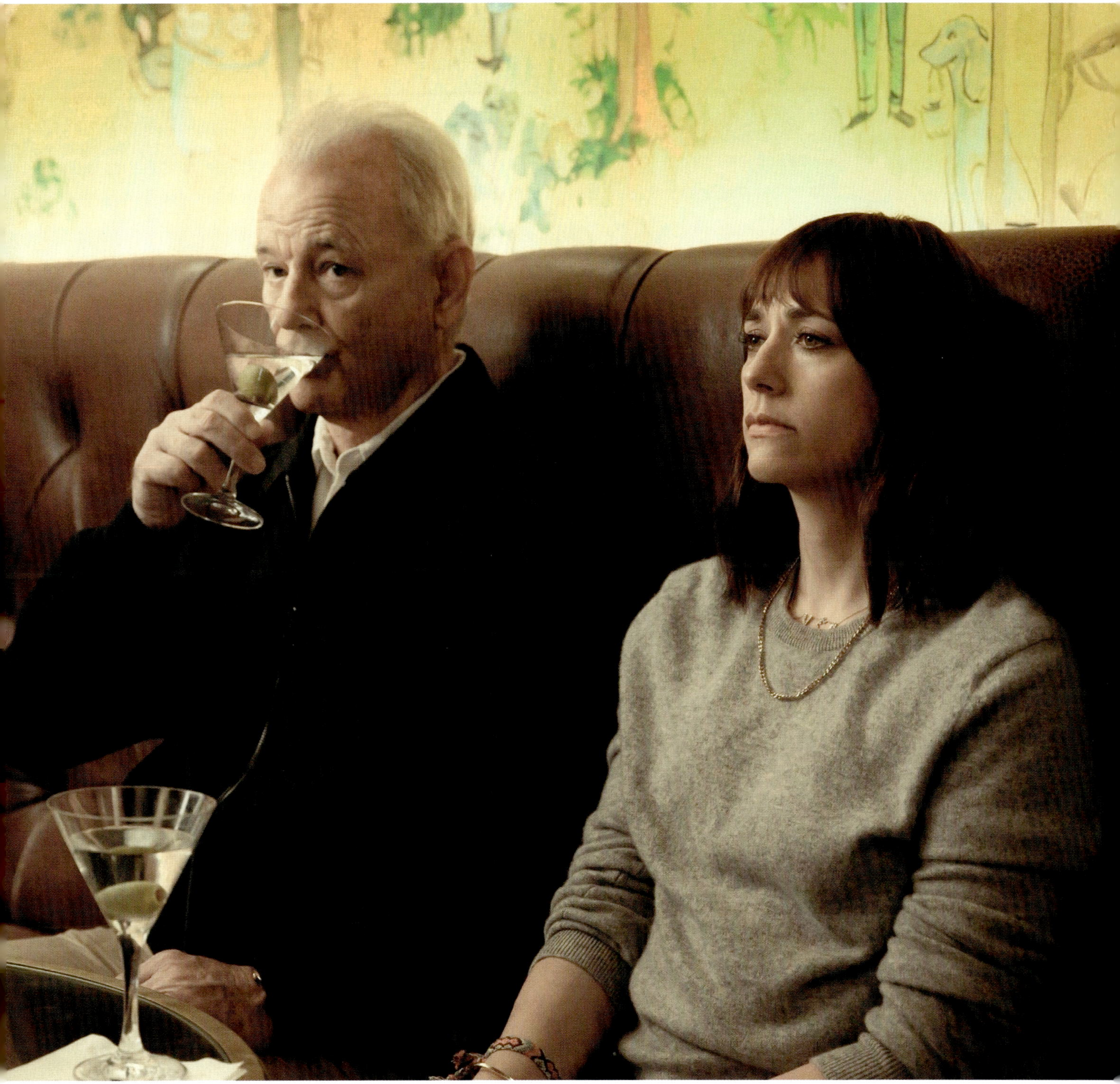

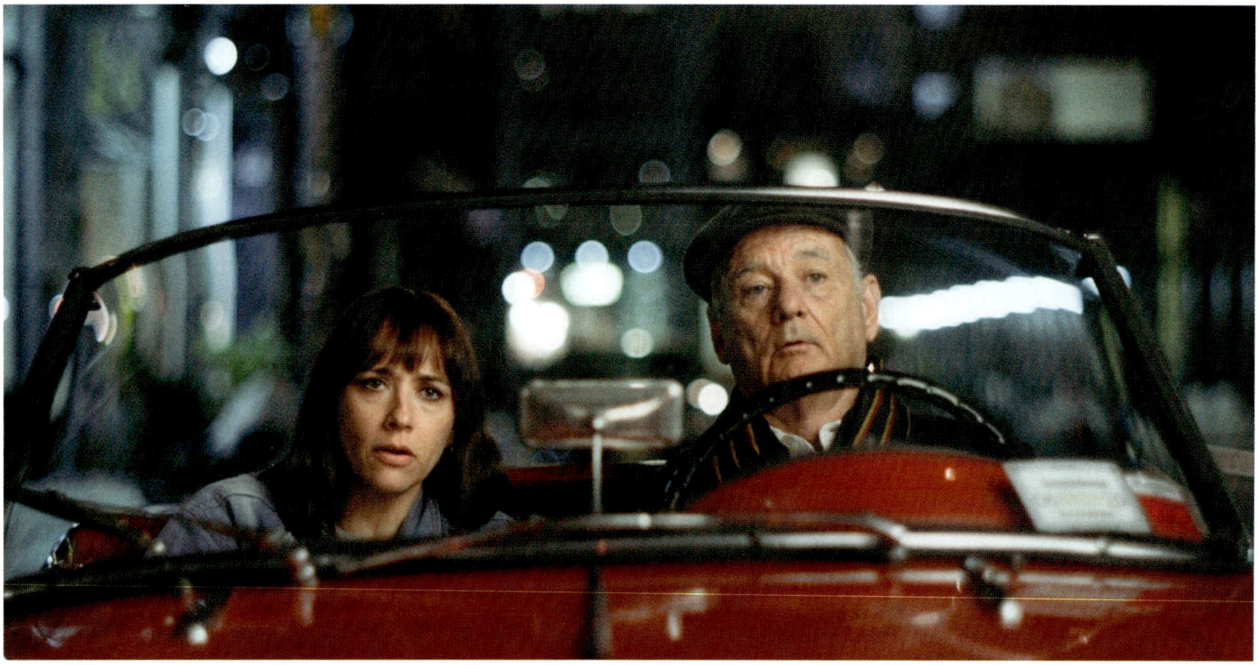

Above: *Follow that cab – flirting with movie conventions, Laura (Rashida Jones) and Felix (Bill Murray) trail Laura's husband on a work night out.*

Coppola poses. They are in pursuit of her husband, prime suspect in a case of marital infidelity, currently getting away in a cab.

Seventeen years before, on another fateful night in New York, Coppola had first met Murray in her attempts to persuade him to take what is now considered his greatest role – the unhappy serenity of Bob Harris in the aforementioned Tokyo drift. After dessert at an Austrian joint he knew, they had strolled back through the city to where Murray had parked his car. She mentioned that she had never driven in the city, and with an impish grin he tossed her his keys and they set off through the mythical streets. Her second feature film with the mercurial star was partly drawn from that moment. The idea that he would play a father with a convertible.

On a warm summer night in 2019, while hardly the metallic furies of William Friedkin or Paul Greengrass, this was demonstrably a car chase in a Coppola movie. 'Sofia likes a challenge,'[2] laughed cinematographer Philippe Le Sourd. Clocking in again as second unit director, her brother Roman helped storyboard a sequence that couldn't be left to her usual loose-limbed improvisations.

'We looked at different car scenes together and I put together different references,' explained Le Sourd, 'so we had an idea of what we liked and what we didn't.'[3] They shot between 9 p.m. and 4 a.m., across the scant four blocks the City of New York had been willing to give up, which meant they had to really figure out the angles. They used two identical Alfas and a Biscuit Rig – basically a driveable platform on which the car is mounted, originally designed for the mechanical horses on *Sea Biscuit* – where it only looks as if Murray is driving, though he did his fair share behind the wheel (and with aplomb). It was a chase scene as much about aesthetic as action, comedy value over thrill, and more about what was going on *inside* the car. They had three cameras locked onto the hood to peer at their faces. A nonchalant male smile met by a female scowl.

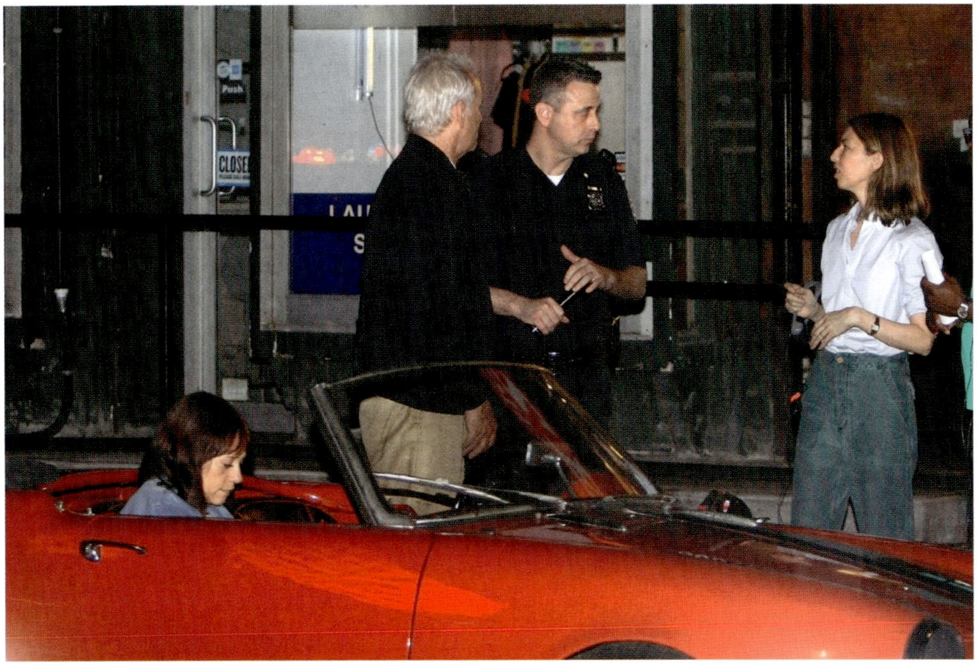

Left: *Sofia Coppola, action director – on location in nighttime Manhattan, Coppola co-ordinates elements of what is still her only true (but still ironic) car chase, centred on a scarlet convertible Alfa Giulietta Spider...*

Below: *... which includes the debonair Felix (Murray) talking his way out of a ticket with local police. Much to Jones' disgust as Laura.*

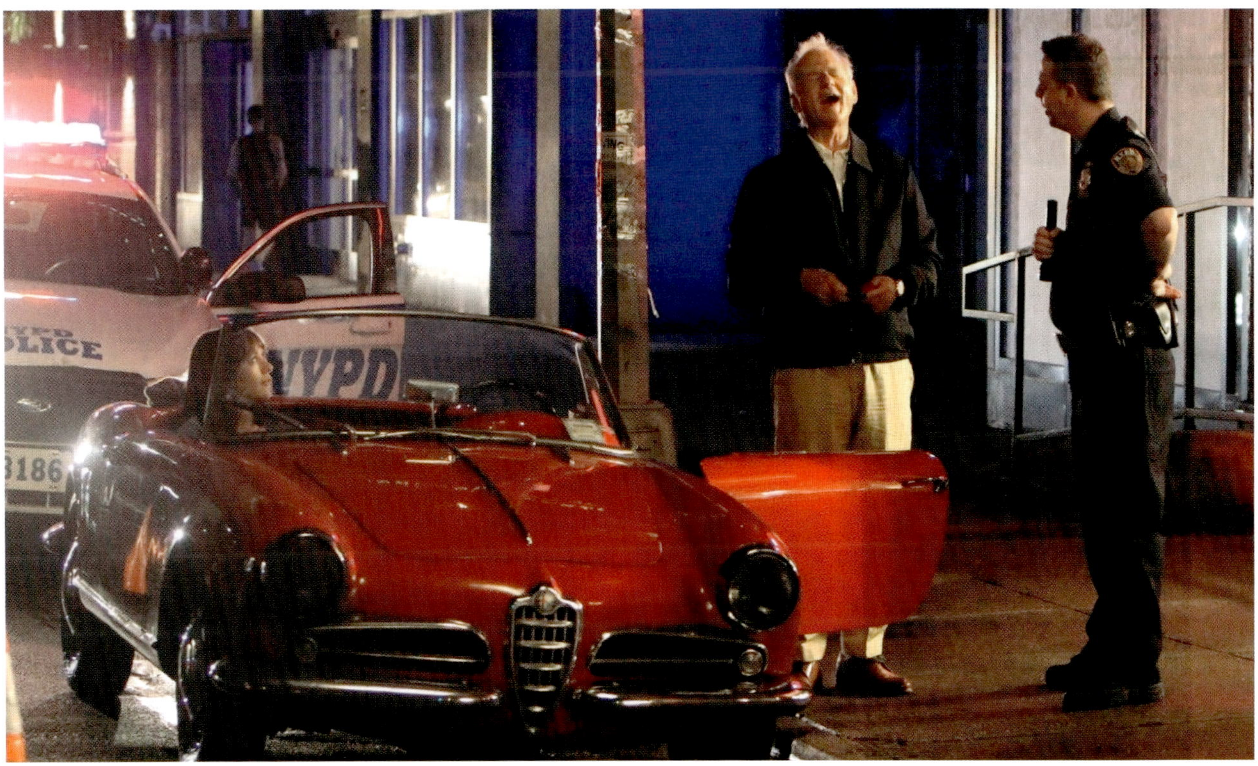

On the Rocks gestures toward a Hollywood movie but never quite fits: a romcom without the rom, a detective movie without a crime, a father and daughter trading quips over Martinis in the heart of photogenic Manhattan. It is also a clear return to first principles: the metropolis as dream space; countercurrents of funny and heartfelt; a laconic surface stirred by formless hurt. After the detour to a poisoned past with *The Beguiled*, we are back in the cool modernity with which Coppola has made her name. 'That's the filmmaking I like,'[4] she insisted.

The kind you can't quite decipher.

'I start with a feeling, or a mood,'[5] she added: plot always comes later with her original stories (which always follow her adaptations), those not based on any particular source bar herself. She was older, forty-eight, trying to balance home life with her creative needs amid this bustling, nagging city. In the evolving story, Jones' Laura is a writer, negotiating both a persistent block and the demands of motherhood. From photos and podcast backdrops, we know the sanctity of Laura's office to be the spitting image of Coppola's pristine workspace.

As she keeps trying to remind herself, Laura has the perfect marriage and two lovely young daughters (like Coppola). But her husband Dean (Marlon Wayans successfully playing it straight) is preoccupied with advancing as an internet entrepreneur, and Laura can't help feeling neglected. Especially as the quotidian routines that come with young children are playing havoc with her muse. She's already a little cranky and out of sorts. When the increasingly absent Dean begins to behave out of character, and she discovers his leggy co-worker's wash bag among his things, she suspects the worst.

Laura is the closest we have come to a Coppola cypher since Scarlett Johansson's Charlotte. However, the director was now closer in age to Bob, and troubled by similar middle-aged ruminations. This is a different stage in her cycle of female identity crises – Laura is her first fully realized mother. Though when pressed on any likeness to herself, the writer-director naturally deflected. Yes, it was about what was going on in her life, but in her friends' lives as well. In fact, it was a friend who handed her the high concept.

'Her husband was travelling a lot with a co-worker, and she really went and spied on her husband with her dad. They were hiding in bushes. Hearing that, I thought I would love to see a father-and-daughter buddy-detective movie.'[6]

Laura's answer to her dilemma is to recruit her somewhat estranged father, Felix, partially retired art dealer and master in the

> He loves to shake up people that are rigid, and I wanted a sense of that in the character too...
> **SOFIA COPPOLA**

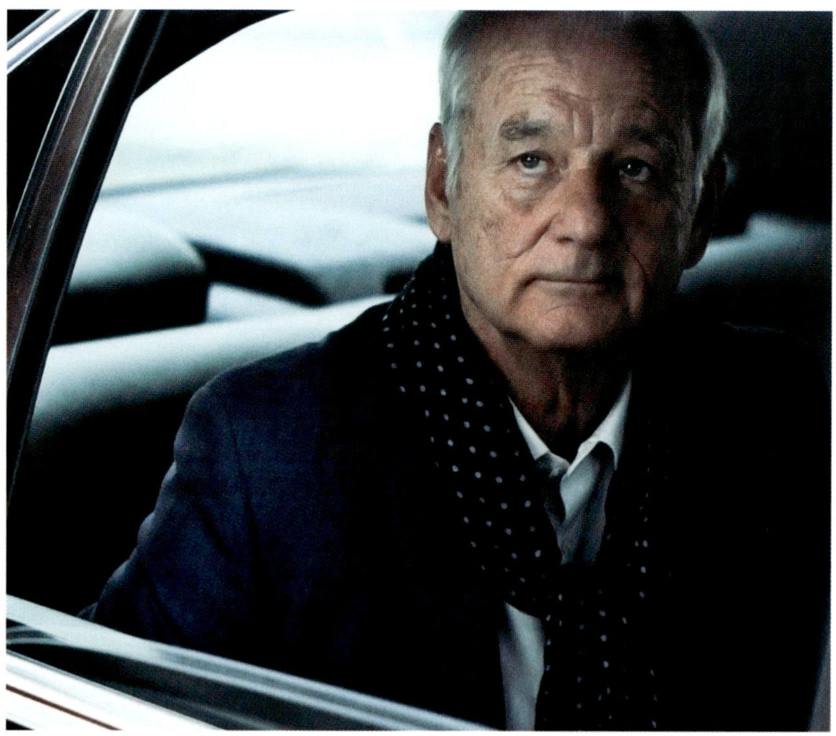

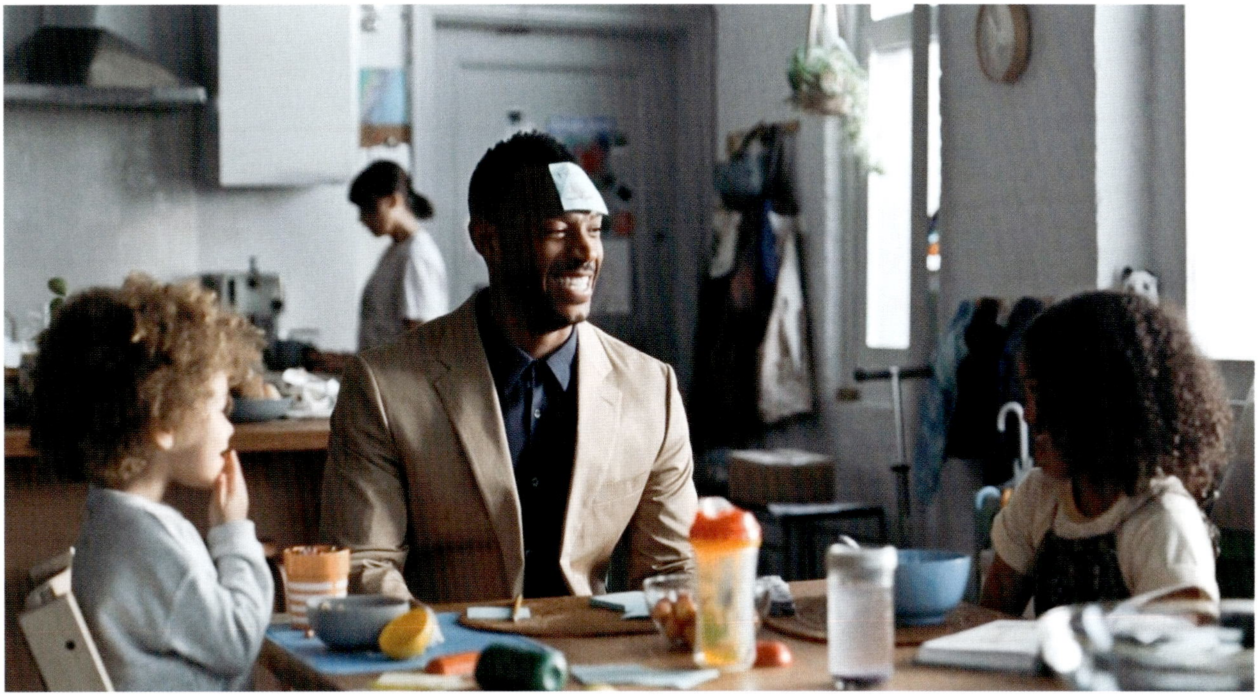

Above: *Happy families? Laura (Rashida Jones) starts to have doubts about her perfect family set-up, with a loving husband (Marlon Wayans) and two lovely children.*

Opposite: *Felix was an amalgam of many things – Coppola's father, friends' fathers, and, of course, a good dash of Murray's mercurial persona.*

arts of emotional subterfuge and infidelity, still fashioning himself as a Manhattan dandy, still an incorrigible flirt, and played with that fountainhead of charm and mordant wit that comes less by design than by simply being Bill Murray. Though his dashing array of Battistoni suits and scarves were picked out by the director.

Written over five years, *On the Rocks* works its ennui by stealth; the cover story is an odd-couple comedy. Coppola was trying to embrace, she said, 'something sillier than my usual realm…'[7] Dean, the errant husband, is only the MacGuffin. This is not the story of a faltering marriage, but of a father and daughter in search of understanding. It is another of Coppola's 'cross-generational stories,'[8] a companion piece to and reflection on earlier films, but given a bold, new, funny context, only with that familiar Murray face.

'With all due respect to Jim Jarmusch and Wes Anderson, Coppola's loose trilogy of *Lost in Translation, A Very Murray Christmas*, and this year's *On the Rocks* arguably qualifies her as the bard of 21st-century Murray,'[9] declared Chris Stanton in *Paste*.

Which begs the question: how close is Felix to Bill? According to Coppola, 'It's him and not him.'[10] She had to get over her initial worries about casting her old friend (and therefore easier to get hold of), accusations of repeating herself already ringing in her sensitive ears. In any case, there was no getting away from the fact she had written Felix with Murray's sourpuss *joie de vivre* in mind, and it was impossible to see the character without the actor's softly creased face. Quite literally, as she had a picture of them both – at some film festival bash, clinking Martinis – pinned up on her corkboard. Like Felix, Murray changes the atmosphere in any room (or car) he enters. His personality is simply too strong to divert.

'He loves to shake up people that are rigid,' said Coppola, 'and I wanted a sense of that in the character too, because she's very uptight and locked into all the mundane details of domestic life.'[11]

Felix was all the things that made Murray a superstar (albeit one operating in his own universe), combined with something more personal. Coppola had been going through the first stages of a divorce during *Lost in Translation*, and she remembered Murray opening up to her in a sincere, 'big brotherly'[12] way, something that people rarely saw on screen yet was always present. 'That side always stayed in my mind,'[13] she said.

This was the trick to casting Murray. You need to mine for something else within his genie-like talent. So what is it that makes Felix Keane different from Bob Harris? Felix is older, obviously, and far more adept at hiding his loneliness. His attitude toward women is frankly archaic, with a line in pithy Darwinian justifications for his terrible behaviour. 'Males are forced to fight and dominate and to impregnate all females,'[14] he sighs, as if shouldering a burden. Yet his boorish persona is softened by the whole Murray thing.

'Murray is at his best in performances where he appears to be in a different movie from everyone else,'[15] noticed Walter Chaw in *Film Freak Central*.

'His indirect directness is a lot like Coppola's; instead of forcing a movie into shape, she gives the impression that everything has just settled into place of its own accord,'[16] noted Stephanie Zacharek, reviewing the film for *Time*.

Felix needed to be complex in that lovely, unfixed Coppola way: someone who simultaneously thrilled and enraged his daughter. Someone who refused to conform to life's rules. Someone like Murray. 'I needed someone like Bill who's so loveable, but can bring both sides.'[17]

Coppola had been talking to the great comic writer Buck Henry, a hero of hers, responsible for the more directly sexual cross-generational escapades of *The Graduate*. He admonished her to 'write some dialogue for once.'[18] So she went away and did the unthinkable – wrote pages and pages of dialogue. The first draft was solely comprised of rambling conversations in bars and restaurants. All this back-and-forth between the leads, contrasting takes on relationships between men and women from the outlook of different generations.

The point is less whether Dean may or may not be having an affair, but that Felix is projecting his skewed morality onto the situation. He thinks every man is like him.

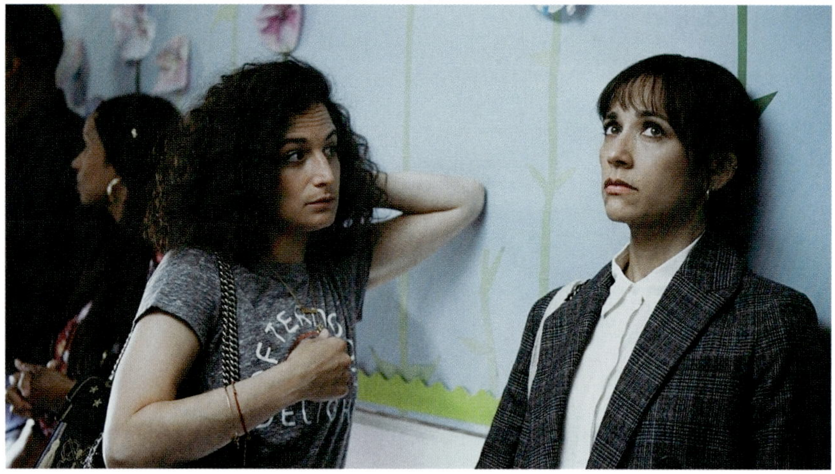

Top: *The interminable self-absorption of Jenny Slate's Vanessa on the school run is another catalyst for the self-doubt experienced by Laura (Rashida Jones).*

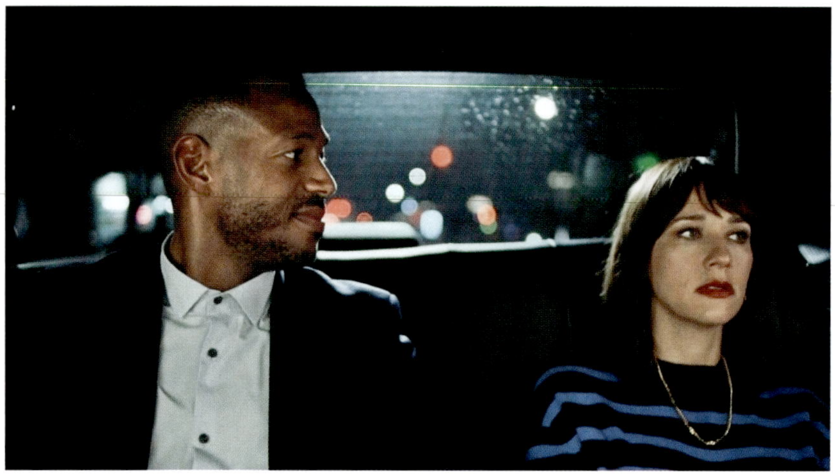

Above: *Dean (Marlon Wayans) and Laura (Jones) share a backseat miscommunication. The motif of car travel becomes crucial to the film's dynamic.*

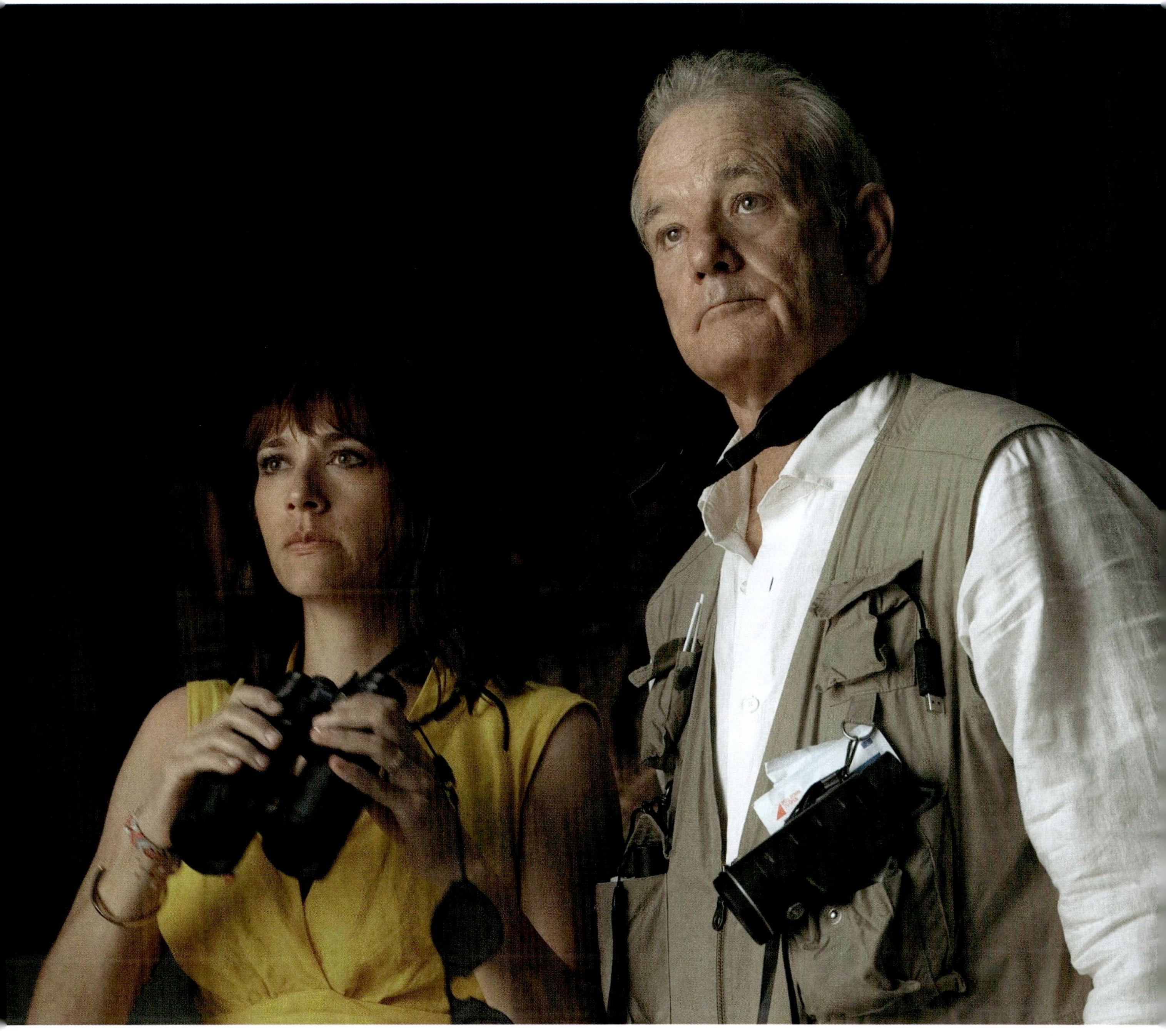

Above: *The central device of* On the Rocks *is how father (Bill Murray) and daughter (Jones) come to resemble a pair of private eyes on a case. A personal story becomes refracted through movie conventions.*

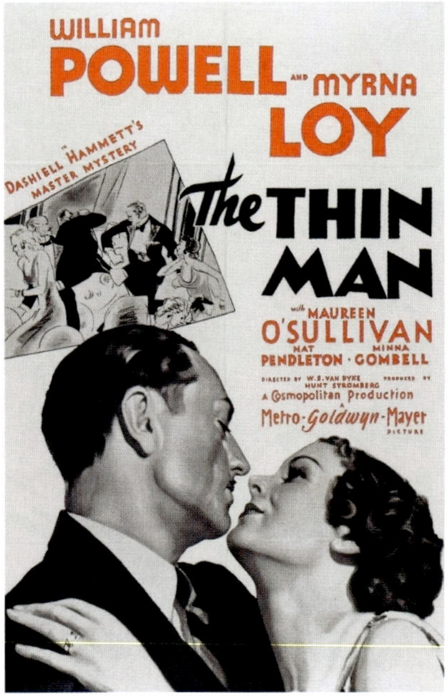

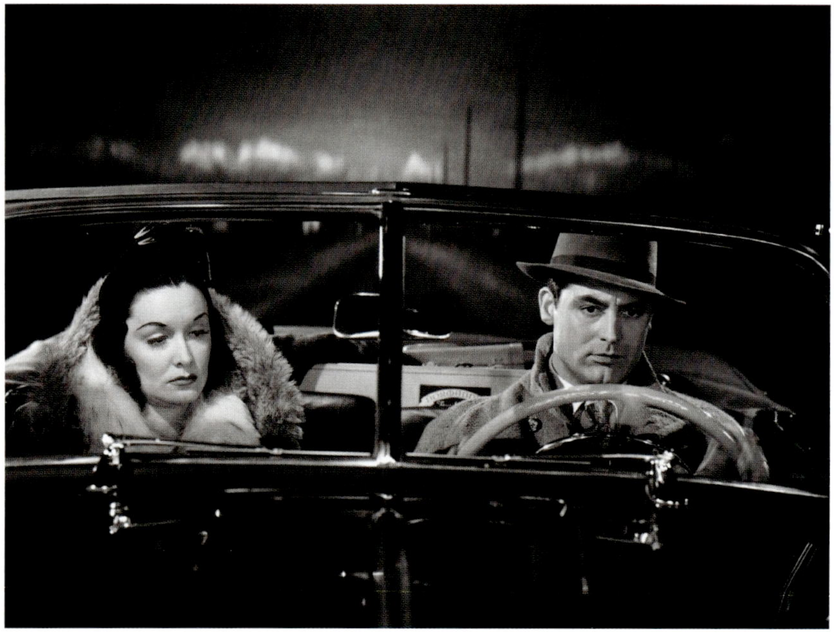

Above left: *For* On the Rocks, *Sofia Coppola was drawing on classic black-and-white Hollywood, including the famous* Thin Man *series of private eye films from the thirties…*

Above right: *… and such frothy comedies as* My Favorite Wife *(1940) with Gail Patrick and Cary Grant.*

Yet, delivered with Murray's nonchalant worldliness, there's a hint that such unbridled narcissism is a bit of a put-on, in order to stir a reaction from his daughter. There is a layer of regret hovering over his monumental denial. It is only with Laura that Felix is able to open up another side to himself. That is why he yearns for her company – a chance to let down his guard. 'That relationship is unlike any other woman in his life,'[19] explained Coppola.

She was aiming for the kinds of films they just don't make anymore. The absurdly straight-faced nuttiness of Blake Edwards' social comedies. *The Thin Man* series of the thirties with Myrna Loy and William Powell solving crimes between Martinis. The screwball vibe of *The Awful Truth* (1937) or *My Favorite Wife* (1940). Le Sourd received a list of classics to watch, and realized it was less about the images than the rhythm of the dialogue. They were romantic movies in a sophisticated, adult idiom. The difference, noted Coppola, was that *On the Rocks* 'was about finding romance in your own life.'[20] She joked that if she made a sequel it would be called *Make it a Double* – it's a delicious if unlikely thought: father and daughter reuniting as genuine private detectives, still bantering about their own problems.

Giving so many lines to Murray ran the risk of stifling his precious spontaneity. But Coppola left room for what she called 'Bill-ness.'[21] The unexpectedness she had come to expect. Take the scene with the flowers. With Dean away on business, Felix is picking up his daughter for a last-minute birthday celebration, and Murray broke free from the straightforward blocking to appreciate the outsized bouquet of pink roses Felix has sent her. The character is, after all, an art dealer, he is drawn to beauty and floats toward the flowers with the distracted air of a honey bee. And Coppola uses the whole, uninterrupted motion, letting the entire film ebb and flow to a mix of Laura's frenetic paranoia and Felix's slow-motion suavity.

Alongside the exterior beauty of the city, captured over the early summer of 2019 (note that it only rains at the end), we are back among the lingering glamour of high-end hotels. And back in Bemelmans Bar for a cocktail, wherein Coppola poses her couple – Murray tall for a movie star, Jones tiny by comparison – sat side by side on a leather banquette, gazing in different directions, on separate trains of thought, a conscious echo of Bob and Charlotte in *Lost in Translation*. Alongside Bemelmans, Coppola and her discreet crew were granted access to such classy joints as Raoul's, Indochine, and the 21 Club, where, as Felix points out, they filmed at the table where Bogart proposed to Bacall. There's a passing joke that Laura has lost the knack of whistling that her father once taught her – a recontextualization of Bacall teaching Bogart to whistle in *To Have and Have Not*. Felix partakes of an oak-lined fantasy that might as well be Golden Era Hollywood.

The vibrant score fits the bill. A mix of jazz and classical, with musical quotations from Chet Baker, Thelonious Monk, and Franz Schubert. Rather than Death in Vegas, when Felix arrives eighteen minutes into the film he is accompanied by 'Madamina, il catalogo è questo,' an aria from Mozart's *Don Giovanni*, about a man with thousands of lovers. To her eye-rolling resignation, Laura is mistaken for Felix's latest floozy.

Compared to her father's gilded myth (and indeed the melancholic electronica of Charlotte's interior life), Laura's daily routine is accompanied by a chorus of construction sites and squealing schoolyards. Her apartment is impressive but lived-in – Coppola and production designer Anne Ross decided that Felix must have helped out. Is it a stretch to imagine it is along the lines of the director's own place in the West

Below: *Laura (Rashida Jones) attempts to face Felix (Bill Murray) with a few home truths in the legendary surroundings of New York's 21 Club.*

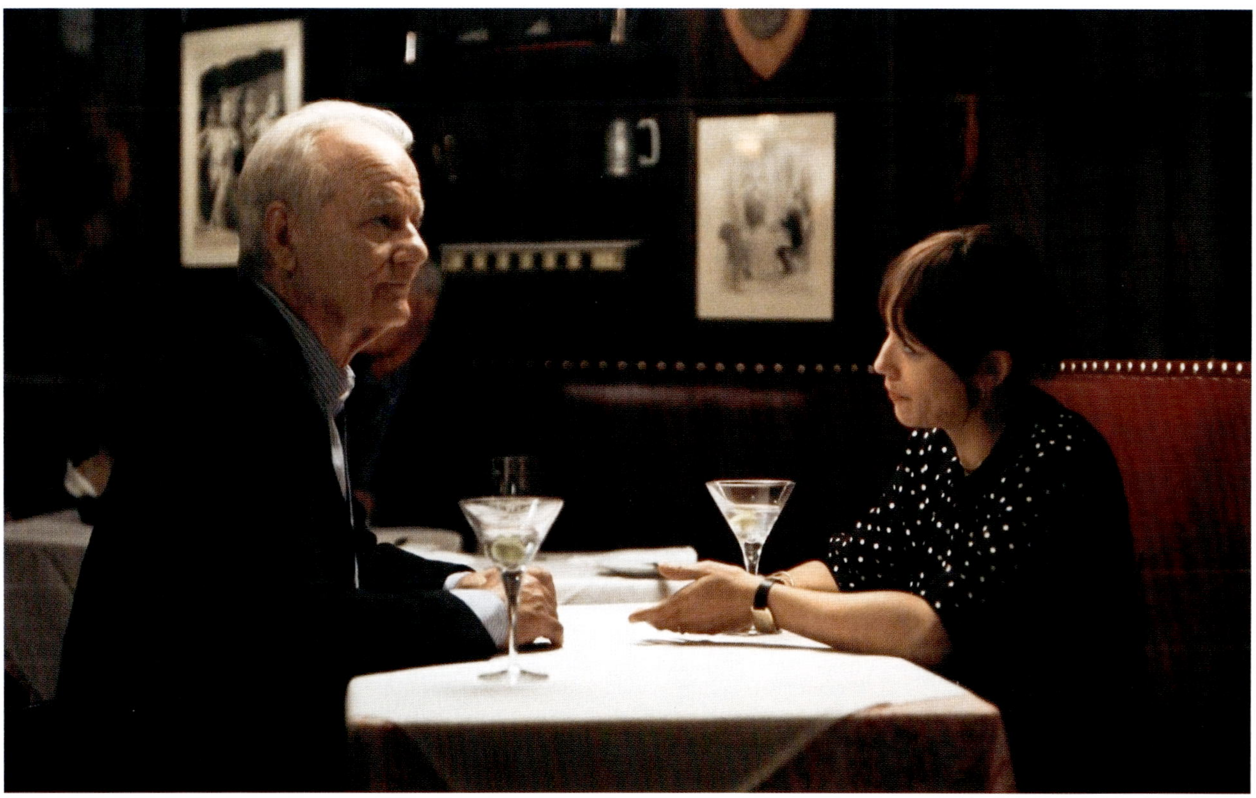

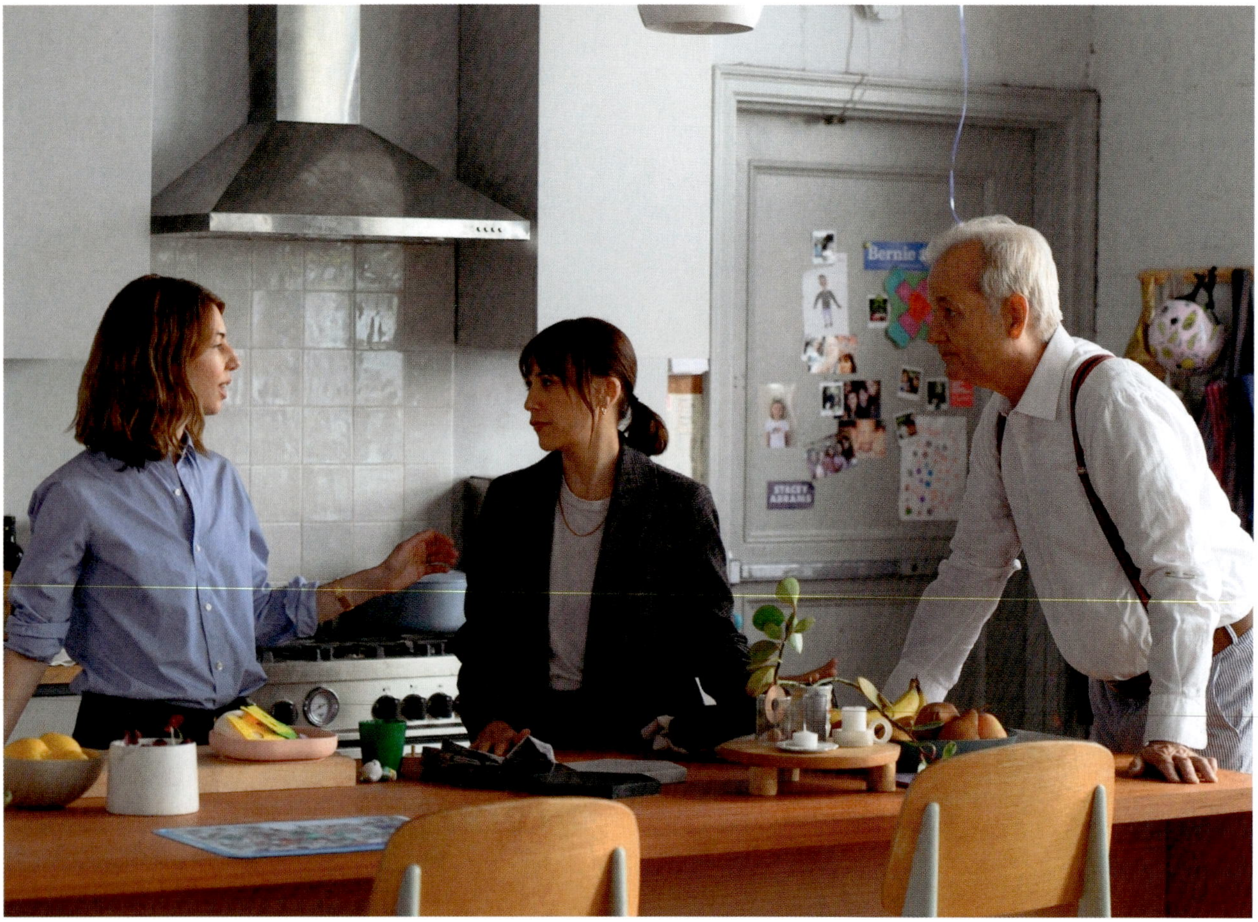

Above: *Close to home? As she is wont to do, Sofia Coppola was drawing on her own life for* On the Rocks, *including much of the interior décor of Laura's life.*

Village? The film was doing nothing for the more cynical view that Coppola only makes films about the privileged few.

On the Rocks is not a satire. The comic element, its spin on detective movie motifs, gives shape to the sudden burst of energy that Felix brings to Laura's drab routines. This might even be the book she is supposed to be writing (we never learn its actual subject).

The critic Elvis Mitchell wondered if he could spot the influence of her father's great (if wildly different, tonally speaking) conspiracy thriller *The Conversation*, the story of an investigator who is ultimately led back toward himself. 'Wow, I never thought of that,' responded Coppola. 'Maybe in my subconscious. I love the ending. That is one of my favourite endings of all time.'[22]

During the endless promotional push for the film, she hit upon an apt and knowing sobriquet for Felix: 'He's sort of a fairy godfather,'[23] she smiled. Backed by Apple, the film would be released during lockdown straight onto streaming, where its success remains impossible to gauge. During those time-lapsed months, Coppola hunkered down at the family estate in Napa, alongside her brother and cousins. They would show their latest films in the family screening room, and she gave them a preview of *On the Rocks,* while her father unveiled his new, improved (if not transformative) thirtieth anniversary cut of *The Godfather Part III*, given the rather prolix new title of *The Godfather Coda: The Death of Michael Corleone*. And there she was like a ghost of the past, a reminder of the time her father had sped her down paths she would come to regret.

Which gives rise to the next question. How much is the film an examination or even a celebration of Coppola's relationship with her own highly charismatic father? The answer to which remains much the same – it's him and not really him.

Francis Ford Coppola could light up a room in exactly that same, dangerous way as Felix. 'He was bigger than life growing up,'[24] Sofia accepted. As with *Somewhere*, her first exploration of father-daughter dynamics, there are moments lifted wholesale from her experiences. She did indeed come home to find the babysitting Francis watching *Breaking Bad* with his infant grandchildren

Below: On the Rocks *marked the third collaboration between Coppola and Bill Murray, and it felt like second nature. Nevertheless, she was keen to explore a different side to the star's persona, rather than simply replaying an older version of Bob from* Lost in Translation.

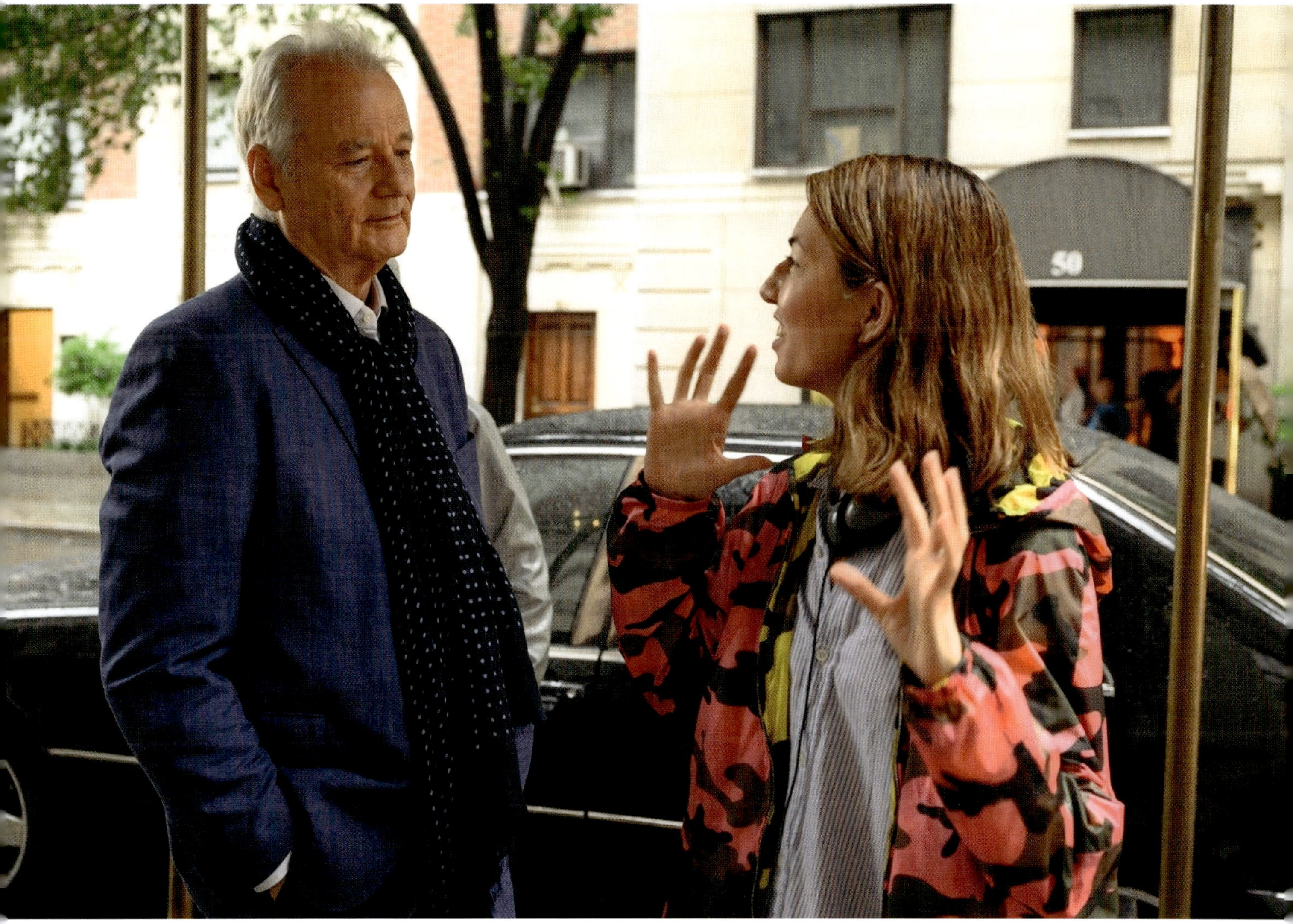

on the grounds he had heard it was a great show. The reasonable tone, the comebacks, the endless advice all have the ring of her father. And there is the car, of course – the Alfa from his flashy youth.

One of the themes of the film is how, as we grow older, our parents begin to reveal themselves outside of our relationship with them as children. Laura is seeing Felix not as a parent (even an unreliable one), but as his own flawed person. Was this a way of processing her own father's waywardness?

Pressed on any likeness closer to home, Coppola would simply declare that the character was a cocktail of so much: Murray, Francis, her father's friends, her friends' fathers, and her father-in-law (hardly a shrinking violet himself by all accounts).

Felix embodies an entire generation of men who can't shake their addled attitudes toward women, even as values evolved around them. In its breezier, boozier way, *On the Rocks* returns to the sexual politics of *The Beguiled*, even if Coppola brushed off the idea she was evolving into a figurehead for feminism. 'I just try to do my thing,'[25] she implored. Still, in different ways, the probing of masculinity becomes the major theme of her later films, with *Priscilla* (2023) grappling with another older man-younger woman relationship from an entirely new angle.

Return to *On the Rocks*, and you realize it belongs to the superb Jones. Felix might be the centre of attention, but this is Laura's story. And Coppola needed a leading lady who could go toe-to-toe with Murray. Someone who could play the straight man. Coppola had spotted the chemistry between them during their brief interactions in *A Very Murray Christmas*. What struck her the most was that Jones was an equal and opposite to his flamboyant tricks. Which goes double for the double act of *On the Rocks*.

'When he zigs, she zags, challenging him to follow,' applauded *Time's* Stephanie Zacharek. 'Their dance has a prickly, electric warmth.'[26]

And so we hit upon another question: how much is Laura like Rashida? Jones was at a similar stage of her life, moving into her forties, uncertain of where her career was going. She shared with Coppola and Laura the burden of a heavyweight dad. Jones was the offspring of legendary music producer Quincy Jones, who had found a sound for Frank Sinatra and Michael Jackson, and worked on numerous film scores.

'It was personal for me on the page,' admitted Jones. 'And then it was even more personal for me when we filmed it. There's a dynamic for sure with my dad where I grew up loving being in the bask of his love and charm.'[27] Prior to filming, she had completed a six-year journey directing a documentary on his life. Fathers were very much on her mind.

Born in Los Angeles, Jones was prodigiously intelligent. She went from high school to Harvard, where she discovered theatre. She had an exasperated, chatterbox vulnerability that offset her leading-lady beauty and gravitated, via

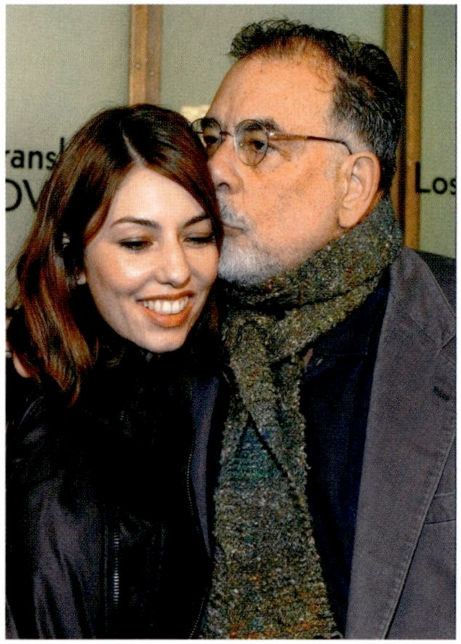

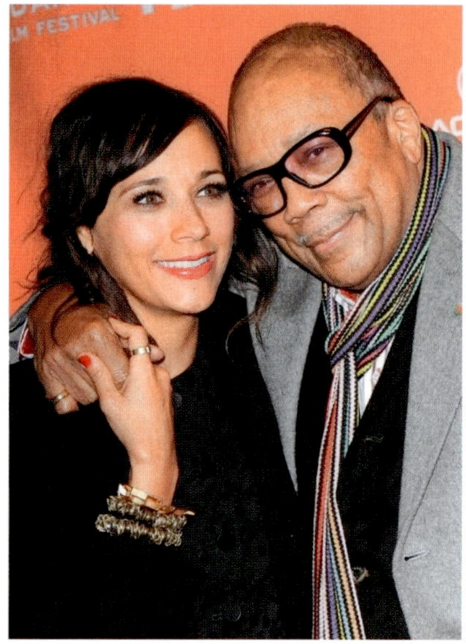

Above left: *Art resembling life with artists – Sofia Coppola obviously drew from growing up with a flamboyant father in Francis Ford Coppola…*

Above right: *… just as Rashida Jones recalled the complexities of having a loving but famous dad in legendary record producer Quincy Jones.*

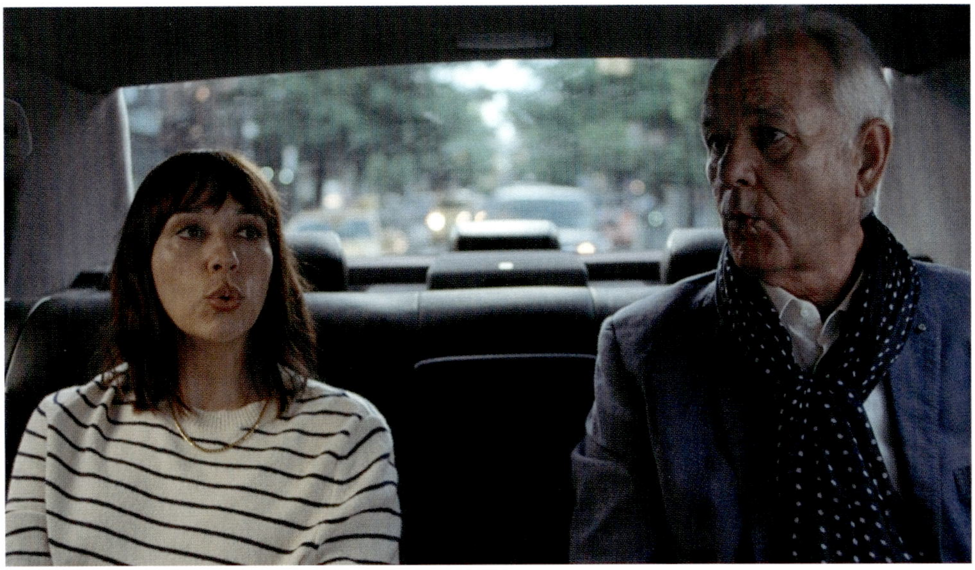

Left: *The scene of Laura trying to recall how her father once taught her to whistle recalls Lauren Bacall teaching Humphrey Bogart to whistle in* To Have and Have Not *(1944).*

Below: *The superb Jones as Laura, who still has those lonely, reflective qualities of a quintessential Coppola character – only relocated to middle age, exactly the stage of life the director had reached.*

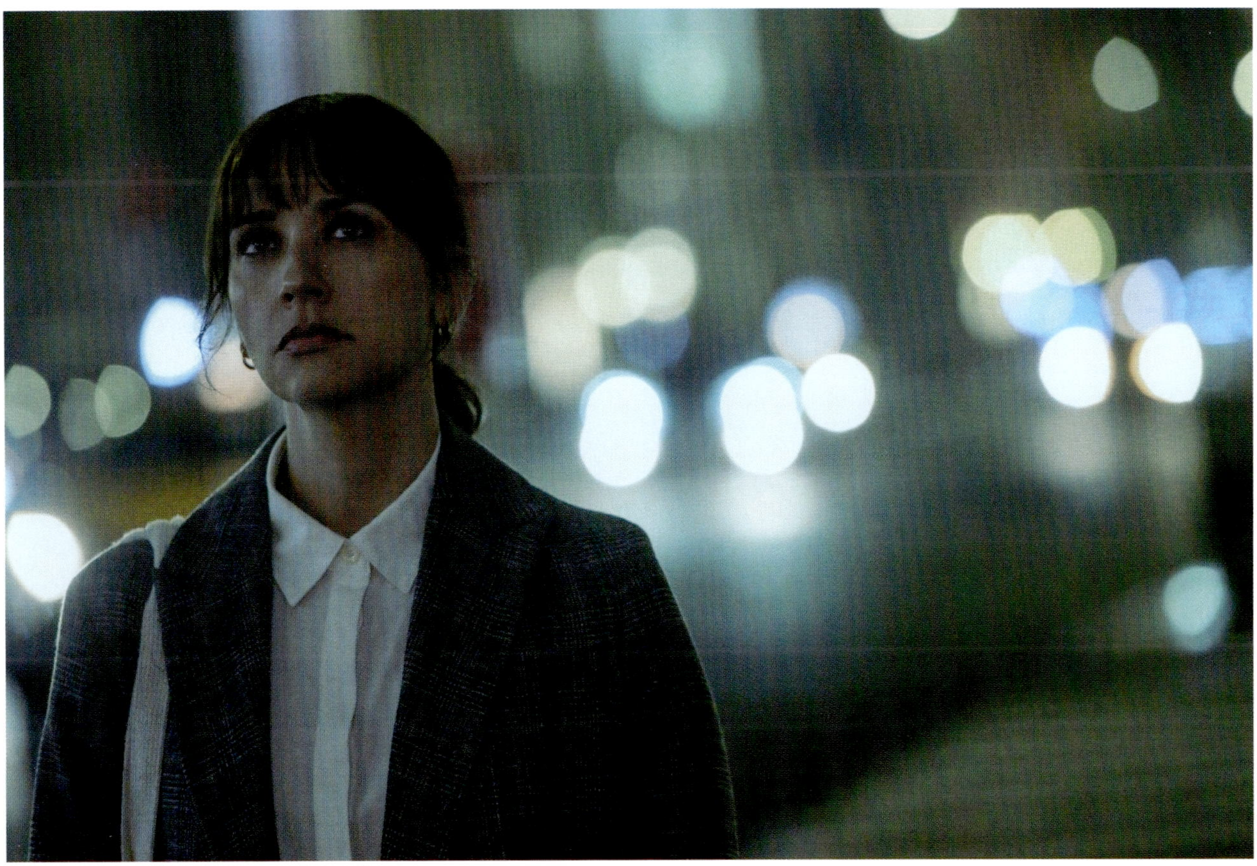

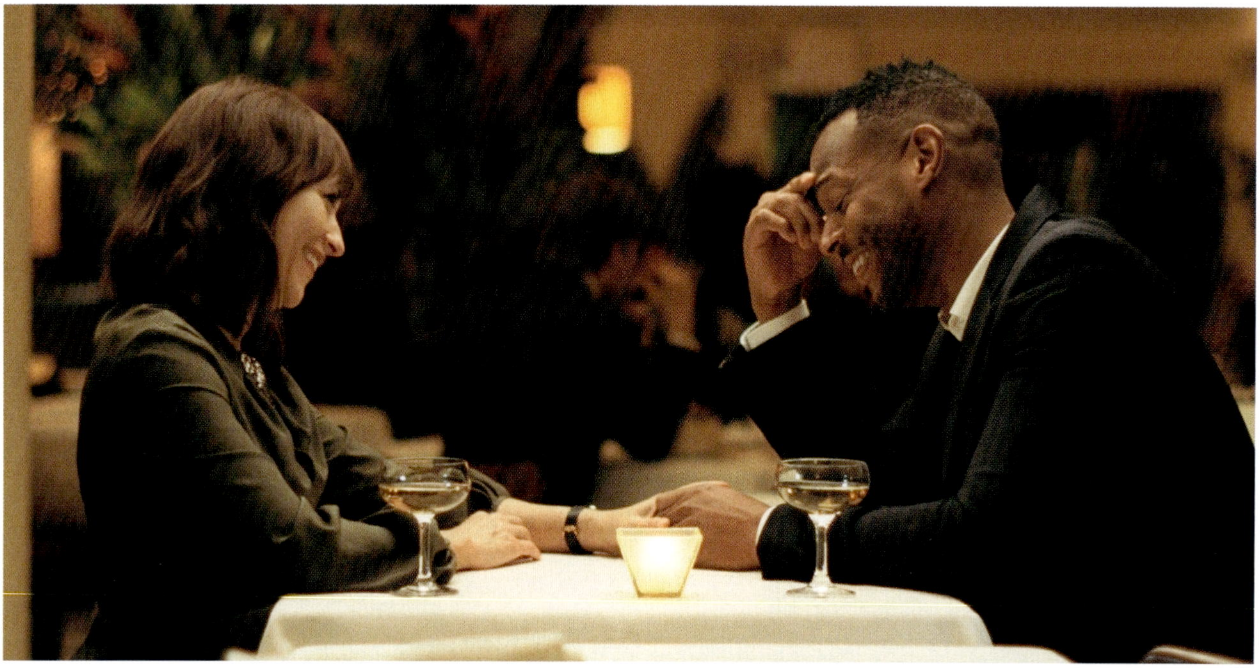

music and modelling, into comedy with *The Office*, *Angie Tribeca*, and a recurring role on sitcom *Parks and Recreation*. But movies had kept their distance. Her only previous lead was in divorce comedy *Celeste and Jesse Forever* in 2012.

Like Felix, Laura is complex. Timing her reactions to perfection, Jones captures her character's divided feelings about her father and in deeper ways her own worth, which circle back to his casual cruelty anyway. She is having to grow up all over again.

'My God,' she gasps. 'What if what we find out is that Dean's just busy, and I'm in a rut?'[28] She may have it figured but already, but she needs this misadventure as much as Felix does.

Our oddest of couples will finally follow Dean to a Mexican resort where the showdown will not, of course, be with a husband (who has, unbeknownst to the preoccupied detectives, returned home early to be with his family), but with the father who has led her such a merry dance.

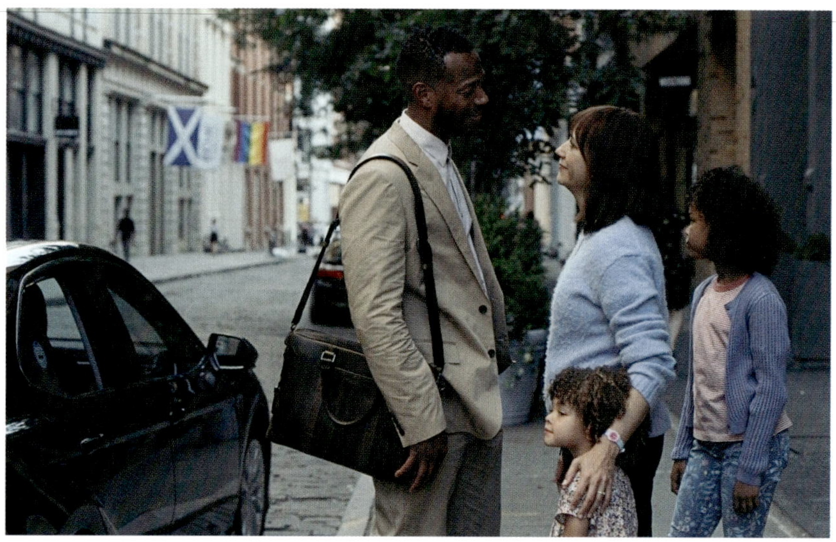

Top: *Order restored – back in a swish New York with cocktails, only now Laura (Rashida Jones) finds her marriage to Dean (Marlon Wayans) is still very much intact.*

Above: *After the controversies that dogged the portrayal of race (or not) in* The Beguiled, *Sofia Coppola was keen to centre her story on a beautiful family of colour.*

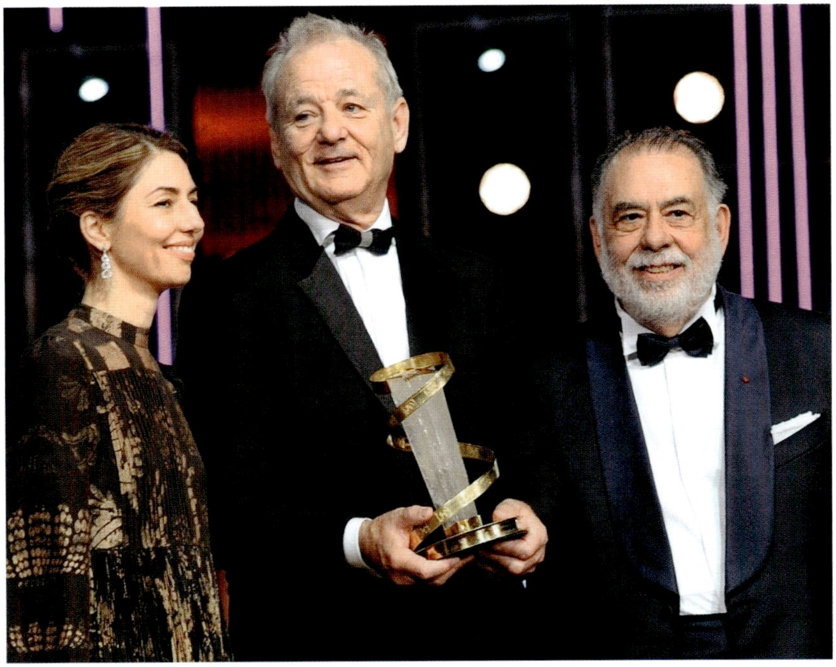

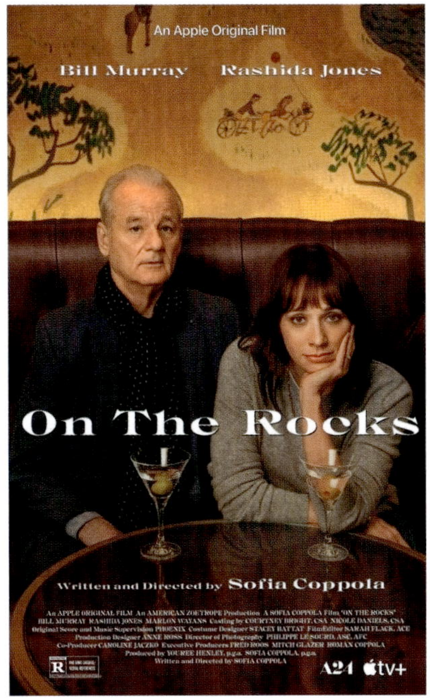

Above left: *Life and art again – Coppola poses with a fictional father, Bill Murray, and the real thing at the 2015 Marrakech International Film Festival, where Murray received the Tribute.*

Above right: On the Rocks *works as a sister film to* Lost in Translation *(sharing so many themes – and Murray), but stands in its own right as one of Coppola's finest accomplishments.*

When things get frank between the leads, Coppola strips out tunes entirely and lets the breaking waves accompany the sadness that finally breaks the surface of the film. At last, Laura will let decades' worth of feelings loose. And Felix responds with a rare and telling (if tangential) moment of honesty recalling the one true love he let go – not, as it happens, Laura's mother. Now his own hour is late, and there is an abiding nostalgia that he is an endangered species, the love that matters most to him is that of his daughter.

One last thought. Interviewed for the film, cinematographer Philippe Le Sourd casually noted something that feels significant about Coppola's methods. 'If there's a scene with a lot of emotion, she tried to always shoot it at the end of the shoot,'[29] he explained. The amputation scene in *The Beguiled*, for instance, or Laura and Dean's fraught conversation on the New York kerb at the end of *On the Rocks*. The point the marriage gets back on an even keel.

So very different from her father, Coppola is an introvert by nature, and, fascinatingly, an introverted filmmaker. Her work is about underlying emotions, what lies behind the fizzy dialogue and ambiguous frowns. The beauty of which is that both she and her films are impossible to pin down. But they suggest multitudes. Or as Jones put it, Coppola has the gift of 'how to say little and get everything…'[30]

LONESOME TONIGHT

Priscilla (2023)

Her eighth film was a biopic featuring the most iconic American of all time. But this was the edifice of Elvis seen through the eyes of his troubled young wife

When she was fourteen, Sofia Coppola developed a crush on a rock star. Not an unusual turn of events for any impressionable teen – it is virtually a rite of passage. Nevertheless, it says a lot about her unconventional spirit that her romantic daydream wasn't focused on the typical pretty boy idols, but rambunctious punk frontman Joe Strummer, lately of The Clash. And it spoke a great deal about her unconventional upbringing that at the height of her yearning, Strummer came to record some music on the Coppola estate in Napa. 'I always remember feeling kind of mortified, but also so excited that Joe Strummer was at our house!'[1] she laughed.

While the fixation passed, as they tend to do, what stayed with Coppola was the mystery of what might have happened if he had said, 'Run away with me.'[2] What would it be like to give in to that longing? What if the dream became real? Which is exactly what happened to Priscilla Beaulieu, who married Elvis Presley at the age of twenty-one, having met him at fourteen, to become Priscilla Presley, the subject of Coppola's eighth feature film – a story that required the director to turn off her middle-aged-parent brain and get back in touch with her teenage self. The result is another collage of love, youth, fame, and isolation, but the mood is uneasy, the time span involved longer, and the real person at the centre of the story had been at the end of a phone.

This reflective biopic was born in the wake of another passion project run aground. Coppola had spent much of lockdown adapting Edith Wharton's 1913 novel *The Custom of the Country* into a five-hour miniseries for Apple, her first venture into prestige television. But it was not to be. Just as *The Little Mermaid* faltered over differing visions, cracks began to appear in her relationship with the Apple executives, and the budget came under increasing scrutiny. 'The idea of an unlikable woman wasn't their thing,'[3] she reflected, though given the novel is a satire of New York society, in which the mercenary, scheming Undine Spragg strives to make her way, quite what they thought she was intending is hard to fathom. Again, we can only lament for what was lost: a mix, perhaps, of the jostling for social advantage in *The Beguiled* and the brats on the make in *The Bling Ring*.

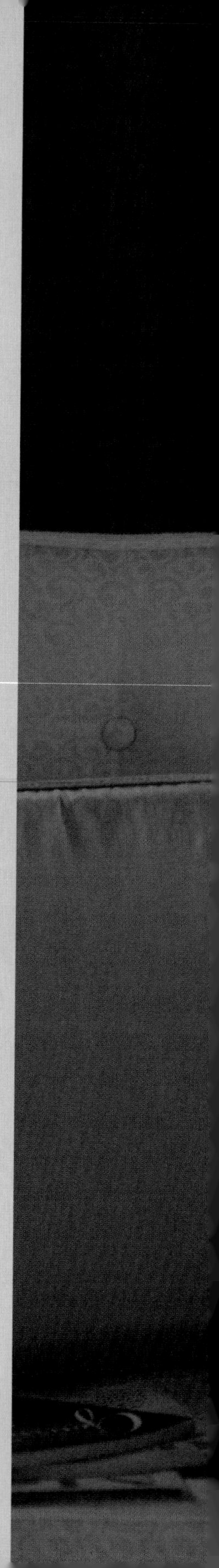

Opposite: *The wife's story – Cailee Spaeny as Priscilla Presley catching up on the latest gossip about her world-famous husband Elvis in Sofia Coppola's haunting biopic* Priscilla.

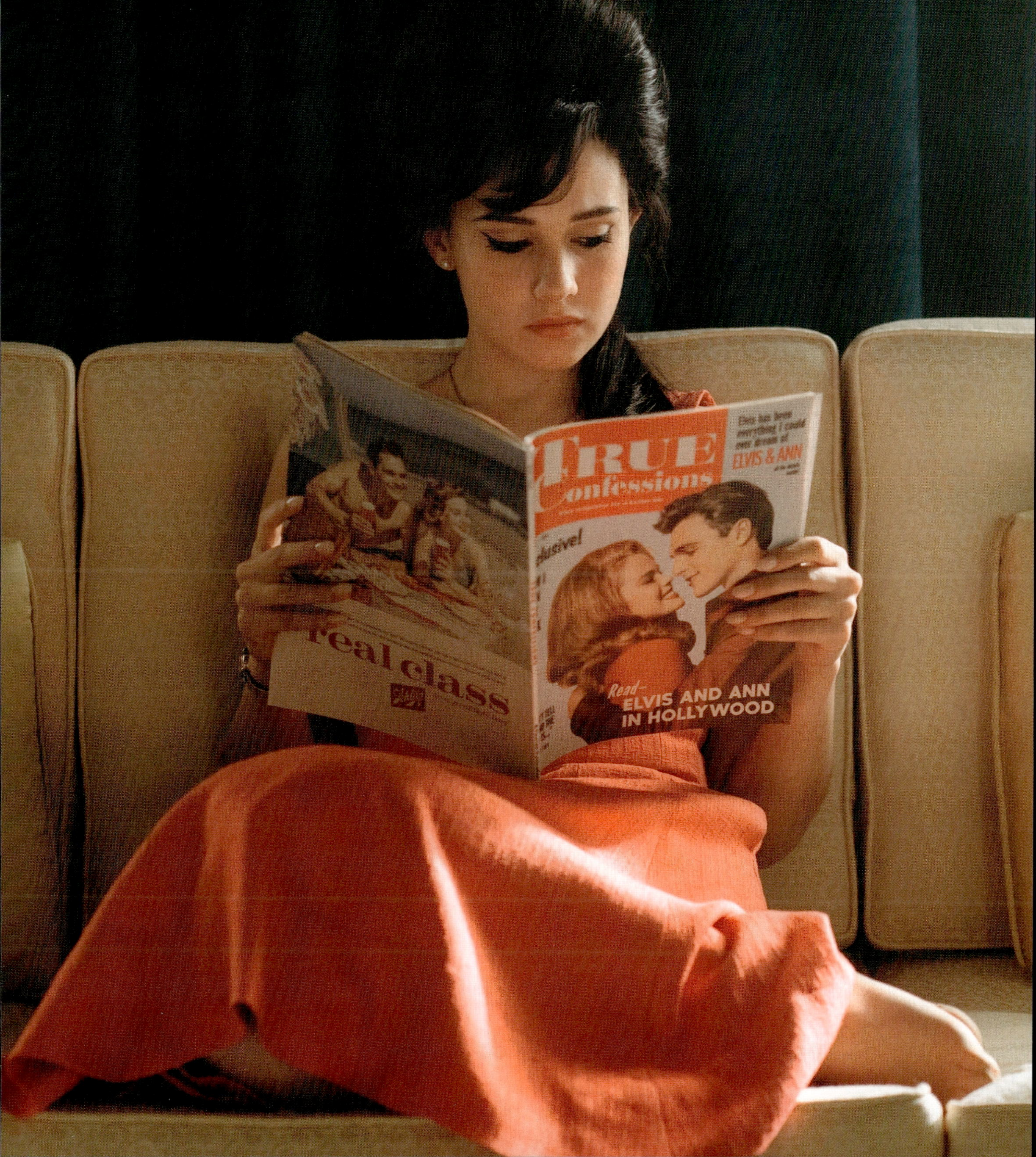
TRUE
Confessions
Elvis has been everything I could ever dream of
ELVIS & ANN
clusive!
Read—
ELVIS AND ANN
IN HOLLYWOOD
real class

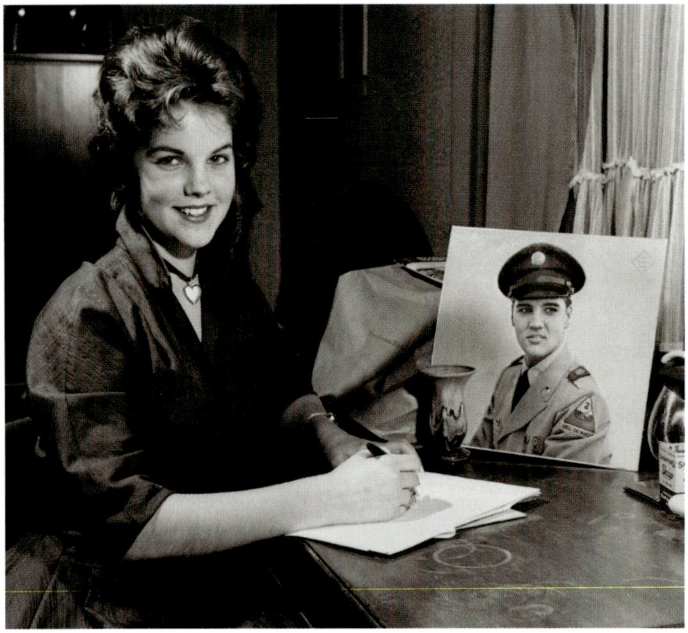

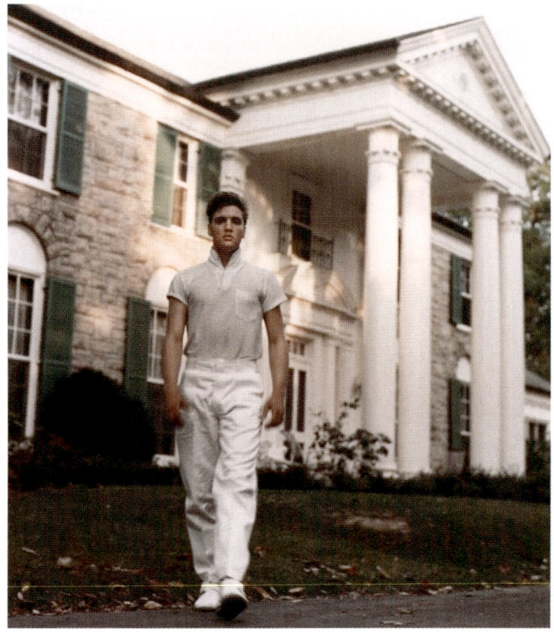

But while Priscilla Presley's tumultuous 1985 autobiography was a much-needed palate cleanse, it made sense in Coppola terms. Stoic Priscilla was a very different character to Spragg, certainly, but likewise another variation on that Coppola tradition of a young woman (or indeed an ageing male) negotiating a strange new environment. Where once there was Tokyo and Versailles, now came Graceland. And, following *On the Rocks*, the story evolved into another variation on a marriage running aground. Priscilla will find herself at the point where she decides to leave the dream behind.

Coppola had picked up the paperback ten years before; with its gaudy typography and tabloid title, *Elvis and Me*, she was expecting titillation, only to be shocked by how moving she found the story. Instinctually, she began to imagine what kind of film it would make, but was wary it ran too close to *Marie Antoinette*. There is truth in that: the prisons of fame and wealth, the prescribed social roles; a teenager, barely that, sucked into a baffling world in which she strives to find herself; kings behind closed doors.

The idea had lain dormant until, by chance, she had got talking to a friend about Priscilla's story, which inspired her to dig out the book. 'Re-reading it, it grabbed me in a way where I could see this enticing, inspiring visual world of Graceland and 1960s Memphis. It was something I'd never done, and it was so Americana,'[4] she relished.

As they always did, the images came first. For the opening shot, delicately painted toes luxuriating in the thickness of a pink shagpile. There had never been such a candy-hued carpet at Graceland, yet the sensory effect of the image evoked something for Coppola. The idea of sinking into this plush world. 'How could you ever leave that place behind?'[5] she wondered. *Priscilla* unfurls in a *Marie Antoinette*-like flurry of sensations, textures, and surfaces in close-up. The smooth veneer of China figurines, the velour of banquettes, gusts of hairspray, pills, fake eyelashes, and the caress of eyeliner curling like Egyptian kohl.

Above left: *The real Priscilla Presley pictured at the age of sixteen in Germany, which was where she first met Elvis.*

Above right: *The real Elvis Presley taking a stroll through the grounds of Graceland.*

Opposite: *Living the dream – Priscilla (Cailee Spaeny) walks down her high school corridor with the secret knowledge that she is Elvis' girl.*

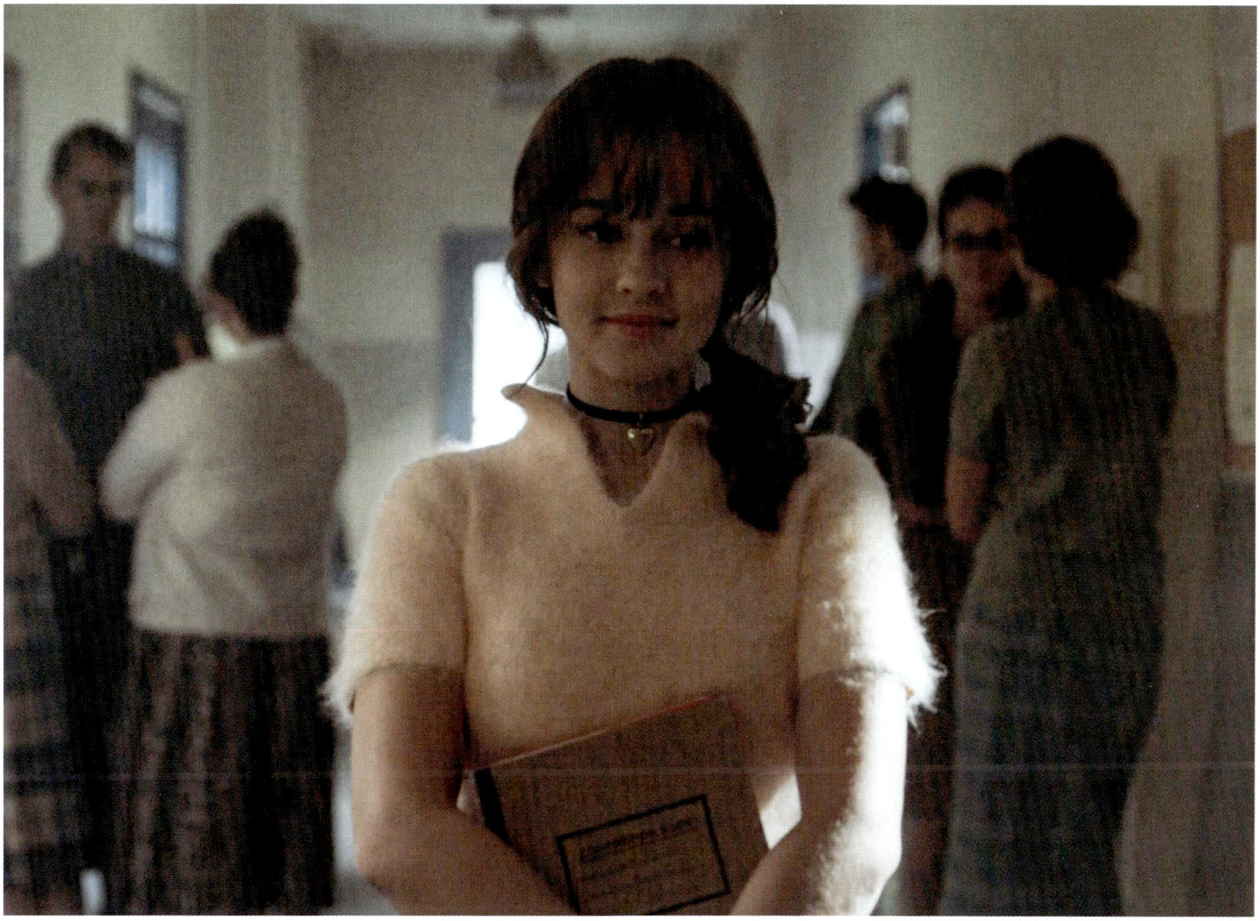

'To point out that *Priscilla* is superficial, even more so than Coppola's other films, is no derogation, because surfaces are her subject,'[6] Anthony Lane assured us in the *New Yorker*.

This was a new kind of reality. She savoured the chance to recreate the news footage of Priscilla leaving hospital with their newborn baby, fully dolled up, her hair in a beehive. Or that famous wedding-day shot of a pensive young couple framed by a flowered arch. She had Chanel create an interpretation of Priscilla's original dress; Valentino provided suits and knitwear for Elvis. She imagined them as a fairytale couple, perfect enough to put on top of a wedding cake. There was a line in the book about picking which gun goes with which outfit. 'That utterly weird part of Americana,'[7] she said.

Her film would melt away from the reality of those moments into somewhere more subjective – Priscilla's interior life.

We knew so little about her, Coppola realized, it was shocking. And she was so young. She was still in high school when she moved into Graceland. This was to be a biopic of Priscilla not Elvis – he will only ever be seen through her eyes, described by her story, framed as a distant, mercurial dreamboat, twenty-four when he met her, but not much more than a boy.

> "…I could see this enticing, inspiring visual world of Graceland and 1960s Memphis. It was something I'd never done, and it was so Americana.
>
> ***SOFIA COPPOLA***

What was it like to have to grow up in paradise? What was it like to try to connect with the volatile man rather than the legend? Coppola never saw *Priscilla* in strictly biopic terms (genre is simply part of the design), but as a film about feelings. 'I really wanted to capture how overwhelming that first brush with love is and how confusing it can be trying to understand a man who's so hot and cold,'[8] she explained. It was a universal experience in a heightened environment.

If there was a familiarity about all this, isn't that what makes a director an auteur? It was a new spin on recognizable Coppola-isms: the intoxication and toxicity of fame, the challenge of forging an identity in a world that seeks to define you, the ennui that lurks behind the perfect life, the perfect hotel (Graceland covers that). After her study of the French queen and the rogue teens of *The Bling Ring*, this was her third film dancing with fact. Like *Marie Antoinette*, Priscilla is anointed into a marriage and a gilded cage in which she begins to suffocate. This is the rise and fall of a romantic ideal.

They meet in Germany in 1959, where Elvis (Jacob Elordi) is stationed during his stint in the U.S. Army, and shy, bobby-socked Priscilla Beaulieu (Cailee Spaeny) is living on the base with her mother (Dagmara Domińczyk) and military stepfather (Ari Cohen). It was one of the ways in which Coppola related to her story. Growing up, she had felt like an Army Brat, always on the move with her father's shoots. It was during one of those restless productions that she had first

Below: *A million rivals - Priscilla (Cailee Spaeny) begins to understand that she will always have to contend with swathes of adoring fans.*

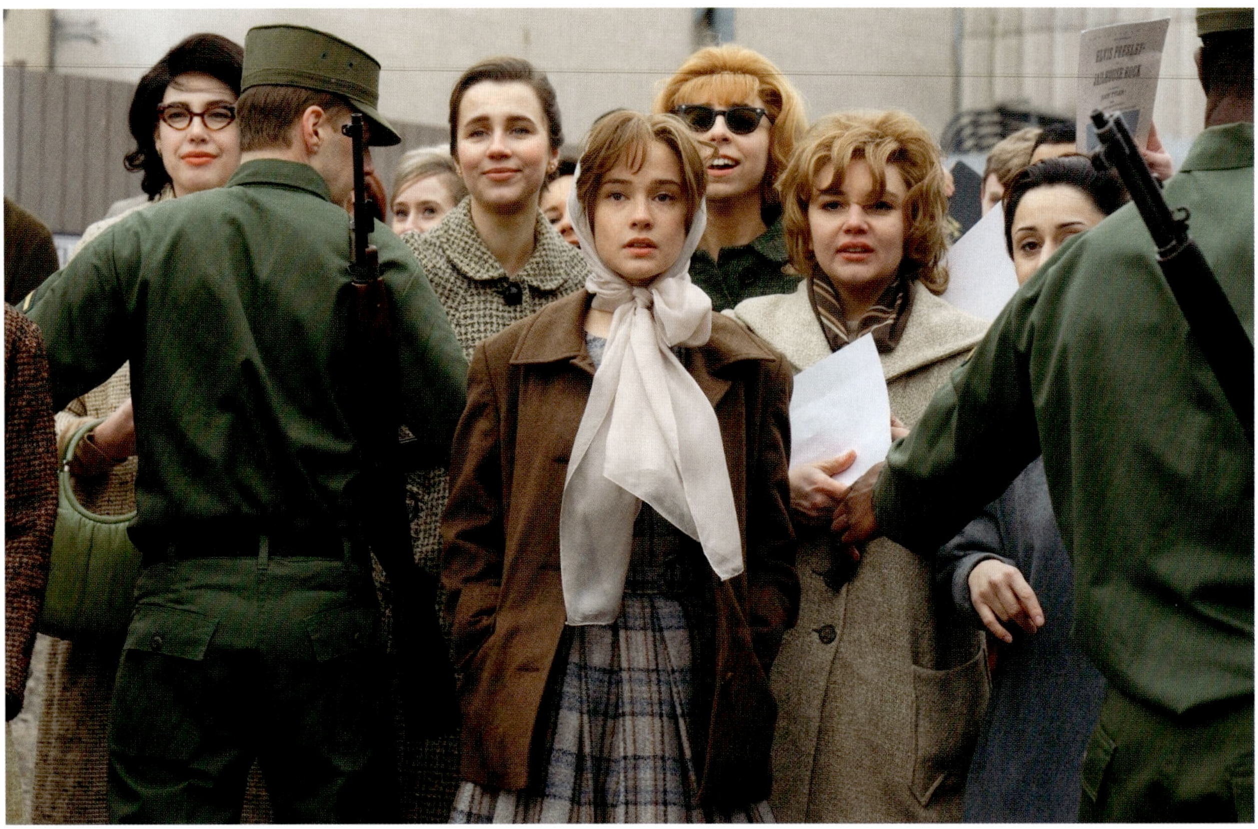

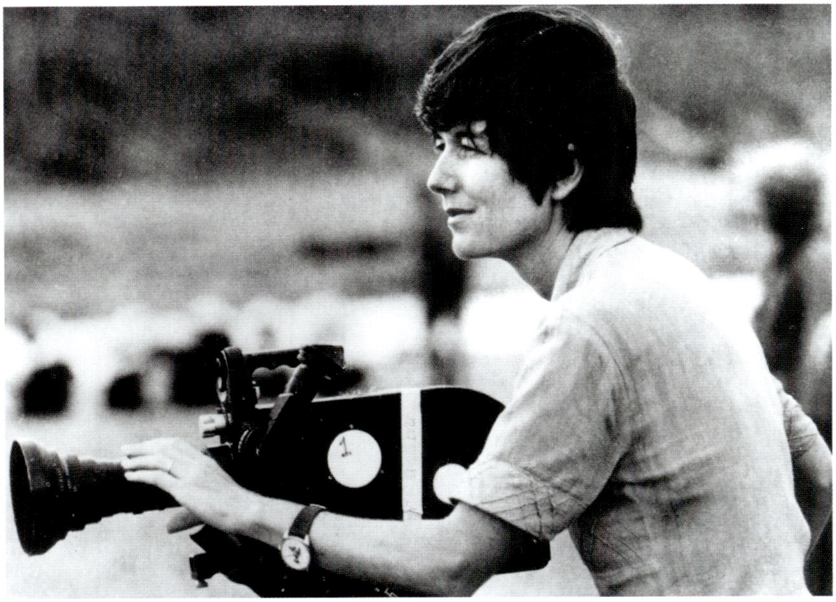

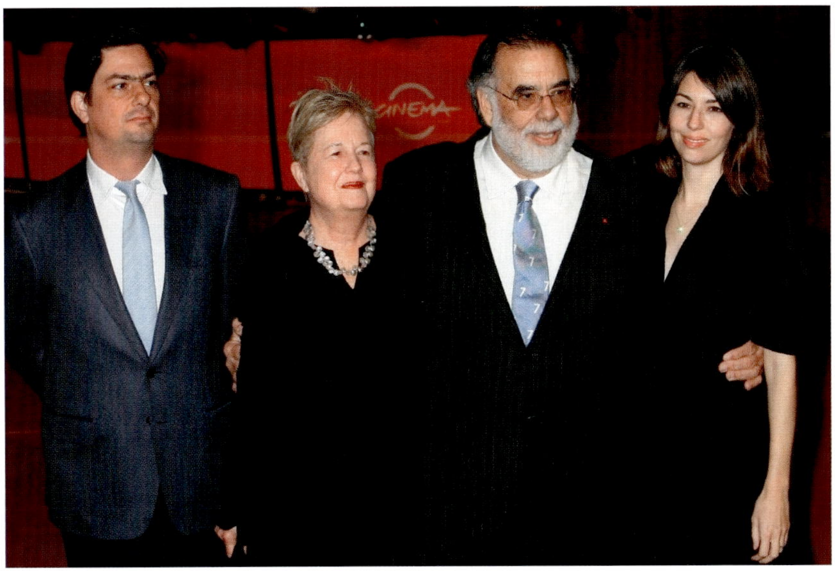

Top: *Eleanor Coppola filming what would become the documentary* Hearts of Darkness, *during the tumultuous production of* Apocalypse Now. *Sofia Coppola would see a lot of her own mother in Priscilla's story.*

Above: *Sofia (right) often credits her mother as the power that held the family together. She's pictured here with her son Roman Coppola and husband Francis at the Rome Film Festival.*

visited Graceland. He was in Memphis filming *The Rainmaker* when she took the short trip to Elvis' sanctified home and National Historic Landmark – it was a mad place, so incongruous, like Versailles, a human-sized doll house. Recreated for the 2022 Toronto shoot, the Corinthian columns and Colonial Revival styling also recalled the lethargic Napoleonville manor at the centre of *The Beguiled*, and the kind of show home that would be raided by the kids of *The Bling Ring*.

The impossible happens to tiny Priscilla: Elvis, the most famous man in the world, invites her back to stay in Graceland, unfathomably winning the trust of her parents. They are like Lux and Trip from *The Virgin Suicides*, young and foolish, but she will be married and posed among his figurines. As the calendar pages are torn away, she will surrender to motherhood and loneliness, before finally summoning the strength to leave the fading monument behind.

Coppola saw herself in that journey too. Her dilemma was different: she was trying to escape not a marriage but the reputation of her family name – the expectation that came with it. Where she refracted her relationship with her father through *On the Rocks*, she mused that this film said so much about the women of her mother Eleanor's generation. The expectations of them to stay at home.

'I know that she struggled with having a creative life of her own,' recalled Coppola, 'and was expected to be a mother and a wife; or at least, those were the priorities.'[9] Overshadowed by both her husband and daughter, Eleanor Coppola was an experimental artist, memoirist, and filmmaker in her own right. It wasn't in her mother's nature to seek the limelight, but Coppola recognized that, as a director, she was closer in sensibility to Eleanor than Francis.

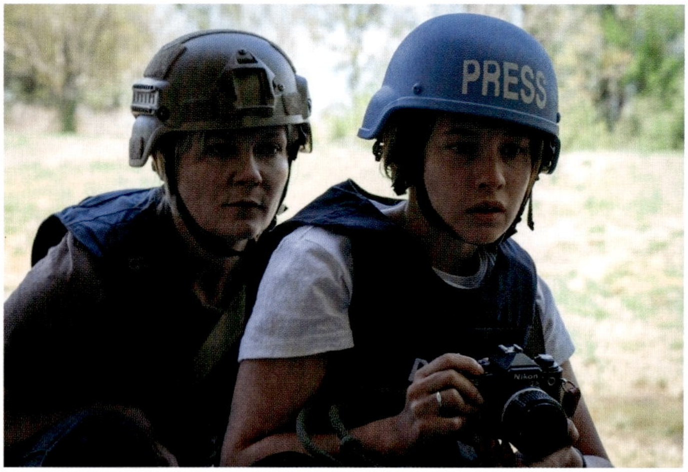

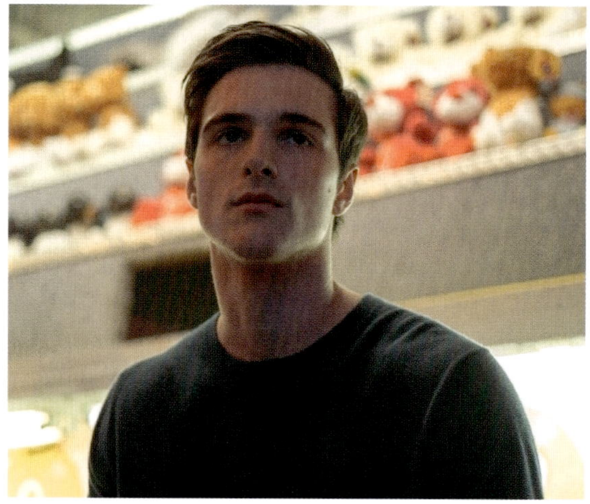

Above left: *Cailee Spaeny was a relative unknown at the time, having had only small roles in films such as* Civil War *(2024) with Kirsten Dunst…*

Above right: *… while Jacob Elordi was probably best known for his role in hit HBO drama* Euphoria *(2019).*

'My mom is more of a quiet observer, which I think I've taken from her into my work. I think that comes through; that aspect of her personality, or what I've inherited from her. That side of myself is deeply connected to her.'[10]

Elordi's Elvis is a new type for Coppola: insidiously unlikeable, prone to mood swings and self-doubt, mercurial in ways more sinister than Bill Murray's idiosyncratic moves, more of a brute than McBurney in *The Beguiled*. The actor is as handsome as Elvis but feels more oppressive, a ghostly presence, not quite there. So different from Austin Butler's puppy-dog superstar in Baz Luhrmann's carnivalesque biopic *Elvis*, released a year earlier.

The news of a rival project didn't perturb Coppola. She had already written her script when she heard, and watched Luhrmann's film just before heading into production. 'It's like, okay, and then next year you get to hear Priscilla's story.'[11]

She was telling the alternative tale with the sure knowledge that her choices, from French history to a Christmas Special to the bride of Elvis, would always be embalmed in her subdued mood. 'Coppola finds a way of telling… without being in any way sensationalist, or overtly judgemental but allowing the audience to see,'[12] enthused Mark Kermode on *Kermode and Mayo's Take*.

'I do like movies where things aren't all spelled out,'[13] she explained with a credo that she has carried through an entire career.

For the leads, Coppola had deliberately sought out unknowns, avoiding the distractions of celebrity (there was enough of that already), but it speaks volumes to her eye for a captivating face that both have gone on to become major stars (just as Kirsten Dunst, Scarlett Johansson, and Elle Fanning have done). Australian-born Elordi, a successful junior athlete, had toiled on glib Netflix romcoms before his talent surfaced as the narcissist jock in hit drama series *Euphoria*. Coppola met him in a New York coffee shop, sold by the effect his presence had on passing women.

Quite what Elvis is ever thinking is an enigma. At times, he seems as trapped as Priscilla is, surrounded by beer-swilling cronies (filled by local Toronto actors), bound by the rigours of stardom. Only once does Coppola show him on stage, as mythical Elvis, strategically shot from behind as Elordi expertly works through the trademark moves in silhouette, a man isolated in the spotlight with the hungry clamour of the Vegas crowd ringing in his ears.

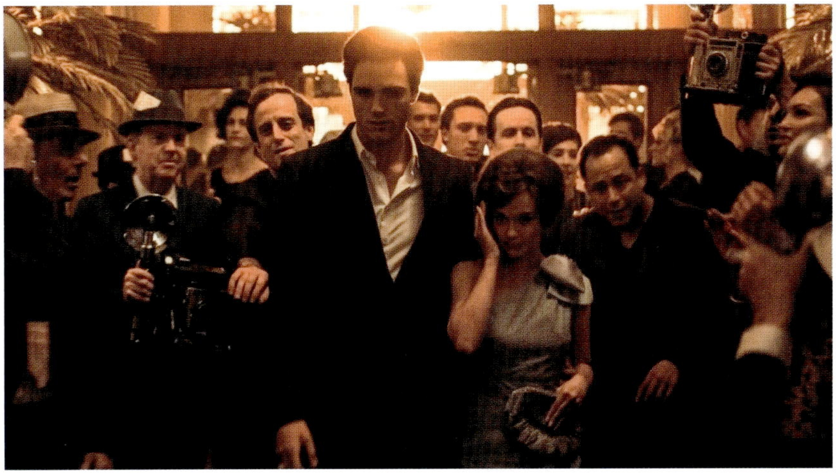

Left: *The most famous couple on the planet – Elvis (Elordi) and Priscilla (Spaeny) are constantly on show to the massed cameras of the paparazzi...*

Below: *... but* Priscilla *is far more the story of what it was like on the inside of Graceland, for good and bad.*

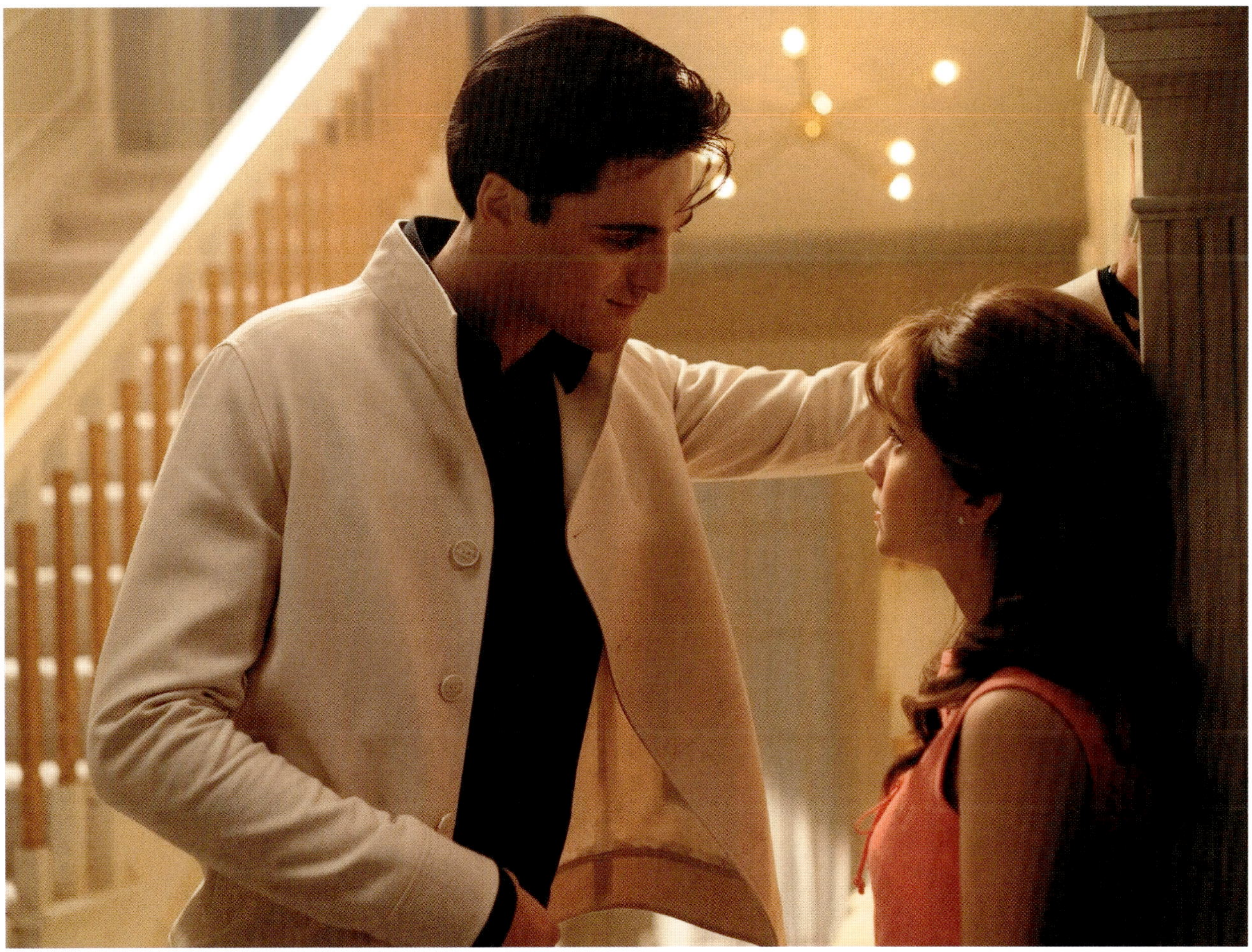

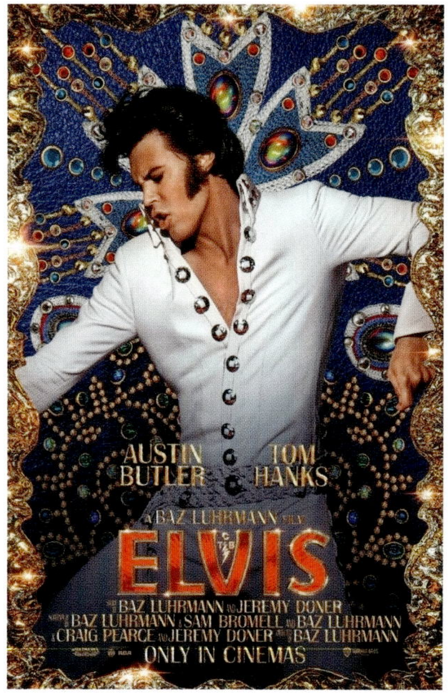

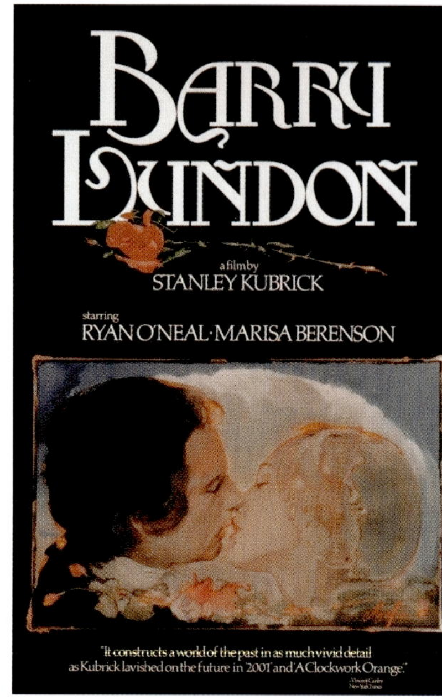

Above left: *As she wrote her script, Sofia Coppola would discover that she had a rival Elvis biopic in Baz Luhrmann's elaborate* Elvis *(2022).*

Above right: *Among the array of fictions that inspired Coppola was the strange marriage at the heart of Stanley Kubrick's* Barry Lyndon *(1975).*

Opposite: *Coppola would dwell on close-ups of Priscilla (Cailee Spaeny) making herself up like a doll. It is the act of putting on the face of Elvis' wife, which may not actually be her own.*

In typically Coppola fashion, the music is consciously anachronistic. Apart from a sliver of 'Love Me Tender', there is not a single Elvis classic to be heard: instead her husband Thomas Mars (the rock star Coppola did end up marrying) and his band Phoenix provided the score, including a spacey cover version of Frankie Avalon's 'Venus.' Coppola wanted a vibration of the era – a dream take. 'I wanted to find a way to include music from that time period that connects with Priscilla's story but also still aligns with my taste.'[14]

As she kept reiterating, the film was called *Priscilla*, and 'her experience was unique and interesting enough just to present.'[15]

No other Coppola film has rested so heavily on the title role. She needed a leading lady who could convincingly mature from fourteen to twenty-nine: all the stages of the Coppola life cycle from girlhood to grown woman. She had seen Cailee Spaeny in *Mare of Easttown* and was stunned to discover she had been in her twenties playing fifteen. Having recently worked with Spaeny in *Civil War* (shot before *Priscilla* though released after), Kirsten Dunst was effusive in her praise for the actress. As with Elordi, Coppola preferred to meet Cailee in a coffee shop and chat rather than going through the stresses of auditioning. There was always that sensation that Coppola was subconsciously casting versions of herself.

Spaeny turned out to be a huge fan, obsessed with *The Virgin Suicides* – she had been the right age, with the right sensibility. 'That movie rocked me in a way that I had never felt before,'[16] she admitted.

Coppola showed Spaeny certain scenes from other films, fixing on specifics. The carriage ride from *Barry Lyndon* for the shot of Priscilla and Elvis travelling silently in a limo. For the first time the singer takes her to Vegas, she showed early parts of *Sid & Nancy* for the us-against-the-world feel of the relationship. On YouTube, they watched the Presley home movies that gave such a strong impression of how the couple acted at home. Coppola mentioned *Alice in Wonderland*, a life that gets curiouser and curiouser.

Spaeny was more than up to the task of conveying what she called the 'human moments'[17] within this marriage. And with limited time they had to shoot out of sequence – the 120 costume changes formed a psychology for the character, her changing hairstyles marked the changing fashions. She would be awarded the Volpi Cup for Best Actress at the Venice Film Festival.

'Cailee can convey so much with so little fanfare,'[18] declared Keaton Bell in *Vogue*.

Variety praised her 'slow-motion melancholy.'[19]

Where Luhrmann's studio-backed *Elvis* had \$85 million to play with, Coppola's independent path meant things were forever tight, even eight films into her career. They shot in wintery, adaptable Toronto for the value it offered. In October 2022, only days from production, they lost a portion of the money and a week off the shoot, which

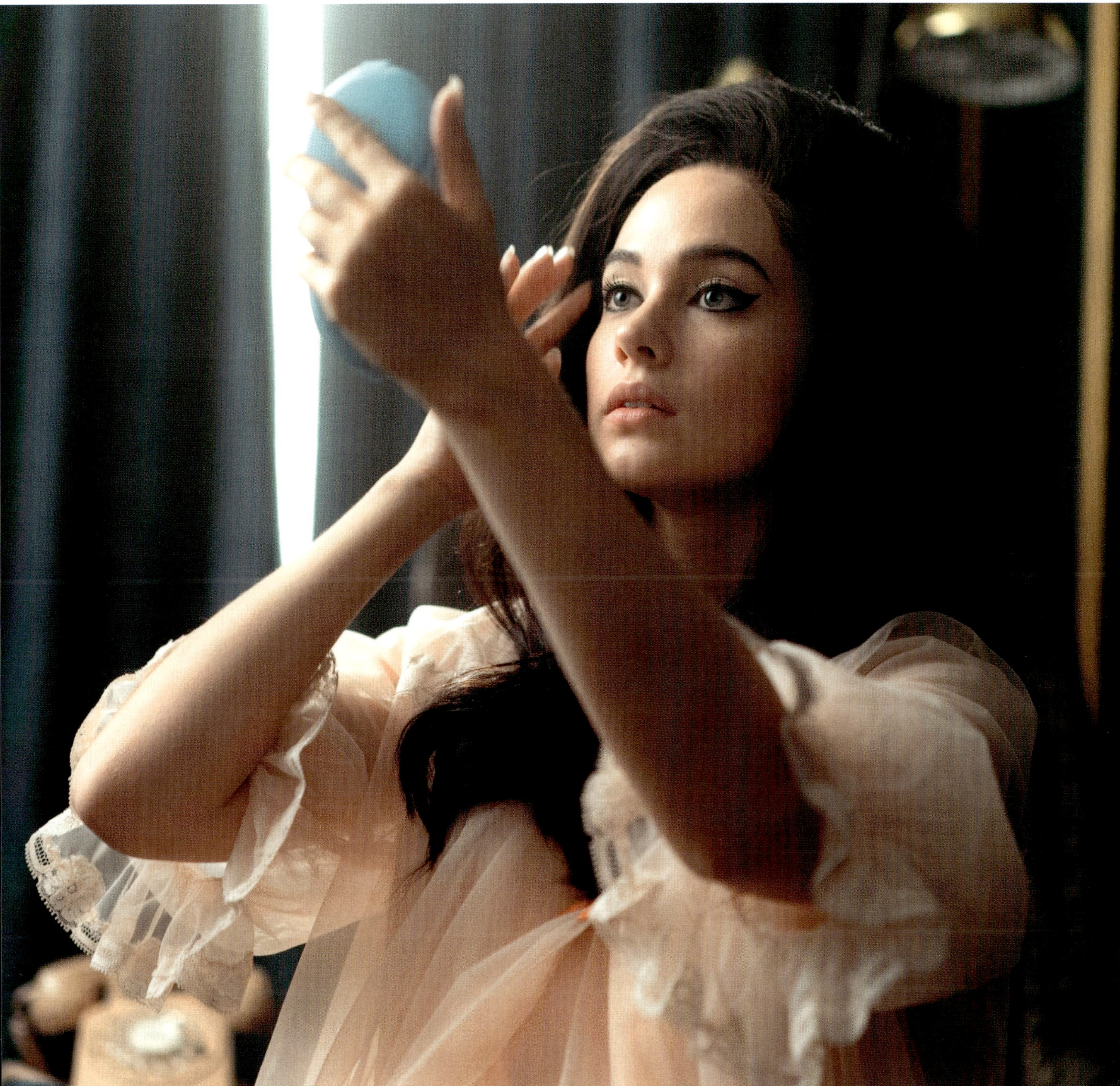

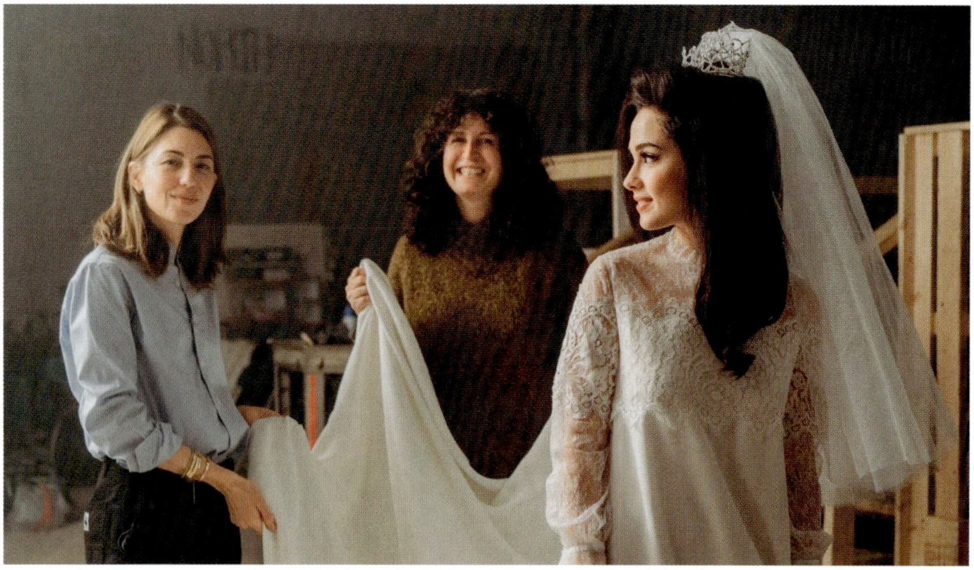

Left: *Sofia Coppola and costume designer Stacey Battat check out the film's version of Priscilla's wedding gown, being worn by Cailee Spaeny. More than any of her other films,* Priscilla *amplified Coppola's love of fabric and fashion.*

Below: *Slave to fashion – Priscilla's evolving looks were a way for the film to chart the passing of time. She had everything she could want, but was given so little of what she needed.*

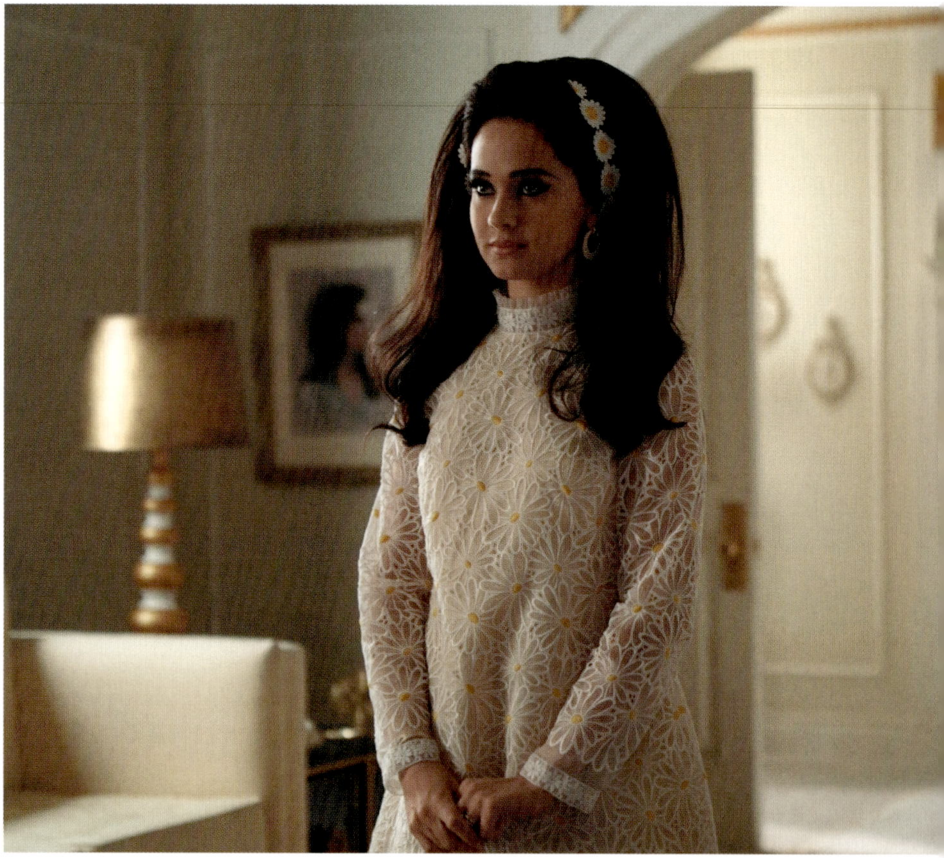

meant cutting ten pages from the script. The final budget was $20 million.

'We lost a scene of Priscilla riding motorcycles when she was eight months pregnant,' recalled Coppola. 'I thought it was so touching that she's trying so hard to keep up with Elvis, even in that condition.'[20]

Naturally, it was a difficult time, but there was something to be said for limiting your means. It crystallized what was important in the story, and she loved that handmade quality that comes with lower-budget films, everyone in it together, without a studio executive leaning over her shoulder. Walking onto the cramped soundstages at Pinewood Toronto Studios, she would see Lisa Marie's nursery in one corner, then turn around and walk into a Memphis hair salon. She was so proud that the work of production designer Tamara Deverell still had a certain muted grandeur – and a distorted sense of luxury. Nothing ever feels homely.

Coppola got to create her own hermetic Graceland, moving through the sixties to 1972, when Elvis and Priscilla separated. After the modern New York of *On the Rocks*, she had craved another immersion in the

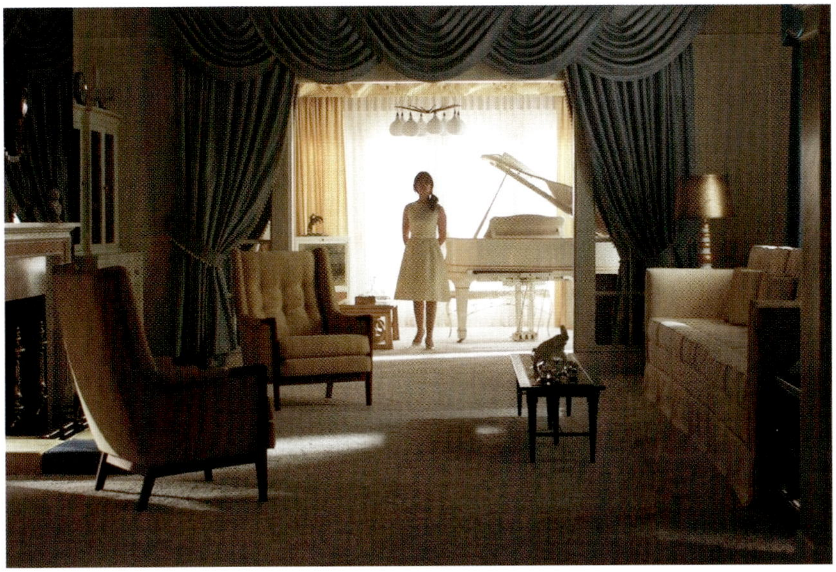

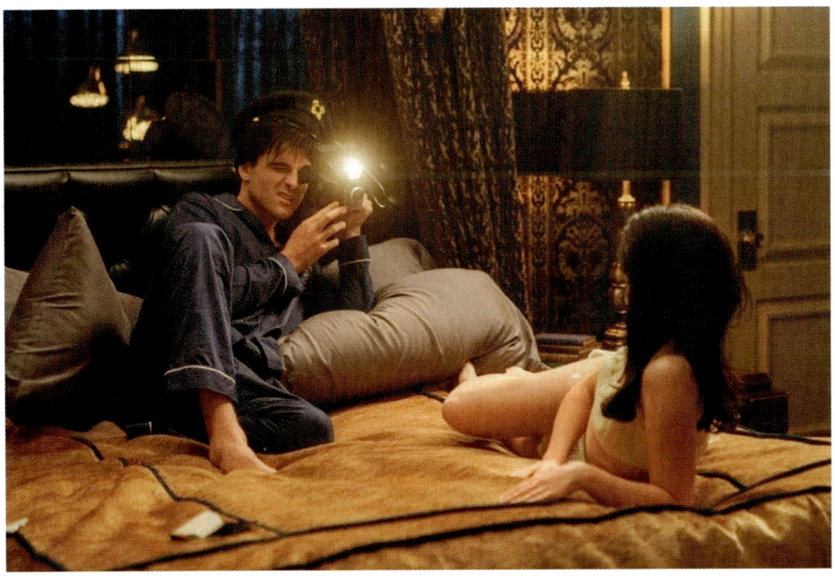

Top: *An exile in her own home – Priscilla (Spaeny) becomes more ornament than wife within the sterile luxury of Graceland.*

Above: *Lighter moments – Elvis (Jacob Elordi) and Priscilla share an intimate bedroom moment. In advising for the film, the real Priscilla Presley had insisted that there was love there.*

past. Elvis' sense of interior decoration was almost as playful as that of Coppola's *Marie Antoinette*. The ironic affectation came built in, but there is still a stylized authenticity at work – the truth of the world bending to the truth of the story. They weren't making a documentary. For instance, they invented the couple's marital bedroom entirely, as few photos existed of this inner sanctum.

Priscilla had described the bed as intimidating. All she could think of were the women who came before her. Beds are another running motif throughout Coppola's films, the most intimate and varied of locations. Picture Bob and Charlotte lounging just about chastely on the hotel bed in *Lost in Translation;* the struggles to consummate the marriage in the voluminous bed of *Marie Antoinette*; or Johnny lingering numbly between the sheets in *Somewhere*.

What made *Priscilla* a unique and fulfilling, though in its way intimidating experience was the proximity of Priscilla. Coppola had gained her approval for the project – thankfully, Presley loved her work and claimed she was 'quite honoured'[21] by the attention. They went through the script together, page by page, often over long phone calls, like girlfriends. Coppola could ask for those tiny details, a sense of the things that went unwritten, but Presley never came to set – to give the production space, and not make Spaeny nervous.

It was a complex relationship – Coppola wanted her to like the film, but also wanted to make something that felt true to herself, wondering how far could she pry into this woman's intimate memories. Showing Presley the finished film was terrifying.

'Oh my God, it was maybe the most nervous I've ever felt,'[22] she admitted. When it was over, Presley turned and looked at her. 'That was my life,'[23] she said softly. Spaeny, she went on to say, had expressed all of the emotions she felt during her time at

Left: *At six foot five, Jacob Elordi towered over Cailee Spaeny, which gave the film an unforeseen thematic heft, as the leading man would always dominate the frame.*

Below: *Love me tender – Elvis (Elordi) and Priscilla (Spaeny) with the baby Lisa Marie. It amazed Coppola that even having just given birth, Priscilla was fully dolled up.*

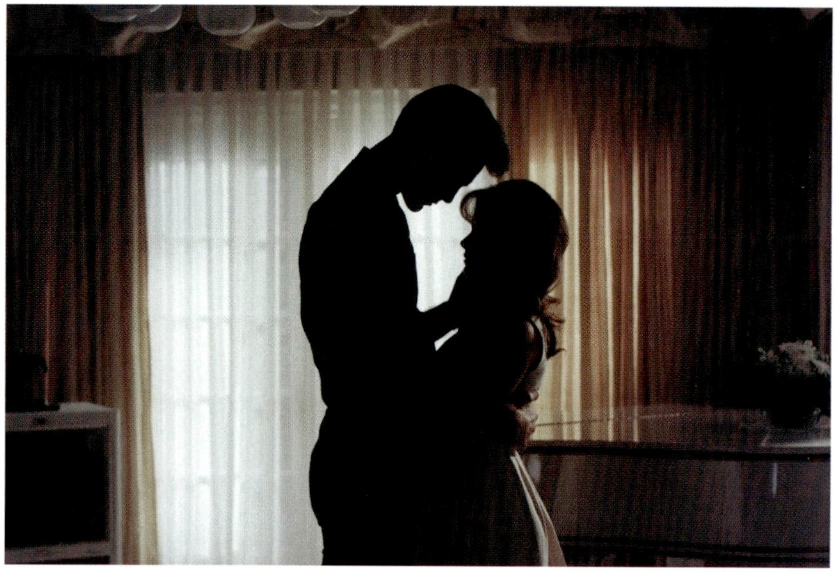

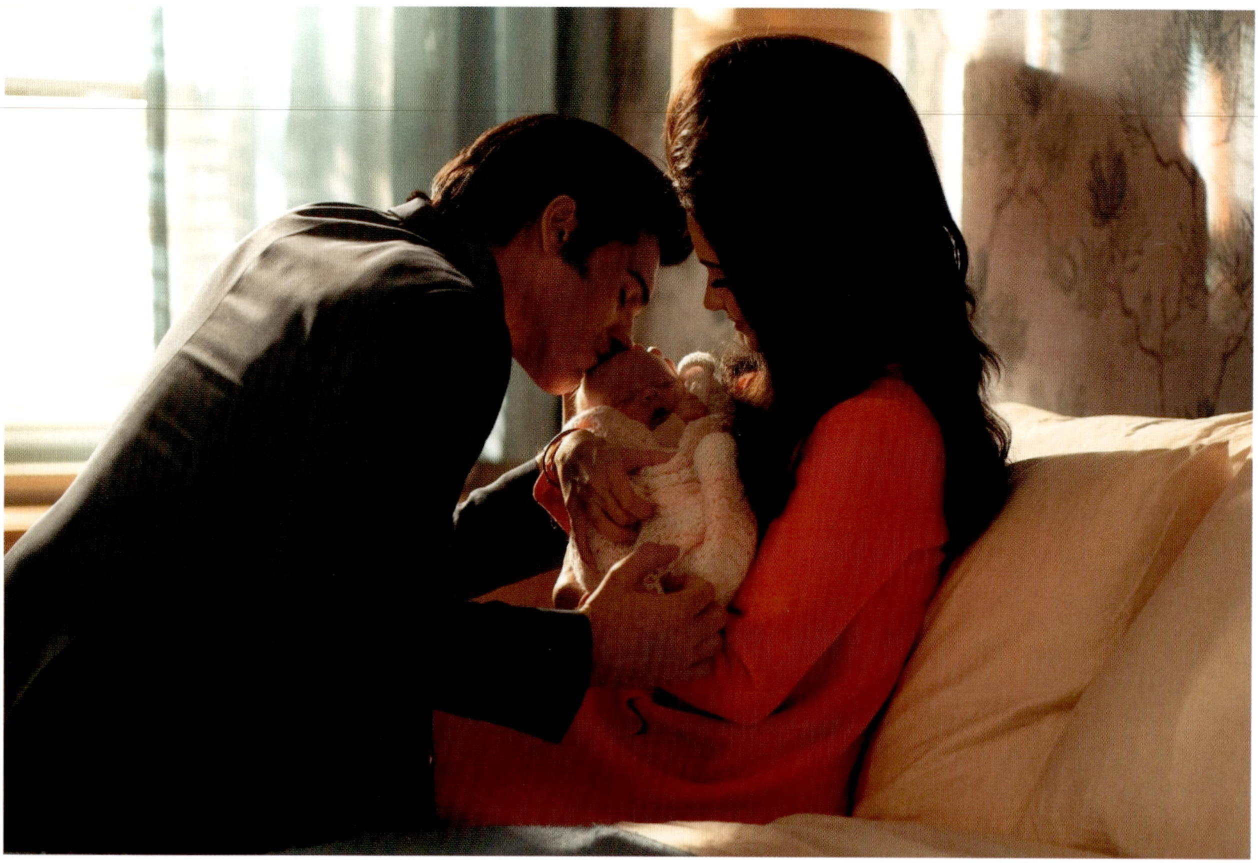

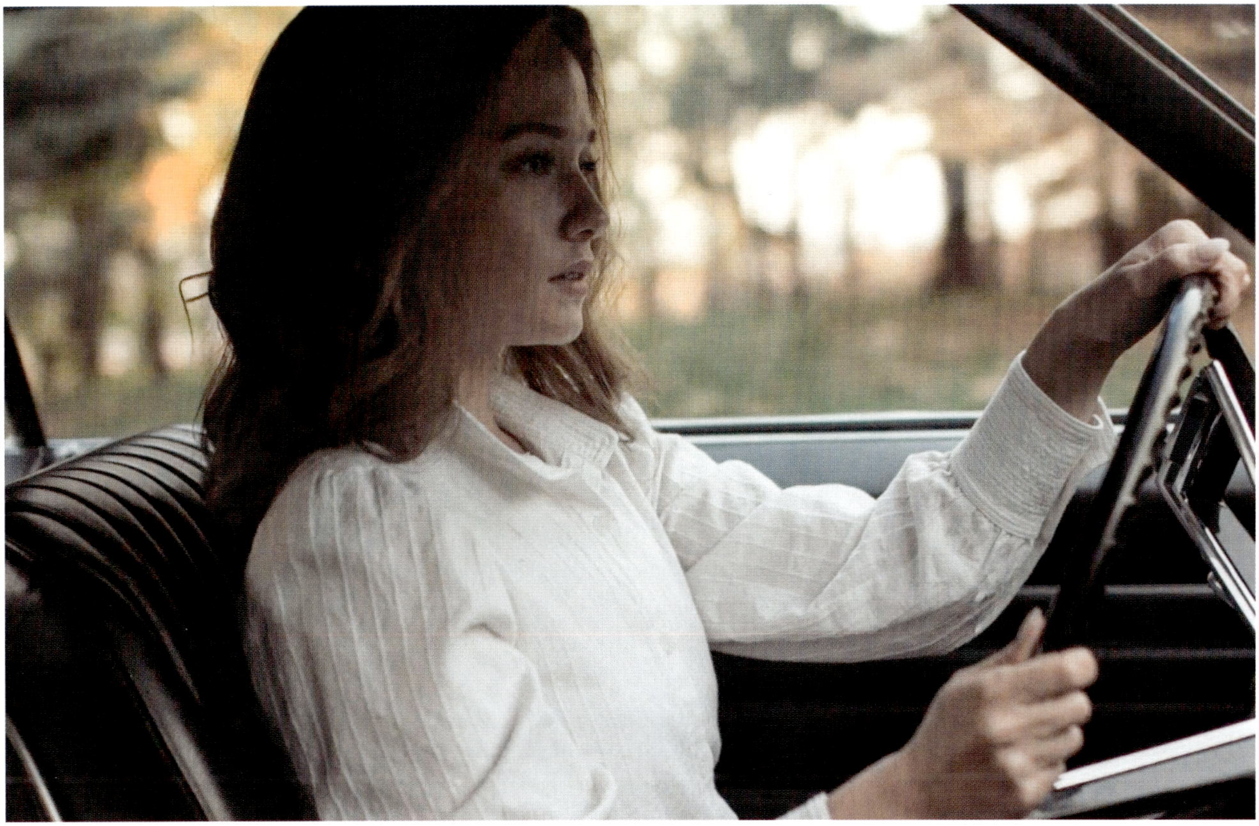

Above: *Farewell to Graceland – the film concludes at the moment when Priscilla (Spaeny, visibly more mature) takes control of her own life, and drives out through the gates of her former marital home.*

Graceland. Her only misgiving was that the eventual breakup was not as coldly emphatic as Coppola painted it for dramatic purposes, with Spaeny's Priscilla driving out of the gates of Graceland – a shiver of Marie Antoinette departing Versailles – accompanied by Dolly Parton's 'I Will Always Love You,' a song Parton had refused permission for Elvis to record due to contractual issues.

Coppola loved that the number had its own place in Elvis-lore, but had known from the writing stage that she had to have that level of heartache. 'I also thought it was important to end on a woman's voice.'[24]

The seventy-nine-year-old Presley would attend the Venice Film Festival premiere, crying through the seven-minute standing ovation, vociferous in her praise. However, shadows would gather over the production when Priscilla and Elvis' only child, Lisa Marie, emailed her in defence of her father, saying she would publicly denounce the film. Coppola was shocked. Hadn't the book been out for decades? Was this a mother-daughter issue? Did she feel betrayed? Presley maintained they were still on good terms.

Coppola hadn't set out to make people feel uncomfortable about Elvis, she neither wanted to condone nor condemn – the audience should make their own minds up. He had his struggles, not least with the prescription drugs waiting in his bedside cabinet, one of which he bestows upon the palm of his wife like a love token. She wanted to capture the pressure he was under. There was love as well as darkness. You can be moved by Priscilla's plight and still love Elvis' music.

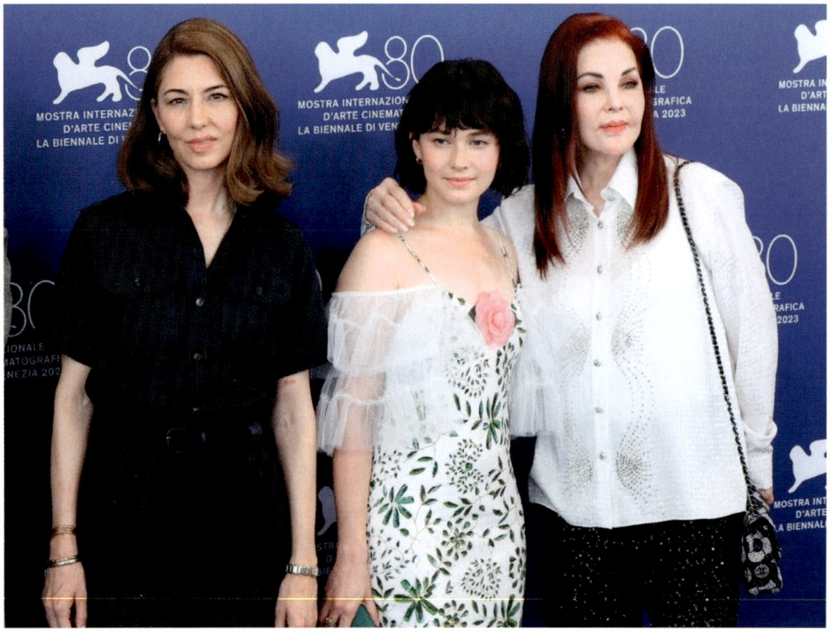

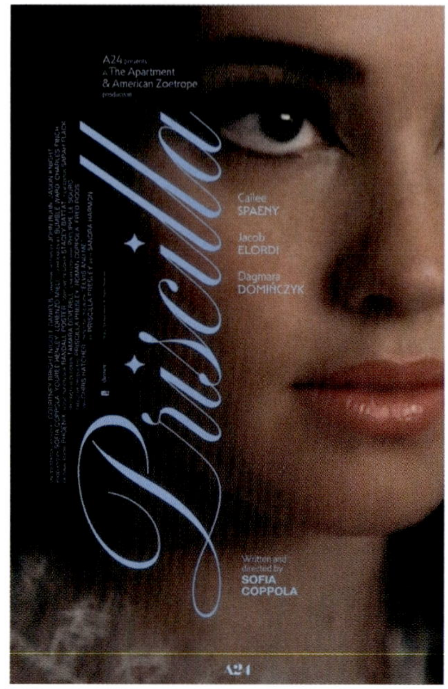

Above left: *United front – Sofia Coppola, Cailee Spaeny, and the supportive Priscilla Presley stop for a photo call at the Venice Film Festival premiere of* Priscilla *in 2023.*

Above right: Priscilla *encompasses so much of what we think of as Coppola's style and themes, but it has a darkness that is all its own. In a sense, it is her prison movie.*

Adding more tragedy to the family saga, Lisa Marie Presley died four months before the film came out (from complications due to weight-loss surgery). Elvis, of course, had passed away at forty-two, though Coppola's film concludes long before his sad demise.

Priscilla was released on 23 October 2023 to decent enough rewards at the box office, with a worldwide total of $33 million. On the whole, critics appreciated Coppola's ability to tell a different kind of Elvis story – a Priscilla story. There were those who felt it lacked dramatic heft, the blow-by-blow of events, and those who understood it is Coppola's restraint which speaks so loudly. 'The film is deliberately airless and suffocating, letting viewers feel how trapped Priscilla is in her situation,'[25] understood Gary M. Kramer in *Salon*. Like the jaded spirit of *Somewhere* and the sexual swamp of The *Beguiled*, there is a discomfort here that seeps into you. Celebrity, the director confirms, is not what it is cracked up to be.

Coppola has reached the stage of her career when books are written about her, laurels given, conclusions drawn. Indeed, in the lead-up to making *Priscilla*, she had been putting together her own, naturally arty-leaning book, *Sofia Coppola Archive*, made up of her pictures and letters and notes from all eight of her films. Essentially, a mood board of her career. Only now did it dawn on her how connected her movies were. She understood that this is her 'vocabulary.'[26]

In twenty-six years she has made only eight films, a Christmas special, and a documentary, but we get a true sense of her as a filmmaker – and a person. She knew it wasn't exactly a prolific output.

'I'm just not one of these people that has a bunch of things cooking all at once,' she admitted. 'I kind of put my heart totally into one thing, and then I have to get my energy back before going back in.'[27]

She never set out to be a filmmaker, it was the films that called to her. 'You have to do it, because it bugs you until you do,'[28] she laughed. *The Virgin Suicides* (now such a totem), *Lost in Translation* (surely her masterpiece), *Marie Antoinette* (no longer misunderstood), *Somewhere* (her most ephemeral, and perhaps most personal film), *The Bling Ring* (which allowed to her to find an edge), *The Beguiled* (arguably her most mainstream work, but completely her own), *On the Rocks* (the indulgence we all craved), and now *Priscilla* (a bittersweet cocktail of so many of her preoccupations).

We know her style so well, but putting it into words, even over an entire book, is a challenge.

On one level, it still feels as if she is only just getting started, as if that thing she needs to express, an interpretation of human nature or just her own state of mind, remains out of reach.

That sense of reluctance combined with absolute determination trembles through her characters. She is the reluctant Coppola who has risen far above accusations of nepotism. Say the name 'Coppola' in 2026 and it is Sofia that comes to mind. Intimate, feminine, otherworldly, resolutely independent: she is so different from her father's great seventies heyday, though they both have such an eye for cinematic detail and are defiantly personal artists. Ironically, being a Coppola is something she can only process by making films. She understands that knowing who we are is the biggest mystery of all.

Her worlds may be rarified, her hotels five-star, she might explore celebrity and wealth, and coax great performances from attractive movie stars, but she assures us that these things are no guarantee against loss and loneliness. Her eight films could have been made just for us.

'I feel like I want to put beauty into the world, even if I have doubts about things,'[29] she once said.

The great joy and power of Coppola's vocabulary is the whisper we will never hear.

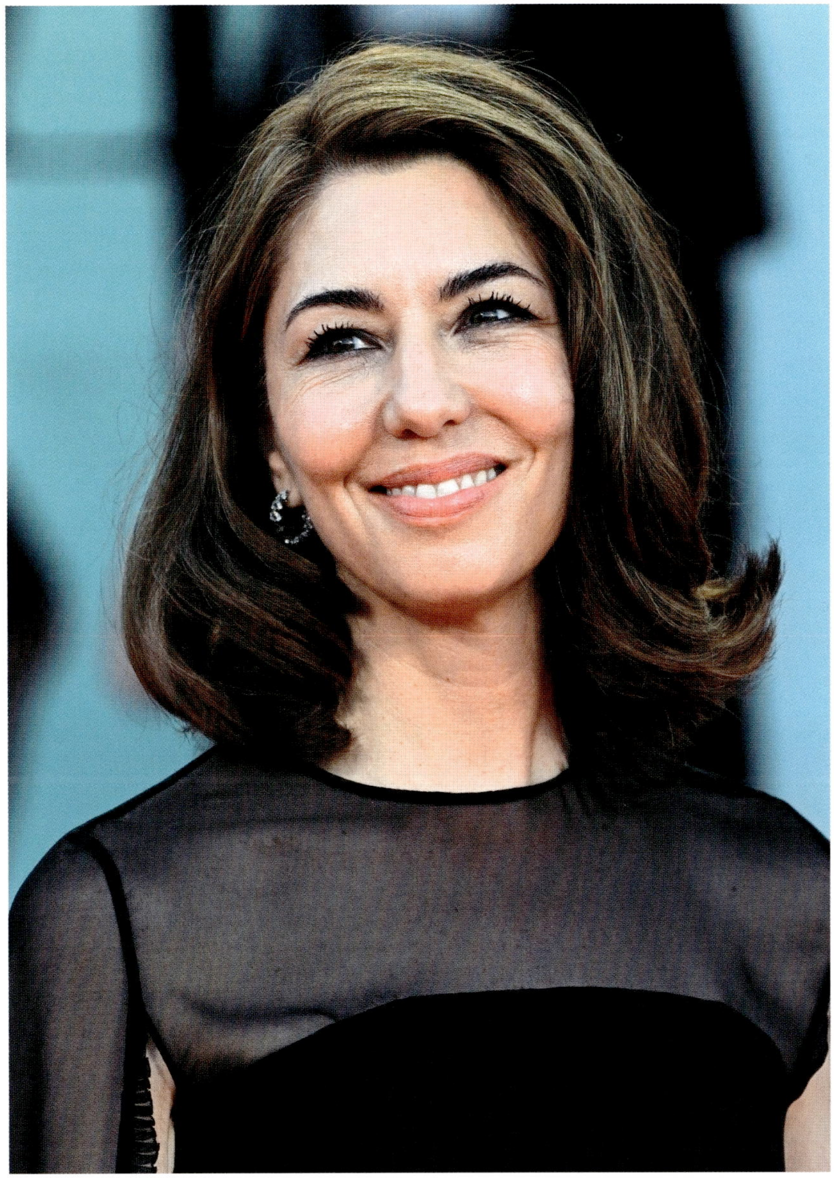

Above: *Coppola in 2023, established as a major director, feted as a great artist, but with surely so much still to share.*

SOURCES

BIBLIOGRAPHY

Coppola, Eleanor, *Notes on a Life*, Nan A. Talese/ Doubleday, 2008
Coppola, Sofia, *Sofia Coppola Archive 1999-2023*, Mack, 2023
Ferriss, Suzanne, *Lost in Translation – BFI Film Classics*, Bloomsbury Publishing, 2023
Monaghan, Amy N. (editor), *Sofia Coppola: Interviews*, University Press of Mississippi, 2023
Nathan, Ian, *The Coppolas: A Movie Dynasty*, Palazzo, 2021
Strong, Hannah, *Sofia Coppola: Forever Young*, Abrams, New York, 2022

DOCUMENTARIES

The Beguiled: Colin Farrell On Sofia Coppola's 'Laid-Back Environment' On Set, Entertainment Weekly via YouTube, 30 June 2017
Jeffrey Eugenides' First Time, Paris Review via YouTube, 2016
The Making of 'Marie Antoinette', Marie Antoinette DVD, Sony Pictures Home Entertainment, 2007
The Making of Priscilla, A24 via YouTube, 8 October 2025
Sofia Coppola Breaks Down the Dinner Scene, Vanity Fair via YouTube, 22 June 2017
Sofia Coppola Looks Back on Growing Up Cinephile, Criterion Channel, 24 May 2019
Sofia Coppola on Directing On The Rocks and Casting Rashida Jones and Bill Murray - On Directing, BAFTA Guru via YouTube, 22 March 2021
Sofia Coppola on Priscilla, Lost in Translation and her filmmaking career - BFI in conversation, BFI via YouTube, 3 January 2024
Sofia Coppola on the Writing Process, On Stage Q&A for The Beguiled, Angelika Film Center, 23 June 2017
Sofia Coppola: Spotlight on Conversations, AFI Film Festival, 11 November 2017
Sofia's Touch featurette, Universal Pictures Home Entertainment, 2017

INTRODUCTION

1. Syme, Rachel, *Sofia Coppola's Path to Filming Gilded Adolescence, New Yorker*, 22 January 2024
2. Ibid
3. Ibid
4. Hirschberg, Lynn, *The Coppola Smart Mob, New York Times*, 31 August 2003
5. *Sofia Coppola Looks Back on Growing Up Cinephile*, Criterion Channel, 24 May 2019
6. *Sofia Coppola on the Writing Process, On Stage Q&A for The Beguiled*, Angelika Film Center, 23 June 2017

FAMILY TIES

1. Coppola, Francis Ford & Coppola, Eleanor, *Lost and Found Sound: Five-Year-Old Sofia Coppola, All Things Considered*, 27 February 2004
2. Ibid
3. Syme, Rachel, *Sofia Coppola's Path to Filming Gilded Adolescence, New Yorker*, 22 January 2024
4. Monaghan, Amy N. (editor), *Sofia Coppola: Interviews*, University Press of Mississippi, 2023
5. Chuba, Kirsten, *Sofia Coppola Recalls Early Career 'Before Nepo Babies Were Charming' and was considered Actress Who 'Ruined the Godfather Films', Hollywood Reporter*, 13 November 2025
6. Syme, Rachel, *Sofia Coppola's Path to Filming Gilded Adolescence, New Yorker*, 22 January 2024
7. Ibid
8. Nathan, Ian, *The Coppolas: A Movie Dynasty*, Palazzo, 2021
9. Ebert, Roger, *New York Stories review, Chicago Sun-Times*, 3 March 1989
10. Jones, Eileen, *Sofia Coppola Wants You to Feel Bad for the Very Rich and the Very Sad, Jacobin*, 4 December 2020
11. Chuba, Kirsten, *Sofia Coppola Recalls Early Career 'Before Nepo Babies Were Charming' and was considered Actress Who 'Ruined the Godfather Films', Hollywood Reporter*, 13 November 2025
12. Corliss, Richard, *Cinema: Schemes And Dreams for Christmas, Time*, 24 December 1990
13. Kael, Pauline, *The Godfather Part III review, New Yorker*, 14 January 1991
14. Anderson, Wes, *Sofia Coppola, Interview*, October 1999
15. Ibid
16. Bell, Keaton, *Sofia Coppola on the 20th Anniversary of The Virgin Suicides: 'It Means a Lot to Me That It Has a Life Now', Vogue*, 21 April 2020
17. Insdorf, Annette, *Sofia Coppola on Filmmaking, 92Y Reel Pieces*, 20 April 2020
18. Syme, Rachel, *Sofia Coppola's Path to Filming Gilded Adolescence, New Yorker*, 22 January 2024
19. Ibid
20. Nancy Spiller, *Coppola Puts Own Career in High Gear : The Daughter of a Famous Director Has a Few Goals of Her Own, Los Angeles Times*, Feb 4 1995
21. Coppola, Francis Ford & Coppola, Eleanor, *Lost and Found Sound: Five-Year-Old Sofia Coppola, All Things Considered*, 27 February 2004
22. Unattributed, *Sofia Coppola, Metro Pop*, Spring 2002
23. Ibid
24. Syme, Rachel, *Sofia Coppola's Path to Filming Gilded Adolescence, New Yorker*, 22 January 2024

THE LOST GIRLS

1. Coppola, Sofia, *Sofia Coppola on making The Virgin Suicides: 'When I saw the rough cut I thought: Oh no, what have I done?', Guardian*, 25 January 2018
2. Anderson, Wes, *Sofia Coppola, Interview*, October 1999
3. *Jeffrey Eugenides' First Time, Paris Review* via YouTube, 2016
4. Ibid
5. Ibid
6. Ebner, Mark, *Like a 'Virgin', Salon*, 1 February 2000
7. Abbott, Megan, *'They Hadn't Heard Us Calling'*, Criterion Collection, booklet, 2018
8. Bell, Keaton, *Sofia Coppola on the 20th Anniversary of The Virgin Suicides: 'It Means a Lot to Me That It Has a Life Now', Vogue*, 21 April 2020
9. *The Virgin Suicides* blu-ray, Criterion Collection, 2018
10. Ibid
11. Ibid
12. Coppola, Sofia, *Sofia Coppola Archive 1999-2023*, Mack, 2023
13. Bell, Keaton, *Sofia Coppola on the 20th Anniversary of The Virgin Suicides: 'It Means a Lot to Me That It Has a Life Now', Vogue*, 21 April 2020
14. Coppola, Sofia, *Sofia Coppola on making The Virgin Suicides: 'When I saw the rough cut I thought: Oh no, what have I done?', Guardian*, 25 January 2018
15. Nolfi, Joey, *Sofia Coppola: Studio was 'Afraid' of Girls Watching The Virgin Suicides*, Entertainment Weekly, 23 April 2018
16. Coppola, Sofia, *Sofia Coppola Archive 1999-2023*, Mack, 2023
17. Ibid
18. Tijerina, Daniela, *Sofia Coppola on the Film Execs Afraid of The Virgin Suicides, and the 'Guys Version' They Didn't Make, Vanity Fair*, 16 May 2025

19. Bell, Keaton, *Sofia Coppola on the 20th Anniversary of The Virgin Suicides: 'It Means a Lot to Me That It Has a Life Now'*, *Vogue*, 21 April 2020
20. Flam, Charna, *Kirsten Dunst Admits It Was 'Terrifying' Kissing Josh Hartnett in The Virgin Suicides as a Very innocent 16-Year-Old'*, *People*, 4 June 2025
21. Tijerina, Daniela, *Sofia Coppola on the Film Execs Afraid of The Virgin Suicides, and the 'Guys Version' They Didn't Make, Vanity Fair*, 16 May 2025
22. Flam, Charna, *Kirsten Dunst Admits It Was 'Terrifying' Kissing Josh Hartnett in The Virgin Suicides as a Very innocent 16-Year-Old'*, *People*, 4 June 2025
23. Ibid
24. Coggan, Devan, *Sofia Coppola and The Virgin Suicides Cast Reunite to Talk 20th Anniversary, Entertainment Weekly*, 18 June 2020
25. Thomson, David, *The New Biographical Dictionary of Film*, Little Brown, 2010
26. *The Virgin Suicides* blu-ray, Criterion Collection, 2018
27. Saada, Nicolas, *The Remaking of a Masterpiece: Air's Haunting Return to The Virgin Suicides, Manifesto*, 2025
28. Unattributed, *The Virgin Suicides review, Premiere*, May 2000
29. Scott, A.O., *Evanescent Trees and Sisters in an Enchanted 1970's Suburb, New York Times*, 21 April 2000
30. Olsen, Mark, *A World of Silent Hysteria, Sight & Sound*, June 2000
31. Ebert, Roger, *The Virgin Suicides review, Chicago Sun-Times*, 5 May 2000
32. Ebner, Mark, *Like a 'Virgin', Salon*, 1 February 2000
33. Nolfi, Joey, *Sofia Coppola: Studio was 'Afraid' of Girls Watching The Virgin Suicides, Entertainment Weekly*, 23 April 2018
34. Coppola, Sofia, *Sofia Coppola on making The Virgin Suicides: 'When I saw the rough cut I thought: Oh no, what have I done?', Guardian*, 25 January 2018

THEY MEET, THEY BREAK UP

1. Libby, Brian, *The Coppola Clan's Best Director? Salon*, 23 September 2003
2. Ibid
3. Thompson, Anne, *Tokyo Story, Filmmaker*, Fall 2003
4. Coppola, Sofia, *Sofia Coppola Archive* 1999-2023, Mack, 2023
5. Ciment, Michel & Tobin, Yann, *Interview with Sofia Coppola: An Emotion Like Nostalgia, Postif*, January 2004
6. Thompson, Anne, *Tokyo Story, Filmmaker*, Fall 2003
7. Ciment, Michel & Tobin, Yann, *Interview with Sofia Coppola: An Emotion Like Nostalgia, Postif*, January 2004
8. Libby, Brian, *The Coppola Clan's Best Director? Salon*, 23 September 2003
9. Ibid
10. Edelstein, David, *Prisoner of Japan, Slate*, 11 September 2003
11. Stern, Marlow, *Lost in Translation: Sofia Coppola on the Movie's 20th Anniversary, Rolling Stone*, 12 September 2003
12. Ibid
13. Thompson, Anne, *Tokyo Story, Filmmaker*, Fall 2003
14. Ibid
15. Ibid
16. Murray, Rebecca, *Scarlett Johansson Talks About Lost in Translation, liveabout dotcom*, 1 December 2018
17. Ferriss, Suzanne, *Lost in Translation – BFI Film Classics*, Bloomsbury Publishing, 2023
18. Libby, Brian, *The Coppola Clan's Best Director? Salon*, 23 September 2003
19. Ebert, Roger, *Lost in Translation review, Chicago Sun-Times*, 12 September 2003
20. Mitchell, Wendy, *Sofia Coppola Talks About Lost in Translation, Her Love Story That's Not Nerdy, IndieWire*, 4 February 2004
21. Ibid
22. Mitchell, Elvis, *An American in Japan, Making a Connection, New York Times*, 12 September 2003
23. Schwarzbaum, Lisa, *Lost in Translation review, Entertainment Weekly*, 11 September 2003
24. Coppola, Eleanor, *Notes on a Life*, Nan A. Talese/Doubleday, 2008
25. Lovejoy, Alice, *Two Lost Souls Adrift in Tokyo Forge an Unlikely Bond in Sofia Coppola's 21st-Century Brief Encounter, Film Comment*, July/August 2003
26. Rickey, Carrie, *A Tender, Sincere Bill Murray: In Sofia Coppola's Lost in Translation, He Finds the Role of a Lifetime, Philadelphia Inquirer*, 19 September 2003
27. Stern, Marlow, *Lost in Translation: Sofia Coppola on the Movie's 20th Anniversary, Rolling Stone*, 12 September 2003
28. Ibid
29. Brunson, Matt, *Lost in Translation: American Splendour, Creative Loafing Charlotte*, 1 October 2003

LET HER EAT CAKE

1. Gilchrist, Todd, *Interview: Sofia Coppola, IGN*, 17 October 2006
2. Ferrari, Jean-Christophe & Tobin, Yann, *Interview with Sofia Coppola: Characters Breathing, the Rustle of the Fabric, Postif*, June 2006
3. Bell, Keaton, *'It Was Like Hosting the Ultimate Party': An Oral History of Sofia Coppola's Marie Antoinette, Vogue*, 29 October 2021
4. Ibid
5. Coppola, Sofia, *Sofia Coppola Archive 1999-2023*, Mack, 2023
6. Bell, Keaton, *'It Was Like Hosting the Ultimate Party': An Oral History of Sofia Coppola's Marie Antoinette, Vogue*, 29 October 2021
7. Coppola, Sofia, *Sofia Coppola Archive 1999-2023*, Mack, 2023
8. Bell, Keaton, *'It Was Like Hosting the Ultimate Party': An Oral History of Sofia Coppola's Marie Antoinette, Vogue*, 29 October 2021
9. *Marie Antoinette DVD*, Sony Pictures Home Entertainment, 2007
10. Romney, Jonathan, *Marie Antoinette review, Independent*, 22 October 2006
11. *The Making of Marie Antoinette, Marie Antoinette DVD*, Sony Pictures Home Entertainment, 2007
12. Fraser, Antonia, *Sofia's Choice, Vanity Fair*, 17 October 2007
13. Hohenadel, Kristin, *French Royalty as Seen by Hollywood Royalty*, New York Times, 10 September 2006
14. Fraser, Antonia, *Sofia's Choice, Vanity Fair*, 17 October 2007
15. *The Making of Marie Antoinette, Marie Antoinette DVD*, Sony Pictures Home Entertainment, 2007
16. Bell, Keaton, *'It Was Like Hosting the Ultimate Party': An Oral History of Sofia Coppola's Marie Antoinette, Vogue*, 29 October 2021
17. Hohenadel, Kristin, *French Royalty as Seen by Hollywood Royalty, New York Times*, 10 September 2006
18. Rousseau, Jean-Jacques, *Confessions*, Penguin Classics, 1973
19. *The Making of Marie Antoinette, Marie Antoinette DVD*, Sony Pictures Home Entertainment, 2007
20. Bell, Keaton, *'It Was Like Hosting the Ultimate Party': An Oral History of Sofia Coppola's Marie Antoinette, Vogue*, 29 October 2021
21. Hohenadel, Kristin, *French Royalty as Seen by Hollywood Royalty, New York Times*, 10 September 2006
22. Bell, Keaton, *'It Was Like Hosting the Ultimate Party': An Oral History of Sofia Coppola's Marie Antoinette, Vogue*, 29 October 2021
23. Ebert, Roger, *Marie Antoinette review, Chicago Sun-Times*, 19 October 2006
24. *The Making of Marie Antoinette, Marie Antoinette DVD*, Sony Pictures Home Entertainment, 2007
25. Coppola, Sofia, *Sofia Coppola Archive* 1999-2023, Mack, 2023
26. Quinn, Anthony, *Marie Antoinette review, Independent*, 20 October 2006
27. Rozen, Leah, *Kirsten's Marie Antoinette Fizzles at Cannes, People*, 21 October 2006
28. Mendelsohn, Daniel, Lost in Versailles, *New York Review of Books*, 30 November 2006
29. Rife, Katie, *Sofia Coppola's Marie Antoinette was as Misunderstood as its Teenage Queen, AVClub*, 7 May 2021
30. Dwyer, Michael, *The Princess Diaries, Irish Times*, 20 October 2006

31. Bradshaw, Peter, *Marie Antoinette Review – Kirsten Dunst Stars in Dreamily Gorgeous Anachro-Period Drama, Guardian,* 25 May 2006
32. Freer, Ian, *Marie Antoinette review, Empire,* November 2006
33. Honeycutt, Kirk, *Marie Antoinette review, Hollywood Reporter,* 19 October 2006
34. Ebert, Roger, *Marie Antoinette review, Chicago Sun-Times,* 19 October 2006
35. Coppola, Sofia, *Sofia Coppola Archive* 1999-2023, Mack, 2023
36. Bell, Keaton, *'It Was Like Hosting the Ultimate Party': An Oral History of Sofia Coppola's Marie Antoinette, Vogue,* 29 October 2021
37. Rife, Katie, *Sofia Coppola's Marie Antoinette was as Misunderstood as its Teenage Queen, AVClub,* 7 May 2021
38. *Marie Antoinette DVD,* Sony Pictures Home Entertainment, 2007

HOTEL CALIFORNIA

1. Coppola, Sofia, *Sofia Coppola Archive* 1999-2023, Mack, 2023
2. Thompson, Anne, *Oscar Watch: True Grit's Joel Coen Interviews Somewhere's Sofia Coppola, IndieWire,* 22 November 2010
3. Hirschberg, Lynn, *Somewhere, W,* 1 December 2010
4. *Somewhere DVD,* Universal Pictures Home Entertainment, 2011
5. Coppola, Sofia, *Sofia Coppola Archive* 1999-2023, Mack, 2023
6. O'Connor, Clint, *Sofia Coppola Gives Chateau Marmont a Starring Role in Somewhere, Cleveland.com,* 21 January 2011
7. Gross, Terry, *Sofia Coppola Mimics Hollywood Life in Somewhere, Fresh Air,* 20 December 2010
8. Leon, Humberto, *Sofia Coppola Somewhere Interview, Anyonegirl,* 22 December 2010
9. Ibid
10. Brody, Richard, *DVD of the Week: Somewhere, New Yorker,* 1 November 2011
11. Ibid
12. Leon, Humberto, *Sofia Coppola Somewhere Interview, Anyonegirl,* 22 December 2010
13. Coppola, Sofia, *Sofia Coppola Archive* 1999-2023, Mack, 2023
14. O'Connor, Clint, *Sofia Coppola Gives Chateau Marmont a Starring Role in Somewhere, Cleveland.com,* 21 January 2011
15. Gross, Terry, *Sofia Coppola Mimics Hollywood Life in Somewhere, Fresh Air,* 20 December 2010
16. Strong, Hannah, *Sofia Coppola: Forever Young,* Abrams, New York, 2022
17. Ebert, Roger, *Lone Wolf of the Chateau, Chicago Sun-Times,* 21 December 2010
18. Gross, Terry, *Sofia Coppola Mimics Hollywood Life in Somewhere, Fresh Air,* 20 December 2010
19. Coppola, Sofia, *Sofia Coppola Archive* 1999-2023, Mack, 2023
20. Keough, Peter, *Interview: Sofia Coppola provides direction to Somewhere, The Boston Phoenix,* 4 January 2011
21. Ibid
22. Brunson, Matt, *Somewhere DVD review, Film Frenzy,* 2025
23. Turan, Kenneth, *Movie Review: Somewhere, Los Angeles Times,* 22 December 2010
24. Brunson, Matt, *Somewhere DVD review, Film Frenzy,* 2025
25. Coppola, Sofia, *Sofia Coppola Archive* 1999-2023, Mack, 2023
26. Berning, Beverly, *Interview with Sofia Coppola and Stephen Dorff, the Director and Star of Somewhere, Culture Vulture,* December 2010
27. Coppola, Sofia, *Sofia Coppola Archive* 1999-2023, Mack, 2023
28. Ibid
29. Ibid
30. *Somewhere DVD,* Universal Pictures Home Entertainment, 2011
31. Berning, Beverly, *Interview with Sofia Coppola and Stephen Dorff, the Director and Star of Somewhere, Culture Vulture,* December 2010

STEALING BEAUTY

1. Johnson, Zach, *Paris Hilton in The Bling Ring: See Inside Her Immaculate Home!, US Weekly,* 13 June 2013
2. Galloway, Stephen, *Sofia Coppola: The Trials, Tears, and Talent, Hollywood Reporter,* 8 May 2013
3. Scott, A.O., *Twinkly Totems of Fame, Theirs for the Taking, New York Times,* 13 June 2013
4. Hanna, Beth, *Sofia Coppola Talks 'The Bling Ring,' First Digital Shoot, Feeling-Over-Talking Technique, IndieWire,* 10 April 2013
5. Galloway, Stephen, *Sofia Coppola: The Trials, Tears, and Talent, Hollywood Reporter,* 8 May 2013
6. Rickey, Carrie, *Lost and Found, DGA Quarterly,* Spring 2013
7. Sales, Nancy Jo, *The Suspects Wore Louboutins, Vanity Fair,* March 2010
8. Ibid
9. Strong, Hannah, *Sofia Coppola: Forever Young,* Abrams, New York, 2022
10. Coppola, Sofia, *Sofia Coppola Archive* 1999-2023, Mack, 2023
11. Rickey, Carrie, *Lost and Found, DGA Quarterly,* Spring 2013
12. Schepp, Calie, *Reality Star Alexis Haines on the complicated legacy of the Bling Ring, Entertainment Weekly,* 21 September 2022
13. Galloway, Stephen, *Sofia Coppola: The Trials, Tears, and Talent, Hollywood Reporter,* 8 May 2013
14. Aleksander, Ivina, *The Lives They Lived: Eleanor Coppola, The New York Times Magazine,* 20 December 2024
15. *The Bling Ring DVD,* StudioCanal, 2013
16. Ibid
17. Rickey, Carrie, *Lost and Found, DGA Quarterly,* Spring 2013
18. Gevinson, Tavi, *Girls with Power and Mystique: An Interview with Sofia Coppola, Rookie,* 17 June 2013
19. Rickey, Carrie, *Lost and Found, DGA Quarterly,* Spring 2013
20. Ibid
21. Shoard, Catherine, *The Bling Ring – review, Observer,* 7 July 2013
22. Abbasi, Hafsah, *The Bling Ring Surveils a World of Parasociality, Celebrity, and Consumer Culture, Paste,* 28 August 2024
23. Klawans, Stuart, *Thoughtless and Dishonest, The Nation,* 31 July 2013
24. Coppola, Sofia, *Sofia Coppola Archive* 1999-2023, Mack, 2023
25. *The Bling Ring DVD,* StudioCanal, 2013

SOME ENCHANTED EVENINGS

1. Erbland, Kate, *Sofia Coppola Explains Why She Left Her Ambitious Take on The Little Mermaid, IndieWire,* 21 June 2017
2. Ibid
3. *Sofia Coppola's Little Mermaid, Funny Or Die* via YouTube, May 2014
4. Ibid
5. Marchese, David, *Sofia Coppola Talks About Getting Into the Spirit of A Very Murray Christmas, Vulture,* 1 December 2015
6. Bachor, Kenneth, *A Very Murray Christmas Director Sofia Coppola: I Wanted To Do Something 'Joyful', Time,* 4 December 2015
7. Ibid
8. *A Very Murray Christmas,* Netflix, 2015
9. Harris, Bill, *Paul Shaffer praises Miley Cyrus for her work in A Very Murray Christmas, Toronto Sun,* 1 December 2015
10. Bachor, Kenneth, *A Very Murray Christmas Director Sofia Coppola: I Wanted To Do Something 'Joyful', Time,* 4 December 2015
11. Stanton, Chris, *Five Years Later, A Very Murray Christmas Sums Up Sofia Coppola's Nostalgic Holiday Melancholy and Helps Define Her Murray-Verse, Paste,* 4 December 2020
12. Smith, Jeff, *Our Lives in Pink: Sofia Coppola as Transmedia Audiovisual Stylist* in *Transmedia Directors,* Bloomsbury Academic, 2020
13. Strong, Hannah, Sofia Coppola: *Forever Young,* Abrams, New York, 2022
14. Young Ashley, *PopRally Exclusive: Sofia Coppola on Directing Phoenix's 'Chloroform' video, Inside/Out – A MoMA/MoMA PS1 Blog,* 12 November 2013
15. Ibid
16. Strong, Hannah, Sofia Coppola: *Forever Young,* Abrams, New York, 2022
17. D'Addario, Daniel, *Sofia Coppola and Marc Jacobs*

on Venice Festival Doc 'Marc by Sofia', 'I Felt Very Comfortable Exposing Everything to Sofia', Variety, 31 August 2025

18. James, Caryn, *'Marc by Sofia' Review: Sofia Coppola's Marc Jacobs Doc Offers a Colourful but Unrevealing Insider's Take, Hollywood Reporter,* 2 September 2025
19. Povoledo, Elizabeth, *Valentino and Sofia Coppola Make an Opera, New York Times,* 18 May 2016

AN UNCIVIL WAR

1. Buchanan, Kyle, *How Sofia Coppola Reclaimed The Beguiled for Women (and Gay Men), Vulture,* 14 June 2017
2. Ibid
3. Zacharek, Stephanie, *The Beguiled: A Sly Ode to the Sensuality of Deceit, Time,* 24 May 2017
4. Buchanan, Kyle, *How Sofia Coppola Reclaimed The Beguiled for Women (and Gay Men), Vulture,* 14 June 2017
5. Blyth, Antonia, *Sofia Coppola May Have Won Big at Cannes—But There's Still a Long Way to Go for Female Directors, Elle,* 30 May 2017
6. Monks Kaufman, Sophie, *Sofia Coppola: 'I'm Telling the Same Story But From the Women's Point of View', Little White Lies,* 24 May 2017
7. Ibid
8. Ibid
9. Erickson, Steve, *Sofia Coppola's Update on The Beguiled Explores Desire and Exploitation, Nashville Scene,* 29 June 2017
10. *Sofia Coppola Breaks Down the Dinner Scene, Vanity Fair* via YouTube, 22 June 2017
11. *Sofia Coppola: Spotlight on Conversations,* AFI Film Festival, 11 November 2017
12. Rapold, Nicolas, *Interview: Sofia Coppola, Film Comment,* 19 June 2017
13. Kaufman, Anthony, *Sofia Coppola and Anne Ross: For The Beguiled Coppola and Ross Travel Back in Time, DGA Quarterly,* Spring 2017
14. Ibid
15. Monks Kaufman, Sophie, *Sofia Coppola: 'I'm Telling the Same Story But From the Women's Point of View', Little White Lies,* 24 May 2017
16. *The Beguiled,* Universal Pictures Home Entertainment, 2017
17. Monks Kaufman, Sophie, *Sofia Coppola: 'I'm Telling the Same Story But From the Women's Point of View', Little White Lies,* 24 May 2017
18. Rapold, Nicolas, *Interview: Sofia Coppola, Film Comment,* 19 June 2017
19. Zacharek, Stephanie, *Art on Film: Sofia Coppola Returns with 'The Beguiled', Which Builds on Eighteen Years of Considered Work, Time,* June 2017
20. Ibid
21. Ibid
22. *Sofia's Touch* featurette, Universal Pictures Home Entertainment, 2017
23. Monks Kaufman, Sophie, *Sofia Coppola: 'I'm Telling the Same Story But From the Women's Point of View', Little White Lies,* 24 May 2017
24. *The Beguiled: Colin Farrell On Sofia Coppola's 'Laid-Back Environment' On Set, Entertainment Weekly* via YouTube, 30 June 2017
25. *The Beguiled,* Universal Pictures Home Entertainment, 2017
26. *Sofia's Touch* featurette, Universal Pictures Home Entertainment, 2017
27. Gilby, Ryan, *Sofia Coppola's The Beguiled brings one refreshing element: a female eye, New Statesman,* 14 July 2017
28. Hoberman, J., *The Snake in the Schoolhouse, New York Review of Books,* 6 July 2017
29. Scott, A.O., *Review: 'The Beguiled', Sofia Coppola's Civil War Cocoon, New York Times,* 22 June 2017
30. Turner, Lauren, *Elle Fanning on her 'scandalous' character in The Beguiled, BBC Culture,* 11 July 2017
31. Anderson, Melissa, *Sofia Coppola's Southern Comfort, Village Voice,* 21 June 2017
32. Kohn Eric, *Sofia Coppola: How She Survived 'The Beguiled' Backlash, Why She Won't Do TV, and Why Her Dad is 'Over' Film, IndieWire,* 27 November 2017
33. Ibid
34. Ibid
35. Strong, Hannah, Sofia Coppola: *Forever Young,* Abrams, New York, 2022

THE ODD COUPLE

1. Clarke, Donald, *On the Rocks: Bill Murray and Rashida Jones are perfect in Sofia Coppola's latest film, Irish Times,* 22 October 2020
2. Strong, Hannah, Sofia Coppola: *Forever Young,* Abrams, New York, 2022
3. Ibid
4. *Sofia Coppola on Directing On The Rocks and Casting Rashida Jones and Bill Murray - On Directing, BAFTA Guru* via YouTube, 22 March 2021
5. Ibid
6. Hattersley, Giles, *'We Didn't Know We Were Making a Period Movie': Behind the Scenes of 'On The Rocks' With Sofia Coppola, Vogue,* 11 October 2020
7. Olsen, Mark, *How Sofia Coppola and Rashida Jones Put Their Own Family Lives into 'On the Rocks', Los Angeles Times,* 23 September 2020
8. *Sofia Coppola on Directing On The Rocks and Casting Rashida Jones and Bill Murray - On Directing, BAFTA Guru* via YouTube, 22 March 2021
9. Stanton, Chris, *Five Years Later, A Very Murray Christmas Sums Up Sofia Coppola's Nostalgic Holiday Melancholy and Helps Define Her Murray-Verse, Paste,* 4 December 2020
10. *Sofia Coppola on Directing On The Rocks and Casting Rashida Jones and Bill Murray - On Directing, BAFTA Guru* via YouTube, 22 March 2021
11. Mitchell, Elvis, *Sofia Coppola: On the Rocks, The Treatment,* 3 November 2020
12. Ibid
13. Ibid
14. *On the Rocks,* Apple TV, 2020
15. Chaw, Walter, *On the Rocks, Film Freak Central,* 16 December 2020
16. Zacharek, Stephanie, *Bill Murray and Rashida Jones March Each Other Beat for Beat in Sofia Coppola's Wistful On the Rocks, Time,* 23 October 2020
17. Nathan, Ian, *The Coppolas: A Movie Dynasty,* Palazzo, 2021
18. Insdorf, Annette, *Sofia Coppola on Filmmaking, 92Y Reel Pieces,* 20 April 2020
19. Mitchell, Elvis, *Sofia Coppola: On the Rocks, The Treatment,* 3 November 2020
20. Ibid
21. Kohn, Eric, *Sofia Coppola on the Identity Crisis That Led Her to Make On the rocks with Bill Murray, IndieWire,* 12 October 2020
22. Mitchell, Elvis, *Sofia Coppola: On the Rocks, The Treatment,* 3 November 2020
23. Nathan, Ian, *The Coppolas: A Movie Dynasty,* Palazzo, 2021
24. Ibid
25. Kohn Eric, *Sofia Coppola: How She Survived 'The Beguiled' Backlash, Why She Won't Do TV, and Why Her Dad is 'Over' Film, Indiewire,* 27 November 2017
26. Zacharek, Stephanie, *Bill Murray and Rashida Jones March Each Other Beat for Beat in Sofia Coppola's Wistful On the Rocks, Time,* 23 October 2020
27. Olsen, Mark, *How Sofia Coppola and Rashida Jones Put Their Own Family Lives into 'On the Rocks', Los Angeles Times,* 23 September 2020
28. *On the Rocks,* Apple TV, 2020
29. Strong, Hannah, Sofia Coppola: *Forever Young,* Abrams, New York, 2022
30. Olsen, Mark, *How Sofia Coppola and Rashida Jones Put Their Own Family Lives into 'On the Rocks', Los Angeles Times,* 23 September 2020

LONESOME TONIGHT

1. Strong, Hannah, *Sofia Coppola on struggling to get Priscilla made: 'Straight men with money don't always relate to me', GQ,* 30 December 2023
2. Ibid
3. Buchanan, Kyle, *Sofia Coppola Makes It Look Easy. It Isn't., New York Times,* 27 October 2023
4. Utichi, Joe, *Sofia Coppola on the Roots of 'Priscilla' and Paying Tribute to the Woman Behind the Myth: 'It's so Hard to Fathom That Her First Kiss was Elvis Presley', Deadline,* 22 November 2023
5. Hirschberg, Lynn, *Sofia Coppola Finds Her Latest Muse, W,* 28 September 2023
6. Lane, Anthony, *'Priscilla' Presents the Echoing Void of Elvis's Fame, New Yorker,* 3 November 2023

7. *Sofia Coppola on Priscilla, Lost in Translation and her filmmaking career - BFI in conversation, BFI* via YouTube, 3 January 2024
8. Bell, Keaton, *Sofia Coppola on Priscilla, Dolly Parton, and Whether She'd Ever Direct a Britney Spears Biopic, Vogue,* 3 November 2023
9. Utichi, Joe, *Sofia Coppola on the Roots of 'Priscilla' and Paying Tribute to the Woman Behind the Myth: 'It's so Hard to Fathom That Her First Kiss was Elvis Presley', Deadline,* 22 November 2023
10. Ibid
11. Ibid
12. Kermode, Mark, *Kermode and Mayo's Take,* 28 December 2023
13. Utichi, Joe, *Sofia Coppola on the Roots of 'Priscilla' and Paying Tribute to the Woman Behind the Myth: 'It's so Hard to Fathom That Her First Kiss was Elvis Presley', Deadline,* 22 November 2023
14. Bell, Keaton, *Sofia Coppola on Priscilla, Dolly Parton, and Whether She'd Ever Direct a Britney Spears Biopic, Vogue,* 3 November 2023
15. Utichi, Joe, *Sofia Coppola on the Roots of 'Priscilla' and Paying Tribute to the Woman Behind the Myth: 'It's so Hard to Fathom That Her First Kiss was Elvis Presley', Deadline,* 22 November 2023
16. Hirschberg, Lynn, *Sofia Coppola Finds Her Latest Muse, W,* 28 September 2023
17. *The Making of Priscilla, A24* via YouTube, 8 October 2025
18. Bell, Keaton, *Sofia Coppola on Priscilla, Dolly Parton, and Whether She'd Ever Direct a Britney Spears Biopic, Vogue,* 3 November 2023
19. Gleiberman, Owen, *Priscilla Review: Sofia Coppola's Piercingly Authentic Inside Drama About the Troubled Love Story of Priscilla and Elvis Presley, Variety,* 4 September 2003
20. Strong, Hannah, *Sofia Coppola on struggling to get Priscilla made: 'Straight men with money don't always relate to me', GQ,* 30 December 2023
21. Chamlee, Virginia, *Priscilla Presley Says Priscilla Movie Got Everything Right — Except for 1 Thing, People,* 11 February 2025
22. Bell, Keaton, *Sofia Coppola on Priscilla, Dolly Parton, and Whether She'd Ever Direct a Britney Spears Biopic, Vogue,* 3 November 2023
23. Ibid
24. Ibid
25. Kramer, Gary M, *Priscilla: Sofia Coppola Delivers a Sympathetic but Ultimately Suffocating Portrait, Salon,* 2 November 2023
26. Coppola, Sofia, *Sofia Coppola Archive* 1999-2023, Mack, 2023
27. Utichi, Joe, *Sofia Coppola on the Roots of 'Priscilla' and Paying Tribute to the Woman Behind the Myth: 'It's so Hard to Fathom That Her First Kiss was Elvis Presley', Deadline,* 22 November 2023
28. Buchanan, Kyle, *Sofia Coppola Makes It Look Easy. It Isn't., New York Times,* 27 October 2023
29. Strong, Hannah, *Sofia Coppola on struggling to get Priscilla made: 'Straight men with money don't always relate to me', GQ,* 30 December 2023

ACKNOWLEDGEMENTS

Capturing the spirit and talent of Sofia Coppola, or at least trying to, is almost like the proverbial grasping of smoke. Her work is so wonderful because it doesn't make sense – not in some logical, storybook way. Emotions figure over plots. Her sets are as hushed as churches, or lit up by laughter, contented places. There are none of the titanic struggles with the filmmaking gods that have marked out her father's career. What became clear as I rewatched her eight precious features (and one Christmas Special) is how intensely personal they are – to her and to me, the watcher. She is present in every frame, and somehow so am I. And that is what has made this such an extraordinary book to write. We were on some level in this together.

So above all I thank Sofia, and all who have elevated her art. She is a precious commodity in an era of – ever increasingly – formula.

Thanks, as ever, are also due to those who work so hard to make me look good. To my editor Jessica Axe, a velvet hammer if ever I knew one. To Sue Pressley at Stonecastle Graphics, who contributes so much to the look and feel of these books, and stays endlessly patient when the words slow down. To my copy editor Nick Freeth, who has taught me more about a hanging participle than my entire schooling – and remains invaluable to making sure my prose makes sense. And to the friends and colleagues, who have spent years making me a far better writer: Ian Freer, Simon Braund, Steve Hornby, Nick de Semlyen, Mark Dinning, Julian Alcantara, Lyndy Saville, Stephen Armstrong, and Neil Norman.

Finally, this book is dedicated to Wai Bing Hui, whose opinions and support I cherish more than anything, and who has shared so many midnight conversations. Thankfully, we have never had to part.

PICTURE CREDITS

Abaca Press / Alamy Stock Photo 111a, 152l, 155l; adsR / Alamy Stock Photo 119ar; AFP / Getty Images 13; AJ Pics / Alamy Stock Photo 51a, 99c; Album / Alamy Stock Photo 25, 32, 41, 55b, 59, 86r, 110, 130, 148l, 166a; Allstar Picture Library Ltd / Alamy Stock Photo 42r, 91; amana images inc. / Alamy Stock Photo 42l; AMERICAN ZOETROPE / RGR Collection / Alamy Stock Photo 161a; andrea sabbadini / Alamy Stock Photo 26; Anwar Hussein / Alamy Stock Photo 119br; BFA / Alamy Stock Photo 19l, 39, 64, 69r, 121r, 155r; booksR / Alamy Stock Photo 21r; Capital Pictures / Alamy Stock Photo 120b, 162l; cineclassico / Alamy Stock Photo 126l; Cinematic / Alamy Stock Photo 37, 47b, 65a, 70b, 73, 81, 83, 99l, 164r; Collection Christophel / Alamy Stock Photo 18b, 38a, 133a; David Livingston / Stringer / WireImage / Getty Images 90b; dpa picture alliance / Alamy Stock Photo 139a; Entertainment Pictures / Alamy Stock Photo 78l; Everett Collection, Inc. / Alamy Stock Photo 15l, 19r, 28c, 28r, 31l, 33a, 36a, 54l, 78c, 87a, 109, 115, 116b, 117a, 129r, 138l, 148r, 153b; Fausto Marci / Alamy Stock Photo 139b; FlixPix / Alamy Stock Photo 157, 164l, 165, 166b; Independent Photo Agency Srl / Alamy Stock Photo 171; INSTAR Images LLC / Alamy Stock Photo 143a, 143b; Jesse Grant / WireImage / Getty Images 118a; Jim Spellman / WireImage / Getty Images 132l; LANDMARK MEDIA / Alamy Stock Photo 49a, 128l, 141, 142, 144, 145, 146a, 146b, 147, 149, 151, 154a, 154b, 159, 160, 162r, 163a, 163b, 167b, 168b, 169; Masheter Movie Archive / Alamy Stock Photo 29a; Maximum Film / Alamy Stock Photo 56, 99r; MediaPunch Inc / Alamy Stock Photo 8, 29b; Michael Ochs Archives / Getty Images 158r; Moviestore Collection Ltd / Alamy Stock Photo 28l, 44l, 46a, 46b, 50, 61b, 127a; NEIL SPENCE / Alamy Stock Photo 60l; PA Images / Alamy Stock Photo 57r; PASCAL GUYOT / AFP / Getty Images 4-5; Paul Bruinooge / Patrick McMullan/ Getty Images 138r; PBH Images / Alamy Stock Photo 44r; Photo 12 / Alamy Stock Photo 12l, 15r, 16, 17, 31r, 33b, 35a, 51b, 54r, 67a, 68, 69l, 71, 74, 107, 150, 153a; PictureLux / The Hollywood Archive / Alamy Stock Photo 11, 88al, 158l; Retro AdArchives / Alamy Stock Photo 119al; Robin Platzer / Getty Images 12r; Ron Galella, Ltd. / Getty Images 22r; Sipa US / Alamy Stock Photo 120a, 152r, 170l; Skip Bolen / Getty Images 118b; TCD/Prod.DB / Alamy Stock Photo 7, 14, 18a, 23, 27, 30, 34, 35b, 36b, 38b, 43, 45, 47a, 48, 49b, 52a, 52b, 53a, 53b, 55a, 61a, 62-63, 65b, 66, 67b, 70a, 72, 75, 76-77, 78r, 79l, 79r, 80, 82, 84a, 84b, 85, 86l, 87b, 88-89r, 90a, 93, 94, 95, 96, 97, 98, 100, 101, 102, 103, 104l, 104r, 105, 106a, 106b, 113, 114, 116a, 125, 127b, 128r, 129l, 131, 133b, 134, 135a, 135b, 136, 137, 167a, 168a, 170r; THA / Alamy Stock Photo 88bl, 132r; Tsuni / USA / Alamy Stock Photo 9; UPI / Alamy Stock Photo 161b; Yasuko Kageyama / Teatro dell'Opera di Roma 122a, 122b, 123; ZUMA Press, Inc. / Alamy Stock Photo 20, 21l, 57l, 111b, 112, 117b, 126r; Creative Commons 22l, 121l.

The author and publishers would like to thank © Yasuko Kageyama / Teatro dell'Opera di Roma for kind permission to use the images of *La Traviata* at the Teatro dell'Opera di Roma on pages 122 and 123.

Every effort has been made to trace the copyright holders of images used in this book. If application is made in writing to the publisher, any omissions will be included in future editions.